W9-CUL-400

Sails

By the same author:
Teach your Child about Sailing (C. Arthur Pearson Ltd)
Racing Dinghy Sails (Adlard Coles Ltd)
Crewing for Offshore Racing (Adlard Coles Ltd)
Out in Front (Sailing film by ICI Fibres) Technical Adviser
Night Intruder (David and Charles)
The Care and Repair of Sails (Adlard Coles Ltd)

Jeremy Howard-Williams

Sails

Diagrams drawn by J. D. Sleightholme

John de Graff, Inc.

First published 1967 by Adlard Coles Ltd, London.

First published in USA 1971
Third edition 1972
Reprinted 1974
Fourth edition 1976

John de Graff Inc.
Clinton Corners, N.Y. 12514

ISBN 0—8286—0054—6
Printed in United States of America

Acknowledgements

I would not attempt to write a book of this scope without obtaining a second opinion on many items of both fact and fancy. I am indebted to many friends and, in particular, to the following who, nevertheless, should not be held responsible for any of the views expressed in this book, which are entirely my own.

The Royal Yachting Association; Mr Frank Carr of the National Maritime Museum, Greenwich; Mr Fred Cross BSC, AFRAeS; Mr David Cheverton; Mr Austin Farrar MRINA; Mr Ernest Hayward; Mr John Hayward; ICI Fibres Ltd; Mr Christopher Ratsey; Mr Michael Souter; Mr Thos Tanner of Southampton University; and Mr E. Vallender, Foreman (now Manager), Ratsey & Lapthorn Ltd. All these kind people read various drafts and made many valuable suggestions.

In addition I am grateful to the International Yacht Racing Union for permission to publish their Sail Measurement Instructions; to ICI Fibres Ltd for their Instructions on Laundering and Dry Cleaning Terylene Sails; to the Editor, *Yachting World*, for his permission to reprint two articles on the spinnaker gybe; and to the Editor, *Yachts and Yachting*, for his permission regarding a similar article.

The list would not be complete without the names of those Sail Makers who have been kind enough to allow me into their lofts, some when I was a practising Sail Maker myself, and some when I was writing this book; their hospitality has broadened my outlook. My appreciation is extended to Bruce Banks of Sarisbury Green, Carlsen of Denmark, Paul Elvström of Cannes, Goldfinch of Whitstable, Hood of Lymington, W. G. Lucas of Portsmouth, Nickels of Liverpool, W. Penrose of Falmouth, Harry Shirlaw of Cowes, and Mrs Williams of Hamble. Not least are my thanks due to Franklin Ratsey-Woodroffe of Ratsey & Lapthorn Ltd of Cowes, from whom I learned what I know about sailmaking, and who has kindly allowed me to use much material and photographs in this book.

Finally I must mention my wife, who nobly typed the manuscript, my Publishers who read the entire book in draft form and put me on the right lines and J. D. Sleightholme who did the drawings.

The finished article would have been the poorer without all this support, and I am glad to record my gratitude.

Warsash 1967 JHW

Techniques in the sailing world have changed since I first wrote this book ten years ago. In particular the International Offshore Rule – like it or lump it – has arrived on the scene. Over the years the book has been kept up to date and in this, the fourth edition, I have once again examined critically all that was originally written. New ideas, new materials and new designs all require flexibility of thought, so some passages have been revised – radically in places. But the principles of sail shape and driving force remain constant, and I am glad to see that much of what I first wrote remains unaltered. I must record my thanks to Sir David Mackworth of South Coast Rod Rigging for checking my revision of the chapter on Design and Rating.

In these days of leech Cunninghams, Barber haulers, control luff headsails, wind tallies and hydraulic boom vangs, it is hard to recall that, when this book first appeared, the majority of owners and crews were too often content to hoist their sails and pay little further attention to them. This always distressed me, but notice now how often a Sail Maker figures in the crew list of a winning boat. If I could ask for only one achievement for *Sails*, it would be that it has helped bring about this great awakening to the importance of the sailmaker's craft.

Warsash 1976 JHW

Contents

Appendices

List of Plates

Introduction

One of the great joys of sailing is that it is still not a scientific pastime and, try though we will to iron out the many variables with which we have to contend, there are always some problems left unsolved.

Our knowledge increases with experience – often bitter – and it is a great help when those who really know, give of the fruits of their experience in readable form. Far too many experts are incapable of communication and far too many books are written by those who are more skilful with the pen than at the helm.

Jeremy Howard-Williams is, however, one of those lucky few who both know and can communicate their knowledge. He has spent a number of years with Ratsey & Lapthorn of Cowes making good sails and listening intelligently to the ideas, some good and some not so good, of many keen yachtsmen. He has sailed in all sorts and sizes of boats from the largest in the Fastnet Race to a children's Scow, and has taken the trouble to keep up to date in his thinking.

Because of this, he knows as a helmsman what a helmsman wants; as a crew – and I know from personal experience that he is a first-class one – he has learned the techniques and the drill in handling sails, while as a Sail Maker he has applied a good brain to making the yachtsman's 'engines' as efficient as possible.

The result of his experience is this book, informative, authoritative and right up to date. Many distinguished yachtsmen do not bother to read books on yachting subjects, feeling that few of them contain anything new. I feel, however, that this book will become a yachting classic and one which every keen yachtsman should have on his bookshelves, for even the pundits will find some nuggets here and there.

There has been an absolute spate, in the last few years, of books on most of the many different aspects of sailing but there has been a lack, since the days of cotton and until now, of a good book on sails.

It is an honour for anyone to be asked to write an introduction for a friend's book, but I am especially pleased to write this one because I am sure this book will help us all to obtain a better performance from our particular boats once we realize more clearly the many problems which all Sail Makers have to face.

Stewart Morris

CHAPTER I

History

Although my subject evokes tales of handling acres of hand-sewn Egyptian cotton, the reader will look through these pages in vain for illustrations of gaff-cutters and schooners. This book is about synthetics and the present, and there is little room in it for nostalgia.

The shorter *Oxford English Dictionary* tells us that canvas is 'a coarse unbleached cloth made of hemp or flax, used for sails, tents, etc.'. The misconception that canvas means cotton to the exclusion of synthetics probably springs from this definition. In fact, if we read on further in the dictionary, we find that canvas also means sailcloth, and this is the meaning of the word as used by sailing men today. In other words, Terylene and Dacron are just as much canvas as cotton is.

The earliest sails were probably developed from palm-fronds erected in Egyptian boats for shade or ornamentation. The Romans used hide and homespun cloth, as did the Vikings, and their sails were made in a number of panels sewn together by the womenfolk. They even used to case the edges of the sails with leather for protection, in much the same way as we sometimes do today, and sealskin was particularly popular for this application.

The first record of a sailing boat built purely for pleasure in England refers to the three-masted vessel called *Disdain*. She was some 30 ft long and was built for the young Prince Henry in 1604.

Yachting got its real start in this country, however, from King Charles II. Soon after the Restoration in 1660 he was presented with two yachts, *Mary* and *Little Bezan*, by the Dutch East India Company, and they brought the very name yacht with them from the Dutch language.

The King's friends soon built yachts of the same size, and races took place. With the death of the King, however, the sport lost its initial impetus and died out for about a hundred years. The Starcross Yacht Club of Devon was founded as long ago as 1773, and is the doyen of English sailing clubs. The Cumberland Fleet, which was later to become the Royal Thames Yacht Club, followed it in 1775, and the sport started up again. Rigs developed slowly, and there evolved the straight-stemmed gaff-cutters with large jackyarders and long booms which we know so well.

The next major landmark in the history of English yachting was the arrival in our waters of the schooner *America* from the United States in 1851. Her whole concept was radically different from the bluff lines and single mast of her competitors. She was fore and aft rigged on both masts, and her sails were made of well-woven cotton, as opposed to the flax universally used in England; they were also unusual in that the mainsail and foresail were laced to the boom. This is important, for it gave her the power to take advantage of her fine entry and raking bow, because the sails were much smoother and flatter than those of her rivals, and they were also a good deal less porous.

British yachts switched to cotton after this, but they did not learn their lesson properly. They reverted to flax about thirty years later and did not go back to cotton again until the turn of the century. Terylene, Dacron and nylon did not appear until after the Second World War.

Before the Second World War, international yachting was the prerogative of the rich man, and it was not until afterwards that it became more widespread, ranging from the smallest dinghy through the international day-boats to the ocean-racing fleet. This great intercourse of racing men has meant that there is a constant effort to improve performance. Ideas are tried on the smaller boats, found to be useful and then find their way to the bigger yachts. We have now reached the stage where the margin of possible improvement is so small that everything must be perfect if a boat wants to stay at the front of an international fleet.

This is a good thing as far as the Sail Maker is concerned, because it means that sails are coming in for their due measure of care and attention. And so they should, for a yacht would not get very far without them.

CHAPTER II

Theory of Sailing

For a better understanding of how to set and trim sails, we must first of all know what it is we are seeking. To decide this, we must know something of what the sails are doing, and why. This will also help in following the various complexities of making sails and looking after them.

In 1955 the now defunct Yacht Research Council of Great Britain carried out a comprehensive series of tests with a 5·5 metre, including sailing it on a reservoir and on open water with different helmsmen. One of the deductions to be drawn from the graphs obtained as a result of the tests is that one helmsman is liable to get better results than another, because they sail the boat differently. Certain helmsmen have an uncanny ability to anticipate wind shifts and puffs; they can beat gauges and pointers in steering a boat properly to windward. Most of us will agree that it is better this way, for if science could enable us all to steer the optimum course at all times, then the fun would be taken out of racing.

We cannot control the basic forces which act on our boat as she sails along with a bone in her teeth, any more than we can arrange instruments to tell us how best to select the fastest course every time; but this is not to say that we cannot profit from a study of the problem in order to have a say in the effect those forces have on our speed.

To the student of the subject there is a mass of information available. A look through the correspondence columns of any yachting magazine, over a period of a year or so, will produce enough hypotheses to fill a book on their own. What emerges as certain is that everyone is not agreed as to why a yacht sails to windward, but there is enough wheat among the chaff to help us understand our sails a good deal better than we do.

The forces acting on a yacht moving through the water come from two sources; the yacht's speed through the water and the apparent wind. When a yacht is sailing steadily, that is to say that she is not accelerating, turning or slowing down, the total forces exerted by the wind must be balanced by equal and opposite forces exerted by water pressure on the hull.

It has been shown elsewhere[1] that angles of heel up to 20° make little change in sail forces; we shall accordingly only consider the upright position. In any event, if we can understand the one situation, we should be able to understand the other; if we can improve the one, we should thereby improve the other.

Windward Work

The most difficult case to explain is when a yacht is beating to windward. This is the most obscure, and it is the hardest to improve; it is also the situation where improvement is the most desirable and rewarding. In any case, a yacht sails better with the wind flowing across its sails rather than straight into them, so we shall consider windward work; this will cover all cases where there is movement of air across the sail.

Forces

It is common among aerodynamicists to express forces in terms of coefficients. This is a method of reducing the actual forces by a factor which varies, in the case of sail forces, with the density of the air, the square of the relative wind-speed, the sail area and the relative wind angle. The resulting figure for a particular sail can then be compared directly with the similar coefficient of another sail under different conditions, in order to establish relative superiority. It is a sort of efficiency yardstick.

[1] SUYR Paper No. 9, March 1963.

Sails

The coefficient of any force F can be expressed as:

$$C_F = \frac{F}{\frac{1}{2}\rho V^2 A}$$

where C_F is the coefficient, F is the force, ρ is the air density, V is the relative air-speed and A is a reference area. Providing a consistent, or standard, set of units of measurement is used, the resulting coefficient will be the same regardless of the system, and can be compared with coefficients also using consistent sets of units.

We are not, however, seeking to estimate the speed of a particular yacht from tank and tunnel tests, neither do we want to compare specific cases. We are trying to find out what affects the performance of sails, so that we can try and get the best out of what we have got. To do this, it will be helpful if we understand a little theory, but it will be enough for us to consider only the total forces acting in a given direction and not their coefficients. We do not even need to specify our forces in terms of pounds or kilograms. If there is more driving force, the yacht will normally go faster; if there is more heeling force she will heel more.

Parallelogram of Forces

The first mathematics with which we need concern ourselves is our old friend the parallelogram of forces. I know that it is fashionable to decry the traditional bird's-eye-view of a yacht with its neat aerofoil-shaped curve representing the sail, but it happens to be a simple way to explain it all. I make no apology for using it.

If we look vertically down on a mainsail at its mean chord position, and draw an arrow F_T to represent the magnitude and direction of the total force produced by the sail, we shall find that it acts through the centre of pressure, slightly forward of rightangles to the mean chord. This force line can be resolved by a parallelogram of forces into its components acting athwartships and fore and aft. F_Y represents the heeling or lateral component, and the driving force component is F_X acting along the track of the yacht, allowing for leeway.

The diagram at figure 1 is not necessarily to scale, but it fairly represents a typical case. F_Y is the force trying to push the boat to leeward, and is usually about four and a half times F_X which is driving her forward. Leeway, of course, is resisted by pressure of

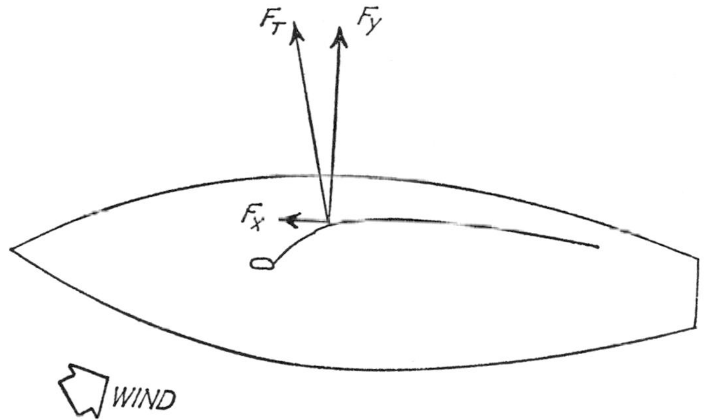

Fig. 1. Parallelogram of forces in a sail.

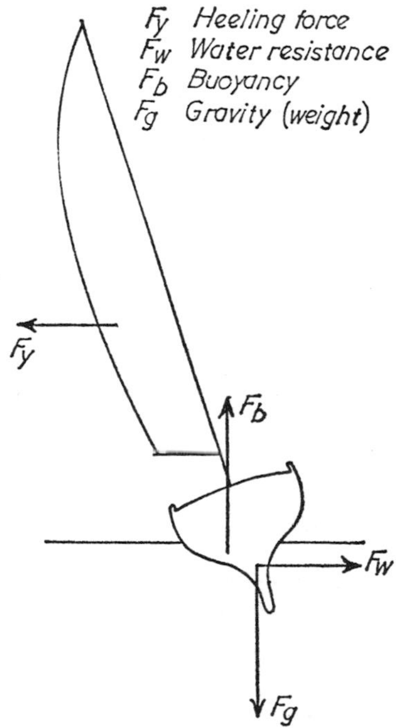

Fig. 2. Opposing force couples in lateral plane. Not to scale.

water on the keel or centreboard (F_W), and the ensuing force couple gives a heeling moment. This, in turn, is opposed by another couple made up of weight (F_G) and buoyancy of the hull (F_B) as shown in figure 2. The weight of the fixed keel (or the crew sitting out in a dinghy) is one arm of the opposing couple, and the natural buoyancy of the hull is the other. In fact, there is a similar balance of forces in the pitching plane, but we need not concern ourselves with it.

We have now balanced out the heeling force – if we have not, we shall either fill and sink, or capsize! Let us refer back to figure 1, and we can see that we are left with F_X acting in the fore and aft line of the yacht and driving her forward. This is opposed by forces set up by the resistance of the water, which we can call drag.

Lift and Drag

We are not concerned here with hull drag and wetted area. The total sail force (F_T) can be resolved into lift (L) and drag (D) acting at right angles to the relative wind and in the same direction respectively. This is shown in figure 3.

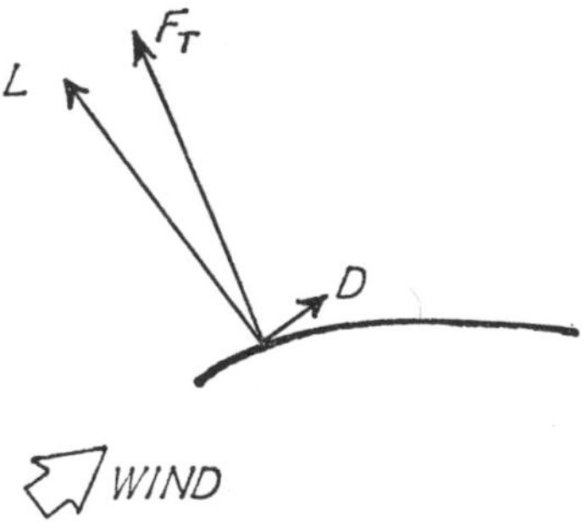

Fig. 3. Lift and Drag.

It will be seen that F_T depends on lift and drag or, to put it the other way, a given F_T will resolve differently for different values of L and D. Thus, if drag is increased, F_T must also increase if the driving force F_X is to remain the same, as shown in figure 4.

Conversely, if thrust F_T remains the same for more drag (D), F_X will be lower. So we need to try and reduce sail drag and to increase lift as much as possible.

Drag. Sail drag can be divided into three kinds:

(*i*) *Induced Drag*. This is a function of lift and of the aspect ratio. It increases with lift, and decreases as the aspect ratio is increased. There is not much we can do about the head of the sail, but a wide boom will act as an endplate to stop the escape of air curling under the foot from windward to leeward, and thus increase the effective aspect ratio. This will lower the proportion of induced drag relative to the area of the sail.

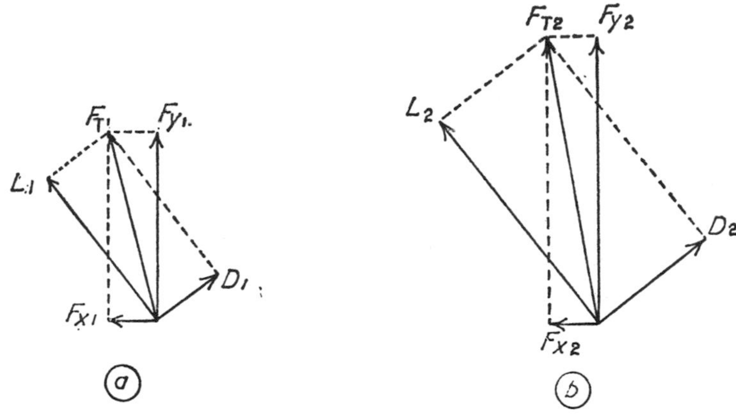

Fig. 4. Increase in total thrust (F_T) necessitated by increased drag (D), to maintain the same driving force (F_X).

(*ii*) *Form Drag*. This is the drag produced by the shape of the sail itself, that is to say the frontal area presented to the apparent wind. A full sail, having more camber, will present more frontal area than a flat one, and thus will produce more form drag. We may, perhaps, add parasite drag here. This is the drag produced by the mast and its associated rigging which, while not directly attributable to the sails, must also be taken into consideration.

(*iii*) *Friction Drag*. The boundary layer at the sail will be directly affected by the nap of the cloth, so we must select a smooth material. Everything must be as clean as possible aerodynamically, and this means the exclusion of too many reef points and large cringles.

Lift. Lift is a function of the shape of the sail and the way in which it transforms the energy of the wind into driving force. If we simply increase the value of F_T, that is to say we increase the total force acting on a sail, then we shall get more lift but we shall also get more drag. The value of F_X may increase, but F_Y will also increase to a point where the angle of heel becomes significant. We have seen that this is around 20°. If, however, we want to increase lift for the same value of F_T, we must decrease drag, decrease F_Y and increase the driving force F_X. This is merely a reversal of the situation prevailing in figure 4, where drag was increased. Equally, if we can incline the angle of F_T so that it is directed more forward, even if we do not increase its value, we shall increase the forward component F_X and at the same time reduce the heeling force F_Y.

Fig. 5. Standard thrust
$F_T = 4\frac{2}{3}\times$
$F_X = 1\times$
$F_Y = 4\frac{1}{2}\times$

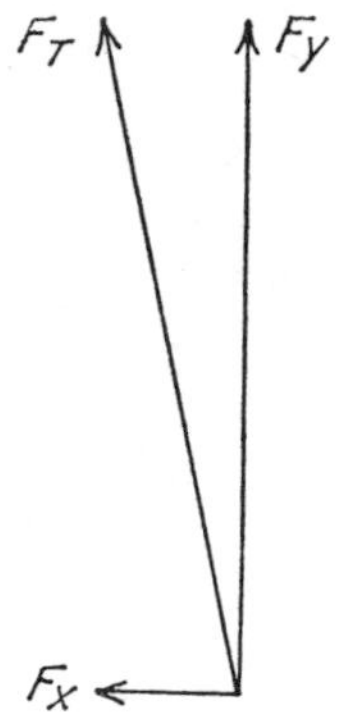

Fig. 6. Thrust increased at same angle
$F_T = 7\times$
$F_X = 1\frac{1}{2}\times$
$F_Y = 6\frac{3}{4}\times$

In figure 6 above, 50 per cent more thrust produces a similar increase in both F_X and F_Y. If, however, the same original total thrust is angled a mere 5° further forward, F_X is again increased by 50 per cent, but F_Y is actually reduced (figure 7). A forward inclination of 10° results in even better figures (figure 8). These results can often be achieved by easing the sheets slightly.

Airflow Pattern

We now come to an examination of the airflow pattern round a sail, and how this results in the total force in the sail.

If we may make an analogy with the section of an aircraft's wing approaching to land at a relatively high angle of incidence, we shall see the sort of pattern we can expect. The earliest wings were made of one layer of cloth stretched over spars and ribs, rather like a fully battened sail lying on its side. More data is known from wind tunnel tests of aerofoil sections, however, so I have used the more advanced shape in figure 9. In particular, the effect of the slot is better documented for aerofoils, and this is important as we shall see.

The streamlines represent the direction of airflow, and their distance apart shows speed: the closer they are together the faster

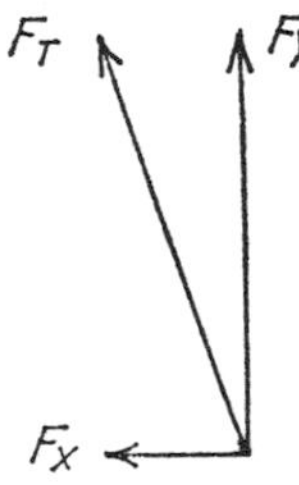

Fig. 7. Original standard thrust is angled forward by 5°

$FT = 4\frac{2}{3} \times$
$FX = 1\frac{1}{2} \times$
$FY = 4\frac{1}{3} \times$

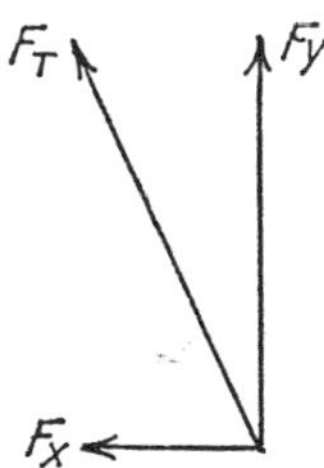

Fig. 8. Original standard thrust is angled forward by 10°

$FT = 4\frac{2}{3} \times$
$FX = 1\frac{3}{4} \times$
$FY = 4\frac{1}{4} \times$

the wind speed at that point. Note how the streamlines start to diverge from their course some way in front of the leading edge, and how they bend from the lower to the upper surface to pass the leading edge. They leave the trailing edge at an angle to their original direction, and do not take up their ordinary path again for some distance. This is the effect which produces the dirty wind which acts principally to leeward and astern, although there is a small element to windward as we all know.

It is normal for streamlines to bend from high towards low pressure. In figure 9 we have the opposite taking place, and this can only occur when there is a barrier such as the aerofoil, or the sails, between the two pressure systems.

Due to the acceleration imparted as they move from the lower surface, round the leading edge and across the upper surface, the upper streamlines increase their local velocity relative to the lower streamlines, which have been able to follow a more direct route along the lower surface. This means that their pressure will be lower, in obedience to Bernoulli's law which requires that pressure in a fluid (and air is a fluid) remains constant for constant speed and reduces for increased speed.

Thus we have a basic situation in which air is deflected from its original path, thereby imparting lift. Alternatively, the airflow over the upper surface of the aerofoil is faster than that over the lower surface, thus reducing pressure so that there is a tendency to move from high to low pressure.

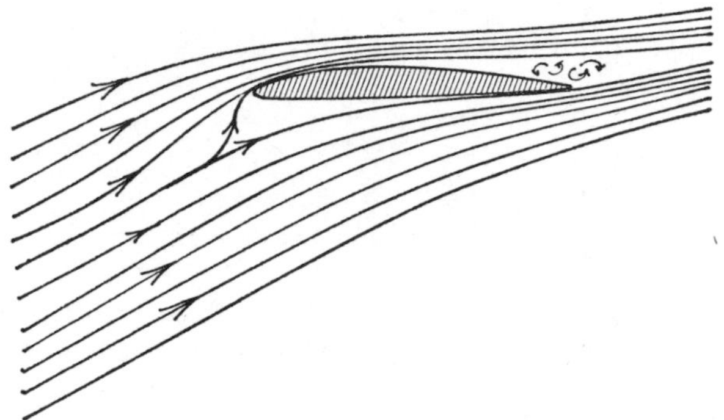

Fig. 9. Aerofoil section at 30° angle of incidence.

It will be noticed that the main streamlines are closest together on the upper surface at a point about one-quarter of the way from the leading edge; this means that pressure will be low at this point and the centre of lift will be somewhere in this region.

If the camber of the section is increased too much, the air cannot cling to the upper surface and is forced to separate under the influence of its original momentum. This is the stall, and pressure in the turbulent air associated with this condition immediately returns to normal, thus reducing lift (figure 10).

The air on the upper side has a high velocity, as it tries to follow a longer path over the large camber. This gives it a lower pressure and much friction drag, to the point where the boundary layer breaks up and turbulence sets in. A mainsail on its own will have an airflow similar to the highly cambered aerofoil, and will produce a pattern on the lines of figure 11. It will be noted that the streamlines break away from the lee side of the sail near the position of maximum camber, and this is a point to remember when it comes to making sails for a cat-rigged boat like the Finn and OK classes.

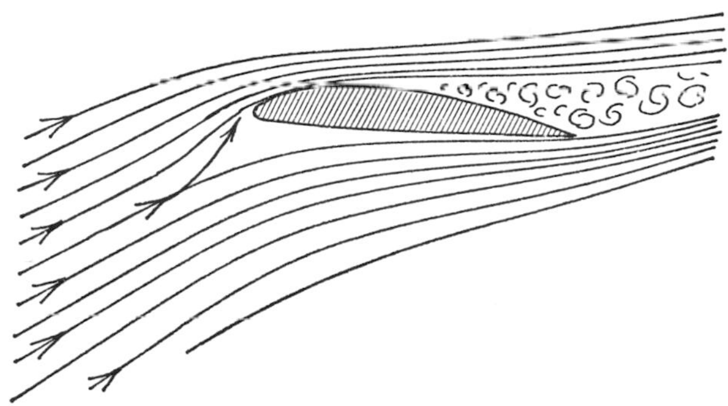

Fig. 10. The stall.

Returning to the aerofoil, if we now introduce a slot through the section, so that some of the lower speed, higher pressure air on the under surface can be bled off to the upper surface, the top flow will be revitalized and the stall delayed.

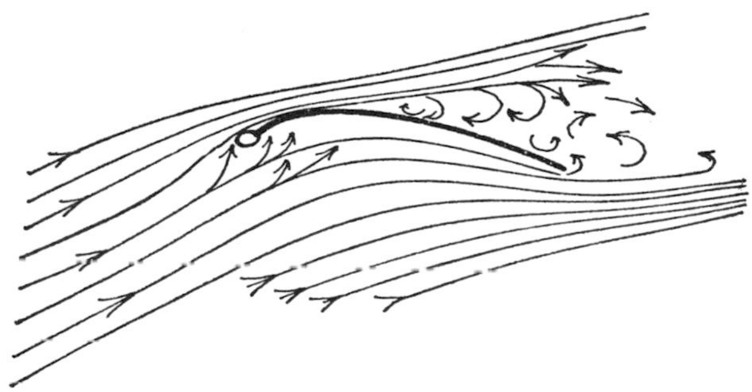

Fig. 11. A mainsail on its own.

We now have the basic situation of the headsail and mainsail acting together, as shown in figures 12 and 13. We must learn to think of these two, not as separate shapes, but as one aerofoil with a slot, exactly as we have just examined. We must therefore consider the flow round the whole of this combined aerofoil.

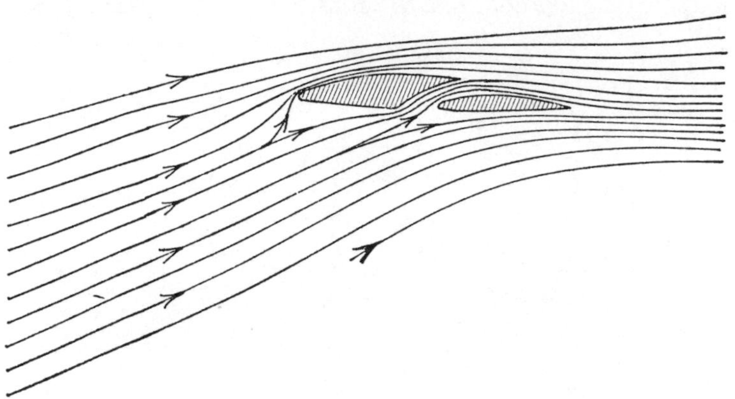

Fig. 12. Effect of a slot in an aerofoil.

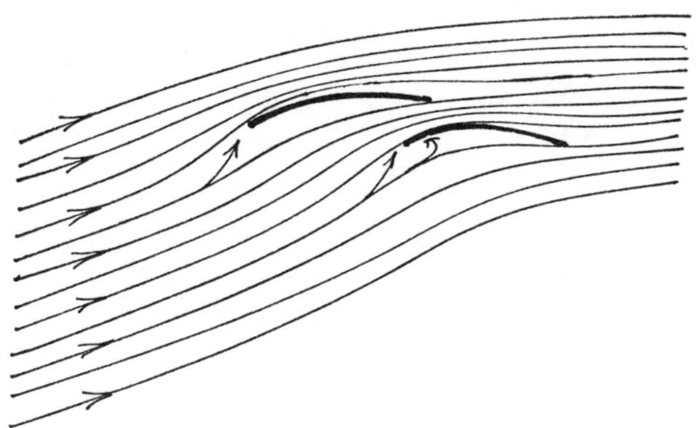

Fig. 13. The combined aerofoil of headsail and mainsail, showing slot effect on the stall.

Task of the Headsail

The principal task of the headsail is therefore twofold:

(*i*) To carry the main driving force in its capacity of leading edge of our combined aerofoil.

(*ii*) To produce an efficient slot.

Driving Force. Theory can quickly be confirmed in practice by the simple act of lowering the mainsail when close-hauled. The pull on the headsail sheet when both sails are up and drawing will be far greater than when the headsail is on its own. The greater thrust developed when the mainsail is set acts largely through the forward quarter of the combined aerofoil (i.e. the headsail); as soon as the mainsail is lowered, the rear half of the aerofoil is removed and the thrust in the headsail diminishes.

Slot. If the slot is too narrow, not enough high-pressure air will get through to leeward to revitalize the airflow on that side, fig. 14 (a). If the slot is too wide, the two sails revert to being independent aerofoils, fig. 14 (b), and lose slot effect; in addition the venturi effect of the slot will not be enough to speed up the air passing to leeward, in order to lower its pressure.

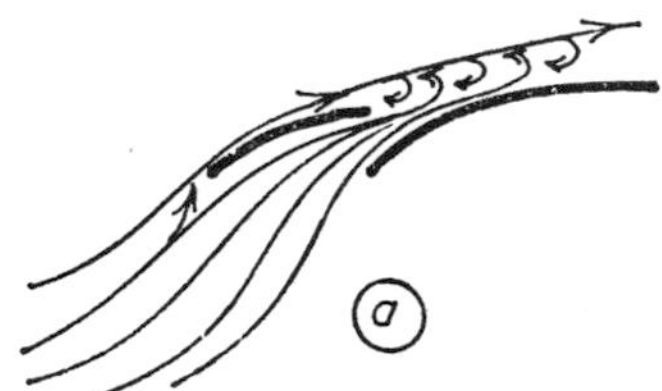

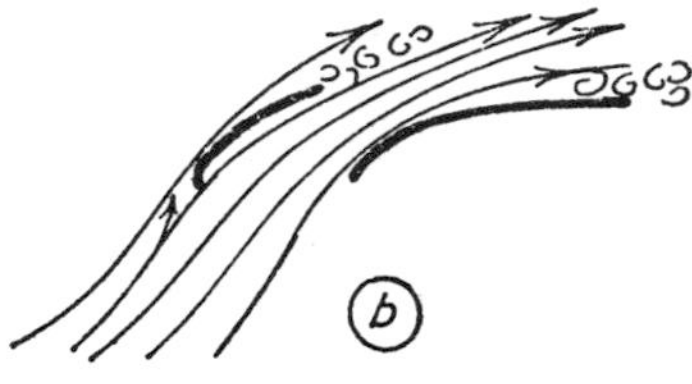

Fig. 14. Slot width
(a) Slot too narrow. Air bunches trying to get through, and becomes turbulent.
(b) Slot too wide. Venturi effect not enough to speed up air in the slot sufficiently.

Overlap. An exact parallel can be drawn in the case of an overlapping headsail or genoa. If the overlap is too little the wind will be dissipated through too great a slot. If it is too great, then the genoa leech starts to come too close to the mainsail, and blockage occurs.

I have also shown in figure 15 the effect of a genoa with a curling leech. Not only does this physically close the gap between the two sails, it also directs the airflow off the leech of the genoa into the lee side of the mainsail, thus further slowing down and disturbing the even flow of air through the slot, and also spoiling the clean aerofoil shape of the mainsail and promoting friction drag and turbulence.

Sails

All this leads one to the conclusion that, for a given combined area, headsail overlap is critical. In assessing a particular boat, however, we are most often presented with the amount of overlap we

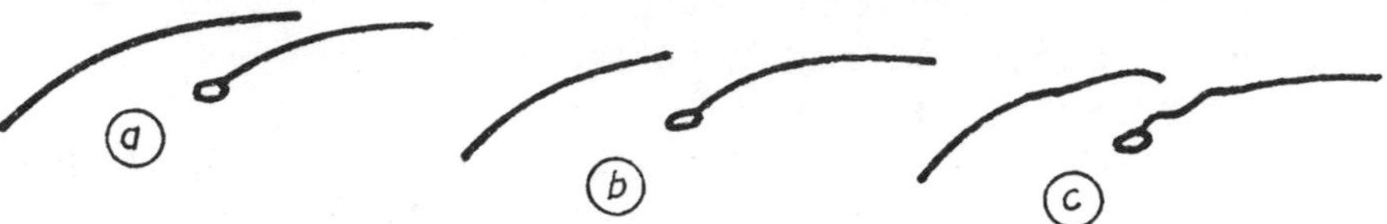

Fig. 15. Genoa Overlap
(a) Too much overlap. The effect will be the same as shown in figure 14(a).
(b) Insufficient overlap. The effect will be the same as shown in figure 14(b).
(c) Curling leech. This is worst of all; not only is there blockage in the slot, but also the wind is directed into the lee of the mainsail.

must use, due to the design of the sail plan or the rule we must follow. We must therefore play with the amount of camber, or flow, in the mainsail and with the amount of hollow in the leech of the headsail, until we get the relationship correct.

Camber

What is the right amount of camber for a sail, and where should it be? The answers to these two questions vary with the type of boat and the conditions for which the sails are intended. There are, however, some assumptions on which we can base our ideas.

Experiments. Southampton University conducted a series of wind-tunnel tests on rigid sails in the unheeled position, and published a preliminary note[1] on the results in 1961. These tests were unrealistic not only in that the sails were made of metal, but also because almost all the investigations were conducted at such low angles of apparent wind that they were outside the working range for ordinary sails. Nevertheless, we can profit from a study of the results if we remember these limitations.

The report's main conclusion concerning fullness of the sails was that the 'position of maximum camber on the mainsail should be

[1] SUYR Paper No. 6, February 1961.

forward of the trailing edge of the foresail, for maximum advantage to be taken of the sloop rig'. This is a corroboration of our discussion above of the effect of the headsail in smoothing out the airflow to leeward of the mainsail, and in the venturi it forms.

The report commented on results of varying the point of maximum camber (the powerpoint) through three positions: 50 per cent, 25 per cent and 15 per cent aft of the luff. It was found that the second two were superior to the first, but I have never been sufficiently happy about the conditions of the tests to accept the results for conventional sails at lower wind speeds without misgivings.

Part of the discussion read as follows: 'The main effect of the foresail on the mainsail would be to delay separation of the flow from the leeward side of the main. In the absence of the foresail this is most likely to occur at, or aft of, the position of maximum camber. If the leech of the foresail is forward of this position, it is doubtful if it will have a big effect in delaying separation.' We know that separation of the airflow causes a breakdown of the low-pressure system which we need to leeward in order to increase our total thrust, and the above passage is therefore particularly important.

Of equal interest is the report by the same source on wind tunnel tests of a one-third scale model of an X class boat.[1] Talking of the interaction between mainsail and headsail, it states that the general direction of airflow on the leeward side of the mainsail in the overlapping region should be tangential to the surface of the mainsail. If the camber of the headsail is too large, excessive convergence of the slot produces a velocity component perpendicular to the mainsail. The report goes on to suggest that a flat headsail should be used, with a mainsail fairly well cambered in the overlapping region, in order to reduce back-winding. It further suggests that altering the trim of the headsail gives relatively large changes in driving force (F_X) but, unlike similar alteration to the mainsail, very small changes in heeling moment (F_Y). This does not immediately concern us at this point, but it should be remembered when we come to the section on trim.

A final point culled from Southampton University reports (and, incidentally, confirmed by me in the Ratsey & Lapthorn wind-tunnel at Cowes) will gratify all helmsmen. In *Sailing Theory and*

[1] SUYR Paper No. 11, October 1962.

Practice Marchaj discusses the relative merits of cambers. Taking as a proportion of the chord, cambers of 1/7 (14·3 per cent), 1/10 (10 per cent) and 1/20 (5 per cent), he concludes that the first two are best in light winds, with little to choose between them, and that 5 per cent is better than the other two in a 20-knot wind. It has thus been established that light airs require a full sail, and heavy weather needs a flat one. We all know this to be true in practice.

Practice. Practice, of course, goes back a long way, and its results have stood the test of time to a point where its devotees will take a good deal of persuading before they throw overboard the experience of a lifetime. The average boat's mainsail should be fuller as the wind gets lighter, and the position of maximum fullness should progress from just aft of the mast in heavy weather to about half-way aft in ghosting conditions. It has been shown under test conditions[1] that the heeling forces generated at low wind speeds are insignificant when compared with the importance of increased thrust; this is the concept of the very full sail. On the other hand, heeling forces become more important as the wind increases, and the emphasis switches from a desire for driving force regardless of heeling moment, to the need to keep down heeling moment at all costs; this demands flat sails.

Back in the 60's, American Sail Maker and Olympic and World Star champion Lowell North went so far as to suggest figures for the camber related to a typical boat of about Star proportions, sailing in force 3 on smooth water. He recommended that the maximum camber of the mainsail should be 10 per cent of the chord at any particular point, and that this flow should be positioned about half-way back in the sail. Comparable figures for the headsail were given as 8 to 10 per cent for the upper two-thirds of the sail, and 6 to 8 per cent for the rest, positioned between a third and half-way aft. Experience has borne out these generalisations, because the modern tendency is to go for mainsail draft almost back to the mid-point, relying on a fine entry to give the ability to point high. When sailing in winds of force 3 and below in smooth water, with a mainsail cut in this fashion, a boat can use Barber haulers to trim sheets well inboard, and climb up to windward without appreciable loss of speed. The headsail needs to be flat rather than full, and have its

[1] SUYR Paper No. 9, March 1962.

camber forward if it is not to direct the wind into the lee side of the mainsail. The important point is to see that the wind runs parallel with the lee of the main as it comes off the leech of the headsail. This usually means that a genoa will have its flow relatively farther forward than a headsail of higher luff/foot ratio, such as the working headsail of a Star or Soling.

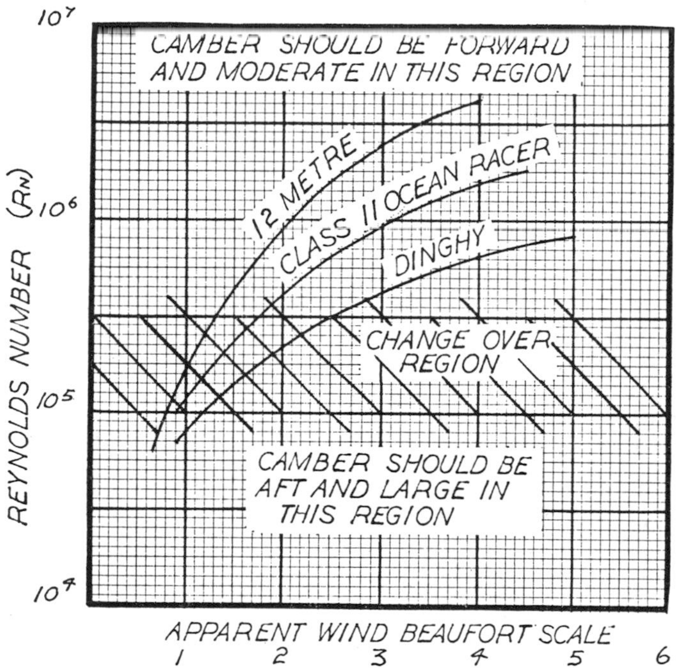

Fig. 16. Effect of RN and wind force on best camber or flow. The larger the mean chord of the combined aerofoil formed by the mainsail and headsail, the flatter should the mainsail be for a given wind strength.

The theoretical optimum camber for a mainsail varies with the mean chord of the sail, as well as with the wind strength for which the sail is designed. Above about force 2, the greater the mean chord, the flatter the sail should be. I am indebted to Mr Fred Cross BSC (ENG.), AFRAeS, for the graph at figure 16, which shows Reynolds Number plotted against wind-speed. This graph was drawn up from data collated by him from early experimental work.

Reynolds Number (R_N) is the ratio of the momentum, or inertia forces, to the viscous forces. When momentum is low (i.e. the Reynolds Number is small) it is easier to make the wind stick to the lee side of the sail, and therefore a large camber can be used. As the Reynolds Number is increased, the camber must be decreased and moved forwards.

It is interesting to note that the actual measurements of a 12 metre mainsail designed for wind-speeds from 10 to 15 knots showed an average camber in the lower two-thirds of the sail of 9 per cent; the greatest measurement recorded was 12 per cent at about half height, while the figure reduced to 6 per cent 5 ft above the boom. Similar figures for a National Enterprise show an average of 13 per cent, a maximum of 15 per cent, and 8 per cent 1 ft above the boom. I have known light weather mainsails for the Dragon class which have exceeded 20 per cent maximum camber.

So far we have been considering a mainsail and headsail in conjunction, but we must not overlook the small cat-rigged boat such as the OK or Finn. We have seen that, in the absence of a headsail, the streamlines over a sail will tend to separate from the lee side at, or aft of, the powerpoint. This of course means that the farther forward the camber, the sooner the airflow will break up with resulting loss of thrust. It is reasonable to suggest, therefore, that a cat-boat sail should have its maximum fullness fairly well aft in order to delay this separation effect as long as possible. This is borne out in practice, for OKs and Finns have always liked fullness near the half-way point in order to go best to windward; if it were any farther aft there would be a loss of driving force due to the centre of effort being too far aft and angling the direction of F_T too much backwards.

Without a headsail to worry about, the cat-boat can have a mast which is a good deal more flexible than a sloop's. This, in turn, means that the sail can be fuller than usual, because it can be flattened more completely in strong winds.

Wind

Two aspects of wind behaviour are relevant to this chapter: gradient and pressure.

Gradient. Largely due to friction, the wind is slower at the surface of the sea than it is higher up. The difference in speed also depends partly on temperature, so that different meteorological conditions give rise to different wind gradients. The graph at figure 17 shows the ratio of the wind speed at any height up to 100 ft to that found at 100 ft (V /V100).

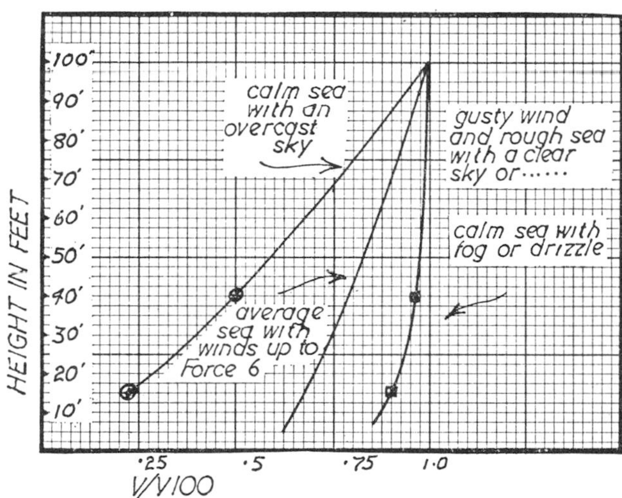

Fig. 17. Ratio of wind speed below 100 ft to wind speed at 100 ft.

The graph illustrates why a tall narrow rig has a greater advantage over a squat one on a calm day, with an overcast sky, than it has under similar wind conditions but when fog or drizzle means a greater temperature loss. In the former case the wind at 15 ft will be just under a quarter of the value at 100 ft, while at 40 ft it will be half; in other words the wind doubles in strength between these two heights. In the latter case, however, the proportions are 0·90 and 0·96 respectively, so there is little increase.

Pressure. The pressure in a sail under given wind conditions can be roughly calculated by using Martin's formula:

$$W = 0{\cdot}004\ V^2A$$

where W is the total weight of wind in the sail in lbs, V is the relative wind speed in m.p.h. and A is the sail area in sq. ft. This formula holds good as an approximation for most points of sailing, but remember that local areas may have a greater or lesser weight per sq. ft than the average, due to aerodynamic forces; the formula gives the *total* weight in the whole sail. Remember this sum next time you have your 700 sq. ft light spinnaker out in a 20 m.p.h. relative reaching wind: you will have half a ton in the sail.

CHAPTER III

Sailcloth

Before going into technical detail about how to make sails, it is as well to get a little background on sailcoth and how it is produced. A woven material is made by arranging a suitable number of threads (or ends) on the beam of a loom to establish the warp, or lengthwise threads, and then passing the thread back and forth through the warp, to form what is known as the picks or weft. The resulting weave is tightened by beating up the weft so that the picks lie more closely together. It will be seen that a given weight of cloth can be established by weaving at what is known as a low sett, which means having a smaller number of thicker threads, or by achieving a larger number of thinner threads through a finer sett. The thickness of an individual thread is known as its count, or decitex (usually written as d'tex) in metric terms: the finer the thread the lower the d'tex.

The density of weave of a particular cloth, as achieved by the closeness of the ends on the beam and the degree to which the weave is tightened by beating up the weft to drive the picks closer together, is expressed as the cover factor. The highest theoretical cover factor which can be achieved for either the warp or the weft threads in a fabric is 28, which represents threads placed so close together that there is no gap between them. A higher value than 28 can, in fact, be achieved by crimping the threads slightly on top of one another, and sailcloth with a cover factor of 32 has been recorded. A logical mind would, of course, raise this magical figure of 28 (which is based on the cotton system of calculation; there are others giving different figures) to 100, thereby converting a measure which is almost meaningless to the layman into a percentage; but sails and sailmaking are full of illogical systems which have grown up with piecemeal development.

A cloth of high d'tex warp and weft, therefore, and a low cover factor, will have fewer threads, a more open weave, and consequently greater porosity than one of the same weight per square yard, but containing thinner threads more closely woven.

With few unsuccessful exceptions, sails in recent centuries have been made from woven cloth. The principal qualities required from sailcloth are as follows:

1. *High Modulus of Extensibility.* The *readiness* with which a material stretches, as opposed to the *degree* which it stretches, is indicated by its Modulus of Extensibility. In sailcloth the modulus should be high, that is to say the fabric should have a good resistance to stretching at low loads.

2. *Stability.* Once a cloth has stretched under load, it should either retain its new form as far as possible, or else it should recover consistently when the load is removed. In either event, its behaviour should be predictable.

3. *Tensile Strength.* Both the yarn and the thread should have a high tenacity allied to a reasonable extension at break (a minimum in the order of 10 per cent – see figure 20(a)); it will thus have a good capacity for absorbing energy and standing up to the shock loads inherent in close weaving on modern looms. The resulting cloth should, of course, be strong enough to withstand hard use.

4. *Impermeability.* Porous sailcloth allows air to permeate from one side of the sail to the other, thereby tending to equalize the pressure distribution to the detriment of thrust. Spinnaker cloth, being particularly thin, suffers more from porosity than cloth for fore and aft sails.

5. *Water Absorption.* Water attracts dirt, and the combination encourages the growth of mildew – it will even grow on glass if the conditions are right. A good sailcloth should not absorb water

either through a porous weave or into the thread itself. In addition, water in sails adds to weight aloft, and thus promotes inefficiency. The requirement, therefore, is for a sailcloth with a low moisture regain percentage; see figure 20(b).

6. *Smoothness.* We saw in the previous chapter how friction drag affects the performance of a sail; a smooth sailcloth reduces friction drag.

7. *Resistance to Chemical Reaction.* Besides mildew, industrial smoke, sun, heat and cold can all affect sailcloth to a greater or lesser extent, in addition to the effects which ordinary chemicals can have if they are accidentally or deliberately brought into contact with the fabric. Resistance to these effects is a factor which should have consideration.

Since sailcloth is woven, with warp and weft forming a close-knit web of yarn threads, there is a certain amount of inherent porosity, depending on the weave and the degree of dressing, or chemical fillers (e.g. resins) put into the cloth in the finishing stage. In addition, any woven fabric must pull out of shape, or stretch as we call it when referring to sails, if a loading or tension is applied on the bias, particularly at 45° to the line of the thread: the small squares formed by the threads crossing each other will be deformed into diamond shapes as the threads move against one another. There will also be a certain amount of linear stretch along the threadline, depending on the nature of the fibre and the amount of twist in the make-up of individual threads, which tend to untwist slightly under load.

The strength of any particular form of sailcloth comes from the basic strength of the individual threads forming that cloth. Where these threads are made up of individual staples, or fibres, from a plant such as flax or cotton, the staples will in turn determine the quality of the thread. Because these staples are closely interlocked in the thread, their length and degree of roughness control the breaking strain of the individual thread, and also the amount of extensibility in it. If, however, the threads can be made up of filaments of one long homogeneous substance, such as occurs in synthetics, individual thread strength will be greater weight for weight than, say, cotton with its separate staples.

Sails

Flax

The first sailcloth with which we need concern ourselves is flax. The herb has narrow, pointed leaves and blue flowers, and its name comes from the Old English word *fleax*. The staples produced when the stems are separated in the retting process are tough, fibrous and fairly long, being as much as 4 ins. or more. These qualities make flax difficult to spin very fine, and it is inherently a coarser thread than cotton. It is about 20 per cent stronger when wet than dry. The resulting cloth is therefore one which pulls out of shape a good deal, but which is particularly suited to hard use.

To this day flax is sometimes chosen for storm sails because it is soft to handle when wet, and also it is stronger than cotton. Storm sails do not always have to be particularly flat, so a little extra stretch can be accepted as the price of easier handling and greater strength – but mildew will strike if they are allowed to remain wet for any length of time, so soft synthetic cloth is best.

Cotton

After flax, chronologically speaking, we come to cotton. The Arabic word *qutun* came to Europe through Spain (where it became *coton*) and France. Egyptian and Sudanese cotton are the best for sailcloth to this day, although the American variety also makes a good cloth. The staple formed by separating the lint from the seed, in a process called ginning, is shorter and finer than flax, being seldom more than an inch long, but it is of a woolly and spiral character which causes resistance between the fibres when they are spun into thread, and naturally produces a uniform cloth.

Being a finer thread, cotton can be woven more closely than flax, and so its advent meant a considerable advance in sail efficiency. Virtually its first appearance as sailcloth in Europe was with the schooner *America*, whose celebrated victory round the Isle of Wight in 1851 started something we have not yet heard the last of. Her cotton sails were much flatter than the baggy suits of flax on her rivals, thus making her closer-winded.

Nylon

Nylon is the generic name for the polyamide fibre plastic derivative of coal, which was developed in America as a result of a long series of experiments started in 1932 by Carothers and his collaborators; it was not used for sails until after the Second World War. Due to its inherent elasticity it is particularly suitable for spinnakers, which can accept a certain amount of give in their cloth to help them achieve their shape. It is also sometimes used for light reaching sails such as mizzen- and spinnaker-staysails. It is not damaged by mildew, but is subject to weakening through prolonged exposure to sunlight.

Polyester

In 1941 J. R. Whinfield and J. T. Dickson of the Calico Printers' Association of Lancashire, England, invented Polyethylene Terephthalate, from which comes the word Terylene, a registered trade mark of Imperial Chemical Industries Limited; the generic name for the fibre is polyester. The war prevented much immediate action on the discovery but ICI agreed to help with development, and they produced their first Terylene yarn in January 1944. Early in 1947 ICI acquired from the Calico Printers' Association the rights for Terylene throughout the world, except for the United States of America, where the rights had already been acquired by DuPont. ICI's affiliated companies abroad produce the polyester material, and the company licensed various manufacturers in other countries to produce it, which is not then allowed to be called Terylene. Tergal in France, Trevira in Germany, Tetoron in Japan, Dacron in America, Terital in Italy and Lavsan in Russia, it is all made to the same chemical formula. These licences started expiring in 1967 and, from that date, there has developed a 'free' market, i.e. a manufacturer of polyester fibre in one country is now allowed to sell the yarn in other countries without restriction as, indeed, he has always been able to sell both the fabric and the article into which the fabric is made. Equally polyester fibre may now be manufactured in some countries by companies other than the original licensee – for instance Fiber Industries Inc. produce it in the United States of America under the name of Fortrel.

Although directly related chemically, there are variations in the types of polyester yarn commercially available throughout the world. For instance, the availability of counts or deniers varies somewhat between the United States of America and Great Britain.

The first sails made from Terylene in England were by Gowen &

Co. of Essex, in the winter of 1951–52, and the 8-metre cruiser/racer *Sonda* had the first one they made commercially – a genoa.

Terylene and Dacron polyester fibre is made from the polymer polyethylene terephthalate, a condensation product of terephthalic acid and ethylene glycol (familiar to motorists as anti-freeze), both of which are derived by chemical synthesis from products of mineral oil cracking. The filament yarn used in sailcloth has no individual staple, each filament being one long extrusion, and the thread is made up of many filaments twisted together. When this thread leaves the manufacturer it has up to about one twist per inch according to denier, in order to bind the individual filaments together. This thread is then processed by a specialist called a Throwster, who twists it further to the Weaver's specification. The more the thread is twisted the greater resistance it has to filamentation in the weaving process, since it holds together better, but the more linear elasticity it will have as the twists tend to unwind slightly under tension.

Polyester sailcloth can be, and often is, woven with warp and weft of different denier, as was flax and cotton. In the early 1950s original cloth constructions were based on lessons learned during the cotton era, and concentration was applied to seeking a high weft factor.

Flax and cotton sailcloths, however, were merely calendered as the final and only finishing process. Polyester sailcloth is scoured and dried, and may have various resin fillers added to improve stability and bias stretch; it is then heat-relaxed to shrink and settle the material, helping the threads to lock together. These processes are normally carried out by specialist firms of Finishers on both sides of the Atlantic.

Cotton constructions proved wrong, and a whole new series of lessons had to be learned. In recent times, Weavers have turned their attention to over-sett cloths with a higher warp factor, but it has been the Finishers who have had to grapple with the major problem. A slack weave has to have chemicals added in order to give it any semblance of stability; a really good, well-woven cloth can easily be turned in the finishing stage into a harsh and brittle fabric which will tear like paper. The final sailcloth can have a hard and stiff finish, which was popular in America at one time, or a soft handle which is difficult to sew up without puckering and tends to have a high stretch factor on the bias. Finishing can make a poor or slackly woven cloth look pleasing for a time. A poor fabric can be so heavily packed with resin fillers that it may appear to be near perfect when new. In use, the filler will eventually break down and detach itself from the cloth to run off with rain or salt spray in a liquid which appears like milk, or else the surface will deteriorate into typical marble crazing as the filler cracks.

The requirement is for a well-woven cloth made of the finest yarns possible, tightly woven together. The ratio of count or decitex between warp and weft must be so arranged that resin additives or fillers are kept to the minimum required to produce the handle and stability desired after the resulting cloth has been heat-relaxed. This is really another way of saying that cloth must be woven to such a standard that chemical additives are not necessary in order to give it the required characteristics, unless special considerations apply.

Commercial Weavers were discouraged for a long time by the economic factors in producing such a cloth. Sailcloth represents such a small proportion of the average Weaver's output for all uses, that they could not justify the close supervision and special machinery necessary to achieve such perfection.

The introduction of polyester fibre, however, made the vital role played by sailcloth in yacht propulsion increasingly apparent. It was Ted Hood of the United States of America who first decided (in 1950) that, if he were to get exactly what he wanted, he would have to weave it himself. He was followed in this by Ratsey & Lapthorn Limited of England in 1964.

For these two Sail Makers better sails, have, of course, been the sole reason for their entry into the textile field. They have been able to concentrate on the single aim of producing the highest quality sailcloth, without the distractions of diverting calls from more commercial materials. The effort put into the product is out of all proportion to the amount of cloth produced – for instance, the Sail Makers have one weaver for every two or three looms, whereas commercial Weavers sometimes have twenty times as many looms to each supervisor when producing large quantities of cheap material for household use. This close supervision is part of the price which has to be paid for sailcloth to the high specification required.

I am not able to speak first-hand for Hood's, but I was Ratsey &

Lapthorn's Manager when Franklin Ratsey-Woodroffe took the decision to start weaving at Cowes. For a year I had a ringside seat as all our energies were thrown into the task, and I have followed progress with interest since leaving them in 1965.

Ratsey's call their sailcloth Vectis, after the Roman name for the Isle of Wight where they weave it. The high quality demanded has meant that the cloth has to be woven on heavy, slow speed looms under great tension. Fortunately, the inherent strength of Terylene means that it can withstand this tension, and the weft can be beaten up hard so that the picks lie really close together, as we have seen is desirable. I suppose the project really stemmed from the failure of the British challenge for the America's Cup with *Sovereign* in 1964. At that period the superiority of Hood's sailcloth had been recognized for some time by far-sighted persons. A close analysis was made of his material, and an attempt was made to produce in England a cloth incorporating all the best features of his construction. Part of this analysis is shown in the table opposite, which also compares the construction of comparable Vectis cloth.

Early Vectis cloth was woven on commercial looms adapted for the job. Meanwhile a fund of experience was gained, so that the specification for the building of special production looms could be laid down with assurance.

In the initial stages there was a strong temptation to retain a small amount of chemical additives in the finishing process. This would have dressed a lower standard of cloth to an acceptable state of stability in its early life, and would have saved a great deal of research, effort and money. The fillers would have eventually broken down, however, revealing the cloth in its true quality, so the decision was taken to eliminate resins and fillers entirely, leaving heat-relaxation as the only finishing process. Incidentally, this has the desirable secondary effect of making the cloth much softer, so that sails are easier to handle; they also stow in less space. It has also meant, however, that an extremely exacting standard must be met if the cloth is not to be loosely woven, porous and subject to a good deal of stretch. The answer has been found in slow weaving under great tension, and constant supervision at all times.

Naturally, constant maintenance of this high quality demands close control and a good deal of test equipment. The principal test

	1964 Terylene. Commercial British weave, based on Hood's construction		*1964 Dacron.* Woven by Hood Sailmakers Inc.		*1969 Terylene.* Vectis cloth Woven by Ratsey & Lapthorn	
	Warp	Weft	Warp	Weft	Warp	Weft
Fabric weight oz/yd² (gm/m²)	14 (465)		14 (465)		14½ (480)	
Nominal denier*	3/250 H.T.	5/250 H.T.	3/250 M.T.	1/1100 1/220 H.T.	2/250 H.T.	3/250 H.T.
Ply twist t.p.i.	5 'Z'	3 'Z'	6 'Z'	2 'Z'	10 'S'	2½ 'Z'
Resultant denier*	895	1460	865	1460	567	810
Denier* uptake %	19·3	16·8	15·7	10·6	13·4	8·0
Threads per inch	65	32	63·4	33	88	48
Cover factor	21·6		21·4		26·0	
Yarn crimp %	6·9	0·7	11·6	0·9	14·0	0·5

H.T. = High tenacity. M.T. = Medium tenacity. * Divide by 0·9 to convert to decitex
t.p.i. = twists per inch. 'Z' and 'S' = direction of twist.

Fig. 18. Analysis of early polyester sailcloth construction.

which Sail Makers all over the world apply to sailcloth in one form or another is one which involves measuring bias stretch. Methods of doing this vary from hanging a weight of about five pounds on a two inch wide strip of cloth cut at 45° to the threadline, and then measuring by a ruler the resulting elongation and recovery, to electronic measurement by means of sophisticated machinery. The hysteresis curves at figure 19 show typical results from an Instron tensile tester when examining three cloths of comparable weight.

It will be noticed in particular how cloth 'A' stretches a good deal, then recovers badly to stretch a good deal at the second loading with an equally poor recovery; this pattern is repeated at each cycle. Cloth 'B' stretches less and recovers very well, to stretch again with an equally good recovery each time. Cloth 'C' stretches once to a similar degree to cloth 'B' and then settles down to a very small stretch with an almost complete recovery – the equivalent really of stretching once and then stabilizing.

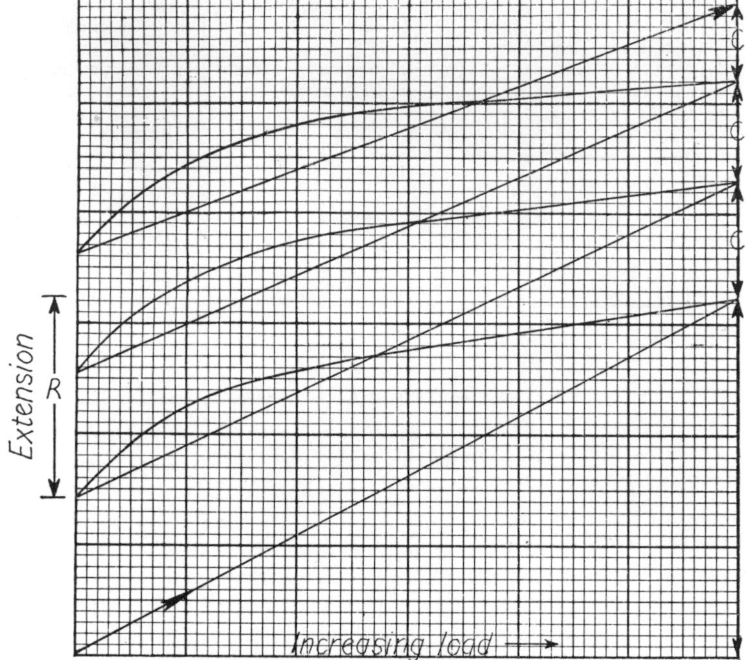

Fig. 19 (a) I = Initial stretch
R = Recovery
C = Creep after successive loading

Cloth 'A'. Slack cloth with excessive stretch and poor recovery.

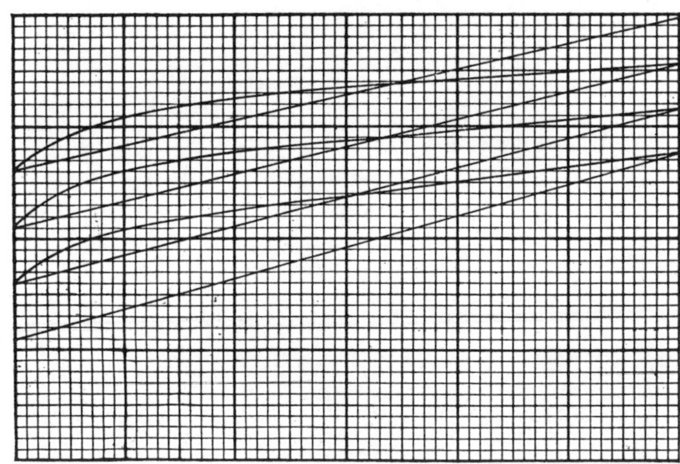

Fig 19 (b) *Cloth 'B'*. Good cloth with fair stretch and good recovery each time.

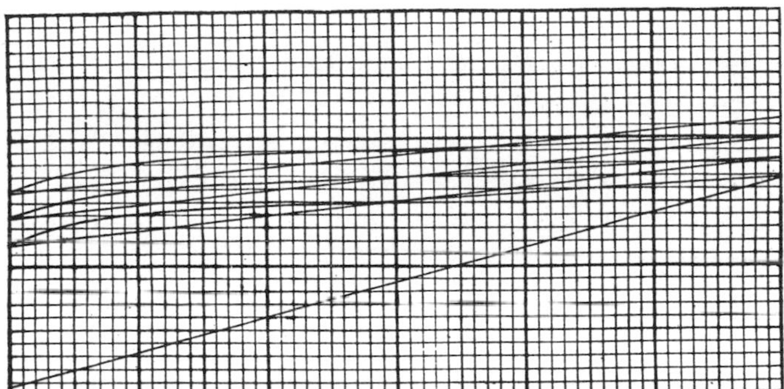

Fig. 19 (c) *Cloth 'C'*. Good cloth with low stretch after one initial movement.

The Sail Maker must decide whether he wants to tailor the flow into his sail to a specific shape, allowing for an initial stretch but being sure of stability thereafter (cloth 'C'), or whether he wants the cloth to stretch a little each time to help the sail achieve its flow, providing it recovers properly when the load is off (cloth 'B').

It should not be thought from all this that commercial producers are being left behind by the amateurs. There is a general realisation of the significance of all aspects of sailcloth. ICI decided some time ago that the relatively small commercial return on this side of their business is more than outweighed by the fact that many Top People in industry indulge in sailing, and that some research would help their image in the right places.

The aim of the ICI programme was to improve the yarn, so that Weavers might produce a better cloth. The Company already has unrivalled laboratory facilities for testing yarn and cloth at all stages of its manufacture, prior to delivery to the Sail Maker. It was decided, therefore, to try and evaluate the movement (or stretch) of cloth while under normal operating conditions. To do this, a test mast was erected in the open so that full size sails could be examined.

Measurement of wind speed and direction was recorded, as was the force generated by the sail (as registered by a load cell introduced into the main sheet). The sails were marked at 12 in. vertical and horizontal spacing, and photogrammetry was employed to record the amount and direction of distortion induced by different wind strengths. This is a system of twin stereo cameras much used by map makers to establish contours by aerial photography; it has the merit that no direct contact with the sails is necessary, so the wind flow is undisturbed.

Test conditions and results were carefully recorded, fed into a computer and analysed by a stereo-autographic plotter, which produced three-dimensional co-ordinates together with both plan and elevation views.

Initial results indicated that stretch in different parts of a sail is not always what might be expected. For instance, in a mainsail cut with cloths running at rightangles to the leech, stretch in the head of the sail closely follows the line of the weft *providing the cloth is well woven*; it is more conventionally on the bias if the cloth is slack and of poor quality, while it is on the bias anyway in the lower half of the sail. This points the way to the possible use of two different cloths in making a mainsail: one for the upper half, where construction would be aimed at containing stretch on the weft, and one for the lower half which would aim at reducing bias stretch.

Reverting once again to the Sail Makers who weave their own cloth, it is perhaps fortunate for the yachtsman that there is more than one: each will always be keen to see that the opposition does not get too far advanced in development. As long ago as 1967 Ted Hood produced a mainsail for a 12 metre (*Intrepid*, defender that year of the America's Cup) made from $9\frac{1}{4}$ oz/yd² ($7\frac{1}{2}$ oz US) fabric. The principal advantage of a lighter cloth, besides the ability to take up its proper shape in light winds and when running and reaching, is a reduction in weight aloft; this cuts down the pitching moment as well as the heeling moment. A secondary advantage is that the lighter material does not flog so much when the boat is head to wind.

This lightweight sail was used by *Intrepid* throughout the series, despite the fact that the cloth was not much more than half the usual weight for a 12 metre; it kept its shape even in the stronger wind ranges. This remarkable achievement was made possible by a combination of improvements in the yarn filament, in cloth construction and in weaving technique. The result is expensive, but price is no object in this kind of competition. The cruising man reaps the benefit of a better cloth as soon as production can be stepped up to commercial proportions.

From the foregoing you might be forgiven for assuming that a non-resinated cloth is the answer to the yachtsman's prayers, and is the solution to all our problems. A measure of the difficulties involved, however, is provided by the teething troubles suffered in producing KAdron, a sailcloth without fillers produced in Australia.

After the acceptance by the Americans in 1964 of the Australian challenge for the America's Cup in 1967, it was decided to weave a synthetic sailcloth without fillers in Australia; it was christened KAdron. It is interesting to note that even the resources of a large textile concern, concentrated over three intense years, were not able to guarantee success at the first, or even the second attempt. The final cloth still left a good deal to be desired, although perhaps the designers were not able to take full advantage of its properties because they were at that time still some way from fully understanding the implications of such a fabric.

A sailcloth without fillers will, as we have seen, be softer than one which is resinated. As you might expect, it therefore usually has a certain amount of inherent elasticity. This is not necessarily a bad thing provided, first, that it is kept within reasonable bounds and, secondly, that it recovers well. Under the action of the wind, the flow will move aft as the sail bellies due to elasticity. Obviously, this should not be excessive, nor should it be such that the sail will not resume its original shape when the pressure is off. This stretch can be compensated by the correct use of bendy spars where a mainsail is concerned; a headsail is another story, however, and may not be able to absorb variations in shape so easily – particularly where the luff is not adjustable.

Where the sail shape, or flow design, cannot be altered while sailing, therefore, there is a case for a highly resinated cloth. The sail will have been tailored to a particular shape for specific conditions, and that shape should be allowed to alter as little as possible. The use of fillers in the cloth will ensure a more stable material in the initial stages of its life (cloth 'C' in figure 19), and will thus help to retain the shape which has been scientifically cut into the sail, rather than induced by means of tension on the cloth. This also holds good for those sails which might otherwise endanger their good shape if they stretch too much in different places due to a multitude of bias angles. Breakdown of the chemicals can, moreover, be postponed very considerably if the sails are not subjected to excessive stretch, and are meticulously rolled each time they are taken off. This virtually restricts use of this cloth to boats of up to day sailer size.

Other Synthetic Cloths

Ever since synthetic sailcloth started, the search for improvement has been constant. In the sphere of the spinnaker, the goal has been a finer material than the one-ounce nylon which for long represented the lightest available (although nylon of half an ounce is now claimed on both sides of the Atlantic). In recent years attention has been turned to polypropylene because of its high tenacity, high toughness, low moisture regain and low density [see figure 20(b)]. This material is called Ulstron when produced in England by ICI Fibres.

Low density means that a very lightweight polypropylene fabric can be produced with a fair degree of impermeability, because the thickness of thread for a given weight is greater than nylon. One of the major snags, however, is that the resulting cloth – be it polypropylene or nylon – is very thin at the half-ounce weights we are considering, and it deteriorates rapidly in sunlight. Polypropylene is more susceptible than nylon, but use of a stabilizing agent to inhibit the effects of ultra-violet rays somewhat reduces this degradation. Hood Sailmakers Inc. did some tests to show polypropylene to be at least half as resistant to sunlight as nylon, which is good when the other advantages are considered.

Various other synthetic cloths have been tried but, although some of them have advantages, they usually fail in other areas such as modulus of extensibility (like Melinex) or flexing fatigue (like Kevlar or Fiber B).

Cloth Testing

I have already mentioned the bias stretch test made by Sail Makers to test sailcloth; this section is meant more for the owner who wishes to test samples of sailcloth for himself. A simple bias test can be conducted by pulling the cloth at 45° to the threadline between the hands. Stretch should be low, and the resulting crease should not remain too prominently after the pull is slackened. Another good way to test synthetic cloth which is suspected of being overfilled with resins, is to crumple it in the hand to observe the crazing of the surface as the chemicals break down. If you have time, it is also a

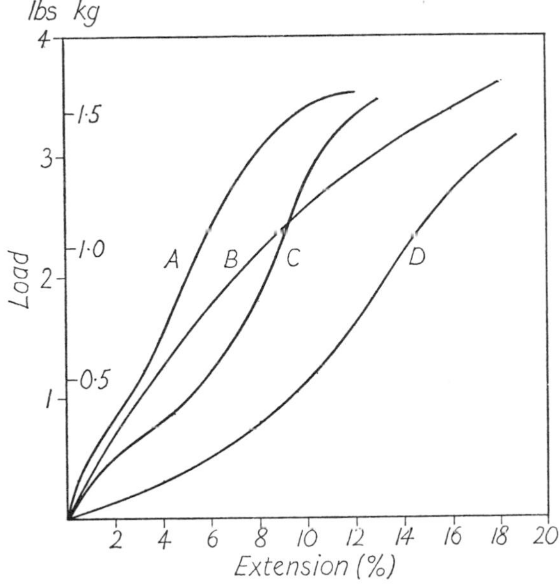

Note
Divide denier by 0·9 to convert to decitex.

A = 250 den Terylene (H.T.), dry or wet.
B = 190 den Ulstron, dry or wet.
C = 210 den nylon (H.T.), dry.
D = 210 den nylon (H.T.), wet.

Figure 20(a). Load extension curves for sailcloth yarns.

Property	Ulstron	Terylene	Nylon	Flax	Cotton	Glass
Tenacity (g/den)						
Dry	8·0–8·5	6·5–7·5	7·0–8·8	2·4	1·5–2·0	6·3–7·0
Wet	8·0–8·5	6·5–7·5	6·0–7·9	2·9	1·8–2·4	5·4–5·8
Extension at break (%)						
Dry	18–22	10–14	16–26	2–3	3–10	3–4
Wet	18–22	10–14	19–28	4	2·5–8·0	2·5–3·5
Elastic recovery (% from 5% extension)	88	90	98	Breaks	45	Breaks
Initial modulus (g/den)	90	110–130	40–50	136	12–70	330
Moisture regain (%)	0·1	0·4	4·2	12	8	0
Specific gravity of fibre	0·91	1·38	1·14	1·54	1·54	2·5–2·6

The tensile properties quoted for flax and cotton refer to spun yarns, which have an overall tenacity lower than that of the individual single fibres.

Figure 20(b). Table of Comparative Filament Yarn Properties. (Reproduced by kind permission of ICI Fibres) good idea to nail a sample to a mast for twenty-four hours and then look at the results at the end. An overfilled cloth of poor quality will quickly have the stuffing knocked out of it by this treatment, and both bias stretch and recovery will suffer.

Where chemicals are used, they have to be forced into the cloth under pressure using rollers, and then 'cured' by heating. After the cloth has been made up into a sail, therefore, there is no way in which an old synthetic sail can be renovated by redressing the cloth as can be done with cotton.

Nylon is tested mainly for porosity and, with practice, a good deal can be told by trying to blow or suck through it. Sail Makers use a more exact method which usually takes the form of some kind of hollow cylinder made to fit vertically into a container of water. The nylon to be tested is fastened over the upper end, thus restricting the passage of air, and the time taken for the cylinder to descend a given distance into the water is a direct indication of the porosity of the cloth under test.

These simple tests are given as a guide only. Your Sail Maker is the expert, and you should normally be guided by him in preference to your own assessment. Sail Makers have a wide experience in judging cloth and, indeed, all other matters relating to making sails, and nothing will be more calculated to get you off to a bad start than ill-informed criticism and comment, or over-insistence on your own point of view with no more grounds than, say, a quick glance through this book.

Sail Outline Design

Before the Sail Maker can get down to the task of selecting the right cloth for the sail under consideration, and then to deciding how he is going to make it, he must know its outline shape. This is sail design proper, and should not be confused with the design of the camber, or flow, of the sail together with the round or hollow built into the edges of the sail in order to achieve the desired performance; I prefer to call this flow design, and I shall refer to it in some detail later.

In most cases the outline design of a sail will be decided for the Sail Maker. Either the yacht is a one-design boat, with strict limits and tolerances on the sizes allowed, or else there will be a sail plan, and he will be required to follow the sizes set forth by the Naval

Architect or the rule. It may be, however, that the owner will ask the Sail Maker to make a sail for a specific task, and that this sail does not figure on the sail plan – or indeed that no plan exists.

Not many Sail Makers have a qualified Naval Architect on their staff, but most of them have sufficient practical experience of sailing and sailmaking to design a reasonable sail to most plans. It should be remembered, however, that they will almost certainly be working without the underwater lines of the boat, and that their answer will at best be an experienced cock-shy and not a qualified calculation. Such a course has, for the owner, the advantage that design fees are saved, but there can be no redress if the result is not all that could be desired. Redress from a Naval Architect would, however, be hard to come by, and the Sail Maker has years of experience in interpreting sail plans from a wide variety of designers, so you need not be chary of asking his opinion.

Naturally it will be a comparatively easy task to draw a maximum size no-penalty IOR genoa on to an existing sail plan. All that has to be done is to draw the LP one and a half times the J measurement, and then to see that adequate clearance is allowed at the head, tack and clew. It is a slightly more delicate calculation to suggest a suitable intermediate genoa or working jib, and it becomes a major task when a complete redrawing of the sail plan is required, in order perhaps to alleviate weather helm or to reduce the rating. These last two aims are best met by calling on the services of a qualified Naval Architect, unless you are quite certain that you know what you want or that your Sail Maker can be relied upon.

I shall refer in more detail to this question in the chapter on 'Design and Rating', but I would refer the reader anxious to draw up his own sail plan to the chapters on sail design in Captain Illingworth's admirable book *Further Offshore*. He will find there many of the finer points explained at some length.

Cloth Weight

I shall assume here that the outline shape of the sail is known to the Sail Maker. The next task is to establish what weight of cloth will be used for the sail in question. I propose to deal exclusively with synthetic cloth in this connection, as many excellent books and articles have been written about cotton. I refer the reader in particular to the earlier editions of *Yacht Sails, Their Care and Handling* by Ernest Ratsey and Ham de Fontaine, and *Offshore* by John Illingworth – both of which, let me hasten to add, have been revised since the advent of synthetic cloth.

Terylene and Dacron are strong enough to resist hard use, but this causes one of the most common errors to be made: too light a weight is selected. What is too often forgotten is the stretch factor. I can do no better than to quote John Illingworth on this subject, as his views coincide so closely with my own:

'In the case of headsails the answer in brief is to use the lightest weight of cloth *which will keep its shape*, in the wind strength for which the sail is designed . . . care must be taken to choose a mainsail cloth which will be *fully adequate to its task* but no heavier.' (The italics are mine.)

A light cloth, while being easier to stow and handle, will stretch more readily than a heavy one, and the sail will consequently blow out of shape, usually manifested by the flow moving aft to an inefficient position. Steps must then be taken to correct the situation by pulling harder on the halyard or luff adjustment. As we shall see later, on pages 63 and 65, this has the desirable effect of drawing the flow forward again to restore the proper aerodynamic shape. Besides the size and function of the sail, the weight of cloth for a particular sail is also a function of the size and type of boat, and the winds which the sail can expect to meet. Thus a beamy cruising boat will have heavier sails than a slim racer of the same length. Similarly for any particular boat the larger the headsail the lighter the weight of cloth in general, for the sooner the sail will be replaced by a smaller one as the wind increases. The heaviest canvas, therefore, will be used for the storm headsail (in practice usually no heavier than the working headsail); the intermediate genoa and the genoa each becomes progressively lighter. The question of light weather headsails is slightly different, and receives attention later.

Continuing the practical approach to the problem, on a cutter we normally have the jib lighter than the staysail, because the former is usually taken off first as the wind gets up. Some owners of twin headsail yawls and ketches, however, prefer to sail in really heavy weather under mizzen and jib rather than mizzen and staysail, because the boat is better balanced; it partly depends on where the topmast stay arrives at the deck, for it may be dangerous in a blow to handle a jib on the end of a bowsprit. If the jib is the last working headsail to come off before storm canvas is set, then its weight should be sufficient to maintain shape in all winds up to this moment. Conversely, if the jib is set on a bowsprit, it will be taken off sooner and, in any case, it is not desirable to have too much weight to handle so far beyond the end of the boat.

Before we get down to actual figures, I should say something about the various methods of denoting cloth weight. The Americans measure sailcloth in ounces per yard of cloth 28½ in. wide, whereas in Britain the square yard is used. There is thus an apparent difference of 20 per cent in our respective cloth weights, for a yard of cloth in Britain will have more material to be weighed (being 36 in. wide) than a yard in America (being only 28½ in. wide). Thus 3½ oz. (US) is the same cloth as 4½ oz. (Br.), while 6½ oz. (US) = 8 oz. (Br.). Countries using the metric system use grammes per square metre, and the two examples above would be 155 gm/m² and 275 gm/m² respectively. I have attached a comparison table at Appendix A.

Working Sails. The best way to establish the weight of cloth for a particular boat's sails is to decide the mainsail and working headsail first. It is not possible to be dogmatic because different types of boat need different solutions, but it is always useful to have a yardstick. A good method is to relate cloth weight to the water-line length of the boat. It is a direct indication of the size of the yacht and, unlike tonnage, there is only one interpretation of a given figure; it also has the advantage that it can be scaled straight from the sail plan. You may consider that sail area would be an equally good method, but you would be surprised at the number of owners who do not know the area of their sails. In addition some yachts carry more or less sail than the average and, in any case, headsail sizes can vary between yachts of the same size: a masthead genoa will be a good deal larger than the largest headsail which can be set on a yacht of similar proportions which only has a three quarter rig; yet they will both be used under similar wind conditions. In addition, there is always a risk of confusion between rated and actual areas.

Below is a table showing the recommended weights of cloth for average boats of various water-line lengths. These should be varied either way if the boat is especially heavy or light for her size, or if she habitually sails in light winds or Atlantic gales. Besides the working sails, I have shown my thoughts on genoas. In this connection it should be remembered that owners are tending nowadays to hold on to these sails in stronger winds than they did ten years ago. The tremendous pulling power of the genoa has been appreciated at last, and it is common practice to take two or three rolls in the mainsail and leave the genoa on, as the wind increases. In this case it becomes the equivalent of a working headsail, and its cloth weight should be calculated accordingly.

For those who want to carry some sort of figure in their head, a very rough guide to working canvas weight can be obtained from the following formula:

$$Wt = \frac{L}{3} - 10\%$$

where Wt is cloth weight in oz/yd² and L is the waterline length in feet.

The cloth for the mainsail of a yawl or ketch should normally be decided in accordance with the table opposite, tending to go slightly lighter if there is any doubt. This is because the sail will be rather smaller than a mainsail for a comparable sloop, and probably smaller than for a cutter, so it will not have as large a total pressure in it for a given wind strength. On the other hand, beware of going too light for it will not be reefed as often, due to its smaller initial size.

A mizzen should normally be not more than two weights lighter than its mainsail. It is here that calculation according to area can lead one astray, and I take issue with John Illingworth on this point. A yawl of 30 ft water-line may have a mainsail of 350 sq. ft and a cloth weight of 9 oz/yd². Its mizzen, however, may not be larger than 60 or 70 sq. ft, which *Offshore* would have us give 6 oz/yd² cloth. Yet this is the sail which may well have to stand up to the weight of a near-gale, when the mainsail has been removed. 7½ or 8 oz. is the minimum for such a task, even at this small area. We did, in fact, make one mizzen of about 60 sq. ft at Ratseys out of 6 oz. cloth for a French owner. It was a complete failure, for the leech stretched badly out of shape and, though we recut the sail twice, it was never a success. The owner, of course, blamed poor sailmaking, and I suppose he was right, because we should have refused to accept instructions to use such a light material. We were in a difficult position, because there was no doubt what had caused the leech to stretch, but we could not put the blame on the Naval Architect concerned without incurring his displeasure, to the possible jeopardy of future orders from him. On the other hand, the owner was most

TABLE OF RECOMMENDED CLOTH WEIGHTS

Weights are expressed in oz/yd². To convert to oz/yd × 28½ in. (US system) or to gm/m², see Appendix A.

Yacht	*Mainsail and Working Headsail*	*Genoa*	*Intermediate Genoa*	*Light Genoa*
Small dinghies	3½– 4½	—	—	—
Stout dinghies	5 – 6	5 – 6	—	—
Small keelboats	6 – 7½	5½– 7½	—	—
Larger keelboats:				
Dragon, Soling	7 – 8½	5½– 8½	—	4 – 5
L.W.L.:				
20 ft	5½– 7	5 – 8	—	3 – 4½
21–25 ft	7 – 8	6 – 9½	7 – 9½	3 – 5
26–30 ft	8 – 9	6 –10½	8½–10½	3 – 5½
31–35 ft	9 –10½	7½–12	9½–12	4 – 6
36–40 ft	10½–12	8 –13	11 –13	4 – 6
41–45 ft	12 –13½	9½–14½	12 –14½	5 – 6½
46–50 ft	13½–14½	*	*	*
51–60 ft	14½–16	*	*	*
61–70 ft	16 –18	*	*	*

*requires individual assessment.

displeased so we just had to grin and bear it. As I say, it was partly our fault for allowing ourselves to be talked into such a light material in the first place.

Reverting to the table, you will notice that light genoas do not increase their cloth weight in proportion to the other sails. This is because they should never be used in winds above force 3, and the total weight of wind in the sail will thus not be great, no matter how large an area is involved. I must here make the first of several warnings about using such sails in winds too strong for them; this also applies to ghosters and drifters, with even more effect. It is a natural temptation to hold on to a sail which is pulling well, even though the wind increases a good deal. If this occurs, the sail may be ruined for all time as it is blown out of shape, and the owner must make up his mind whether the race is worth it.

Let me repeat that this table is only a guide, and that each boat's sails should be the subject of an individual decision in the light of all the factors: size and type of boat, size and role of sail, winds expected, life expected from the sail, stability of the canvas. This latter factor reminds me that a weight lighter all round can be used if the sail is made from panels which are narrower than the usual 33 to 36 in. This is because a shorter length of cloth is exposed on the bias which, in turn, means that there will be less stretch for a given material.

Before closing this chapter on sailcloth, I must mention one more British Sail Maker who has entered the textile field. Following his close association with *Sovereign*'s challenge for the America's Cup in 1964, Bruce Banks initiated an intensive campaign to develop sailcloth to his own specification.

Late in 1966 this development work started to pay off, and a limited range of sailcloths began to emerge. Banks now hires loom time on contract from an established firm of Weavers, who produce his Challenger range of cloths to his own specification. The high cover factors obtainable with modified looms and techniques ensure a fabric so tightly woven from high tensile yarns that it needs no synthetic fillers to promote stability, when used for large cruising and off-shore racing sails. The smaller class racing boats often require a slightly different approach and, in this case, it had been found that a hard finish gives added power and speed. Banks, therefore, produces a Challenger cloth specially treated to give a rock-hard finish suitable for constructing these fully moulded sails.

CHAPTER IV

Sail Flow Design

After the general shape and outline form of the sail have been decided, and the cloth selected, the Sail Maker must make up his mind how he proposes to achieve the flow which has been agreed. To differentiate it from the sail design involved in drawing up a sail plan, I have called it flow design.

Not only must the controlling dimensions and weight of cloth have been decided at this stage, but also the general degree of fullness required in the finished product and the conditions under which it will be used should be known. By this I mean not only what wind speeds it will encounter, but also the characteristics of the spars or stay on which it will be set. Thus, a headsail made for a forestay which is nearly straight (the optimum) will be cut differently from one which is to be used on a wire which sags a good deal; the luff of the latter will have to be cut to allow for a predetermined curve. The same holds good for a mast which bends.

There are five principal ways in which a sail can have flow designed or controlled:

1. Rounding the luff and foot.
2. Tapering the cloths (broad seam).
3. Tension on the cloth.
4. Tension on the rope, tape or wire.
5. Lay of the cloth.

Rounding the Luff and Foot

If the luff and foot of a mainsail destined for a straight mast and boom are cut in a convex curve, the surplus cloth will be pushed back into the sail as flow when it is put on the spars and the edges are forced into straight lines.

This flow will lie fairly close to the mast and boom, and the Sail Maker will have no control over where it settles unless he adopts other measures as well. There are, however, many successful sails which

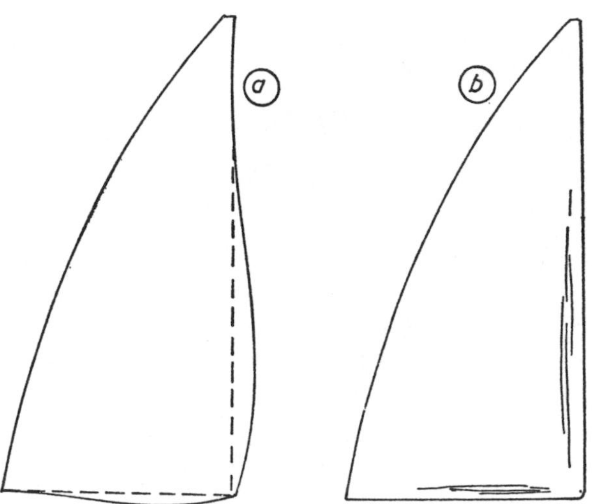

Fig. 21. (a) Luff round and foot round in a mainsail laid flat on the floor before roping.
(b) When the sail is hoisted on straight spars the extra cloth is forced back into the sail as flow.

have their flow arbitrarily induced in only this way. The less round built into the sail, the flatter it will be, so there is none built in at the head, which may even be slightly hollow if it is desired to keep the sail particularly flat at this point. Bendy spars must have more round, so that the sail can take up the shape of the spars under maximum flexion, and still provide the extra cloth required for camber.

A headsail receives similar treatment along its luff. Round is built into the lower half of the sail to provide flow, and it is taken away from the upper half where the sail needs to be flat. In the same way that a mainsail luff is cut to take up the curve of the mast it will use, so a headsail must be shaped to allow for the curvature of its stay. No forestay can ever be absolutely straight, so the Sail Maker must allow for the sag which will occur. Unlike that of the mast, this bow will be towards the rear and to leeward, which will tend to throw cloth into the bunt of the sail and thus make it fuller. The luff must therefore be hollowed to allow for this. The longer the luff the more sag there will be to the stay, so the more allowance must be made.

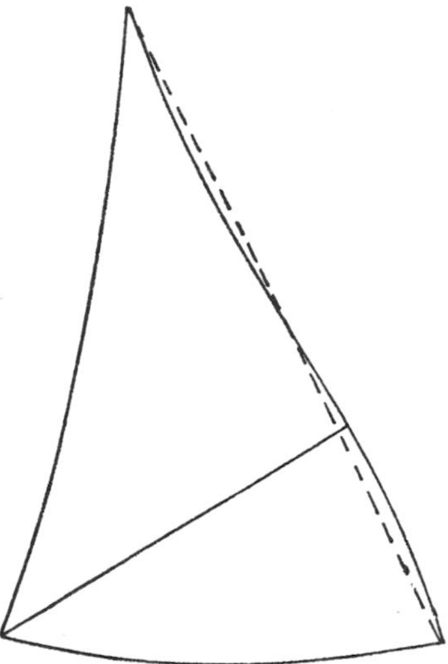

Fig. 22. A headsail is usually hollowed in the upper luff to counteract forestay sag, and slightly rounded in the lower luff to give flow.

The Sail Maker is usually very much in the hands of the owner in this respect, and is sometimes given misleading information. Word has got round that a straight forestay is a good thing aerodynamically, and owners do not like to be thought unaware of this requirement. The tendency is therefore to assure the Sail Maker that the forestay is 'as stiff as I can get it. We have the permanent backstay ground right down, you know, and there's very little sag.' A photograph would surprise that owner, if it were taken from dead ahead, or at right angles from down to leeward. A certain amount of fullness is required low down, so we get a shape as shown in figure 22.

It is interesting to note that this basic shape, which has been used by Sail Makers for centuries, was confirmed after extensive wind tunnel research at Southampton University.[1]

Tapering the Cloths (Broad Seam)

If some of the cloths are tapered, the sail will alter shape accordingly. If, in addition, the sail has a certain amount of extra cloth built in, in the form of luff and foot round, the position of the resulting flow can be controlled by means of tapering the appropriate cloths to a predetermined point.

This tapering of cloths is called 'broad seam', and is subdivided into luff seam, tack seam and foot seam. The overall flow given to the sail in the form of luff and foot round will have its point of maximum draft along the line where the inner end of taper ceases. The first time a particular sail is made, this basic line is established on the cloths as they lie side by side after being cut out on the full-size pattern, and before they are sewn together. We shall see more of this in the next chapter.

The horizontal cut is efficient as regards broad seam, because its cloths arrive at the luff at a convenient angle for this purpose. It is for this reason that sails cut in this manner usually have a seam exactly striking the tack, for this is where maximum shaping is required. A radial or a mitre cut mainsail, however, must inevitably rely more on darts specially put in for the purpose, with the attendant danger of small knuckles appearing where they end.

The leech can also be shaped by means of these tapered seams. In this area, however, it is not curvature which is required, but complete flatness to allow the wind to run off cleanly. Thus, leech seams which have been tightened right out to the tabling should be suspect, because they will tend to hold the leech to windward. Rather should we expect to find these seams eased slightly, particularly near the head and clew, to help free the leech where it has to come up to windward a little to rejoin the top of the mast and the outer end of the boom. Care must be taken to not overdo it, or the whole leech area will go slack and sag to leeward.

Similar broad seam can be put into headsails, although they need less flow or camber, and can usually be relied upon to take up more

[1] SUYR Paper No. 11, October 1962.

nearly their correct shape with only the mitre being adjusted and without the necessity for darts. A horizontally cut headsail will, of course, present plenty of scope for adjustment in this manner.

The mitre cut is the most common way of making a headsail, and it is becoming common to tighten the mitre seam along its middle section. This has the effect of flattening the centre of the sail, which we saw in the chapter on theory is desirable.

Fig. 23. (a) Conventional horizontal cut. Suitable cloth joins available in luff and tack for introduction of broad seam. If no suitable join is in foot, one cloth can be split here.
(b) Radial, or sunray, cut. Darts must be put in foot and/or tack if broad seam is required.
(c) Mitre cut. Darts must be put in luff and/or tack if broad seam is required.

Tension on the Cloth

As cloth stretches on the bias, so it causes a fold to appear near the line of tension. To check this, take a clean handkerchief and fold it corner to corner diagonally in half, so that it forms a triangle. Let the two ends hang down while you pull on the other two corners. A fold will appear in the 'luff' of the handkerchief as tension is applied on the bias of the cloth by pulling outwards, and this will deepen as you pull harder.

When the cloth in a sail is treated in the same way, a similar fold

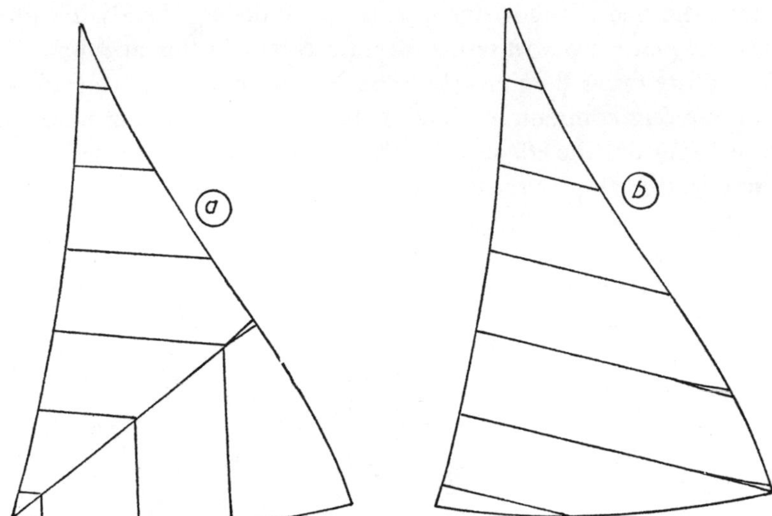

Fig. 24. (a) Mitre cut headsails can have broad seam built into luff end of mitre.
(b) Horizontal cut headsails present plenty of scope for luff seam.

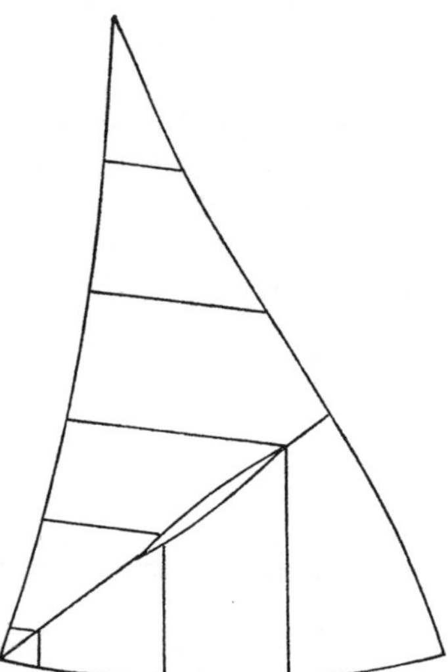

(c) If the mitre of a headsail is tightened along its middle section, the sail is flattened at this point without curling the leech.

will appear along the line of tension. If it is correctly controlled, this tension can be used to induce further flow in a sail. A mainsail is deliberately made shorter on the luff and foot than its full size, so that tension applied by means of the halyard and outhaul will induce flow near the rope. If this tension is applied only lightly, there will be little induced flow, as I call it, and the sail will take up the shape given it by the round and broad seam also built into it. As the wind blows harder, this flow will move aft and up into the sail under the influence of pressure and friction drag. It can be brought back nearer to its starting point again by further tension on the luff and foot. This is one of the principal ways in which an owner can control the shape of his sail in use. If the halyard and outhaul are stretched to their maximum, the flow will appear as a tight fold near the bolt rope, and only the strongest wind will move it further into the sail to the correct place. The flow in a headsail can be controlled in a similar manner if the luff is adjustable in some way – either by being sewn to a rope or tape like a mainsail, or by being free to slide over the luff wire. We shall deal with this more fully in the chapter on trim, but it is as well to know exactly what is happening and why.

Tension on the Rope, Tape or Wire

To be effective, induced flow must be properly controlled. It is no good allowing a sail to be stretched as far as the cloth will go, for this will almost always result in too great a fold appearing in the adjacent area. First and foremost, allowance must be made by the Sail Maker so that the sail does not stretch beyond its marks. Left to itself the cloth would pull out a great deal too much, especially under the influence of powerful halyard winches. However, there is usually a rope (or tape) on the luff and foot of a mainsail, and this will restrict the distance to which the sail can go. The Sail Maker uses a rope with known elasticity, which he first of all pulls to a certain tension before sewing on to the sail. This ensures that there is less rope than sail, thus restricting the amount which the sail can stretch. The exact calculation of the right amount of pre-stretching for the rope is another of the Sail Maker's secrets, and each one has his own ideas, which extend to varying the preset tension along the rope, in order to vary the induced flow up the luff.

Some Sail Makers prefer to use pre-stretched polyester rope for the luff and foot of mainsails, particularly for small sails. This has no elasticity at all, and the sail can be cut to its exact shape without having to take account of induced flow through bias stretch. It will still be necessary to pull the sail out to its marks with a certain amount of tension, because the action of sewing the sail to the rope causes a degree of puckering. Alternatively the rope can be sewn on slack, so that the cloth is pulled a little as the rope straightens out under tension.

The use of luff tape, pioneered by Ike Manchester of the United States of America, is now common practice in Europe; its adoption gives the headsail an adjustable luff free from corrosion. It is important to use the right weight and type of tape for each particular weight of cloth, so that the tape will allow the correct amount of stretch to take place in the cloth. In both cases the luff of the sail will stretch just about the right amount to reach the designed length, while at the same time inducing the right amount of flow by stretching the cloth on the bias. We shall see later about how to pull less on halyard and outhaul in light winds, and how to pull more when it is blowing hard.

Headsails. When a headsail is made with a conventional luff wire, the Sail Maker ensures that the length of the luff is slightly shorter than the wire on which it has to be fitted. The allowance varies with the type of sail and with the Sail Maker concerned (secrets again), but it is in the order of two or three per cent. The tack eye is worked into the sail and the luff is pulled until the cloth stretches the full distance along the wire. The head is then seized at its stretched position and the sail made fast to the head eye. The induced flow is left to lie along the luff as a fold.

The exact amount which the sail is pulled depends on a number of factors, including the weight and quality of the cloth, the type and role of the sail, the size of winch which will be used for the sheet and whether the sail should be full or flat. No two sails pull exactly alike, even if they are supposed to be identical; the cloth or stitching will vary sufficiently to cause a slight variation to be inevitable, so each headsail has to be finished off individually by someone who knows what he is looking for and how to achieve it. The sail may then either be seized at intervals along the luff wire, which is sewn close up all along its length so that it lies at the edge of the luff tabling at all times, or else the wire is left to lie freely inside the luff tabling. In either case, when the headsail is spread on the floor without pulling the wire taut, the wire will lie in a series of S-bends, either taking the luff with it, or else lying loose inside the tabling. This is because the cloth will only spread to a certain size and the wire, being longer, must zigzag to stay confined within the length of the unstretched luff. Not until the wire is pulled taut will the luff of the sail stretch to its designed length, producing induced flow as it stretches.

There seem to be popular misconceptions about two facets of stretch. First, nearly every mainsail and many foresails will appear to be under size if they are laid flat on the floor and measured. We have seen that a mainsail is deliberately made under size so that it shall stretch to its designed length under the influence of its halyard and outhaul, thus achieving induced flow. In addition the rope or tape is sewn on tight, to prevent the sail being stretched too far; this will cause the sail to pucker slightly when little or no tension is put on the rope. A headsail is also made under size, but it is often easier to see the intended length of the luff if it is seized at intervals to the wire along its length. This is because the line of the wire can easily be seen, and it is obvious that it must be straight for measurement. If, however, the wire is loose inside the luff tabling, its sinuous course will not easily be seen as the sail lies on the floor, and so the luff may not be properly tensioned before the tape measure is put along it. See figure 128 (page 283).

The second point is that stretching a sail on the luff and foot does not make it any bigger. All you are doing is to cause the threads to move against any other, thus transforming the little squares formed by the warp and weft into little diamonds. To enable the luff to increase in length beyond the size it was cut, some cloth must come from elsewhere, and it usually comes from the leech. The more you pull on the halyard the less roach you will have. You cannot get something for nothing, so there is no point in pulling the sail as hard as you can in light airs in the mistaken belief that you are getting maximum area by so doing. The reverse is desired from a flow point of view, as you will not want the induced flow hard against the bolt rope. I shall revert to this in the section on setting sails.

Lay of the Cloth

Since Terylene and Dacron stretch as soon as tension is even slightly on the bias, the Sail Maker has to pay great attention to the way in which he lays the cloths of a sail. Cloth stretch is the greatest single factor to be considered in making sails. By manipulating his cloths so that the strain is either on or off the threadline, the Sail Maker can control how much a sail stretches in a particular place. Similarly, the faulty lay of a cloth by as little as one or two degrees can upset the shape of a sail to a point where it is useless. This explains why most leeches have cloths running away from them approximately at rightangles, since stretch on this part of the sail is undesirable, and the threadline must be followed. The cloths are therefore often tripped round the roach of a mainsail and the hollow of a headsail so that the weft follows approximately the line of the leech.

Mainsails. This is not the full picture, however, and we can look at a typical horizontally cut mainsail leech to see why.

There are basically two stress lines on the leech of a mainsail: one goes straight from the clew to the head, and the other runs along the perimeter of the leech itself. It is obvious that we cannot have threadlines running along both lines of stress, particularly in the upper and lower thirds of the sail, where these directions are anything up to 20° different from each other. There is a greater chance of coincidence occurring in the middle third, where the two stress lines are more nearly parallel. However, we are particularly interested in having the leech very slightly slack in the upper and lower thirds, otherwise the sail will tend to hold up to windward, because one part of the sail is fixed on the centreline in each case (the headboard in the upper third, and the clew in the lower third). On the other hand, the middle third is free at either end, and will thus tend slightly to fall away more of its own accord. Equally, if we have the threadline parallel to the leech all the way, then the cloth must be on the bias along the straight line head to clew, particularly in the upper and lower thirds. This means that the sail would go slack inside the leech edge, principally between the clew and bottom batten, and between the head and top batten.

If, however, we set the threadline parallel to the straight stress line (head to clew), you will note from figure 25 that the cloth is slightly on the bias at the leech in the upper and lower thirds. This gives us the slight stretching we require near the head and clew, so that the sail will not hook to windward at these two places. It also reduces the stretch in the middle third, where the sail will naturally tend to sag more to leeward, because the leech edge and threadline more nearly coincide.

Once again this is not the final picture, because a very small variation from the threadline makes a big difference in the degree of stretch. Each sail has to be studied, therefore, according to how much roach it has (and hence the divergence of the upper and lower leech from the straight line head to clew), and each Sail Maker has his own closely guarded secrets about how much bias he allows in different places. The thickness and type of tabling will alter the amount of leech stretch, and some Sail Makers prefer no bias at all, with a very light tabling so as not to hold the sail too tightly; some prefer rather more bias (around 5°) with a stout tabling to help cut down stretch, which can also be controlled by tightening one or two seams the appropriate amount.

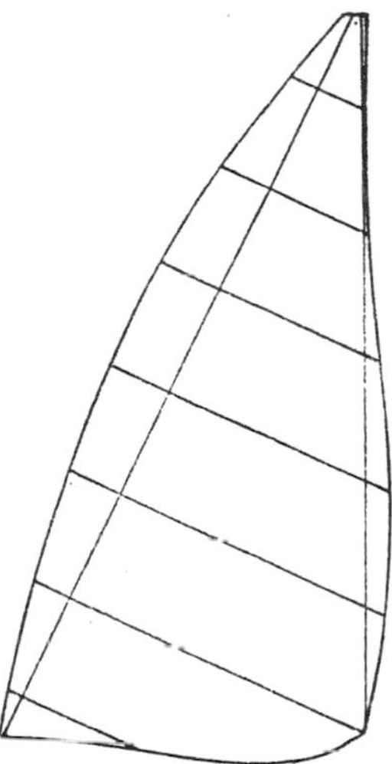

Fig. 25. Thread line of the weft set exactly at rightangles to the straight line joining clew to head.

You will see from figure 26 (*a*) that the conventional horizontally cut mainsail allows the cloths to strike the luff and foot with plenty of bias, so that induced flow can be made to play its part to the full.

If the cloths were on the threadline at the luff or foot, there would be little or no fold as a result of applied tension. This is one of the drawbacks of the mitre cut mainsail, which has to have the foot cloths deliberately offset from the line of the weft if induced flow is to be encouraged [figure 26 (b)].

Radial Cut. When the cloths depart from these conventional patterns, strange things happen to the leech. This is not always detrimental to the sail, but often is. A radially cut mainsail presents a leech which has a varying bias angle, and thus a varying stretch, for which there are no ready-made seams for corrective measures. In addition the cloths will arrive at the luff at varying angles, again with different stretch results. Attempts to resolve the leech problem, therefore, by means of a series of short horizontal cloths at the afteredge, only represent half measures, for the luff will still stretch differentially. The sail's chances of success after several hours' sailing are small unless made by a loft which specializes in this cut.

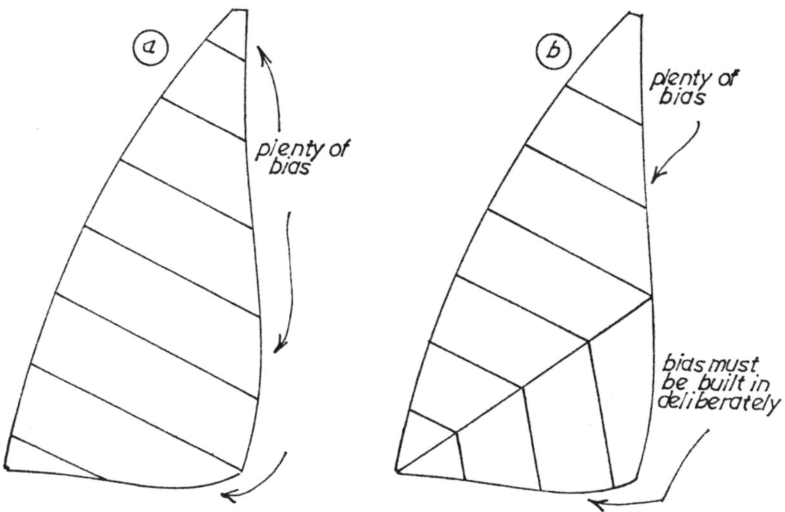

Fig. 26. Mainsail cloth bias.

An additional factor, which the radial mainsail shares with the radial headsail, is that there cannot be threadline selvedges along both sides of the wedge-shaped cloths: one or both of them must be on the bias. Thus uneven stretching and mutual interference may set up between individual panels right across the bunt of the sail.

Headsails. The same basic principles apply to a headsail, which requires careful attention to its leech, so that the clean run off we have postulated on page 29 is achieved, and so that it never hooks to windward. A racing sail with a light tabling (and a designed life

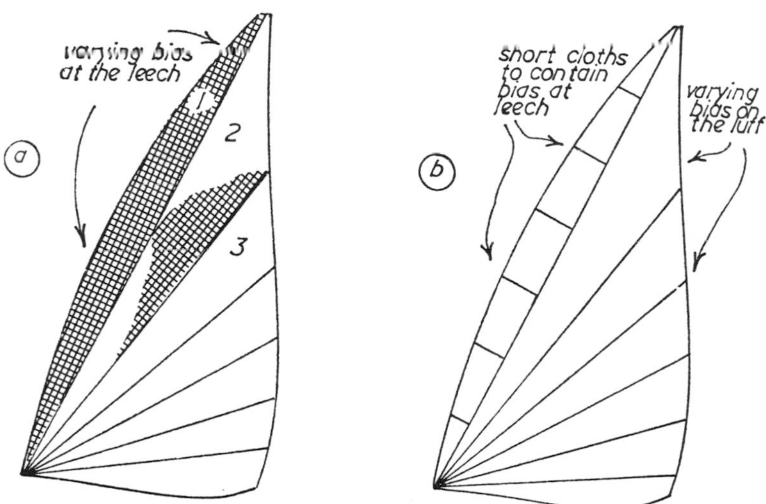

Fig. 27. (a) The leech panel has varying bias along the leech, and none at its forward edge. If panel number 2 meets this with no bias at their juncture, it will have bias at its forward edge – which should be met by similar bias on panel number 3, or uneven stretching will result. But this means that the join between 1 and 2 will not stretch (no bias), while the one between 2 and 3 will – and so on through the sail. (b) Individual panels at the leech are not the complete answer. Besides differential panel stretch as described in 27(a), both (a) and (b) will have differential luff stretch as well, due to varying luff bias.

of a dozen races) may therefore have no bias all the way round the leech. A more robust sail for a long-distance cruiser, with its strong tabling and perhaps even a leechrope, should have one or two degrees of bias to counteract the tightening effect of the tabling. The ocean racer who wants his headsails to last properly for a couple of seasons as racing sails, and then to go on for cruising, should have a tabling graduated somewhere in between, with rather less than one degree of bias on the leech. The foot will also need some stretch – indeed, rather more than the leech, because the bunt of the sail will pull aft under the action of powerful winches. The foot cloths may, therefore, have anything up to 7° or 8° of bias so that the whole sail can move aft, thus flattening the leech area.

Mitre Cut. The conventional mitre cut headsail gives the simplest solution to all these requirements. Its chief drawback is that its cloths strike the luff at different angles above and below the mitre, but it has a leech and foot where the bias angle can be adjusted at will, with ready-made seams for adjustment as necessary.

Horizontal Cut. Due to the doubling of the cloth at the central seam, however, a mitre exerts a restricting influence on the development of draft in a sail. This tends to produce a hard line along the mitre itself and the danger of a flat lower half to the sail. Murphy & Nye of America virtually pioneered large-scale cutting of headsails with all cloths running at right angles to the leech, letting them come as they may at the foot. This allows the clew to draw aft thus flattening the

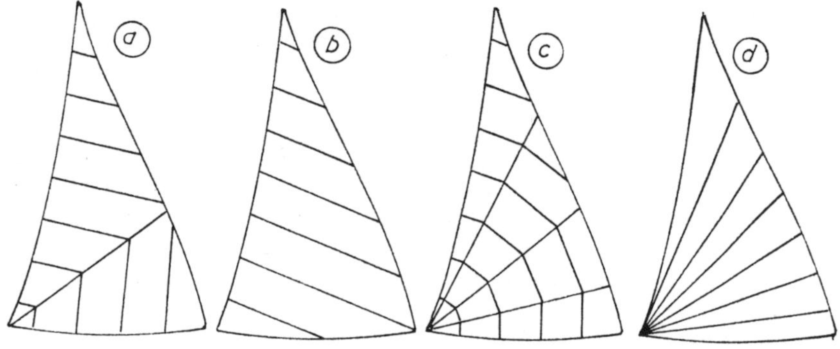

Fig. 28. (a) Mitre.
(b) Horizontal.
(c) Spider-web or multi-mitre.
(d) Radial or sunray.

leech, and is now widely used on headsails of all sizes. Overstretching of the foot needs to be countered by nice calculation of the foot tabling.

Spider Web. The spider web, or multi-mitre, cut has two or more mitres and still retains its weft threadline parallel to the leech and foot. The panels in this type of sail are remarkably small, and stretch is thus reduced to a minimum – perhaps too low in some cases – and this is a style which is only suitable where the sail is large and the stresses are large, such as in the 12 metre. There is a danger here that one or more mitres will be tighter than the rest, equally the bias varies considerably on the luff, with the attendant risk of unequal stretching and therefore unequal induced flow.

Radial Cut. The radial or sunray cut headsail suffers from exactly the same drawbacks as a mainsail cut the same way. Similar attempts to avoid trouble on the leech and foot, such as fitting a number of small panels in the edge cloth, result in a partial cure: the luff will still stretch unevenly due to the different bias angles involved. From time to time a cult for this type of cut arises, but I am convinced that it stems from a couple of leading helmsmen doing well with it, and the rest of the fleet slavishly following suit, in the belief that it is the sail which is winning the race. The truth is all too often that the helmsman would win with any reasonable sail, and I can find no overriding advantage for this cut despite the fact that one or two individual Sail Makers make a habit of producing excellent radial sails.

CHAPTER V

Cutting and Sewing a Sail

The physical task of making a sail once it has been designed and planned, can be divided into five stages:

1. Cutting out.
2. Putting together.
3. Rubbing down.
4. Tablings, patches and pockets.
5. Finishing; this will be treated in the next chapter.

1. *Cutting Out*

The sail is drawn full-size on the floor, with an allowance of several inches all round so that the doubled edges, or tablings, can be put on the luff, leech and foot. The cutter first draws in chalk the three (or four) corners of the sail, marks these with prickers stuck into the floor, and stretches a twine round the basic triangle. He then makes further crosses to mark the amount of round or hollow at predetermined points along the luff, leech and foot. He next bends a spline along the curve he requires or alternatively he 'throws' his tape, or roll of webbing, along the edge to be drawn, by anchoring it at one end with a pricker stuck in the floor and adjusting it to a fair curve by hand and eye from the other end, so that it exactly cuts the several crosses determining the amount of round or hollow. The line of the luff, leech or foot is then chalked on the floor, using the spline or tape as a marker. Where the sail is a recurring one-design, the pattern may be permanently painted on the floor, or the size and shape of all the necessary cloths may be drawn on to a pattern or written in a book, so that they can be cut out on a table. The selected bolt of cloth is then passed back and forth across this pattern according to the flow plan, and the cloth is cut exactly to size; due allowance has to be made, of course, for the overlap of one cloth on another, and for the amount of broad seam to be given to each cloth. It is at this stage that the webbing tape is thrown on the cut-out sail to establish the seam pattern, if the sail has been cut full size on the floor.

Broad Seam. The cutter marks one or two places on the sail where the maximum draft is to be, say one-third aft of the luff at points 6 and 9 ft above the foot. He then throws his webbing tape along the line where he wants the maximum camber to lie. The broad seam will then end at this line, and he marks the sail accordingly.

Each panel is then numbered, and the amount of broad seam it is to have is written on the end of it. This may be as little as $\frac{3}{8}$ in. for a distance of 2 ft 6 in., or as much as 10 in. for a distance of 6 or 7 ft, according to the size and function of the sail and the position of the particular cloth. The surplus cloth can either be trimmed off so the overlap of one panel on another is maintained constant, or it can merely be lapped on the next cloth by the extra amount of the total broad seam of the two cloths. The former is time consuming and, apart from looking nicer, merely serves to make it more difficult for another Sail Maker to find out the broad seam pattern.

A spinnaker will not lie flat on the floor when fully spread, but most modern cuts can be laid out if the sail is folded in half down the centre. Often there is a seam running down the middle, but even if there is not, the cloth will usually double back on itself about the centrefold. The broad seam, or taper, which is put into the sail will lie, as with a mainsail, in a multiplicity of small pleats and folds when the sail has been sewn together.

The tape is 'thrown' on the cut-out sail, as it is on a mainsail, in order to mark where this broad seam shall end.

Cotton used to be made in many different widths, from 12 to 54 in., and sails were made in as many panel widths. They were, however, usually made up of much narrower panels than they are today, due to the lower stretch of a narrow panel. The cloths were either split to as low as 9 in., or else they were false-seamed, sometimes both. This practice has left behind it one or two reminders, such as the batten tolerance in the 14 ft International class. From the point of view of looks, as well as stretch, dinghy panels used to be 9 in. broad, and it was thought desirable at that time to lay batten pockets on the

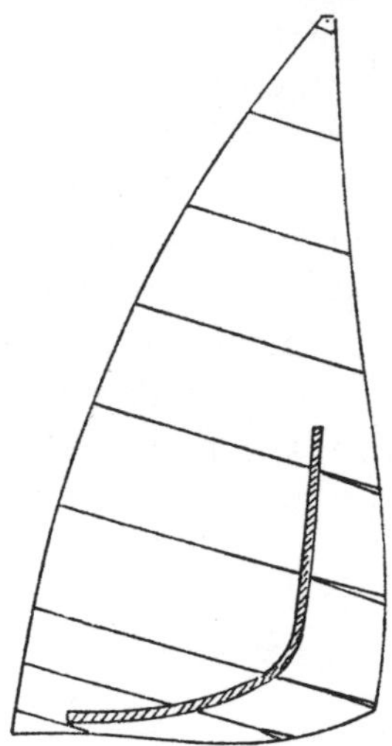

Fig. 29. Webbing tape 'thrown' on cut-out mainsail to mark after end of broad seam.

line of a seam. In order that this could be guaranteed in the Fourteens, it was necessary to have a tolerance of 5 in. either side of the point exactly dividing the leech into five parts, so that the batten could be shifted up or down to coincide with the nearest seam, and this tolerance was incorporated into the rules, where it stands to this day.

Terylene and Dacron are usually woven in widths which vary between 32 and 36 in. The variation is caused by the shrinkage of the heat-setting process. The cloth is quite strong enough for the full 36 in. generally to be used for most sails from dinghies to 12 metres, providing it is heavy enough in accordance with the table I have given on page 57. It is significant, however, that Ted Hood of America and Ratsey & Lapthorn of England are both weaving their own sailcloth in 18 in. widths. This is presumably just another step in the fight to keep bias stretch to a minimum consistent with using as light a cloth as possible. I do not suppose, either, that they are disappointed at the resultant easy identification of their sails due to the narrow panels.

The use of narrow cloths with synthetics is sometimes desirable for two reasons. First, there may not be enough seams in the luff of a sail

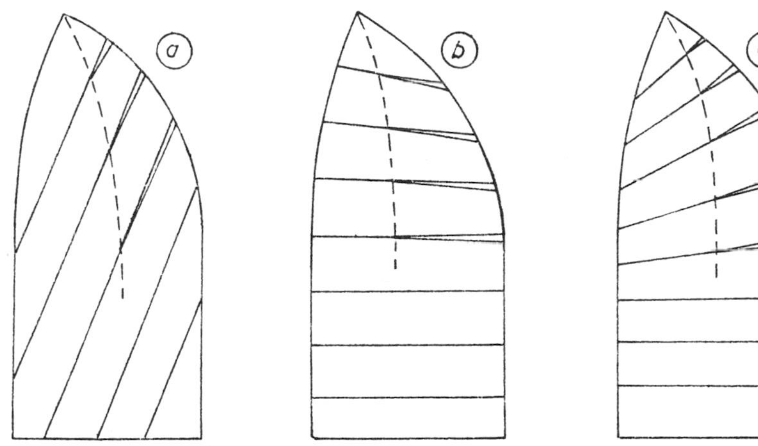

Fig. 30 Spinnaker cuts.
(a) Vertical. Cloths form an inverted chevron when seen from ahead or astern.
(b) Horizontal. Cloths are kept at rightangles to the stays, leading to bias at the centre seam.
(c) No centre seam. Cloths are kept at rightangles to the centrefold, so they may be doubled back on themselves to form the other half of the sail. Dotted lines represent the webbing tape 'thrown' to mark the end of the broad seam.

to allow the Sail Maker to get all the shape he wants through tapering the cloths. This only applies to the smallest sails as a rule, and then more often to those cloths striking the foot of a mainsail, in which case the bottom one or two panels only can be split. An alternative is to put darts into the sail, as we have seen in the previous chapter. Secondly, it may be required to use a particularly light cloth for a certain sail, which would stretch out of shape if full-width panels were used. Splitting the cloth once, or even twice, will keep the stretch down to a minimum. We once made a 35-ft luff mainsail for *Micronette*, a 30-ft sloop owned by John Britten and Desmond Norman. We used a 6 oz. cloth with 11 in. panels, which held its shape very well.

2. *Putting Together*

I am glad to have had the chance of seeing 28 oz. No. 2 heavy cotton being sewn by hand into a 90-ft luff mainsail (in 1964 for Herr Burmester's schooner *Aschanti IV*). But this is a dying requirement, not only because of the advent of synthetics, but because yachts of the right size are few and far between. While they rightly pride themselves on their craftsmanship in this hand-seaming, Sail Makers realise that they must not rest on their past laurels but look to the future. Side by side with these highly skilled craftsmen are young men and women who sew synthetics together with double needle machines equipped with pull-feed and travelling tables.

The standard claw-feed on a sewing machine only operates on the lower of the two cloths being sewn together, and the slippery nature of the material means that this lower cloth goes through the machine faster than the one on top, unless the machinist holds it back with one hand and pushes the top cloth through with the other. This makes it hard to stick to the match marks put across the two cloths as they are 'struck up' when lying side by side on the full-size pattern in the cutting-out stage. A pull-feed does away with this problem, as it squeezes the two cloths tightly together in the sewing machine, and ensures that the top cloth is fed through at the same speed as the bottom one, thus eliminating the need to strike up the cloths in many cases.

Use of double-sided sticky tape permits the cloths to be laid one on the other and held firmly in place, without the attendant danger of one sliding over the other as they are being sewn. This enables inexperienced machinists to sew accurately, but it is time-consuming and not conducive to series production by skilled operators.

Where a cloth is too heavy for a double-needle machine, it must be passed through a single needle twice, or even three times where triple stitching is required – for instance, at the corners and in places of likely chafe. It is useful to use a thread which contrasts sharply with the colour of the cloth, so that any broken or chafed stitching will stand out and receive quick repair. Tan thread is usual for white sails, and white for coloured ones.

Discussion of chafe leads me to the question of hand-sewing. In the days of cotton there was a great advantage to be obtained through hand-sewing, because the stitching (which could be pulled much tighter) was able to bed right into the relatively soft material. Polyester is so hard that this bedding-in process does not occur, with the result that the stitching stays proud and exposed to the effects of chafe. Nevertheless a much heavier thread, waxed for protection (which causes it to lie closer to the surface), is used with hand-sewing, and heavy-duty synthetic sails for the largest vessels should certainly have this refinement. It costs a good deal more initially, due to the time taken and the skill required, but it will save its cost in the long run through longevity and greater security. I would expect to see at least the lowers of any large trading or training vessel hand-sewn, unless the owners want to spend their time repairing the ravages of chafe.

The lap of the cloths should be carefully controlled so that either it is constant or any change, such as is required by tapering the cloths to build in the flow, takes place gradually. If one cloth is allowed to overlap its neighbour unevenly for a short distance, the finished sail will show a hard spot in its surface. The same effect will result from racing numbers or insignia badly sewn on. In this respect, a rolling table top to take the weight of the half sewn sail, makes control easier for the machinist.

3. *Rubbing Down*

When the sail has been joined together, it returns to the pattern on which it was cut, so that the raw edges can be turned over and creased along the line of the final size of the sail. This is called rubbing down, and the crease is formed with a tool called a rubbing iron. The exact shape of this tool is not fixed, indeed a flat piece of steel can be used; the rubbing iron is as old as sailmaking, however, and drawings of them can be found in many old prints and books on the subject.

It is, of course, important to be accurate at this stage, particularly with those sails which have closely controlled dimensions. The turned over raw edge will then become the tabling, to reinforce the outside of the sail.

4. *Tablings, Patches and Pockets*
The next process in sailmaking involves putting on all the strengthening pieces, fitting the rope, tape or wire, and working all the eyes, eyelets, rings, cringles or holes by any other name; slides, hanks and other refinements also come under this heading, but I shall deal with them separately as they merit rather closer attention from the owner than the more routine work of finishing.

Tablings
Tablings are often achieved in dressmaking, where they are called hems, by simply folding, or rolling, the cloth over and tucking the raw edge inside itself (figure 31).

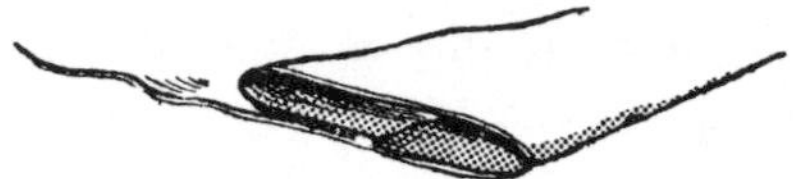

Fig. 31. A rolled tabling.

This can give rise to creases, however, particularly where the edge is a curve, or where the cloths strike the edge on the bias.

The inside radius of any curve will be shorter, and thus a rolled tabling will have to crimp up in tiny pleats as it disposes of unneeded cloth. Where the tabling is more on a straight line, but is on the bias, such as the luff of a mainsail, the action of folding the cloth back on itself will mean that the threadlines of the tabling will cross those of the sail itself at double the angle at which they arrive at the luff. As the sail is stretched on the luff, the cloth may move according to the angle of the threadline, and there will be a significant difference between the action of the tabling and that of the main part of this sail. This may well result in the start of small wrinkles at the luff, which can prove hard to remove.

It is better in both cases (curved leech and angled luff) to trim off the tabling and lift it back on to the edge of the sail without turning it.

The curve at the leech and the threadlines at the luff will then marry up with the minimum risk of distortion (see figure 33).

If, on the other hand, the edge is straight, or a series of straight lines (perhaps from one batten pocket to the next), and the cloths strike it on or near the threadline (either warp or weft), then there is no danger in simply folding the edge over to form the tabling.

A tabling which has been trimmed off and resewn will either be

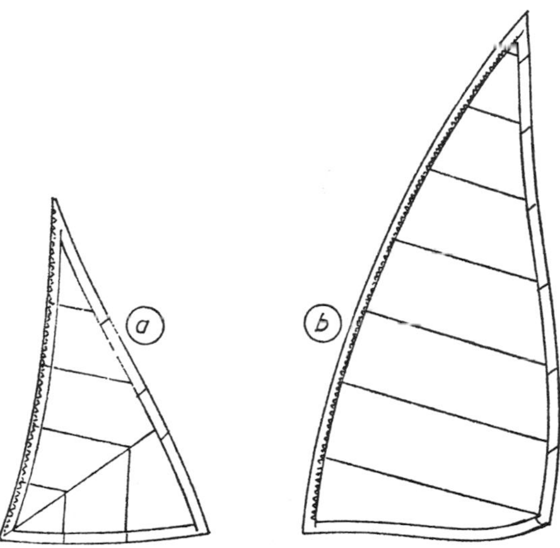

Fig. 32. Rolled tablings.

(a) A headsail leach will crimp up at the very after edge if a fairly wide tabling is rolled.

(b) A mainsail leech tabling will crimp up at its forward edge. In addition the threadlines at the luff will be in conflict, where the tabling is folded over.

turned under at either side, or heat-sealed so as not to fray; similarly with the edge of the sail itself. This means that there may be as many as four thicknesses of cloth at the very edge of the sail, or else two thicknesses plus a double line of heat-sealing. This is sure to have less stretch than the single layer of cloth immediately inside the tabling, with the attendant danger of a 'cup' appearing just inside the leech, unless the Sail Maker has taken appropriate measures to forestall it by means of laying the cloths slightly on the bias, or sewing the tabling on with a little slack.

In addition, great care is needed to see that the tabling is not sewn on too slack, thus causing the leech to 'motor-boat', or be too tight, which will cause it to curl and to aggravate the 'cup' effect. Naturally, the width of the tabling will also affect the amount of stretch it allows the very leech of the sail.

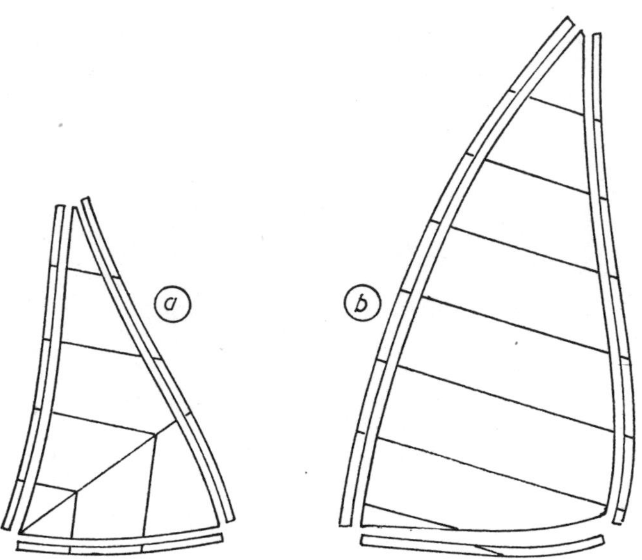

Fig. 33. Separate tablings.
(a) Headsail. The leech tabling lifts straight back on to the leech and fits exactly.
(b) Mainsail. All curves fit exactly. The threadlines at the luff exactly coincide if the tabling is lifted straight back on to the sail.

A rolled tabling will, of course, avoid most of these pitfalls, but its very nature may allow too much stretch to the leech, particularly with large sails which are going to have a good deal of wind in them.

There is thus some reason for doing away with the tabling altogether, at least on the leech, if the sail is not going to be subjected to too much weight of wind, and if the job will be permanent and strong enough. I would like to discount the idea for mainsails straight away, even for the smallest sails. A mainsail's leech has a great deal of stress transmitted through it when beating to windward: there is the steady pull of the mainsheet when the sail is full, and the flogging effect during tacking. I do not believe that heat-sealing the raw edge alone is enough to withstand these stresses and to prevent it stretching too much even if it does not fray out; it is definitely not recommended for mainsails.

Similarly, any boat larger than a small dayboat will have too much weight of wind in its headsails for a heat sealed leech to hold up for long; on any boat which goes offshore it would be a most unseamanlike practice to say the least. This leaves dinghies and

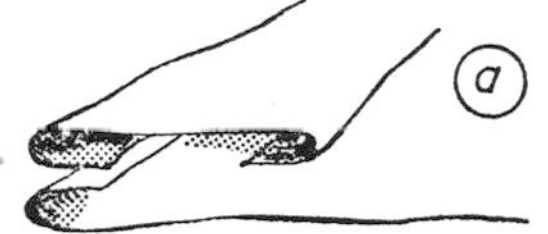

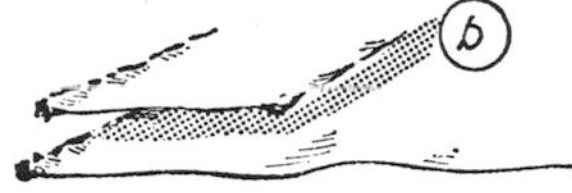

Fig. 34. Separate tablings.
(a) If the cloth is folded over at the raw edge, there will be four thicknesses at the very leech.
(b) If the raw edge of the cloth is heat-sealed, there is a danger of a hard rim where the heat has melted the thread into a globule.

small keelboats like the Dragon and Soling. There is no doubt that a leech without a tabling gives an easy run off to the wind, and will probably never curl to windward. It may, however, easily go slack, which is hard to cure once it has stretched at the edge. Racing dinghies can often get a good jib this way, although it will not last so long as a conventional sail because chafe will soon fray out the most careful heat-sealing (which can always be resealed, however), and the sail will suffer more from mishandling. The small one-designs, whose owners are prepared to have a jib for only a dozen races, can also try the idea with a good chance of success. For an individually cut sail, however, get your Sail Maker to cut the normal tabling when he makes the sail, and put it on one side for later addition; but be prepared to find that later on is too late to cure your problems.

Patches

The loads on a sail are naturally concentrated at the corners, and it is important to see that these parts of the sail are adequately reinforced.

Sails

Several thicknesses of stout cloth should extend well into the sail, so that the strain on the single layer of cloth in the sail proper is well spread. This also gives a strong base into which the cringles or eyes at head, tack and clew can be worked.

The extremely heavy loads imparted by modern sheet winches call for even stronger reinforcement patches. It is good practice to put several lengths of webbing tape looped round a heavy stainless steel clew ring in large headsails, or in those which will be used with powerful winches; also at head and tack eyes. This webbing should extend a foot or so into the sail, to share out the load more evenly.

Sails are carried in much stronger winds than they were even ten years ago. This is the result of keener competition for the top honours. It also means that sails must stand up to increased strains. I am thinking here particularly of spinnakers, and I am sure that the natural desire of an owner to have as light a spinnaker as possible cannot be married to this keenness to hold on to the sail as the wind increases. The Sail Maker can help by increasing the size of his head and clew patches and even, perhaps, by putting a long tongue 3 or 4 ft into the sail, but I do not believe that there is sufficient awareness of the limitations of spinnakers. Whereas most owners know to within 10 per cent the weight of cloth used in their headsails, they are remarkably ignorant when it comes to spinnakers. Yet there is an increase of 33 per cent between a $1\frac{1}{2}$ and a 2 oz. cloth, let alone the 170 per cent increase from 1·1 to 3 oz. To many owners, however, the sail is merely a spinnaker to be used at all times until really strong winds require a heavy weather spinnaker which, as far as some owners are concerned, is distinguishable by its smaller size and the fact that it is flatter in the head, not by its heavier cloth weight.

Batten Pockets

There is little point in having the old-fashioned tie-in battens, unless you are worried that the slip-in type may work their way out. This does not often happen, and it is my belief that the slip-in type is best for all but the deepest deep sea sailor. This may stem from a personal hatred of fiddling about with bits of string, which used to make putting in the battens high on my list of least favourite jobs. I bless the day the slip-in pocket was invented, but must add that there are still some brutes about. It is important that the batten ends be rounded to facilitate easy entry, and ideally the pocket should be slightly overlong with a piece of elastic sewn in its inner end so as to force the batten gently towards the outer end of the pocket, thus keeping it right at the leech. Pockets without elastic must, of necessity, present a tight fit for the batten, which will be hard to fit, and which will tend to chafe the inner end.

The inner ends of full length pockets should have a pair of nylon protectors sewn one each side, to take the chafe which will always occur. The ends of the battens themselves should be carefully shaped

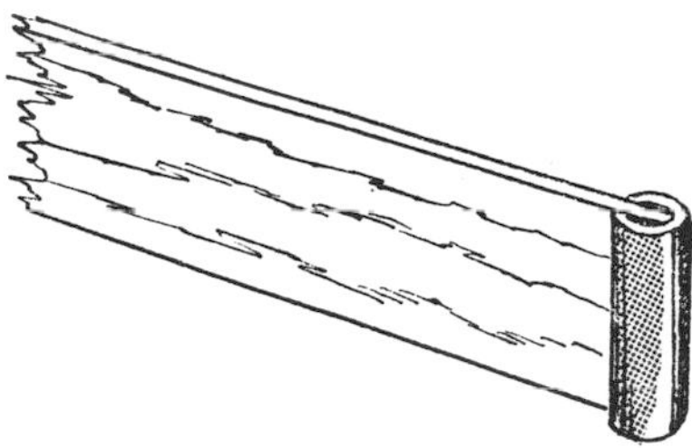

Fig. 35. A strip of split PVC tubing can be fitted to the ends of full length battens where there is no external protector demanding a thin end.

to take up the line of the luff, and they may have a short length of PVC tubing which has been split down its length, fastened to the end. This tubing, however should not be used if external protectors are available, because the batten will not fit snugly into them due to its bulk.

Leech Roaches

Mention of battens leads naturally to leech roach. In most classes this represents 'free area' since it is not measured; it is thus subject to much attention from area hungry owners, who often demand from the Sail Maker more roach than he can safely provide without endangering the set of the sail.

Battens will support approximately one third of their length in roach extended beyond the straight line from clew to headboard. Beyond this the whole leech will tend to fall away in an inefficient manner. This manifests itself in one of two ways, shown in figure 36.

These symptoms are similar to those of a sail which has a slack leech due to incorrect lay of cloth, or poor material. I will not attempt to go into the cures available at this stage, but refer the reader to pages 264–5.

Some classes have maximum cross measurements at various points on the sail, the most usual being the half and three quarter heights; the quarter height is sometimes controlled as well. This is all very well when these measurements are small enough, but their very existence sometimes encourages owners to believe that they represent

Fig. 36. (a) The forward end of the batten sits up to windward in a hard ridge or 'poke'.
(b) The whole leech falls away at the battens.

the norm, and therefore a sail which is below the cross measurements is somehow a bad buy. The 14 ft International class is the classic example of excessive cross measurements. Their half-height measurement is some 4 to 6 in. too big when a mainsail is made for a mast which bends only moderately – say 3 to 4 in. If the mast bends more, the Sail Maker must put more cloth on the luff to allow for the forward bow of the mast, and so the roach is brought in by the same amount. Thus a mast which bends 7 to 8 in. will have a good chance of a well-setting leech.

A large roach which falls off to leeward is inefficient when beating to windward or close reaching. Only when the sail has the wind blowing into it rather than along it does the extra area pay off. Yet the area lost by 4 in. off the leech of a Fourteen is under 5 sq. ft, which can so easily be put efficiently into a spinnaker or genoa for work off the wind. The result would be a faster suit of sails to windward, where seconds so often count.

The ocean racing fleet normally has no limiting cross measurements on mainsails, yet they do not go in for exaggerated roaches at the expense of efficiency. The dinghies should take note, and either be grateful for a sensible restriction if they have one, or else follow this good example.

An instance of the reverse happening, where ocean racers have followed the small boat trend, is the way the mainsail is shaped at the leech. It was found that a fair curve often caused the leech tabling to flutter between the battens, as there was no support for this small area which projected beyond the ends of the battens. Accordingly it

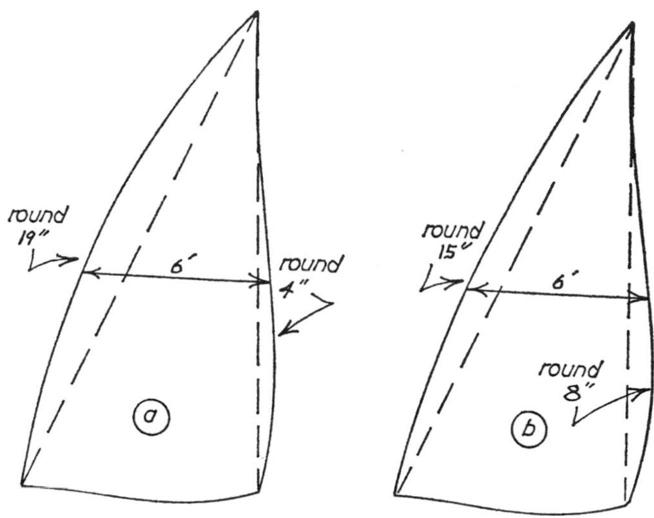

Fig. 37. 14 ft International mainsails.
(a) Made for a fairly stiff mast the 40 in. centre battens must try to support 19 in. of roach.
(b) Made for a bendy mast there is more chance of 15 in. roach standing properly.

is now usual to cut leeches straight, or even very slightly hollow, between the battens, not only on dinghies but on bigger sails as well. The loss of area is negligible, improvement in efficiency is small, but morale goes up out of all proportion!

Headsails

Most headsails are not allowed battens on the leech. The offshore fleet allows them as a rule, if the forward end of the batten comes forward of the mast. They are unseamanlike appendages if they have to come into contact with the mast or shrouds when tacking, and I do not advise them except in certain instances. There are some headsails which are tall and narrow (anything with a head angle of less than 20°), and where the leech comes forward of the mast, which can be made to set better by the inclusion of three or four short battens. There is no point in trying to build up a roach on the leech of such a sail, because this would defeat its own object. The extra cloth would probably cause the leech to foul the mast, which in turn would break the battens. If a greater area is desired in a headsail which is tall and narrow, it is better to draw the clew further aft, so that it overlaps the mast and the sail achieves a lower aspect ratio.

Tufnol is good for headsail battens, because its greater flexibility for a given weight and thickness does no harm in such short lengths. It is more resistant to the rough usage it will get in a headsail, perhaps because of the very flexibility it possesses. Pockets should be securely fastened, and it is perhaps preferable to have the battens permanently sewn or tied in.

As a rule, of course, a headsail has the opposite of a roach on its leech. A hollow leech will stand better than a straight one, and this will help in the slot effect if the sail is an overlapping one. If a correctly graduated leech hollow can be made to follow the curve of the leeward side of the mainsail just aft of its point of maximum flow, the resulting streamlines will be at their most efficient.[1]

Roach to the foot of a headsail is also free area, and is sought after. Certain classes like the 5-0-5 allow a batten in the foot, but most do not. A foot roach of approximately 3 per cent will stand unassisted; beyond this amount (which is about 1 in. of roach for every three feet of foot length), either the Sail Maker has to tighten the foot seams (which means a danger of the foot curling), or else the foot will not stand at all while beating to windward, and the owner reaps his reward of extra area only when sailing off the wind.

[1] SUYR Paper No. 6, February 1961.

CHAPTER VI

Finishing a Sail

Roping

Hand-roping is still a craft on its own, and it takes years of practice to become adept at it. It is still necessary on all ropes of the larger sizes which will not pass through a sewing machine. Indeed, on anything larger than a twenty tonner, machined roping would not be strong enough to be certain of withstanding all that a moderate Atlantic gale can offer. Even below this size, hand-roping gives a much stronger finish to the sail, and is to be preferred for seagoing yachts. The drawback of hand-roping is the difficulty of ensuring even sewing of the rope, particularly if two different men are put on the job. It is for this reason that Sail Makers prize an expert roper.

We have seen that the rope must be pulled somewhat before it is sewn to the sail. This is done by first ensuring that there are no twists in it so that it lies quietly, a line is then drawn along its length to guide the Sail Maker as he sews. The sail is then spread with the luff fair, the rope is laid alongside and the correct amount is deducted from its length; this amount is a function of the length of luff, the size and characteristic of the rope, and the flow required. On one occasion there was a little trouble with Italian hemp rope in the days of cotton. The manufacturer changed the treatment of the hemp in such a minor way that he did not feel it necessary to inform his customers. Sail Makers made a number of cotton sails which did not set too well, and this was enough to cause a major disturbance. Everything was checked and rechecked, until there was nothing left save the rope which could be the cause of the bother. The manufacturer was asked, and the mystery solved. The minor change had altered the stretch characteristics of the rope enough to alter the set of the finished sail.

The rope is next pulled to the stretched length finally required from the sail, to see if it goes correctly (Sail Makers are not going to be caught again); a strain gauge may be used by the progressive at this stage. It is next struck up at intervals, which may be graduated along its length to give a different tension near the head from that lower in the sail, thus varying the flow. The luff tabling is also struck up with similar, but not identical, intervals. The sailmaker then sews to these marks. He must take care that he keeps the rope straight by watching the longitudinal pencil line, and that the marks match correctly, or there will be a tendency for the luff to twist or to gather too much cloth at one point. One of the tendencies in poor hand-roping is for the rope to go on too slack; the rope runs out before the end of the sail is reached.

The advantage of machine-roping is that the stitching will be evenly tensioned throughout the rope, and with little danger of gathering. There will, however, be less flexibility in the relative tension on the rope and sail, and the finished job will not be as strong as a hand-sewn rope. Machining is, of course, quicker and does not have to be done by a highly qualified sailmaker, paid the appropriate wages. Machine work is to be preferred where it is important that all sails should be as nearly alike as possible, such as in classes of rigid one-design like the Firefly or 420 dinghies. There is a third possibility, much used in smaller sails. This is for the luff rope to be allowed to run loose inside the tabling, being merely seized at the head and tack; the same applies to the foot rope. This is all very well on small sails, but anything larger than a five tonner will often have enough weight of wind in its mainsail to cause the seizings to pull away. This will have disastrous results, which are not surprising when you pause to think how the strain is concentrated on three points. It has the advantage, however, that the luff and foot ropes are sure to be absolutely evenly stretched along their entire length.

Luff Tapes

Ike Manchester, of America, has been taping luffs of sails since 1955. Because wire and synthetic rope do not have anything like the same characteristics as synthetic fabric, he felt that they should not be used in conjunction with Dacron. He knew that similar materials will react in a similar way under similar conditions, so he used Dacron cloth throughout the sail.

The adoption of adjustable luff headsails has done as much as anything to accelerate the acceptance of taped luffs. The alternative to this type of sail involves a luff rope, but Manchester's early opinion about dissimilar materials being unsympathetic still holds good. An additional gain is that a headsail without a luff wire will not suffer from oxidization.

A drawback with taped headsails is that the luff tends to set with loops sagging away from the forestay between the hanks in an un-aerodynamic manner. But if a $\frac{3}{4}$ in. circumference ($\frac{1}{4}$ in. diameter) rope is sewn into the luff, and is deliberately made shorter than the tape, the luff will become hard and straight as soon as it begins to reach its designed length; the rope also acts as a check against powerful halyard winches breaking the tape.

If a mainsail has to fit grooved spars, a rope is threaded through the tape itself, which may take the place of the tabling if desired.

Wire

The commonest wire for headsail luffs is PVC covered galvanized, and this is probably the best for temperate climates. Care must be taken to seal the break in the PVC coating where the tack eye is formed, and it is here that most trouble occurs. The head eye is not so subject to frequent salt-water duckings, and is thus less susceptible to corrosion. Galvanized wire is not suitable for tropical climates unless it has a completely sealed covering; it corrodes quickly at exposed places and seldom lasts more than a year. Stainless steel wire is also used a great deal, particularly in the United States of America. It reacts with synthetics, however, and causes discolouring of the cloth which eventually leads to weakness. If stainless steel wire is covered with a protective coating, it will be starved of oxygen which will lead to shielding corrosion. Cranfield and Carter make a number of luff wires for the tropics in monel, which I believe is good, but which has a lower breaking load than stainless steel.

In short, PVC coated galvanized wire is good for temperate climates, but watch the tack eye for corrosion. Stainless steel uncovered is best for the tropics, if a hermetically sealed, covered galvanized wire is not available, but one must accept the stains which will appear on the cloth.

Eyes

For a long time eyes which were pressed or punched in were much weaker than those sewn by hand, and were therefore only suitable for smaller sails. Modern sailcloth, however, is often so closely woven that improved pressing equipment and materials often produce a result which is less damaging to the cloth, while being quite strong enough for the task. Stainless-steel punched eyes are thus often to be found on quite large sails. Hand-worked eyes remain the stronger in coarser cloth, however, and should continue to be used where loadings are expected to be really heavy.

Because of this risk of damage to the cloth from close hand sewing (or of one stitch being pulled too tight and thus starting a crease), where an eye is being hand sewn modern practice is to sew with four parts of thread, and even six on the bigger sails, instead of the more traditional two parts, thereby making half the number of passes with the needle in order to reduce the possibility of wrinkles appearing.

Reef eyelets should have individual patches for extra strength, and the eyes at luff and leech correspondingly larger patches running into the sail, as these will become tack and clew when the reef is taken in. Most other eyes find ready made extra thickness for strength, because they will usually come at the tabling or at the clew or tack patch.

Hand-sewn eyes have a metal ring sewn into the sail to form the basis of strength, with a turnover of the same metal pressed in afterwards to protect the thread from chafe by whatever is to go into the eye: shackle, wire, hank or slide seizing.

Battens

The most common material for battens used to be wood, but this has now been largely overtaken by plastics. There are still plenty about, however, and they should be well rounded and tapered towards the inner end both as to width and thickness, in order to make them bend more at the tip. They should, of course, be well varnished to make them resist water soakage. A good idea, particularly if the end is thin, is to strap the tip with adhesive tape. This both prevents it breaking too easily, and protects the sail if a break does occur. A strip of adhesive tape the full length of the batten serves as a protection from sharp corners in a break, and also enables you to pull the broken end out if the worst should occur.

Tufnol Battens. There is an increasing use of Tufnol for battens these days, and it is a satisfactory material. It does have a tendency to bend rather too much, so care must be used. This flexibility makes it a suitable material for the top batten, which is often the better for having more of a curve than the lower ones, but it means that lower Tufnol battens have to be rather thick if they are to do their job properly. $\frac{1}{16}$ in. is enough for the top batten of a small mainsail, but thickness can range up to $\frac{1}{4}$ in. for the larger yachts. A very rough guide is $\frac{1}{16}$ in. for every 10 ft of water-line length. Width can be the same as wooden battens, and the rough guide here is one inch for every 10 ft of water-line. Thus a boat with a water-line of 25 ft will have Tufnol mainsail battens which are $\frac{5}{32}$ in. thick, and $2\frac{1}{2}$ in. wide; the pockets should be one-third as wide again, if the batten is to slip easily in and out.

GRP or FRP Battens. There are many other synthetic materials which are used for battens with success; plastics in general and GRP in particular spring to mind. One of the advantages which GRP enjoys is that of a high strength/weight ratio; it is also less bulky than wood. This means that a batten can be made which is strong, flexible, light and slim although it tends to stiffen with age. In fact, one of the pitfalls to watch for is a tendency to bend in several directions, which can be countered by ribbing the material. These slim battens usually have spade-shaped ends in order to give a large bearing surface when pushed into batten pockets.

Full Length Battens. Full length battens take some of the inefficiency out of a mainsail when going to windward. The sail becomes much more allied to a solid aerofoil, because its luff does not lift so much under the influence of backwinding by the headsail or, in the case of a mizzen, by the dirty wind off the mainsail. This means that laminar flow is maintained over a greater area with resulting improved efficiency. The powerpoint should be about one-third aft at the head, becoming almost half-way near the foot. To achieve a full camber in light winds, push the battens in hard when you tie them in; use less pressure in strong winds so the sail is flatter. Test for stiffness by standing each batten vertically on a set of bathroom scales and pushing on its upper end until it takes up roughly the right shape. The scales should read between 3–7 lbs; any batten needing more than about 15 lbs is far too stiff. Curvature can also be changed by use of the leech line, although this seems to have most effect in the top third of the sail only. Be careful not to overdo this, because a hooked leech will have a marked braking effect at the high speeds enjoyed by some fully battened multihulls. The forward ends of the pockets are subject to a lot of chafe, so they must be well reinforced.

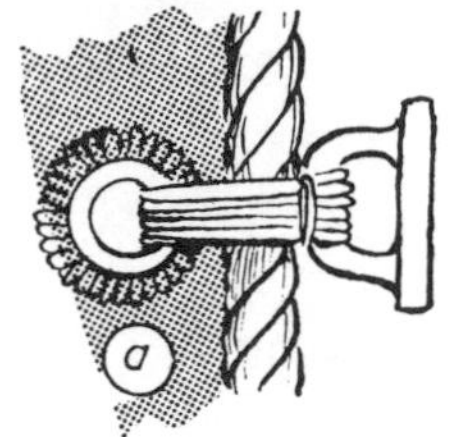

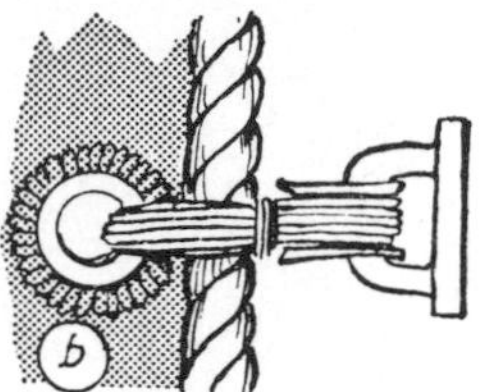

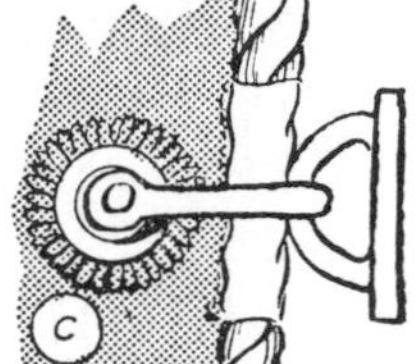

Fig. 38. Slide attachment.
(a) Simple seizing.
(b) Seizing with thimble.
(c) Shackle with hide or cloth casing of the bolt rope in way of the shackle.

Slides

The traditional method of attaching slides is with waxed twine, and this has served well for many years. Its chief drawback is chafe, for only one part of the seizing has to break for the whole thing to be in danger of coming undone. Various methods of overcoming this have been tried, the best being to use a thimble to take the chafe at the slide; sometimes a shackle is preferred.

But this means that the slide is that little bit slacker on the sail, and thus more prone to twist and jam on the track. Shackles chafe the luff rope heavily, which has to be well protected in way of every slide by means of hide or cloth casing. *Thanet* adopted a modification of the shackle during the late forties or early fifties, which proved a slight advantage. The chafe of the shackle pin was eliminated by the simple process of doing away with the pin. The U-shaped part of the shackle was retained in the form of a specially made fitting, with an eye at each end, which was then seized to the sail in the normal way. *Carina* pioneered this system in the United States in 1957.

The two advantages of the shackle are strength, and the fact that it can be quickly and easily fitted by the owner. The disadvantages, however, make a formidable list which more than outweighs the points in favour.

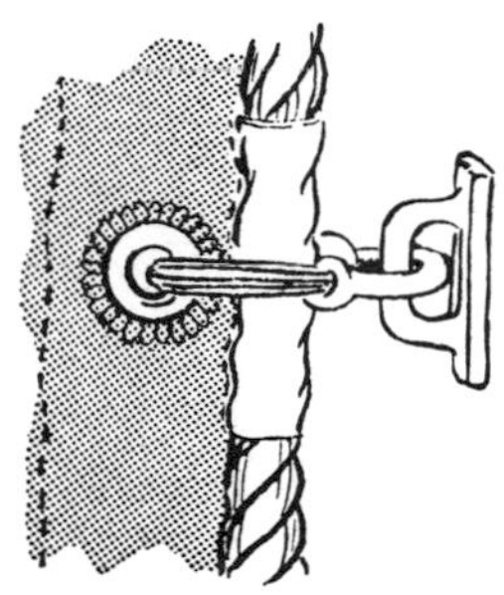

Fig. 39. *Thanet*'s adaptation of the shackle, doing away with the pin.

1. The shackle itself can corrode, so that the pin will not undo. Electrolysis between shackle and slide often accelerates this.
2. The shackle will chafe the bolt rope, which has to be cased with leather or cloth as some measure of protection.
3. The softer of the two metals will chafe, either on the slide or on the shackle.
4. There is extra weight aloft.
5. If an odd sized shackle has to be used for one or two slides, the bolt rope will not run in a straight line.

Which brings me to the question of what the solution is. To my mind the answer lies in the system adopted by *Stormvogel* in 1963. This is to attach the slides by means of synthetic tape. The tape is strong enough to resist chafe by the slide, and is soft enough not to chafe the slide or the sail in return.

One end of about one foot of ½ in. tape is first sewn to the slide. The other end is then passed through the eyelet at the luff or foot, and then back through the slide. This is repeated as many times as it will conveniently go, usually about three or four times to give 6 or 8 parts. Care should be taken to see that a slight amount of lateral play is allowed the slide, so that the sail can swing from side to side on the mast. The loose end should then be sewn through the 6 or 8 parts several times with a stout waxed thread. The result is a neat and workmanlike fitting which will last a good deal longer than most other systems, and which will not damage the slide or the sail.

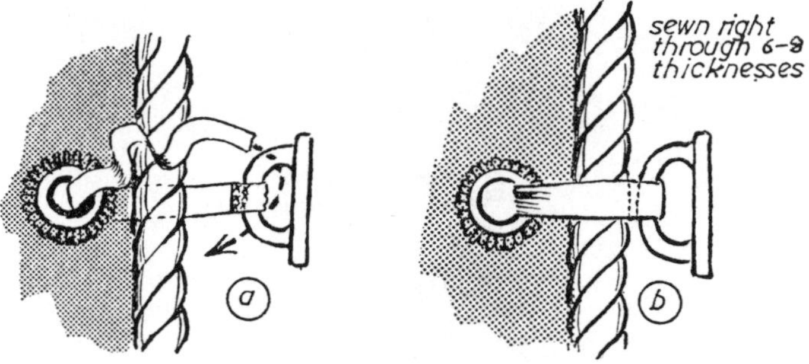

Fig. 40. *Stormvogel's* arrangement, using half inch wide synthetic tape. (a) shows the start of operation, (b) shows the finished job. This method is the best, in my opinion.

Types of Slide. Slides themselves are better from the Sail Maker's point of view if they are made of plastic, because they do not then need greasing. Grease picks up other dirt particles and spreads across the canvas in an unsightly smear; it is most difficult to remove. A certain minimum thickness is necessary if a plastic slide is to be strong enough. This virtually means that external slides cannot safely be made from this material, save for the smallest sails, for the slide would be too thick to pass behind the track. Some of the smaller sizes of internal slide are also suspect when made in nylon or similar material, because they either break at the handle, or elongate at the shoulders.

I tested a number of such slides in 1964 and found that the average breaking strain of the ⅝ in. (16 mm) variety was 550–700 lb. This is enough for a five-tonner, but is low for anything larger, particularly when you remember that it is often shock load which has to be sustained. I have not seen many of the larger type, from $\frac{7}{8}$ in. (22 mm) upwards, which have given trouble.

A standard alloy slide can be coated with a film of nylon which will last a season or so. This does away with the need for grease, and is stronger than an all-nylon slide of similar dimensions. The nylon coating tends to peel off after a year's use.

I do not like external slides, which are so popular in America, for several reasons. Not only can they not be made in nylon thin enough and yet strong enough, but I have yet to see an external slide smaller

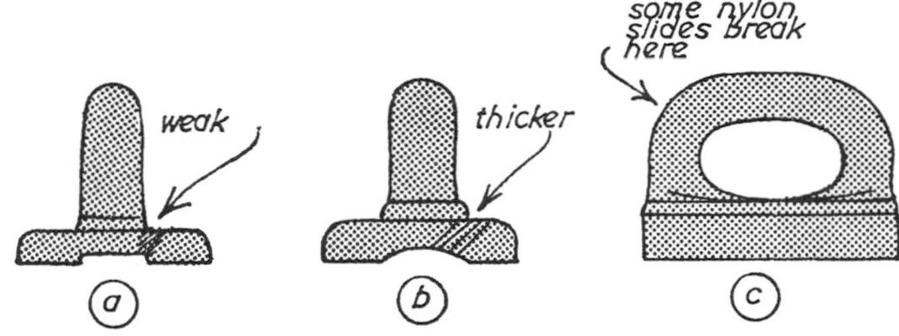

Fig. 41. (a) A common method of hollowing the face of nylon slides to allow them to pass over screw-heads; this gives a weak point, particularly if the shoulders are narrower than the recess.
(b) A curved hollow gives greater strength at the shoulders.
(c) Side view of slide.

than $1\frac{1}{4}$ in. which has a really suitable handle for the synthetic tape attachment which *Stormvogel* developed. The gap left by the usual small handle is not large enough to allow many thicknesses of tape, which normally has to be very narrow to get through in the first place. In addition, the thinness of the metal which is often used, makes them ideal machines for cutting anything which is used to fasten them to a sail, even synthetic tape. It is for this reason that many of them come already equipped with a brass thimble for a grommet or seizing; this makes them very slack on the sail.

In certain very large yachts it is sometimes an advantage to be able to remove the mainsail without taking the slides off the boom. To effect this there are heavy-gauge gunmetal external slides, made by Merriman, which are attached by means of their own screw pins.

When taking the sail off the boom, the screw pins are undone, and the sail lifted bodily off sideways. Yachts which are in the region of 100 ft overall adopt this system, because their mainsails are too heavy to pull forward off the boom. In addition, yachts of such a size usually have an internal track with an external slide. This is because really heavy-gauge track only comes in this form; the slides which go with it are also heavily constructed and able to stand up to the severe loads involved.

Several firms produce a slide which will not only run in a track of the appropriate size, but will also go into a groove. This can be useful, should the owner decide to change his boom from one to the other. They also have the advantage that they are often made of nylon, and thus do not need greasing. The body of the slide is stoutly constructed, and I can thoroughly recommend them.

Finally, some neat little slides originated in France and America (where they are known as slugs) which are cylindrical in shape, also designed to run in a groove. They are about the same diameter as the appropriate rope would be, and they fasten to the sail just like any other slide. It seems to me, however, that it is a waste of opportunity to have a grooved boom and not to run the bolt rope inside it. There are a number of disadvantages associated with slides, and I would not want to go out of my way to fit them, except perhaps on the luff.

Hanks or Snap Hooks

Dinghies have a wide variety of hanks or snaps from which to choose. Besides the end- and side-pull piston type, of either bronze or stainless steel, there are wire clips like overgrown safety pins, nylon and metal twist type attachments, and tab hanks; zip-fasteners also come under this heading. Selection of a particular type is very much a matter of individual choice, and I would be the last to make a single recommendation in this rather specialist field. Whatever I say is bound to displease some people, because there are plenty of dinghy men who spurn hanks altogether in a laudable pursuit of aerodynamic efficiency from a clean luff. Wire clips will not stand up to the heaviest weather without tending to bend, nylon twist hanks chafe on the forestay, metal twist ones are sometimes hard to get off with cold fingers, and gunmetal or stainless piston hanks or snap hooks are not always perfection – although there is not much wrong with them to my mind. Tab hanks may be unfamiliar, so I will describe them for those who would like to give them a try.

A short piece of synthetic webbing, about $1\frac{1}{4}$ in. wide, is sewn to the luff of the headsail so that it protrudes some $1\frac{1}{2}$ in. beyond the luff. This is passed round the forestay and fastened to itself by means of a press-stud. Its advantages are lightness, minimal disturbances of the airflow and unlikelihood of its catching on the spinnaker. Disadvantages are chafe of the tab by the forestay, and the undue reliance which has to be placed on the fastener, which may not always be corrosion free – particularly as regards its spring.

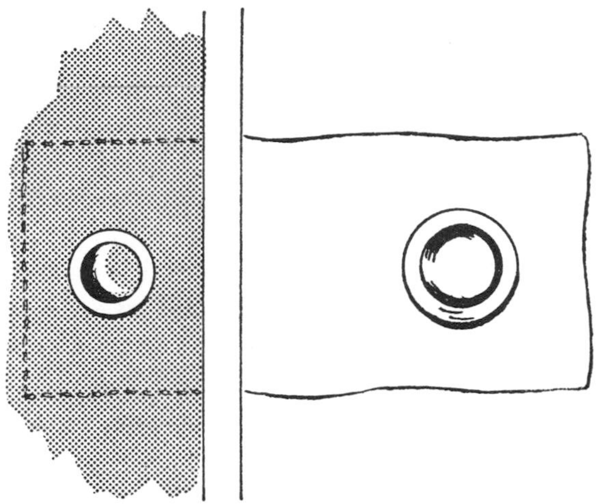

Fig. 42. Press-stud tab hank (full size).

Ocean-racers mostly use piston hanks or snaps of one kind or another, the choice being merely one of materials, and whether the piston should be operated by a side- or an end-pull. A side-pull hank can be worked with one hand, which is a decided advantage when working on a heaving deck; an end-pull hank is possibly more reliable. The traditional material for hanks is gunmetal, and it has stood the test of time well. In the early sixties, however, Goiot of France and Ratsey & Lapthorn of England each came out with an improved material. The latter have their hanks made by an aircraft company, of a metal which is both lighter and stronger than gunmetal. The Strenlite hank, as it is called, is an easily operated, tough hank which takes advantage of modern materials. It has an end-pull operation and is virtually corrosion free (the prototype was hung on a sea wall at half tide for three months, and was as smooth to operate at the end as it was when first put there). A destruction test, which had broken other types of hank at 300 kg tension, was halted at 1,500 kg for fear of breaking the test equipment.

Many piston hanks are still attached to the sail with a seizing. This is an old fashioned system, with drawbacks similar to those attendant upon seized slides. The tendency up to medium-sized sails nowadays is to squeeze a metal arm round the eyelet, possibly using a plastic chafe protector; larger craft can use leather thongs.

Zippers. There is no doubt that a zip-fastener provides a smooth and efficient system of attaching a headsail to a stay. There are no projections for the spinnaker to catch, and the sail is given a clean leading edge aerodynamically. A certain conservatism exists regarding the zipper, not only among owners but also among those responsible for drawing up rules. Far too many classes ban the zippered luff, and I suspect that they would be hard put to it to set down why they ban it. What is certain is that governing bodies have seized upon the pretence that a sail which zips on to its stay is a double luffed sail, and is thus conveniently banned under the rule which deals with such devices. The ban on double luffed sails, however, was brought in to prevent owners from inflating their sails by allowing air to enter at the front of a double sail. To pretend that a zippered luff is attempting the same advantage is nonsense, and I am glad to see that the IOR permits them subject to a minor measurement addition.

The zipper and its slider must be corrosion resistant, and this virtually means that the former should be all plastic and the latter heavily enamelled metal (for the slider has to be thin in places in order to work, and this would weaken plastic too much). The method of attaching the sail to the stay is for the zipper to be open-ended and to close towards the tack. One side of the zipper is passed round the stay, and the two ends are joined at the top, just like the bottom of a zip-fronted jacket. A hand then holds the slider as the sail is hoisted until it is two blocks, and the slider reaches the bottom.

To change sails, the slider on the sail to come off is unzipped for about 6 ft at the tack, while the replacement sail has its head started on the now exposed lower end of the stay. The new sail is then hoisted on a second halyard, while a hand holds the slider as before. The act of hoisting the new sail unzips the old one, so there is never a period when the boat is without a headsail.

I shall refer to zipper stowage of spinnakers and spinnaker nets later.

Grooved Forestay. A grooved forestay has the advantage of a clean aerodynamic entry for the leading edge of the driving aerofoil, and of fast sail changes. Being smooth, as opposed to the serrations of a wire, a spinnaker slides off it more easily and so resists the tendency to wrap round it if the sail falls in (a quality it shares with a rod forestay). A grooved rod forestay is expensive, but has the advantage of simplicity over the cheaper alternatives, which usually involve mating two lengths of metal or plastic extrusion round an existing wire forestay, to produce a pear-shaped entry (which is better aerodynamically) for the headsail luff rope on its trailing edge. Improvement in aerodynamic efficiency is marked, but the IOR takes account of the fore and aft dimension of these stays or attachments when calculating the yacht's J measurement, so the grooved rod will affect your rating less than the cheaper and bulkier alternatives. Twin grooves enable a replacement sail to be set before the old one is lowered.

Windows

Many classes allow windows in sails. They give improved visibility and thus contribute to safety in crowded waters. The material used is resistant to creasing, although particular care should be taken not to maltreat this part of the sail. A window is normally fitted to a finished sail by forming an envelope of the correct size with a second piece of cloth sewn to the sail. The window material is then slipped into one end of the envelope and sewn all round to keep it in place; this ensures that it lies flat in the sail and does not pull at the corners. The middle portion of each side of the envelope is then cut away and the edges tucked under and sewn neatly round. Alternatively, the window material may be sewn straight to one side of the sail, and the sail then cut away on the other side. This leaves a slightly rough surface where the window is not covered at the edge on one side, but it has the advantage of economy.

CHAPTER VII

Rigging

We have seen in Chapter II some of the theoretical factors which affect a yacht's performance to windward. I now want to discuss how the static nature of the boat plays its part *vis-à-vis* the sails, and how you can improve performance by careful attention to it. This covers all those parts of the boat which directly or indirectly affect the set of the sails, such as spars and their rigging, kicking-straps, boom vangs, winches, halyards, etc.

We all have our pet rigging likes and dislikes, some of them for no more valid reason than because we have never used anything else. I cannot hope to set forth the optimum rig for all boats, because each class differs from the next, thank goodness. I say thank goodness, for it would be a dull sport without variety. All that can be done is to point out some of the effects, and to suggest a profitable approach to each problem.

Spars

The earliest masts were tree trunks, on to which the sails were tied at convenient points. The only real refinements over the centuries were for the branches to be trimmed off neatly and for a particular type of tree to be preferred. We thus came to solid spruce masts which were straight and tapered towards the top; girth was decided by trial and error. The same generalization holds good for all other spars.

The rise of the aircraft industry in the twentieth century saw the need for accurate calculation of strength/weight ratios in this kind of structure and, in particular, for cutting down weight while maintaining strength. This led to a more widespread understanding of lamination, hollow construction and, later, to the use of metals and light alloys.

A metal mast of given section will normally be stronger than an equivalent wooden one; equally it will be stiffer and lighter. This means that a good saving in weight aloft can sometimes be made, because the section can be smaller than a wooden one for the same boat, thus also reducing the size of the fittings required. Modern methods of anodizing offer a permanent protection against corrosion, such as is not available against rot in a wooden spar.

You might assume from the foregoing that metal spars are a necessity for all yachts. An expensive, custom-made, wooden mast can sometimes actually be lighter than a metal one, however, and will certainly have a lower centre of gravity. We shall see shortly the advantages of a bending mast, and it should be remembered when reading this section that, while a wooden mast can be made to bend more than a metal one, the latter will be more consistent. It is too broad a generalization to say that no two wooden masts bend alike, but they are more often different than otherwise. On the other hand, the dinghy owner can alter the bend of a wooden mast by carefully planing it down in the appropriate place.

Strength/weight ratios and fittings are largely outside the scope of this book, where I am chiefly concerned with sails and the flow of air over them. This is directly affected by such obvious factors as mast rake and bend, but we must also briefly consider spar shape, how the sail is attached to it, and how it is reefed; neat fittings are desirable in the interests of reduction in parasite drag.

Mast Shape. A clean entry for the wind on to the leading edge of a sail is what we want. The mast and its fittings, therefore, disturb the air just where we least want them to do so. A round, or even a flattened oval, section causes eddies in the airflow which bring a drop in efficiency. When you add to this the fact that the mast section is never at the optimum streamline angle to the wind unless the mast rotates, you can see how important it is to study the shape we present to the wind. The undoubted efficiency of a headsail can be partly explained by the absence of the disturbing influence of a mast at the luff.

Boom Shape. The boom presents a different problem. The shape of its section does not have to be streamlined for efficiency, because the wind flows along it; consistent with adequate strength, therefore, we can allow our desires regarding bend characteristics partly to control the section. However, the boom does perform a useful function in acting as an endplate to the mainsail. The tendency of the wind is to curl downwards under the boom from windward to leeward. If the

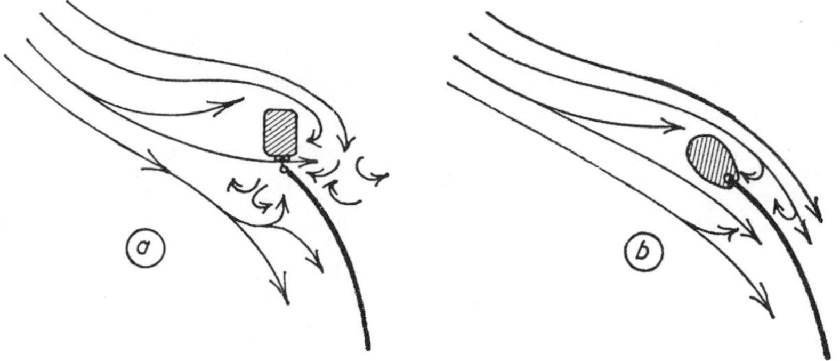

Fig. 43. Mast streamline.

(a) A bluff shape which is at a poor angle to the wind causes excessive turbulence. A sail attached by slides also allows wind to escape from windward to leeward through the gap.

(b) A streamlined shape, which rotates so as to present its best angle to the wind, causes less turbulence. In addition, a groove seals the gap at the mast.

top of the boom presents a moderately flat surface, this tendency will be resisted, thus cutting down induced drag and improving the efficiency of the airflow. In dinghies, a second factor is the free sail area which the boom affords. As deep a spar as the rules allow can give an appreciable increase in area downwind, but it will reduce vertical bend.

Slides or Grooves. Where a sail is attached to its mast by slides, there is a loss of efficiency caused by air leaking to leeward through the gap between the spar and the sail. This reduces the pressure differential between the two sides of the sail. Various methods of stopping this leak have been tried, and the only really successful one is to use a groove for the luff rope. This is all very well for boats which take off their sails every time they stop sailing, but a large mainsail cannot be stowed on the boom without taking it right out of the luff groove and thus detaching it from the mast altogether. This is an unseamanlike operation, as well as being irksome, so we have to accept luff slides as soon as the mainsail gets around 250 sq. ft in area. Whatever the size, however, there is no doubt that a groove is more efficient aerodynamically. Not only does it stop the air-leak, but it shares the load on the luff rope evenly throughout its length. Modern masts are made so that chafe at the luff groove is reduced to a minimum, and I do not think this need affect our choice. This is particularly important since you can now get masts with a groove which has a track running inside it; the groove starts far enough above the tack fitting to allow the sail to emerge and furl on the boom, still retained on the mast by the exposed track beneath the groove entry.

A groove is nearly always best for a boom for several reasons. First, the boom acts as a more efficient barrier to the wind which is trying to curl under it and form flow-disturbing eddies, for there is no leak between sail and spar. Secondly the strain is shared more equally along the foot rope. Thirdly, if a roller reefing system is used, the sail will take up a more even shape when rolled down if there are no slides to cause lumps (and chafe) along the foot. Finally, people will use metal slides which need grease, and this makes a mess on the sail which it is almost impossible to remove. If your spars have already got a track which takes an internal slide, fit one of the modern all nylon variety which does not need greasing to make it run; if you are in doubt about the strength of this type, you can get metal slides which have been coated in a thin film of nylon, but this tends to peel off with use. See that the track is carefully cleaned before bending the sail with its new slides. If, however, you decide to have a grooved boom, be sure to have one or two strongpoints where you can attach a boom vang, because you will not be able to pass one round the boom, as you can with a sail fitted with slides along the foot.

In this connection, a very efficient and usual system is to have one or more rings running on a short length of heavy track recessed into the underside of the boom at its forward end – they might be called ringslides as opposed to ringbolts (which are, of course, bolted into the deck). The vang is then attached to one of these ringslides, which can be adjusted so that it is in the correct position over the strongpoint on deck – railcap or ringbolt – to which the other end of the vang will be made fast.

Reefing. I have long been an advocate of roller reefing, but the advent of jiffy reefing has made me think again. This involves a line rove permanently from just forward of the outer end of the boom, through the leech reef cringle and down to a cleat via a fairlead on the other side of the boom (sometimes the start point and this fairlead are adjustable ringslides). The inner end of the boom is equipped with a downward-facing hook to one side of the tack fitting (another one may be fitted on the opposite side for the second reef). The slack is taken on the topping lift (or the hydraulic boom vang or kicker is pumped up to hold the boom level); the halyard is slackened so that the luff reef cringle can be pulled down over the hook; the leech reef cringle is pulled down to the boom by its permanent line, and the job is done. The bunt of the sail which is left flapping along the boom may then be tidied up at leisure by means of a lacing line but, while helping to spread the load, this is by no means essential if the reef is not expected to be in for long or the situation requires the crew elsewhere.

There are four main drawbacks to roller reefing, which can all be overcome. First, the gear may fail: in this case the wise owner will have had an emergency lacing reef fitted in the two- or three-reef position. Secondly, the sail may not take up quite the desired curve at the foot when reefed, due to the shape of the boom: but a boom which is slightly thicker at its outer end will allow for this, and will raise the clew slightly as the sail is rolled on to it; if you have a straight sided boom, you can either have slats fitted each side at the outer end to increase the diameter, or you can roll some tea towels or old canvas into the leech as you reef down. Thirdly, the leech is not pulled aft on a roller, as it is with a tie reef which has a cringle and positive outhaul: however, John Illingworth recommends that the lower leech of the mainsail should have hauling-aft loops attached from the clew to about the deep reef position, so that a hand can exert a steady pull with a boathook as the boom is being rolled; this will keep the wrinkles out of the foot. Finally, the luff rope tends to bunch on the roller gear as the sail is wound round the boom: a sail made correctly for roller reefing, however, will have reinforcing webbing or tape, instead of rope, on the lower luff so that this does not occur.

A boom vang can be fitted to a rolled down mainsail if a length of synthetic webbing or reinforced cloth is rolled into the sail as the reef is taken in. The free end should have an eye worked into it for the attachment of a purchase.

Through-mast roller reefing entails a fixed gooseneck and a reefing gear which works from the forward side of the mast level with the boom. This method is extremely quick in operation; so quick, in fact, that it is often used for furling the mainsail in harbour.

You should ensure that the boom rises a little with each reef; this will keep it progressively clearer of heads in the cockpit and of the water on a reach, as the wind strength increases and successive reefs are taken in. You should have at least two reef positions, and some-

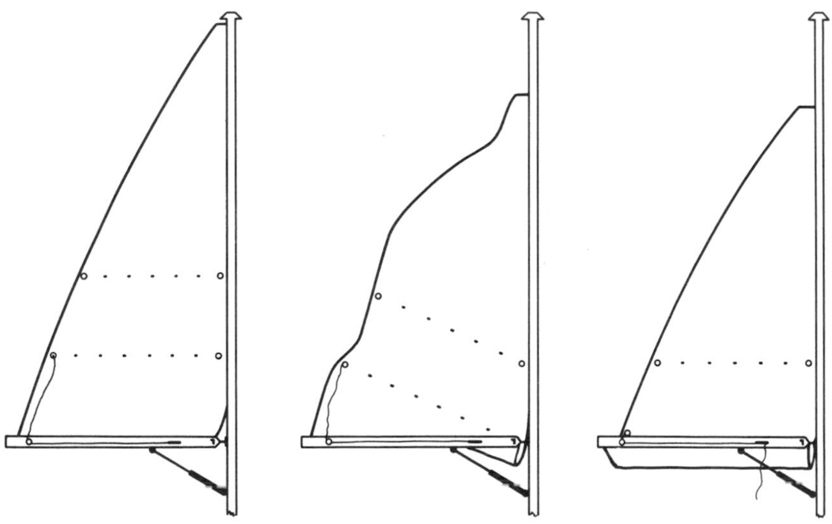

Fig. 44. *Jiffy reefing.* This may also be used with a leech Cunningham, either alone (to top up the clew and flatten the leech), or in conjunction with a luff Cunningham (to flatten the whole foot area).

(a) See that the hydraulic kicking strap or boom vang is holding the boom level; alternatively take up the topping lift.

(b) Lower the main halyard and pull the luff reef earring down over the hook at the gooseneck.

(c) Pull on the (permanently rove) leech reefing line, to bring the leech reef earring down to the bee block or fairlead – it should also pull aft to put tension along the foot. The intermediate reef eyelets or points may then be secured if necessary.

times three if the mainsail is tall and narrow. Each reef should reduce area by about 20 per cent; alternatively you can estimate the luff end of the reef as being approximately one-eighth of the total luff. The leech distance will be about 10 per cent longer than the luff distance.

A jib or staysail can also be reefed. In this case individual points are the best system: they will more easily be tied under the loose foot of the sail. If the distance along the luff is the same as that along the leech, the angle of the luff will ensure that the clew rises a little as the reef is tied in. Aim to reduce area by about 30 per cent with one reef; you should not normally need more than this.

Straight Spars. I cannot, of course, tell you whether you need straight or bendy spars: this is a matter for you to decide. All I can do is to set forth some of the advantages and disadvantages of each rig and leave you to make your own choice. We will deal with straight spars first, as they are uncomplicated.

A straight mast and boom give the Sail Maker the best chance of cutting a sail which responds accurately to your requirements; he knows what the luff and foot of the sail will look like when set on your spars. However, you have to pay for this stiffness in weight and windage. The mast itself has to be of a fairly robust section in order to give it a certain amount of inherent ability to stay straight; it then has to be propped and stayed to hold it dead upright when the wind blows. All these jumpers, diamonds, cross-trees, spreaders, uppers, lowers, intermediates, backstays, forestays and runners create air turbulence and add to weight aloft. Nevertheless, they produce a straight mast. The boom is an easier task, because it does not have the same stresses, and it can be made with a deep section, since this does not affect the airflow over the sail to any great extent. In addition its weight is low in the sail plan, and is therefore not so critical except in light airs.

Bendy Spars. The dinghies have taught us that bending spars increase the range of wind in which we can use a given mainsail. They have also given Sail Makers a headache, because bend characteristics vary from mast to mast, and even on the same mast if the rigging is altered.

A three quarter rigged mast which bends aft at the head normally bows forward in the middle, unless it is restrained. This means that the sail must also bow forward in the middle as the mast bends, thus surrendering some of the round built into the luff. This flattens the sail. A similar change takes place along the foot when the boom bends downwards in the middle, under the influence of a centre mainsheet arrangement. If the mainsheet leads to the boom end, the boom will tend to bend upwards in the middle, and this will increase the fullness along the foot.

It is important for the Sail Maker to know the bending characteristics of the spars on which the sail he is making will be used. If the mast bends more than he thought, the sail will flatten too much and almost certainly will produce a hard spot somewhere up the luff, if not a positive crease running down towards the clew. If the mast bends less than anticipated, the sail, which was cut with extra round in the luff to accept a greater bow forward, will stay too full in stronger winds. Even if the mast bends the correct total amount, but the position of maximum bend is higher or lower than expected, the sail will pull out of shape as soon as bending reaches a certain point, because the correct amount of cloth is not in the right place.

Bending masts are principally used on dinghies, and have not yet won a firm hold on the keelboats (with some notable exceptions such as the Tempest and Star classes). It is therefore not difficult for owners to obtain the exact characteristics of their particular spars. The boat should be laid on its side on dry land while a sail of more or less the desired shape is set, and the mast then bent under the influence of the mainsheet and kicking-strap. Setting the right sail is important, because too flat a sail can restrict the amount of bend, while one which is too full, or no sail at all, will allow the mast to bend too much. A twine should then be stretched between the black bands, and the exact offsets taken every three feet or so.

Ocean-racers and cruisers have so far kept to straight masts, because the stresses on one which bends are complicated. Shroud angles which are all right for a straight spar become doubtful when it bends, and can easily fall to a point where the load becomes unacceptable; this is accentuated with larger masts. The time is coming, however, when the ocean-racing fleet will demand bending masts with an adequate safety factor, for this would confer on their mainsails an ability to cope with a wider wind range. As long ago as 1965 the Editor of *Yachting World* wrote:

Keelboat men must think in terms away from the much loved masthead rig. The future of the $\frac{7}{8}$ foretriangle with a bending spar, even if it means runners to control the limit of the bend, is one of the many things that needs to be explored for larger boats.

For her 1964 challenge for the America's Cup, *Sovereign* tried a mast with a soft top. The idea was quickly abandoned when the unfortunate Sail Maker failed to produce a suitable mainsail at the first attempt. He was working without specific details of the amount of bend, or of its location, and I believe that the attempt should have been allowed to proceed further before being condemned out of hand. This is particularly true in the light of *Constellation*'s successful treatment of the same problem. But if you are going in for a bendy mast, see to it that your spreaders or crosstrees have the ability to accept the change in direction of load which will result. It should be remembered, however, that a bending boom will remove draft from precisely that part of the sail where it contributes most thrust and least heeling moment: low down near the foot. Thrust is still needed, so don't go and throw it all away in an attempt to get the mainsail as flat as a board.

It is a fortunate coincidence that the stronger the wind, the more tension is needed on the mainsheet, and so the more the mast and boom will bend if they are made that way. The more they bend the flatter becomes the sail – which is what is needed in a strong wind.

We have been talking about fore and aft bend so far. Lateral bend is not so good, because it distorts the leading edge of the sail as it is presented to the wind, and will disturb the regularity of the airflow. Nevertheless a slight bend to leeward (and aft) at the head of a dinghy mast helps to feather the head of the mainsail in heavy weather, thus making it easier to hold the boat upright. A light helmsman will therefore probably have a more flexible mast than his heavier rival, who will be able to use his weight to keep upright with more of his sail drawing. This bend to leeward at the head brings with it a corresponding bend to windward below the hounds, which also carries a certain advantage. It has the effect of opening the slot a little between the mainsail and the headsail. When we remember that all this flexibility only occurs in strong winds, it will be appreciated that a slightly larger slot will be beneficial, because it will allow a less disturbed airflow over the lee side of the mainsail.

Mainsails can be cut with the correct flow in them when set on a straight boom, so it does not need to bend sideways to impart this flow, at least until nearly at the after-end. It can pay, however, to allow the final 20 per cent of the boom to sag off to leeward. This frees the lower leech of the mainsail from hooking to windward where it returns to the boom at the clew, and also helps the whole mainsail to present less frontal area to the airflow – thus cutting down form drag. Be careful not to overdo it, however, or you will encourage a slack leech.

It is difficult to generalize about the advisability of flexible masts, but if your dinghy has a lot of sail area for its size, such as a 14 ft International or a Flying Dutchman, or if you are particularly light, without a trapeze, then have bendy spars to help take some of the hard work out of keeping your boat upright. If you own an under-canvassed boat like a Snipe, or if you are heavy, you may prefer to

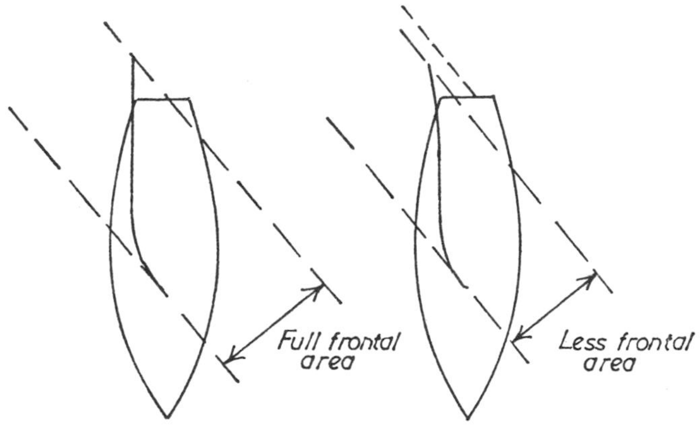

Fig. 45. Effect of a boom outer end which bends to leeward. In (b) above the clew falls away slightly and the sail presents less frontal area, when the wind is strong enough to bend the boom.

avoid the complications of too much flexibility, because you will usually be able to use full power. Secondly, if you are in doubt as to degree, have a stiffer rather than a more bendy mast; you can always bend it by brute force in a blow, yet you will have a straighter fore-stay for light airs, because the stiffer mast will hold it up better.

If you are considering having an ocean-racer built, or are wondering whether to have your present boat remasted, my advice is graded according to your temperament. If you are out to win at all costs, then you should seriously consider the benefits which a bending mast will bring. It will mean abandoning ideas of a masthead genoa, together with the efficient mainsail airflow pattern which this sail confers as a result of its influence on the leeward streamlines right to the head of the mainsail. On the other hand, you will have a mainsail which is full in light weather, yet which will not hold the boat back when it comes on to blow, because you will be able to flatten it.

If, however, you do not treat your racing as a religion, and you are content with the straight spar and masthead rig as developed today, then leave the expense of experiment to others, for there will surely be a number of breakages before the bendy mast comes to stay offshore. Remember that a leech Cunningham and a slab reef go a long way towards flattening the mainsail sufficiently to offset the disadvantages of a stiff mast.

Kicking-straps

I do not propose to argue whether the words 'kicking-strap' correctly describe what is also known as a boom vang and a boom jack; they are understood by all, and form a popular term. The kicking-strap's prime function is to keep the boom down and reduce mainsail twist at the head. In a dinghy it has two secondary roles to perform; those of preventing a Chinese gybe and of helping to impart mast bend. We have already discussed mast bend, and I do not propose to get involved in how best to control the bend you decide that you want. We all know that a Chinese gybe is spectacular and embarrassing; it is not my job to tell you not to do it. But sail twist is very much within the scope of this book, and a few words are indicated.

If a mainsail on a reach is allowed to develop too much twist due to the absence of a boom vang or kicking-strap, the boom must be sheeted in so that the upper part of the sail is not lifting. This means that the lower two-thirds is generating its thrust too much athwartships, and is contributing too much of its effort to heeling the boat and not enough to driving it forward. If we can reduce the twist, we can ease the boom, thereby achieving a greater forward thrust component and reducing the amount of weather helm required to keep the boat going straight ahead. The latter advantage is not always fully appreciated, but it is every bit as important as the former, if not more so.

1. A spreading floor. A large mainsail being cut out at W. G. Lucas Ltd. Note the extra overlap of the cloths in the tack area (lower right) to allow for tack seam. *Wright & Logan.*

2. Half of a 4,000 square foot spinnaker spread at Ratsey & Lapthorn Cowes loft. *Beken.*

3. *Above.* A modern machine shop. *Beken.*

4. *Left.* Porosity tester. The Gurley Meter used by Seahorse Sails Limited for testing sailcloth. It measures the time in seconds for 100 c.c. of air at constant pressure to pass through one square inch of material. 25 seconds is par, 50 is very good and 15 or less is poor. *Seahorse Sails Ltd.*

5. Static test masts in a field. A 14 ft International mainsail, a Dragon mainsail and genoa, and a suit for a cruiser under examination on Ratsey's test spars. *Beken.*

6. Machining light Terylene. *Beken.*

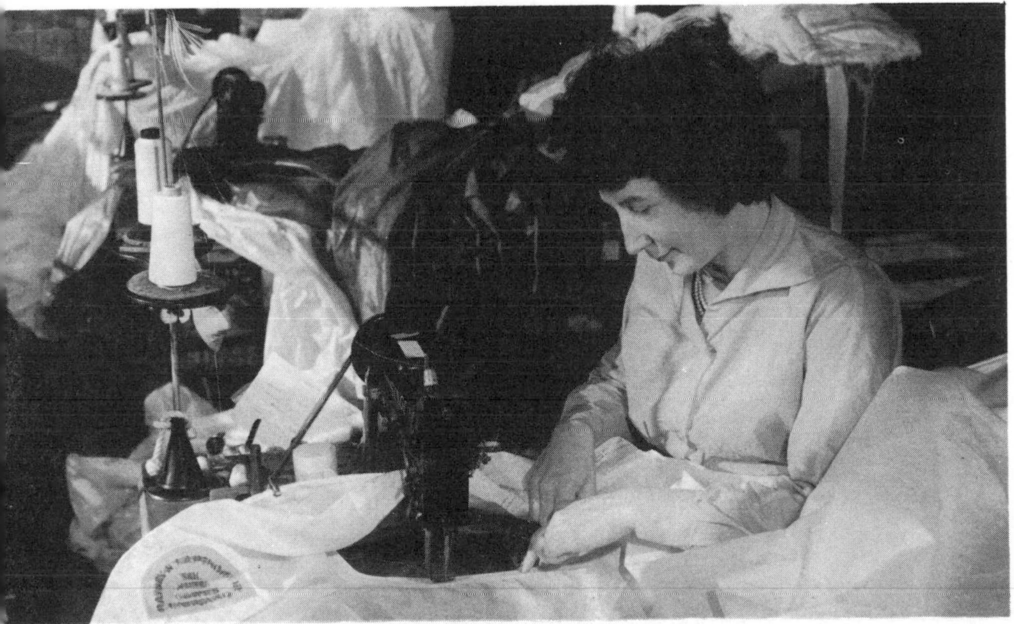

7. Bruce Banks Sails' indoor test rig. General shape and flow, as well as particular faults, can be examined on mainsails up to 800 sq. ft. on this rig. The mast has a groove large enough to take most luff slides. *Yachting World.*

8. Sails for bendy spars need special attention. Here a 505 mainsail is being examined on Bruce Banks' test rig, which can be adapted to suit any degree of bend. *Yachting World.*

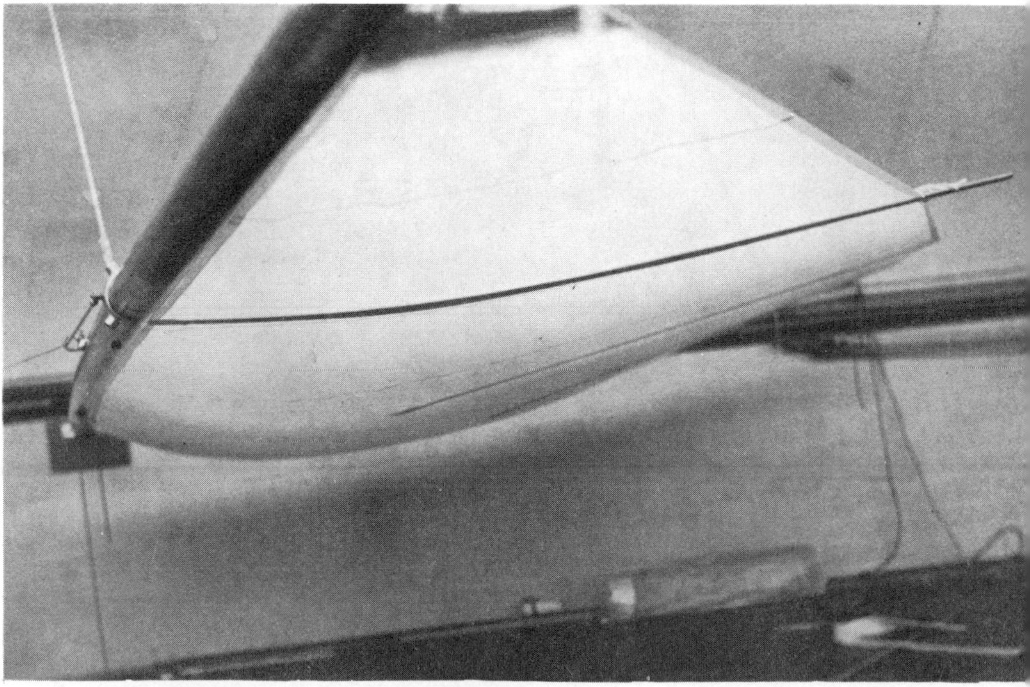

9. A 12 metre mainsail. Measuring the camber from a fire engine turntable ladder. *Author*.

10. This pulpit presents a good safe working platform for the crew of *Eloïse II*. *Author*.

11. A Thames 'A' Rater. A modern rig on an old-timer. The fully battened Terylene mainsail is setting beautifully on a pre-bent mast. Note the flat leech and the flow of the sail, revealed by the cloth seams, gradually flattening towards the head. The boat would probably go better with a full-width mainsheet traveller. *Eileen Ramsay.*

12. *Kurrewa V.* A skirt has been added to this spinnaker in a series of short vertical cloths. As they are laid at right angles to the curved foot, there is a slight bias at the point where they meet the selvedge of the bottom horizontal cloth. Note how the small amount of bias results in distortion of the sail at that point. There appears to be too much broad seam in the sail just above the racing number; the beginnings of a small pucker can be seen. *Beken.*

13. *Sovereign.* Her sunray genoa has a multiplicity of vertical cloths at the foot to try and eliminate excessive stretch. Note how the excessive bias at the luff has caused uneven stretching at the head; there appears to be a patch of uneven sewing at the second hank up. *Beken.*

A full width mainsheet traveller, coupled with a centre boom lead, is aiming at the same result, and these refinements have spread from widespread use in dinghies and the smaller keelboat one-designs into the ocean-racing fleet. Indeed, a centre mainsheet is not easy to accommodate in a two-man dinghy under about 14 ft long, because it gets in the way, whereas the ocean-racers have no such problems. At all events, make sure that your kicking-strap is powerful and easy to use. The hydraulic ram offers the best (and most expensive) solution. It cannot be used with roller reefing, but governs boom angle up and down, and thus gives excellent control over sail shape if used with a slab reef and adjustable clew outhaul. A roller boom, of course, means that a claw has to be used for a centre boom sheet

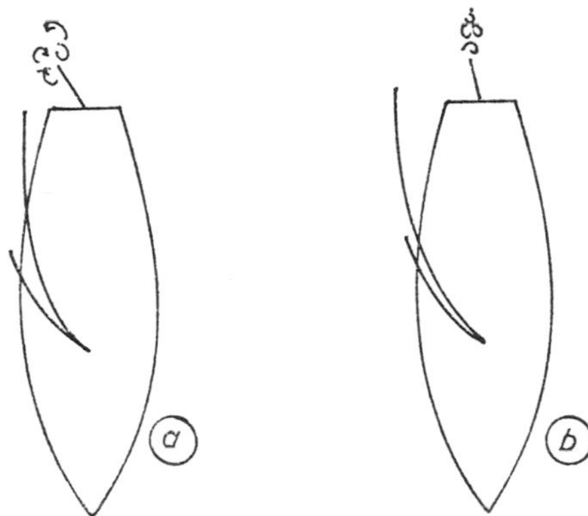

Fig. 46. Effect of twist.
(a) Here the boom is well in, to prevent the upper half of the mainsail sagging off too much.
(b) In this drawing the boom is further out, but the half height section of the sail is the same as in (a) because twist has been reduced. Note how this also reduces weather helm.

lead, and this often gives trouble from jamming and from chafe; it is for each owner to make his own decision as to whether it is worth it.

It is not enough for a dinghy to have a good kicking-strap; it must also have an effective means of controlling the amount of mast bend which it imparts. This often takes the form of chocks of different thickness, which are placed in front of the mast where it passes through the deck or partner. But you should remember that you are most likely to want to vary mast bend as the wind increases, and it is not always possible to change chocks in heavy weather. Cliff Norbury developed a form of jack mounted under the foredeck, and I do not see why a worm drive would not be simpler, if slower, than his suggestion which is reproduced in figure 47.

Dinghies have probably paid more attention to the problem of sail twist than other boats, because the effects are so apparent. It is particularly important to keep a dinghy upright in planing conditions, and the boat with an effective kicking-strap and a full width mainsheet traveller will soon demonstrate its superiority. Besides the

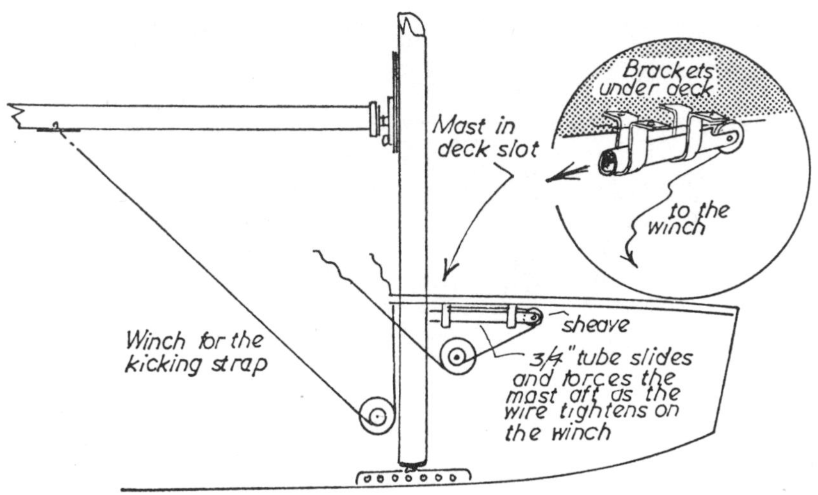

Fig. 47. Cliff Norbury's system of controlling mast bend.

heeling effect caused by the lower half of the mainsail being sheeted too far inboard in order to stop the upper third from lifting on a reach, a rising boom means that the wind is flowing upwards off the upper leech, thus causing the boat to heel more.

One of the drawbacks of a centre sheet arrangement on a planing dinghy is that the helmsman cannot easily strike his sheet to give the boat those sharp kicks needed to get on to a plane, and make the most of the apparent wind suddenly coming farther ahead. Guthrie Penman developed an arrangement on his 14 ft International, whereby a

Novex block at the boom end gave him this ability; the system was also used by Mike Peacock and Jon Allen among others.

On a reach a quick snatch at the sheet brings in the boom end as if on a single part, while the central purchase still acts as a boom bender and kicking-strap. Both centre and boom end parts have travellers, so that easing the sheet when close-hauled lets the boom move sideways on the centre traveller without rising.

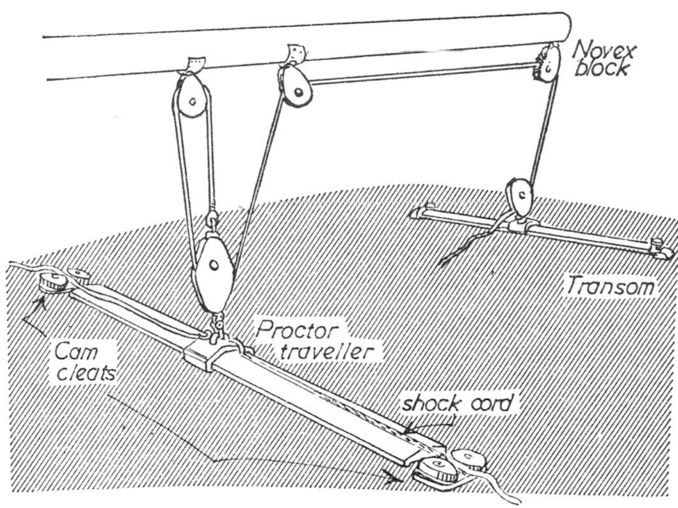

Fig. 48. Guthrie Penman's mainsheet system. This system is claimed to combine the advantages of the centre boom lead with those of the boom end lead.

Winches

The job of a headsail sheet winch is to provide enough power to pull the clew of the headsail concerned far enough aft to flatten the leech of the sail when beating to windward. With many genoas it is the only way of ensuring a flat leech in a blow. Equally, with many winches (and crews) it is the quickest way to overstrain a sail. If you possess powerful winches, therefore, you should tell your Sail Maker when ordering headsails. He can then see that the canvas is the correct weight to avoid distortion, and he can cut the sail appropriately. Many crews feel that 'just one more notch' on the genoa winch is the hallmark of a hard racing man; it is often the ruin of a perfectly good sail.

If you do not possess powerful winches, then your Sail Maker can cut your genoa with a flat leech which does not have to be hauled in bar taut when on the wind. In addition, it is no good making a jib heavily for use on a coffee-grinder, if the boat is not equipped with winches powerful enough to make the sail set properly.

Winches are frequently too powerful. It has become fashionable to own the latest equipment, and to have a higher power ratio than your rival. When you consider that some standard winches have a mechanical advantage of over 70:1 (and I am not talking of coffee-grinders, which are much more powerful), you can imagine the stress you are putting on your sails every time you harden right in. If the sail is cut correctly to start with, there should be no need for more than half this ratio in boats with a water-line length of under 25 ft or so.

Let me here explain that *gear ratio* is represented by the number of turns of the handle, to one of the winch drum. *Power ratio*, or *mechanical advantage*, also takes account of the radius of the winch handle (and thus the leverage which can be exerted on it), and the diameter of the drum (and thus the amount of rope which is pulled in at each turn of the drum); it can be expressed as

$$\frac{\text{Gear Ratio} \times \text{Handle Radius}}{\text{Drum Radius}}.$$

Halyards and Outhauls

Mainsail halyards must be powerful enough to stretch the luff of the sail properly. In dinghies this presents little problem, but the bigger boats need the help of winches. A downhaul is an excellent way of getting that little bit extra when it is needed, and it has the added advantage of providing a first-class system of regulating the flow in the sail according to the weather. A fixed gooseneck means that the main halyard has to be adjusted in order to alter the tension on the luff, and this is sometimes a tiresome process which becomes too much trouble as a result. Remember that rope halyards will stretch with use and spoil the set of the sail if they are not trimmed after you have been out for a while.

An ocean-racer's main clew outhaul should be a positive fitting, preferably a jaw with a through-pin, running on a short heavy track; adjustment can be made either by means of an outhaul line on a purchase, or through a worm drive. The cruising man can stick to the old-fashioned lashing, which gives less trouble from the maintenance angle. Whichever system you adopt, see that the footrope of the sail continues in a straight line throughout its length, and does not rise sharply at the clew.

Dinghies and the smaller keelboats are keenly aware of the importance of adjusting tension on the foot of the mainsail, as much as on the luff, when the wind varies or the boat changes between beat and reach. A lashing cannot be altered easily in a dinghy, and many helmsmen adopt a long outhaul line leading under the boom to a jam cleat; alternatively a worm gear is used, but this means allowing your attention to be distracted for too long at a time and can only be adjusted when the boom end is within reach. John Ogle adopted a good system in his 14 ft International in 1964. He had a footrope entirely made of shock cord, tensioned so that it was about 4 in. short of the black band when lying slack. The clew outhaul was coupled to a Highfield lever which allowed 3 in. of play. The clew was pulled right aft to the black band for beating to windward and was allowed to go forward 3 in. as soon as the boat came off the wind. Admittedly this only provides two alternative positions for the clew, but it has the great advantage that it is simple. Its simplicity means that it is used more often than a more complicated system, even though the latter may give infinite adjustment.

CHAPTER VIII

Tuning

In this chapter I shall look at those aspects of tuning which have an effect on the sails. Such things as a clean bottom, centreboard position, rudder shape and so on are as important as sails and rigging, but they do not directly concern my subject, even though some of them might do so indirectly through affecting the degree of weather helm a boat may have. Before we leave this area, however, I would just like to illustrate that sails are not the only part of a boat where experts can agree to differ.

In 1965 Stu Walker and Mike Peacock both bought new 14 ft International dinghies to the same design and with the same J measurement from Souters of Cowes. Peacock asked for his centreboard to be 4 in. *aft* of the design position, and Walker asked for an adjustable pin. Peacock found that his boat went best when he sat right forward, whereas Walker decided that the best combination was to have the centreboard 4 in. *forward* of the datum, which meant that he finished up sitting right aft in the boat. Both men had tuned to optimum efficiency with two major factors almost as far apart as they could go.

If I use a good many examples from the Fourteens it is not only because they are such a suitable class due to the latitude allowed in their rig, but also because of the nature of the members themselves. I have visited many different classes to advise on sails and help repair them during important meetings, and the owners who stand head and shoulders above the rest for courtesy and consideration are the Fourteen Footers. The attending sailmakers work hard at these meetings to repair and alter sails, often until eleven o'clock at night. At the end of the race, when the plaudits have died down, it is invariably the Fourteen owner who will push his way through the crowd at the club, or walk half a mile to the temporary sail loft, purely to say thank you. They have their foibles like anyone else, and are just as particular about the odd half inch as the next man, besides which their mainsails are not easy to make and are even more difficult to correct once they are not made right, but it is small wonder that I have a soft spot for the class as a whole.

The object of tuning is to balance a boat in such a way that she will sail to best advantage under certain conditions of wind and water. This usually involves ensuring that the airflow over the combined aerofoil formed by at least two mutually interfering sails is efficient, and that the driving force which they generate is optimum in strength and direction. A great many variable factors play their part in this search, as we have already inferred in previous chapters. Not only does the initial shape of the sail make a big difference, but also the size and shape of the slot, the angle of the luff, the run-off at the leech and the way the sail is set and sheeted. Let us, therefore, go through those tuning factors which can affect the set and drive of the sails.

Ashore. If your boat is small enough to be hauled out easily for setting up ashore, so much the better. There is nothing more helpful to an owner than to walk round his boat with a critical eye when all working sail is set. If she is too large for this treatment, a similar result can be obtained at the moorings if you row round her in a dinghy.

Starting Point. First of all you must decide from which basis you are going to start. Don't forget that we are assuming here that all points not connected with sails have been covered, so the position of the mast is probably the most elementary factor. If you do not know how you want the mast placed, have a look at two or three successful boats in the same class as yourself and average their ideas. Decide where you want to put your own mast as a result of this.

The first task is to see that the boat is dead upright. If she is ashore, take care that the chocks are firmly positioned; if she is at her moorings, transfer weight until she is floating exactly to her marks. Next, see that the shrouds on either side are the same length, and that they and the forestay have the right amount of travel on their adjustments.

Classes vary as to whether rigging should be slack or tight. In general, a boat will normally go better to windward with the mast raked slightly aft, and better downwind with it raked forward. In order to achieve this double requirement, many two- and three-man boats use slack rigging. This allows the mast to lean towards the bows when the wind is astern, so that the main shrouds take the weight. When the boat is close-hauled, the mast is raked aft by the pull of the mainsheet; the slack of the forestay and headsail luff is thus taken up, so that the latter in particular is nice and straight. Slack rigging should be somewhat tighter in heavy weather, or the mast will go too far forward on a run and tend to bury the bows to the detriment of speed. Remember also that it is no use spending time finding the exact length for your forestay so that the mast behaves as you want it, only to sweat up on your headsail halyard and thus pull the mast too far forward on a beat. The headsail should be hoisted to the same tension for all races where the rigging is unaltered; the surest way to do this quickly is to have an eye on the halyard and a hook on the mast, so that the headsail luff just takes the weight off the forestay.

Many of the larger boats are putting their masts nearly upright nowadays, for an ocean-racer cannot afford to have a mast which moves backwards and forwards when facing force seven winds offshore.

The competition generated by such series as the Admiral's Cup, the One Ton Cup and the RORC points trophies means that an ocean-racer has to remain in tip-top condition over a long period. The amount of stretch, even in modern wire, is sufficient to interfere seriously with tuning, particularly as regards the forestay. I said something about straight headsail luffs on page 61, and I cannot over-emphasize this point. If the forestay of an ocean-racer stretches, the headsail luff will sag to leeward and the boat will not point properly. For this reason many owners are specifying rod rigging, particularly for the forestay.

When Camper & Nicholson's were building one of the *Yeomans* for

Owen Aisher, an empty lorry drove into their yard in the south of England, having come all the way from Scotland. Peter Nicholson looked mildly surprised at this phenomenon, until he saw tucked along one side of the lorry the rod forestay for the new boat. In those days it was never rolled, as it is now, and road transport was about the only way of delivering it. The rigging itself is expensive enough, and this only added to the final bill.

Once you have decided the basic mast position and whether you are going to have slack or tight rigging, comes the question of the relative tension of the various wires. There is no problem with a simple rig comprising main shrouds and forestay; it is when we come to many shrouded types like the Dragon that complications set in.

Jumpers should usually be fairly tight, to the point where a slight forward bow is induced in the head of the mast; this will straighten out as soon as the mainsail is set. Set the forestay and main shrouds as required, remembering that upper shrouds can usually do with being rather tighter than lowers. Running backstays should be arranged to give the necessary tension to the forestay when they are pulled hard in. The so-called permanent backstay is often adjustable, as on the Dragon; if it is not, then it should be set steady in relation to the combined action of the forestay and jumpers. Be prepared for the backstay to go slack when you are on the wind; its prime function is to restrain the masthead when running. Set the forward lowers, or inner forestay if fitted, as tight as the uppers, and the after lowers rather slacker (to allow some mast bend). Keep checking up the mast to see that it is straight athwartships with possibly a slight bow forward at the head. Now go sailing in a force 3 wind.

A steady bend to leeward as in figure 49(a) means that the upper shrouds, and probably the jumpers, need tightening to control the sag at the head. Tighten both sides at once and make a note of how much you adjust. The bend shown in figure 49(b) is the result of loose lower shrouds coupled with tight uppers. If you are seeking a slack rig, then tighten very slightly the lowers (but do not overdo it), and ease off on the uppers; this should result in the picture at 49(c), bearing in mind that the running backstay should be helping to keep the mast from sagging too far to leeward in the middle.

Do not forget to watch the fore and aft situation. Figure 50(a) is the result of jumpers which are too loose while 50(b) shows either

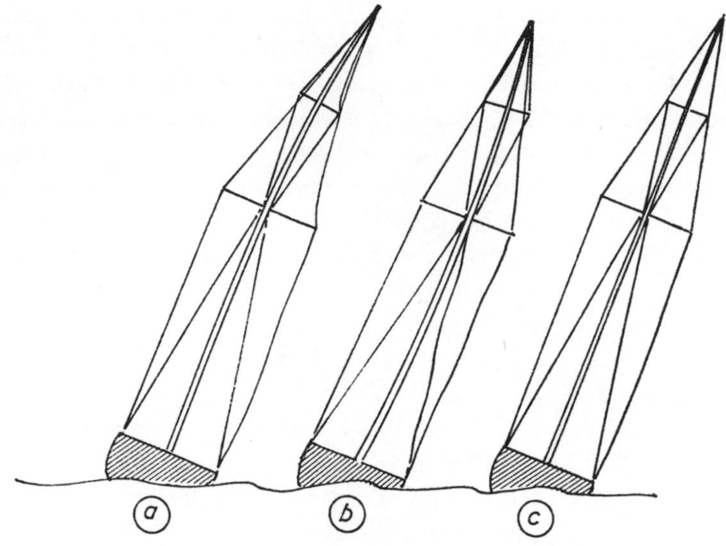

Fig. 49. Shroud adjustment.
(a) Uppers too slack, also possibly jumpers.
(b) Lowers too slack, uppers too tight.
(c) Uppers just slack, lowers slightly tighter, jumpers firm.

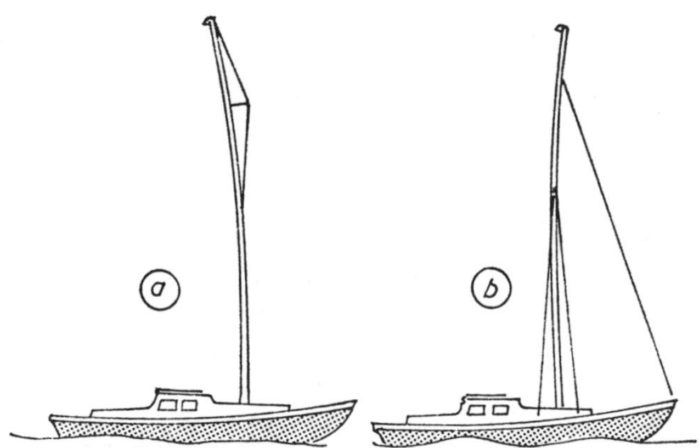

Fig. 50. (a) Slack jumpers will give this effect – but only when under way.
(b) A tight forestay on a $\frac{7}{8}$ths rig pulls the mast forward if the backstay is slack.

tight lower shrouds, if these are led forward of the mast, or tight forestay and slack backstay.

Where there is only one set of shrouds, as on the average dinghy, you will find the effect I described on page 110, where the head of the mast will tend to fall slightly off to leeward above the hounds. This in turn means that the middle of the mast will bow to windward to compensate. Correctly adjusted upper and lower shrouds on multi-shroud masts will have the same effect. This is what opens the slot between the leeward side of the mainsail luff and the windward side of the genoa leech.

Adjustable Rigging

Ideally, you should be able to adjust dinghy rigging to suit the weather. Here again Highfield levers can help by giving a two-way adjustment, which at least gives you an advantage over the boat with no adjustment at all. Some dinghies have this system on their main shrouds. Cliff Norbury had an ingenious method of giving a more variable control over the forestay on his 12 ft National.

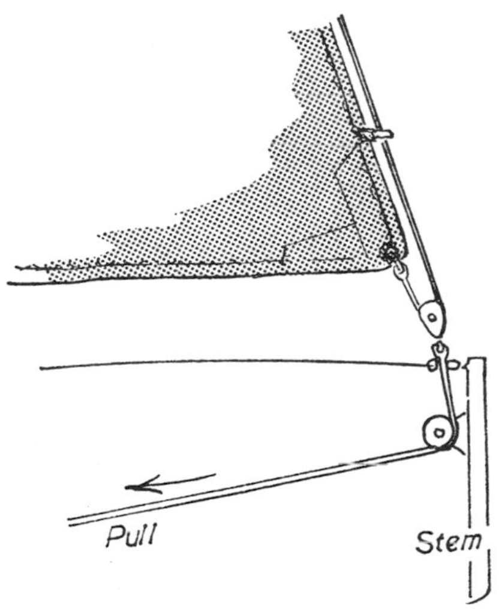

Fig. 51. Cliff Norbury's adjustable forestay and headsail luff. This equalizes the tension on the two wires, and I had a similar idea on my Snipe in Singapore in 1950, although it was not adjustable in use.

The forestay is passed round a block just above the bow, and the tack of the headsail is shackled to it; the headsail is hanked to the forestay and hoisted in the normal way. The block near the tack is free to be pulled downwards under the influence of a downhaul which passes through the deck, through a sheave in the stemhead and so to a winch or jam cleat on the king post. If the headsail is always hoisted to the same point, by means of an eye in the halyard as recommended earlier, the rake of the mast can be adjusted by means of the headsail tack downhaul. The basic advantage of this system lies in the control available when the boat is on a close reach. In these circumstances slack rigging with no adjustment will produce a slack forestay, because there is not enough tension on the mainsheet (as is the case when beating to windward); tighten up the headsail tack downhaul, however, and the headsail luff will become nice and straight. The arrangement will also allow adjustment in the amount of rake when beating to windward – it sometimes pays to rake more in light airs. An added advantage is that any tendency to sag to leeward on the part of the headsail is halved, because the load is shared equally by the luff of the sail and the forestay, and also there can never be any question of the forestay taking all the load of the mast while the luff of the headsail lies slack. In a normal rig, a dinghy headsail should be hoisted so that its luff is marginally tighter than the forestay. In this way the headsail will be pulled straight by the action of the mainsheet when beating to windward, so that the weather shroud and headsail luff are between them holding up the mast. Be sure, therefore, that you have a stout enough wire in your headsails.

All this is of interest and importance to dinghy sailors, and also possibly to those with three-man keelboats like Dragons and Solings. The ocean-racers have yet to come round to this philosophy, and the sterner requirements of offshore weather may preclude such delicate refinements. Nevertheless a straight headsail luff is as important to the large boat beating to windward as it is to the small one. Powerful running backstays are part of the answer, a tackle and winch giving more control than the much easier and constant Highfield lever.

Headsail Leads

We have already seen that the slot between the headsail and the mainsail is critical, so this means that the angle which the foot of the headsail makes with the centreline of the boat viewed from above is important. This is governed by the athwartships position of the headsail sheet fairlead. Some boats have standard one-design positions for their fairleads, others allow latitude. For the latter, the size of the headsail itself will partly affect this position. In addition the degree of fullness of the mainsail will modify the issue, so will the wind conditions. The angle formed by the line joining the headsail tack and clew, and the centreline of the boat, will vary between 7° and 20°. The smaller angles usually apply to narrow closewinded boats like the 12 metre class; beamy ocean-racers and bluff bowed dinghies need the wider angles, particularly in strong winds. The following generalizations also apply:

Wide angle:	Full mainsail;
	Strong winds;
	Reaching conditions;
	More speed, less point.
Narrow angle:	High pointing, less speed;
	Backwinding;
	Flat mainsail;
	Light airs.

Some time ago it was natural to place headsail fairleads as far outboard as the boat would permit. The trend towards greater beam, however, has meant that this is no longer necessarily the correct place, particularly for narrow sails, and many boats go better with the fairlead a little inboard. See Barber haulers below.

The main factor governing what angle to adopt is the moment the luff of the sail lifts as the boat points up to the wind. Sail her in about force 3, and watch the headsail luff as you beat to windward. If it lifts before the mainsail, the fairlead should be moved inboard a little; if it is some time after the mainsail, then you can afford to move it out a little. In general most dinghies seem to prefer 17° to 20° for their headsails, but the slim round bilge boat sailed on calm waters can go down to about 14°; the same boat would need to increase this angle by 2° or 3° if sailed on more open water. A bluff beamy dinghy would need to go to about 20° in similar conditions. Degree lines can be marked on the deck for those boats which permit alteration of the fairlead. In addition, an extra hook should be placed in the outermost position and slightly aft so that the sheet can be slipped under it when reaching, if the class rules permit. This will allow the headsail to free its leech more, while still keeping the luff from lifting, resulting in greater drive.

The more overlap a headsail has on its mainsail, the greater should be its athwartships angle. This used to mean that genoas on ocean racers had to sheet to the railcap to try and get as great an angle as possible. Improvements in sailmaking allow a rather narrower angle nowadays and this, coupled with a tendency towards increasing beam, has allowed the fairlead to be brought inboard slightly to achieve a maximum angle of about 15°, with the ability to reduce it in light airs. The extreme case of inefficiency of this particular angle is provided by the 6 and 12 metres. They are narrow boats, with large overlapping genoas on a narrow sheeting base. It is a sign of the power of a genoa, however, that these sails pull them along in the way they do. A Sail Maker has to remember their rather special circumstances when cutting a mainsail for one of these classes, so that it shall not be constantly backwinded by being too full; he also has to allow plenty of hollow in the leech of a heavy weather genoa, to help open the slot a little when the wind blows up.

A word of warning on boom staysails, before we leave the question of sheeting bases. There is often a tendency to have a fairly short travel for the deck end of a boom staysail sheet. This is a natural enough desire, because a wide horse acts as a hazard to safe passage on the foredeck. But it produces a sail which is trimmed too far inboard, with the result that the mainsail is back winded when close-hauled, and the staysail boom rises inefficiently on a reach.

We now come to the fore and aft position of the fairlead. Before I go any further let me remind those of you with slack rigging to see that the mainsail is hoisted and sheeted hard in, with the headsail hoisted to its usual tension, before you decide how far aft you want your fairlead. Mast rake affects the angle of the forestay, and thus the basic angle of the headsail itself.

The angle of the headsail sheet fore and aft is decided by the shape of the sail. The pull on the sail must be such that neither the leech nor the foot is over-tensioned; this would cause curling of the edge concerned. Adjust so that, as the boat points too high into wind, the whole luff starts to lift at the same time. If it lifts aloft first, move the fairlead forward; move it aft if it first shakes near the tack (see fig. 52).

Barber Haulers. These are named after Californian twins, who developed the system on their *Lightning* in 1963 (although I have a movie I took aboard *Evenlode* at Cowes in 1947, when Tom Thornycroft hung a weight on the light genoa clew to give the sail more

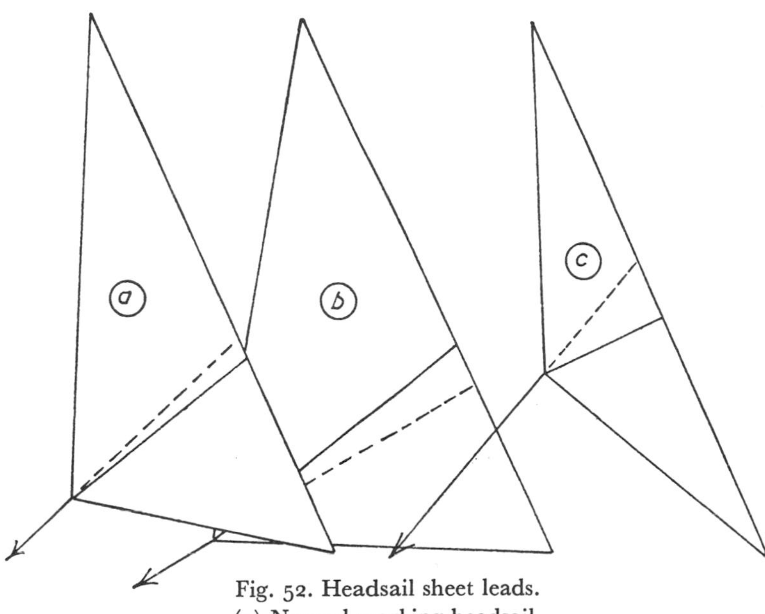

Fig. 52. Headsail sheet leads.
(a) Normal working headsail.
(b) Genoa type headsail.
(c) Yankee jib.

camber on a reach). In light airs and smooth water, some boats can foot as fast yet point higher, if the genoa clew is pulled in towards the coachroof by a tackle or an athwartships traveller. The main boom must also be trimmed amidships, even up to windward, in order to keep the two sails far enough apart to maintain an efficient slot. Another use of the device is to alter the fore and aft headsail sheet lead, thus varying sail shape to suit the wind or point of sailing.

Mainsheet Leads

We can now turn our attention to the mainsail. We have already discussed the question of bending spars, thus touching on centreboom sheet leads. Whether your sheet leads from the middle or the end of the boom, its travel on the deck is important.

If the sheet is permanently attached to the centreline of the counter, its pull will always be down towards the middle of the boat. This means that every time you want to have the sheet hard in, you will have to have your main boom too far in. A wide track for the traveller means that the boom can be well over the counter, yet still pulled hard down to flatten the mainsail (and tighten the forestay where

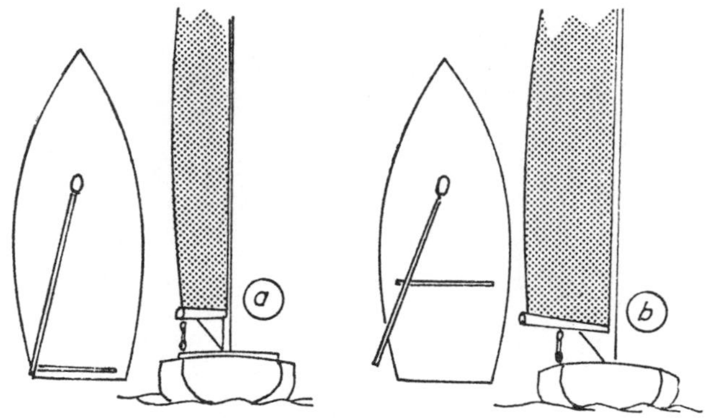

Fig. 53. Mainsail sheet leads.
(a) Transom full width track. Boom end is over quarter.
(b) Full width track under centre of boom – Boom end is well outboard.

slack rigging is used). The same length of track for a centre mainsheet arrangement means a greater range of control than would be the case with a boom end attachment.

This is a field where the ocean-racers can profit to the same extent as the dinghies, and a reinforced coachroof is a ready made base for a centreboom sheet arrangement. The 12 metres developed the recirculating ball-race traveller, which runs smoothly even when full tension is applied to the sheet; Dennis Miller's Sparkman and Stephens designed *Firebrand* came out with one by Lewmar when she was launched in 1965, and so did John Illingworth's *Monk of Malham*; they are now standard items.

Active Tuning

When you have got your mast and rigging set up as you want, go out for a sail in company with another boat of the same class and performance as your own. Set the sails and rigging of both boats to the same adjustment, trim them the same, and sail alongside one another so that you both have the wind free. Now comes a slow process of improvement, during which you must not expect spectacular results.

When you have decided that you know the relative speeds of the two boats, change one item only of the tuning in one of them. Write it down in a book as you change it, and see what effect it has. If it improves performance, make the same change on the other boat and then try altering something else. If it has a bad effect, put it back where it was and try again.

Most boats and helmsmen like a small amount of weather helm when beating to windward. This helps the helmsman feel his way to windward through the puffs, and sees that any slackening of concentration does not result in the bow paying off before the wind. The angle of the rudder under these circumstances also causes the water-flow to curve slightly, in such a way that leeway is reduced. As a rough general guide the tiller should be held between 3° and 5° to windward in medium weather in the average boat; this is about one inch for every foot of tiller.

Weather and lee helm are caused by a slight imbalance between the centre of effort of the sails and the centre of lateral resistance of the hull and keel. If the former is aft of the latter, the resulting force couple will tend to turn the boat towards the wind, which must be counteracted by holding the helm to weather, and vice versa. If the boat does not have enough weather helm, it can be induced by raking the mast aft, thus moving the centre of effort towards the stern. Conversely, if you have decided to rake the mast more in an effort to improve windward performance, be prepared to feel more weather helm.

On the other hand, if the boat has too much weather helm, raking the mast forward will help to cure it. Raking the mast, however, will only effect minor alterations in trim and, if the tendency to weather helm is pronounced, a change in sail plan will cure it most easily. This can best be done by trimming cloth from the leech of the mainsail, to remove area from aft of the centre of lateral resistance.

The International One Design class at Cowes decided in 1962 that they were afflicted in this way, so they had 14 in. cut off the foot length of their mainsails at the clew, and faired the reduction up to the head. This cured the excessive weather helm and actually made them faster to windward. Had they been a handicap class their rating would also have been reduced, due to the smaller E measurement.

It is sometimes possible to have your cake and eat it.

Broaching

Modern fin and skeg offshore designs, while benefiting from increased hydrodynamic efficiency and usually from a reduction in wetted area, sometimes suffer from a tendency to broach, particularly when close reaching in a stiff breeze under spinnaker; this is a case of extreme weather helm in a particular situation. Such craft frequently have fairly firm quarters and a fine bow so that, when the boat heels, the stern tends to lift and the bow digs in; this is accentuated by the downward pull of the spinnaker from the masthead and a shift of the C of E to leeward. The centre of lateral resistance thus moves forward with increasing heel, so that there is a mounting tendency for the bows to push up into the wind.

At rest, therefore, the centre of effort of the mainsail and foretriangle area should normally be some way in front of the CLR, so that the two are correctly balanced when the boat is under way. Movement of the CE to leeward of the keel as the boat heels increases the broaching couple. I will digress into the next chapter at this point and suggest that, if your boat has this habit of broaching badly in a breeze, it is no good raking the mast, or even cutting down the area of the mainsail as an attempt at a *sole* solution.

You should consult a Naval Architect, who may suggest moving the mast, trimming area from the mainsail leech, fitting a dagger plate aft and/or increasing the depth and area of the rudder. But you can't do any of these in the middle of a race, so you should bring the crew right aft to help lift the bow, and you should do all you can to reduce the angle of heel. Letting the mainsail flog will help, but you will almost certainly have to collapse the spinnaker, particularly if it is strapped close alongside to keep it full, for it will be heeling the boat and burying the bows out of all proportion to its driving effect. Read my words on page 209 about the pros and cons of reaching under spinnaker or headsail, and have second thoughts about hoisting the big one when you are less than 75° to the apparent wind above force 3, unless you have a really flat-cut reaching spinnaker, genniker, star-cut spinnaker or what-have-you.

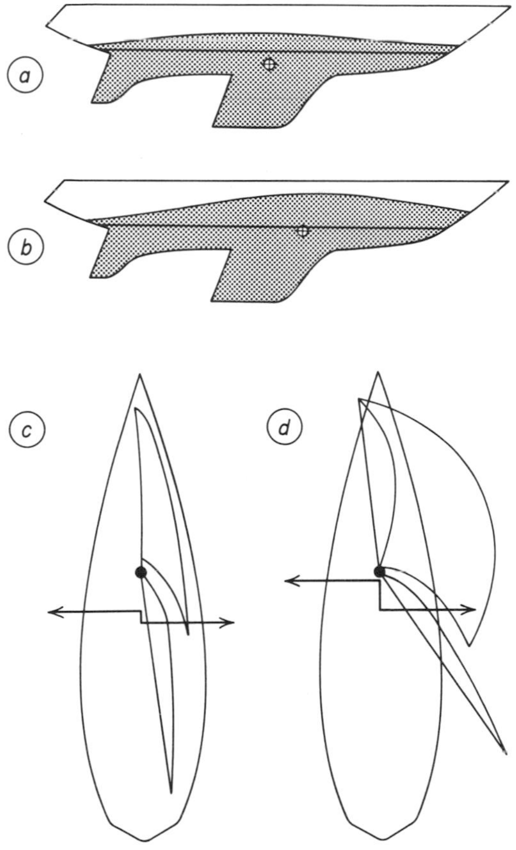

Fig. 54. Broaching.
The shaded portions of (a) and (b) show wetted area when a boat is heeled with an even keel fore and aft, under genoa as in (c), and also with the bow buried on a close spinnaker reach as in (d). The CLR moves forward as the bow goes down, thus increasing the turning arm of the force couple set up with the centre of effort.

CHAPTER IX

Trim

Choice of Sails

Trimming sails starts in the clubhouse with the correct selection of which sails to use. Those ocean-racing men with only one mainsail can smile at the indecision of the dinghy or Dragon owner as he worries over the weather forecast. I recall Stewart Morris at the Prince of Wales' Cup race at Weymouth back in 1962. He used to work up for this race for about six months, and the POW week was the final tuning of a precision instrument, which reached its peak on the day of the Prince of Wales' Cup race itself. He went to bed at nine the previous evening and was awake in time to hear every weather forecast from the farmers' bulletin at 06·45 onwards.

The Thursday of the week dawned with somewhat unsettled weather for the big race. Stewart selected a new medium weather mainsail and started to rig his boat well in advance. All the time his eyes kept wandering to the clouds, and he paced the dinghy park restlessly. Finally he changed mainsails for an old flat faithful which had served him well in the past. But it was obvious that he was not happy, from the way he kept asking his crew, other competitors, and even myself, what we thought the wind would do. After another glance at the sky, he changed back again to his first choice, and we started out on the long push over the sand towards the sea. We had lifted the boat off the trolley, which I was preparing to take back to his berth, when he took yet another look at the sky.

'If any wind comes out of that cloud I'm sunk,' he muttered and hurried up the beach once more. He reappeared with a sail bag and threw it into the boat.

'I can always put it aboard the committee vessel just before the start,' he grinned as he shoved off.

He must have used up enough nervous energy in those thirty minutes to ruin the chances of a lesser man. But the P O W was almost a religion to Stewart, and he is the exception who proves the rule, for he won it again that day; but he was a tired man in the evening. I have always thought that part of the reason for his indecision was that his medium weather sail was relatively unknown to him, for he had not had it very long, whereas his heavy weather sail was tried and proved, and thus was a known factor. None of the top helmsmen likes using gear on an important occasion which has not been proved under actual racing conditions, and this holds especially good for sails.

Stewart Morris usually had two mainsails currently in favour, but there are those who have three. This is too many in my opinion, for you will be haunted by the fear of a wrong decision long after the choice has been irrevocably made. I was a far happier man when I got rid of my very light weather mainsail for the Dragon, and contented myself with two sails. One was for winds up to force 4, and the second was for force 4 upwards. During any season in England, the number of races which are completed in ghosting conditions can be counted on the fingers of one hand. You are more likely to be caught out by winds of force 1–2 increasing to force 3, than by them dying away to nothing. If you have an ultra-light weather sail, all the zippers and Cunningham holes in the world won't stop the boat being knocked down and generally overpowered as the wind increases, unless you have a flexible mast.

The ocean-racing and cruising men carry the problem of choice of sails afloat with them. They will only have one mainsail, but a selection of headsails will be at their disposal. If they are caught out by strengthening winds they can switch headsails accordingly, and can also snug down to the trysail if they have one. But this does not always happen, and I make no excuse for repeating the following warning. Many is the ocean-racing man who has set his drifter of

2 oz. Terylene or Dacron in force 1, only to find that the wind has slowly increased. The boat is going well, however, and it seems a shame to take off the sail; so he hangs on to it into force 2. What he does not realize is that the light canvas is being punished out of all proportion to its strength. Any woven cloth will stretch as the threads are pulled on the bias, and a light cloth will soon stretch past the point where it will resume its original shape as soon as the pressure is relaxed. With the wind forward of the beam a 2 oz. sail should be taken off as soon as the wind goes above force 1, and a 3 or 4 oz. sail should not be expected to deal with anything stronger than force 2.

I always advise that a ghoster should have a cloth of around 3 oz. per sq. yd, but even this will become misshapen if it is carried in force 3; what is more it will never recover. The flow is blown permanently aft, where the hooked leech will both act as a brake and deflect the wind into the lee of the mainsail.

I have digressed enough. We must assume that the correct choice of sails has been made (if, indeed, a choice exists; happy the man in many ways for whom it does not). Now comes the time to hoist them.

Hoisting Sail

Before going further we must recall what happens to a mainsail when it is hoisted. The Sail Maker has built flow into the sail by means of making the luff rounded, and by tapering the appropriate panels. He also makes it slightly shorter than the stretched size, so that further induced flow can be put into it when it is pulled to its designed length. You will find that no successful fore and aft sail is made with the cloths running either parallel or at right angles to the luff; this is because of the bias stretch to which the cloth is subject when tension is off the threadline, and stretching helps it to achieve shape, as we discussed in Chapter IV.

Do not, therefore, be a slave to your black bands. Just because a sail is made to set between certain marks, there is no need always to pull it right out to those marks. You will not make a sail any bigger by stretching it, so you are not gaining area. There is only a certain amount of cloth in any sail, and no amount of pulling can put any more into it. If you increase the length of the luff by stretching it, the round to the leech of the sail must come in to compensate.

Here are half a dozen reasons why a particular mainsail may set better if it is short of its marks, by one or two inches on a dinghy and anything up to 8 or 9 in. on a larger boat; they are in order of likelihood:

1. The sail was cut for wind strengths greater than those prevailing.
2. The luff is roped too tightly.
3. The sail has been altered at some time, changing its characteristics.
4. The gooseneck fitting is not as given to the Sail Maker.
5. The black bands are wrong.
6. The sail has not got enough cloth up the luff.

On the other hand, the sail may come easily to its marks, and still be undertensioned. This is where the Cunningham hole comes into its own, by enabling extra power to be exerted on the luff without overstepping the black bands. I shall go more fully into this device on page 164.

Light Weather. Thus, in light weather, do not set up the mainsail halyard too tight, even to the point where a multitude of small wrinkles appears along the luff. When you have the flow as you want, take in what Uffa Fox called a 'nattigram' to allow for halyard stretch or a slight increase in wind, and make fast. Similar careful attention should be paid to the clew outhaul. It is important not to put too much tension on the foot tape in light weather or a fold will appear along the foot. The clew should be eased forward from its medium weather position, between 1 and 3 per cent of the foot length according to the inherent flatness of the sail. In these circumstances Jack Knights goes so far as to suggest that dinghy owners should have a specially light boom in order not to drag the mainsail down too much and thus flatten it; I would not disagree with this slightly fastidious recommendation.

Heavy Weather. On the other hand, heavy weather demands a firm pull on halyard and outhaul to force the flow forward. It is safer to err on the ham-fisted side under these conditions, because once you have started it is simpler to ease the halyard if it is too tight, than to pull it harder. The sail may look a poor shape in the initial stages, but the wind will immediately blow the flow aft into its correct position, perhaps even too far if the halyard is not tight enough.

Before leaving the question of hoisting sail, do not forget to take the weight off the boom until the sail is up. If you let the boom hang on to a half-hoisted sail which is flogging about, you will quickly overstretch the leech. This may sound obvious, but you would be surprised at the number of mainsails which are returned to the Sail Maker by their owners, complaining of a juddering leech for this reason. While we are on the subject, it may sound even more obvious not to pull a sail down by the leech, but it is amazing how an otherwise top class skipper will do this if he is in a hurry.

Under Way

When checking a sail for correct trim under way there are three cardinal rules: first, always sight up the mast to see that it has no abnormalities on either tack; secondly, see that all leech lines are completely slack, for they can give a false impression if tight; finally, have a look at the sail in question from leeward and in front if possible, it will look totally different from this angle and will reveal its faults more easily.

Mainsails

Apart from the curve of the mainsail, there are two points to watch when beating to windward. The first is the amount of twist you allow the leech of the sail, and from this comes the position athwartships of the mainsheet traveller and the tension on the boom vang or kicking-strap. The second is the interrelation of the headsail and the mainsail, and from this comes the shape of the headsail leech.

Twist. When a mainsail suffers from twist, the head sags off to leeward and lifts earlier than the rest of the sail. To stop this, the boom has to be trimmed closer, which means that the lower half of the sail is too tightly sheeted for its own efficient working, and there will be more sideways thrust than necessary. If the boom is pulled down by a vang, twist will be reduced and the sail can thus be eased to give more forward thrust. It also makes the sail more efficient, because wind flows off the top of a twisted sail. A certain amount of twist is, however, beneficial in light conditions.

Mainsheet Traveller. For smooth water and light winds the traveller should be fairly well in towards the centreline of the boat. This will enable you to point better, and the slight hook to windward which it gives the lower leech will be more than offset by the greater speed made good to windward. Do not, therefore, try to eliminate all twist by pulling hard down on the mainsheet; the sail should not be flattened too much, and a certain amount of twist can be accepted to this end. As the wind increases towards force 4, however, it becomes vital to remove any tendency to hook to windward, so the traveller should be eased until the boom makes an angle of about 8° or 9° with the centreline of the boat. If you do not have a traveller, ease the sheet, having seen that the kicking-strap or boom vang is tight to reduce twist.

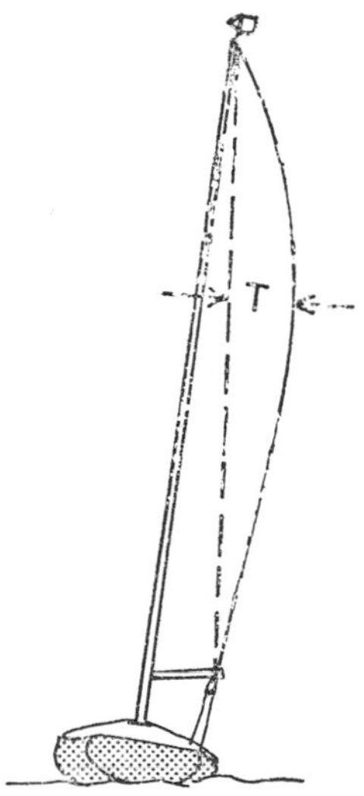

Fig. 55. Twist.

As the sea and wind both increase further, so should the traveller be eased to its fullest extent. If there is a lumpy sea, the boat will move more slowly than if the same wind were blowing over smooth water, so the apparent wind will be farther aft. The boom should therefore be out more to accept this. In addition, most boats go better into a chop if they are freed slightly and driven into it. The mainsail can therefore afford to be a little fuller, so the tack can be eased up if the wind is not so strong that a flat sail is necessary to avoid too much weather helm.

If the mainsail lifts near the head before the main body of the luff falls in, there is almost certainly too much twist. This can be corrected by easing the traveller and hardening the sheet to pull the boom down over the counter.

A boom which is trimmed too close will soon make itself felt through excess weather helm. As the wind increases, the flow of the mainsail will be forced aft and the boom will tend to rise. These will cause the lower leech to curve to windward, which will drive the bow round towards the wind. If the traveller is already eased fully, the luff of the sail should be tightened to draw the flow forward again (either by tacking down harder or by use of a Cunningham hole), and the clew pulled out more to flatten the lower leech. A bendy mast will probably be under maximum curvature already, due to the influence of the tension of the mainsheet; if it can safely be bent more (on dinghies by harsh use of the kicking-strap for instance), then you should do so. The last resort should be to ease the mainsheet so that full power is not delivered, but this should also be done if the boat is obviously fighting the rudder and heeling too much. The loss of power from the mainsail must be weighed against the reduction in weather helm; it pays in many classes to ease the mainsail until it is lifting along its entire length in a stiff blow, because the easier rudder lets the headsail pull her along more quickly.

A leech Cunningham hole, fitted with a permanent line (see fig. 44), may be pulled down in conjunction with a luff Cunningham. This will flatten the whole foot area, raise the boom and reduce weather helm; the boat heels less and is easier to control.

Heavy Weather Mainsails. Most of us know that a heavy weather sail needs to be flatter than one cut for light or medium winds. We should beware, however, of cutting a mainsail so flat that it loses nearly all its drive. The ocean-racing man will have to forgive me for a while, because discussion on the requirements of a heavy weather mainsail does not directly concern him, as he is all too often prevented by the rules from having such a specialized sail. The upper third of a mainsail designed for strong winds for a dinghy or one of the two- or three-man keelboats should be quite flat, so that it presents little or no resistance to the wind and so that it 'feathers' easily on a beat; this will reduce the heeling moment. The middle third of the sail should start to take some shape, so that the lower third can be comparatively well rounded, particularly over the boom. It is from here that the boat will get its drive. The heeling effect is minimized because the centre of effort on such a sail will be fairly low down.

Most authorities agree that it does not often pay to have small mainsails for heavy weather racing in dinghies. Boats with full area may lose a little on the windward leg, but they will more than make up for it off the wind. It is far better to have flexible spars which can be controlled by the helmsman; this will take the excess fullness out of the mainsail, and make the boat easier to keep from too much heel. As explained on page 113, it is not enough to have a number of different chocks to put in front of the mast where it passes through the deck, and this is where Cliff Norbury's jack, or something like it, will pay dividends. The man who can set full sail and maintain control of his boat will normally have the legs of the man who either has a small mainsail or who rolls down a reef. There are, of course, exceptions to this rule but not many, and much depends on what is meant by 'maintain control' of the boat.

It is in heavy weather that the beneficial effects of a boom which bends slightly to leeward at the outer end will be felt. The reduction in drag and the easing of the lower leech will both have a marked effect on performance. Be careful, however, that the boom does not bend so much that it causes the whole leech to go slack, for this may give rise to a crease along the inner ends of the battens, especially in those classes like the 12 ft National which often have too much roach for the battens to support properly; it may also weaken the boom beyond the safety point for heavy weather.

The foregoing remarks are meant primarily for dinghies, but many of them can be applied to the ocean-racing fleet as well, where the rules permit the use of specialized heavy weather mainsails, such as in racing round the buoys. The bigger boats, of course, often meet stronger winds than the dinghy fleet, and I do not pretend that they should seldom reef; we shall see more of this later in this chapter.

Headsails

If you have a large overlapping headsail, either on a dinghy such as the 14 ft International or on an ocean-racer, then you will not be able to ease your mainsail quite as much in heavy weather and still keep an efficient airflow, particularly if the genoa is a mastheader. You will have to be careful not to close the slot between the sails too much, and there will come a time when the boat will go faster with a smaller headsail, because she would otherwise be overpowered. A dinghy cannot switch headsails without too much loss of ground on a relatively short beat, but the ocean-racer will need at this stage either to change to an intermediate genoa, or to take a reef in the mainsail. An intermediate genoa can be sheeted hard in and the mainsail eased slightly because there will be a wider slot between the smaller genoa's leech and the lee side of the mainsail; a reefed mainsail will cause the boat to heel less, thus enabling the full-sized genoa to be kept at the main job of driving the boat along. The tendency nowadays is towards the latter solution.

It becomes progressively more important to examine your headsail leech critically as the wind freshens. The flow in the sail will tend to move aft under the action of the wind, and any tendency to curl at the leech will be accentuated. This can be helped somewhat by pulling harder on the headsail sheet, but be sure that the pull is at the correct angle and beware of overstretching the canvas. A light sail will curl more than a heavy one, and should be changed as soon as this starts to happen. At all events you should avoid the extremely unfavourable airflow created by a tight genoa leech. Make sure that you have not got the leech line tight, and also see that the sheet lead is not too far forward. It is better to have a genoa leech which vibrates, than to have a quiet leech which curls to windward. The former will allow the wind to run off freely, but the latter will direct it into the lee side of the mainsail.

Heavy Weather Headsails. When it comes to heavy weather headsails, dinghies and the smaller keelboats most probably have the one-sized sail, which should be cut flat with rather more hollow to the leech than a medium weather headsail, in order to open the slot. If a small headsail is allowed, one may be used in really strong winds before the mainsail is reefed. This is an efficient way of reducing sail area, while keeping the full sized mainsail for reaching and running. Here again, however, the winning boats are often those who hold on to full sail, while the lesser men change down. For instance, most Dragons no longer reef their mainsails and only use a 1st foresail under special conditions: if the wind is strong and there is a good deal of short tacking to do, such as in a narrow estuary or to keep in a more favourable current. But you must be ready to switch to the full size genoa as soon as you come off the wind; even then the resulting sail change may cost you the ground you have gained. An effective way to overcome this conflicting requirement is to have a full size genoa cut with a good deal of hollow to the leech, thus opening the slot and also reducing sail area less drastically. The bigger boats will have a range of headsails from which to choose, descending in size as the wind increases. With this in mind, it is easy to see why the largest headsails in a boat's wardrobe have the lightest cloth, and vice versa.

Adjustable Luff Headsails. What I said just now about tension on the luff of the mainsail also applies to headsails which have means of adjusting their luff tension. If the sail is adjustable over the luff wire, you will have some form of downhaul at the tack. You will also have a useful datum from which to judge the amount of pull you are applying: when the tack of the sail reaches the bottom of the wire, you have set up the sail for the strongest winds it should encounter. The wire itself is often painted or served by the Sail Maker, so that you can tell how much tension you have applied by noting how much wire is showing at the tack. If the headsail has a tape luff, you may either adjust it on the halyard, in which case you should mark the halyard, or by means of a tack downhaul which should be similarly marked. The former is the more efficient system, because the tack is then always as low as possible, thus keeping the driving force low, but the latter is simpler to operate and therefore preferable. Remember that adjustable luff headsails will alter their clew positions as they adjust, and the sheet lead must be varied accordingly.

While on the subject of headsails, see that the luff is as straight as possible when beating to windward. The forestay must not be allowed to sag too far off to leeward in the pursuit of mast rake and slack rigging as discussed earlier in this book, or the boat will not point properly. No boat can have an absolutely straight luff to her headsail, for this would bring unacceptable stresses to the mast, and this factor must be borne in mind when setting up the forestay. If there is too much sag to the headsail when on the wind, however, equal adjustment to *both* the forestay and its opposite numbers towards the rear must be made if you are not to rake the mast out of its desired position. 'Opposite numbers' can include the pull of the mainsheet, runners, permanent backstays, and shrouds, depending on where the forestay attaches to the mast. You may also have to readjust the jumper stays.

The whole question of a straight forestay can lead to excessive loading on the mast of a large boat, and it is one where the Sail Maker's requirement of no sag to the headsail luff can conflict with the designer's ideas on what the boat will stand. I remember sailing in the 12 metre *Norsaga* when she had her first outing, after re-rigging in 1960 as the Red Duster group's test bed for a new challenger for the America's Cup. Besides the owner Lord Craigmyle, there were on board Arthur Robb who had undertaken the re-design, and Franklin Ratsey-Woodroffe who had been responsible for the sails. Franklin took one look at the genoa luff and ordered more tension on the weather-runner, and on the backstay and forestay turnbuckles. He returned to the bow of the boat, had another look and ordered more turns on the rigging. Arthur Robb watched this for a few moments and then went to have a look up the mast. Finally he called a halt to the proceedings, and the two opposing requirements were forced into a compromise. At all events a straight luff is important for good performance on the wind, and I make no apology for repeating it. This means a tight forestay (preferably a rod) on a boat which has straight spars and tight rigging; and sufficient movement on the mast, coupled with a forestay slightly slacker than the jib luff wire, on a boat which has slack rigging.

A headsail should usually be cut on the flat side rather than the opposite. Naturally a full headsail can be useful in light airs, but a flat sail can normally be given a little extra draft by easing the sheet, whereas over-hardening the sheet will only pull a full headsail out of shape and will not make it much flatter.

If the headsail is too full, the flow will be forced aft as the wind increases in the same way as happens in a mainsail, and it will tend to backwind the mainsail. There will also be a rearward component of the driving force at the leech.

The moral of this is that headsails should err on the flat side and their sheets should not always be pulled hard in unless it is blowing fairly hard; it is the owner's task to check the enthusiasm of his sheet hands. As the wind grows lighter, so should the sheet be eased further and the fairlead brought inboard if there is adjustment. It is good practice when racing neck and neck with another boat to try easing the headsail an inch or two; you will be surprised how often this will make just the difference to your speed. Also check your sheet lead for fore and aft position; a small variation may give you enough extra speed to establish an overlap at the buoy. Don't forget the findings of the Southampton University research team, which reveal that headsail sheeting is more critical than mainsail sheeting.[1] Corny Shields said that he usually had his headsail sheet leads further forward than most people, as he considered that this gives a better shape to the lower half of the sail. It will certainly free off the foot and allow it to take up a better aerofoil shape, but watch out for a curling leech. I do not imagine that the American master advocated more than half a degree or so, and I would be the last person to contradict him.

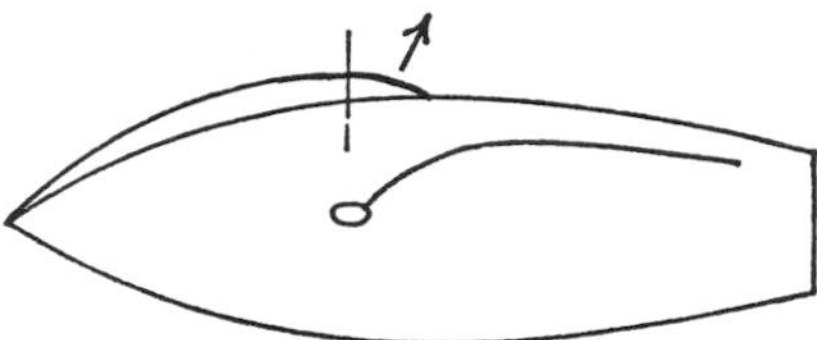

Fig. 56. The rearward component of a curling headsail leech.

On the other hand, let me here say that another American, Jack Sutphen of Ratsey & Lapthorn Inc., says 'as a rule of thumb, it generally is better to have the leads too far aft than too far forward'. This shows that the whole question is open to experiment, and that they are dealing in very small differences. It is more than likely that both are ending at the same point, having started from a slightly different datum. Each helmsman has his own preference and I feel that Sutphen is the more orthodox in his approach; Shields confesses that he is in a minority in his point of view.

Reaching. The question of adjustment holds doubly true when reaching. The headsail hand should play the sheet constantly to take advantage of wind shifts. It may well be that too tight a headsail is backwinding the mainsail and thus giving the helmsman a false impression. Easing the headsail sheet will let the mainsail go off that little bit extra, and both sails will give more drive. Watch the luff of

[1] SUYR Paper No. 11, October 1962.

the sail about a third of the way up, ease until it just starts to quiver and then harden in very slightly; keep feeling for the quiver so that you have always given the sail as much sheet as it will take. If the rules permit, switch the sheet to a hook farther out and farther back than the normal fairlead, as I suggested on page 126. If the sail is not too big and the wind not too strong, the sheet should be held in the hand, either on or off the winch, and the crew encouraged to play it as he sees fit. Wind tallies or tell tales sewn through the luff of the headsail can be a great help here. If a windward tally lifts, sheet the sail harder; if it is the leeward one which shows breakdown of laminar flow into turbulence, ease the sheet.

Reefing

A badly reefed sail will materially affect the speed of the boat, not so much because it does not produce the maximum driving component, but because this component will be heavily reduced by increased drag and knockdown effect, caused through too much fullness aft. If you allow the sail to be sloppy over the boom, you will form a bag near the leech and this will hold the boat back and heel her over without producing any drive. It is here that Illingworth hauling-aft loops and a carefully shaped roller boom pay for their keep. The fixed reef man will be able more easily to adjust a continuous lacing reef than one tied with individual points. Those two great authorities, one on each side of the Atlantic, Wallace E. Tobin and John Illingworth have both written their opinion on reefing. They are united in their verdict that most people roll in and shake out their reefs too late. You will make a neater job of reefing if you do it before the wind gets too strong; when the wind starts to go down, you will outdistance your rivals if you overcome your natural desire to let the next watch increase sail when they come on in an hour's time. There should be no excuse for this laziness now that jiffy reefing (see p. 106) has made it so quick and easy.

When dinghies or small keelboats have to reef mainsails, it is often only really necessary on the windward leg. This is where a simple system like the Banks reefing gear can pay dividends, in that it will enable you to set full sail again for the reaching leg; but remember that you may have to roll down again for the next beat, and you should be confident of making a good job of it.

Heavy Weather Technique

I do not intend to get too involved in technique, but it is difficult to explain the requirements relating to sails in heavy weather without going slightly into the way it should be done. You may not agree with the methods I advocate, but the principles are sound enough; providing you arrive at the same result, and know why you are doing what you are doing, we shall not argue.

Twist is one of the faults which must be corrected as much as

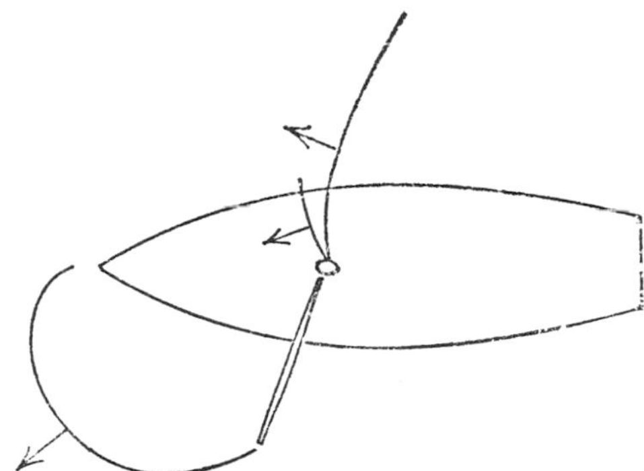

Fig. 57. Rhythmic rolling.
Divergent thrust forces contribute to rhythmic rolling. Note how a section through the top quarter of the mainsail pushes to windward – Also, the spinnaker sheet has been eased too much, giving further windward push.

possible in heavy weather. Not only does excessive twist mean that, when beating to windward, the boom has to be further in than need be the case but, when sailing downwind, it also promotes what John Illingworth has called rhythmic rolling. Because the head of the sail sags far enough forward to contribute pressure to windward, there comes a time when the action of the waves on the hull and the forces acting on the sails combine to cause the phenomenon we all know. This is aggravated when the spinnaker sheet is allowed to slack off too far, thus adding to the windward tendency.

Beating to windward in a dinghy is often a matter of keeping the boat upright and staying as close to the wind as possible. A heavy crew combination can free sheets slightly to drive the boat through the water, keep their sails full and sit right out to hold the boat upright. By playing the sails enough to allow them to quiver, but not to flog, they can hold the boat upright by a combination of weight and minor playing of the sails. A light crew cannot hope to adopt the same tactics without a trapeze, and must rely on a bendy mast. With kicking strap and mainsheet bowsed hard down, the top of the mainsail will feather so as to give least drag and heeling moment. The headsail is kept hard in for as long as possible and the boat is balanced between being too close to the wind and becoming overpowered through being too free. This is a solution which has to be practised assiduously to achieve competence. In both cases remember that it is necessary to have some power in the sail, and that this is best placed in the foot where it has least heeling effect, and will help you climb over the big waves.

The mainsheet traveller should be right out, and the kicker or vang adjusted to bend the mast according to the amount of power you can control, which in turn depends largely on your weight (assuming skill as a constant). As soon as you come off the wind, the kicking-strap should be hard enough to stop the boom from rising too much, but it should not be quite as tight as usual, so that some of the strain is taken off the rig. In addition, a boom end which is constantly dipping in the water stops you spilling wind and slows the boat. A centre mainsheet fitting will help flatten the sail, but may take a little getting used to at the start. It is not my job to tell you how to do this, merely to say that I think that it is a device which amply repays its incorporation and will lead to a more flexible sail. A boom end fitting, in fact, allows the boom to bend upwards in the middle, which is exactly the opposite of what we want as the wind increases, for this will only make the sail fuller over the boom.

Spinnakers

The spinnaker is so important that it has a chapter to itself. Correct trimming of this sail can win a race as easily as its mishandling can lose one.

Sail Handling

It goes without saying that sail handling should at all times be smooth and efficient. A good crew member will spend the first half-hour on board a strange boat finding out where all the various sheets and halyards lead, how the boom vang is rigged, the purpose of all the winches, and the location of all sails not in use, together with ancillary gear such as reefing handle, tack pendants, handy billy, spinnaker net, etc. Some of the best crew drill I have seen was displayed on board the little Dutch sloop *Hestia*. One year the late Mr Van Beuningen had ordered a quadrilateral with such a high upper clew that we had to put three sheets on it, instead of two. The lowest sheet led through the normal genoa fairlead, and the two upper sheets went via a couple of 'monkeys' running on the permanent backstay, the upper one of which needed to be some 20 ft above deck. Besides their sheets, both these 'monkeys' had halyards and downhauls of their own so that they could be trimmed to the correct height. This meant six ropes at the backstay alone.

We set the sail in a light breeze of about force 2 and put her on the wind while we sought the correct angle for the upper sheets. After a certain amount of experiment we felt that we had the sail setting well, and the owner announced that we would try it on the other tack. This meant lowering both 'monkeys' by means of their downhauls, unreeving the two upper sheets, reeving the sheets from the other side, and hauling the 'monkeys' back up the backstay. Meanwhile, the boat was being tacked in the normal way and the lowest sheet had to be tended as well. The whole operation proceeded with the utmost calm and efficiency, just as if it were the most normal operation afloat – but remember that this was the first time that the sail had ever been aboard. I know, for I took it straight from the loft to the boat before we sailed. It was obvious that Mr Van Beuningen had worked out the drill beforehand and had practised his crew in it.

Headsail Cartridges. Headsail changes can be speeded up by the cartridge system. If a foil or grooved forestay is used, special slides are fitted to the sail and a short length of foil is removable from the bottom of the forestay, with the lowered sail bunched on it; the replacement sail, also stowed on its own cartridge, is clipped in place and lines up with the groove in the foil. The sail is thus ready for immediate hoisting, and times for headsail changes can be cut dramatically. Similar systems have been evolved for use with standard piston hanks or snap hooks, but they are not quite so convenient. A grooved forestay, of course, is a great help in speedy headsail changes with or without a cartridge.

CHAPTER X

Working Sails

One of the pleasures of owning a boat, no matter what her size, is to indulge in planning extensions to her wardrobe. This exercise usually takes place during the winter, and has the advantage that it does not cost anything, at least while it stays in the planning stage. The following three chapters are designed to help these daydreams, and I have listed some of the more popular sails to be found in an inventory. I have deliberately stuck to the more conventional sails which may be found on the average yawl, ketch, sloop or cutter, or else the list would have been never ending. The schooner owner will therefore find nothing here to help him design a fisherman staysail or a golly-wobbler; but there are regrettably not many schooners about these days. Similarly, I do not mention the flying jib, the square sail or the mizzen spinnaker, as these are all too rare.

I had thought of writing this section alphabetically, that is to say that balloon headsails would come first and yankee jibs last. This, however, presents problems of natural succession, besides the fact that many sails are known by two or more names. I have accordingly written about them in groups, and the reader will have to turn to the index first if he wants to find one particular sail quickly.

The percentage in brackets immediately following the name of the sail, represents a guide to its cloth weight. All sails are related to a yardstick of the standard weight of cloth for the working sails for that particular boat, which is 100 per cent. Thus a yacht with a mainsail and working headsail of 12 oz. cloth will have an intermediate genoa (85 to 100 per cent) between 10 and 12 oz.; a similar sail for a standard working canvas of 9 oz. would be between 7½ and 9 oz.

Mainsail (100 *per cent of cloth weight of working sails*)

The mainsail and the working genoa are the two most important sails on the boat: the latter because it produces most of the drive when it is set, and the former because it is up most of the time. On a dinghy or one of the smaller inshore two- and three-man keelboats, of course, they will be the only sails apart from the spinnaker. It is important that they should work well together, and they should preferably be made by the same Sail Maker. If you are going to be unwise enough to provide your ship with second rate sails, at least ensure that the mainsail and genoa come from a good firm.

Do not be misled into ordering an all-purpose mainsail of a cloth which is much lighter than the recommended weight, as derived from the table I have given on page 57. This is especially true if a light weight is dictated by reasons of economy and not of aerodynamic efficiency. At the risk of boring you, let me repeat that a light canvas may not tear, but it will stretch out of shape as soon as it is subjected to any weight of wind. I shall have something more to say about this under the section on light weather sails in the next chapter.

An all-purpose mainsail should have its flow at about the forward third of the sail, and it should have a reasonable degree of fullness over the boom. A narrow boat will normally need a flatter mainsail than a beamy one, because the headsails of the former will have a narrower sheeting base than the latter, and will thus tend to backwind more. The amount of headsail overlap also has its effect in this respect: the greater the overlap, the flatter the mainsail. In addition a large penalty overlap may produce a case for having the maximum flow of the mainsail a little farther aft, so that the slot is formed according to the principles we saw in Chapter II; improved sailmaking, with a fine luff entry, has increased this trend in recent years. A dinghy will normally be able to carry a rather fuller mainsail than an ocean-racer because its spars will be able to take out some of the fullness by bending, be it ever so little, and also because a dinghy will not have to stand up to the strong winds which can buffet a yacht offshore; see also the graph at figure 16.

We have already seen that a depth of flow, or camber, of 10 per cent of the chord is a reasonable amount of fullness for medium weather, and that 5 per cent is the figure we can expect to be efficient for a heavy weather sail. In any case, flow should be carried right down a mainsail so that there is plenty of drive low down near the boom, and it can always be flattened with a slab reef.

We have also seen that a high aspect ratio is efficient in reducing the effect of induced drag at the foot. I go more fully into this question later, in the chapter on 'Design and Rating'. Suffice it to say here that a mainsail luff length should not be more than just over three times the length of the foot, unless the yacht is undercanvassed for her size or there are special considerations which apply, e.g. with catamarans or to achieve a desired rating.

Battens are almost always limited in length by the rules under which a particular boat is sailing. The length of batten will, in turn, determine the amount of roach which the Sail Maker can safely put on the leech of a mainsail, and still expect to stand. A batten will normally support one third of its own length outside the straight line from the headboard to the clew. You go beyond this limit at your peril, as we have discussed earlier.

The best aerodynamic efficiency is obtained from a mainsail which runs in grooves in both the mast and boom, because wind will then not be able to escape from windward to leeward between the spar and the sail, as is the case when slides are used. However, a mast groove is not seamanlike where the mainsail would normally be left bent to the spars when sailing is over, because the sail has to come right off the mast when it is lowered; slides are normal in this case, and we can generalize that it occurs where the mainsail area reaches around 250 sq. ft.

Virtually the only disadvantage of a boom groove is that a vang cannot be passed round the boom at any point along its length to make a kicking-strap: either an adjustable ring, or specially reinforced attachment points have to be provided at two or more places, and these have to be recessed if the boom is a roller.

I shall not repeat here all the arguments put forward in Chapter VII regarding roller reefing *vis-à-vis* points or lacing reefing. Suffice it to say that, in the absence of jiffy reefing, I feel that the average offshore yacht of up to 35 ft water-line length would need to consider carefully before adopting anything other than a roller boom, with a row of emergency lacing in the deep reef position.

This does not, of course, preclude a slab reef being incorporated in any mainsail from a dinghy upwards, and I shall have more to say on this subject (and that of Cunningham holes) in the next chapter, when we come to examine light weather sails. It should be remembered here that these devices can be incorporated to add to the flexibility of an otherwise medium weather mainsail.

Mizzen (75 *per cent of cloth weight of working sails*)

The main advantages of a mizzen are twofold. First, it offers a useful quick reef to the cruising man: a yawl or ketch under mizzen and headsail alone gives a most comfortable ride, even in the strongest winds. Secondly, it can help add some bite to the helm if it is strapped in hard on the wind. For these reasons it should be made of cloth which will stand up to a blow. It does not need to be as heavy as the mainsail, because its area is usually substantially less, and thus the total weight of wind in the sail is less. Nevertheless it presents a good argument against deciding cloth weight on area alone and it should not be more than two weights lighter than its mainsail, and only one if its area is more than one-third that of the mainsail. For the racing man, the mizzen is not heavily rated under the IOR, and the second mast confers the relatively lightly taxed area of the mizzen staysail when off the wind.

When beating to windward, the mizzen is operating permanently in the dirty wind of the mainsail, so its apparent wind is at a finer angle (but see my remarks in Chapter XII on the mizzen tallboy). It should thus be cut flat and sheeted hard. It also helps if the leech is not too long, so that a firm downward pull can be exerted on the boom, which is still out of the way of the sunbathers on the after-deck (a serious consideration not to be lightly ignored, let me add). A row of reefing eyelets can be incorporated by the pessimistic, even on the smallest mizzen, in case the foot of the sail should tear.

Working Headsail (100 *per cent of cloth weight of working sails*)

A working headsail should usually be the same weight as its mainsail, with only rare exceptions, such as when the latter is unduly large and therefore is, in fact, one weight heavier than the standard for the size of boat.

Unless considerations of rig or area dictate otherwise, the working staysail of a cutter, or working headsail of a sloop should be cut with the clew approximately level with the main boom, and so that it does not foul the mast or shrouds. This is so that it will not pick up water in a fresh breeze, the helmsman can see under it, and it will not chafe too much. Battens should only be used if the sail is tall and narrow, say with an angle at the head of less than 20°, because the simpler the sail the better. It should, of course, be cut flat since it will normally be used in fairly strong winds. A mitre cut working headsail will usually lead to a fairlead so that the sheet is below an imaginary prolongation of the mitre aft.

One-design dinghies and two- and three-man keelboats with small headsails (that is to say, without overlapping genoa jibs), such as the Enterprise, Fireball, Star, 420, International One Design and Soling, will need rather different consideration from the simplification set forth above. They will certainly need a flat cut headsail for heavy weather, and one with a little more draft in it for light to medium going. Not disposing of a large jib for light weather, they could well have the latter sail made of a canvas one weight lighter than the standard, if the rules allow. In addition, a leech roach will make a significant increase in area on such a small sail. Thus, if battens are allowed by the rules they should be used to this end on a light weather sail, which will also have as much foot round as the Sail Maker can include within the rule.

Boom Headsail (100 *per cent of cloth weight of working sails*)

A working headsail is sometimes set on a club boom. Be it a boom staysail, boom jib, or boom foresail, it will obey all the requirements of a normal working headsail as regards clew height and weight of canvas. The point to watch here is that the sheet has enough travel athwartships, or the sail will backwind the mainsail badly. This requires a fairly wide horse if the clew is not to rise too high, and it can thus become an obstacle on the foredeck; for some reason recessed sheet travellers are not common for boom headsails.

A headsail boom which is mounted on a pedestal gives added flow

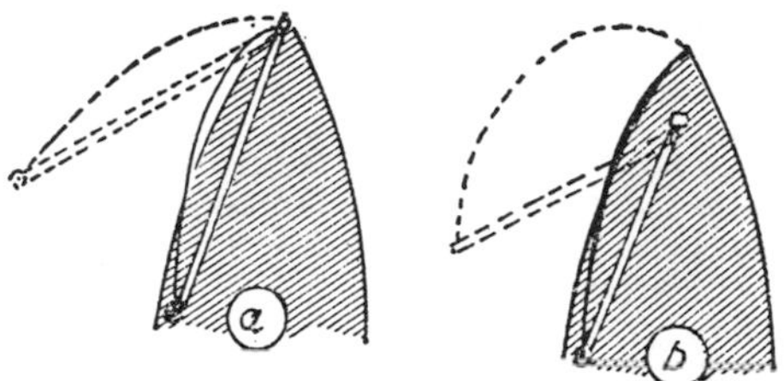

Fig. 58. Headsail booms.
(a) Boom is attached to forestay. Camber of headsail remains unchanged as sheet is eased.
(b) Boom is hinged on a pedestal short of the forestay. Headsail becomes fuller as it is eased on a reach.

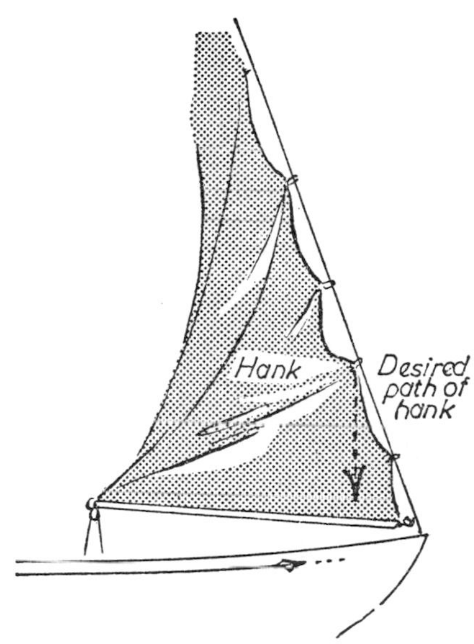

Fig. 59. Lowering a boom headsail – A hank or snap opposite the clew will not slide down the forestay as the headsail is lowered, because the cloth between the clew and the hank will not stretch.

to the sail as it is freed off, and is thus aerodynamically more efficient than a full length boom.

In order that the sail can be fully lowered down the stay, while remaining attached at the clew, some device is needed to allow the clew to come forward, or the luff to come aft, as the sail comes down the stay.

Let us assume there is a hank or snap hook at the luff opposite the clew, so that the line joining the clew and the hank is perpendicular

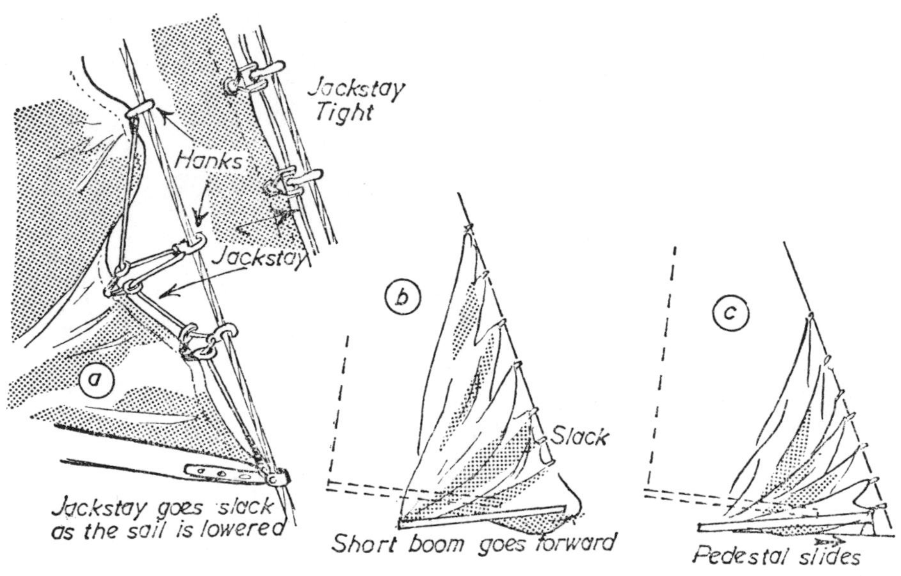

Fig. 60. Methods of lowering a boom headsail on the forestay. (a) Jackstay or relieving line gives slack, and luff goes aft towards clew.
(b) Short boom goes forward, and clew goes towards luff.
(c) Sliding pedestal moves forwards, and clew goes towards luff.

to the luff. This will be shorter than the distance from the clew to any point on the stay below the hank in question, so that the hank will not then be able to slide down the wire since the clew is restrained by the boom.

If a jackstay is fitted to the headsail, the hank or snap hook (and any others at a distance from the clew which is less than the length of the foot) can allow the luff to fall aft as the weight is taken off the halyard. Another system is to have the club boom sufficiently short at the tack to allow the sail to move forward as it is lowered; in this case the boom is attached only to the sail and not to the stay or the deck of the boat. A third method is to allow the pedestal to move in a short track, so that it goes forward as the sail is lowered. Finally, of course, some system of releasing the clew of the sail can be used, but this means another operation to remember when lowering sail.

Jib or Yankee (66 *to* 85 *per cent of cloth weight of working sails*)
A cutter's jib will be used in conjunction with a staysail, and the pair of them can not only confer more area than a genoa for the same fore triangle, but the jib also forms a slot with the staysail. The latter is thus working to better aerodynamic advantage and developing greater thrust. In addition, reduction in sail area is more efficient than handing the genoa and setting an intermediate, because there will always be a sail set and drawing in the fore triangle. Finally, two sails forward of the mast seem to make a boat steadier offshore than a single one.

A working jib, also called a yankee in Great Britain if it is cut with a high clew (a name which is not used in America, by the way), should normally be one or two weights lighter than the standard, if it comes off before the staysail, and particularly if it has to be handled on the end of a bowsprit. There are, however, owners of twin head-sail yawls and ketches who prefer to sail in heavy weather under mizzen and jib rather than mizzen and staysail. In this case, of course, the jib should be 100 per cent of the standard, or one weight lighter at most.

Care must be taken that the jib does not interfere with the airflow over the staysail. To this end there should be a reasonable gap between their respective stays, which are best if they are nearly parallel, and the jib should be cut high in the clew to allow room for plenty of wind to pass to leeward of the staysail. The sheet lead will run slightly forward of the average for a headsail: the higher the sail is cut, the further forward will come the sheet lead. In practice, the height of clew is usually controlled by this requirement. It will be as high as possible and still sheet inside the boat – on or near the counter, providing the base is wide enough at that point to keep the leech free.

Genoas

The genoa in its various forms is such an efficient sail that it is now looked upon more or less as a working headsail. As the wind increases to a point where reduction in sail area is necessary to keep the boat sailing at an efficient angle, modern technique is to hold on to the genoa and reef the mainsail. I have therefore shown as cloth weight percentage guides the lowest figure normal to a particular genoa, where it would be changed for a smaller sail before the first or second reef is taken in the mainsail, and also the full 100 per cent for hard driving.

Working Genoa (70 *to* 100 *per cent of cloth weight of working sails*)

The working, or medium, genoa is the sail which wins races for the sloop, and its shape is all-important. Not only does it provide immense thrust on its own account, but it controls the flow of air over the mainsail. It is vital, therefore, that this sail should hold its shape.

In the vertical plane a genoa should cover as much of the mainsail as possible, and so should be taken as near the top of its stay as it will go and still clear the shrouds; the width of the sail at the head is small enough to outweigh considerations of disturbing the airflow so near the mainsail. It should be cut with its flow well forward, and with a flat run aft to the leech. It is most important that the leech itself should not curl to windward, because the streamlines will then be directed straight into the lee of the mainsail, and the slot will be choked. A well-hollowed leech will open the slot and pass more air, thus backwinding the mainsail less. Modern materials and techniques enable lighter cloth to be used than was common a few years ago, particularly if the sail has a control luff to regulate flow position.

A good idea is to have a kind of jiffy reef. Extra cringles fitted at luff and leech, usually in a horizontally cut sail, can be pulled down in far less time than it takes to change sails; the slack can either be left lying on deck or tied off. This saves a sloop without a twin groove forestay from being bare-headed during a change; it saves another sail (useful where the wardrobe is limited by special rules); and it can be used where conditions are marginal or will be of short duration. Disadvantages are weight of the cringle and its reinforcement at the leech, finding a weight of cloth to suit both conditions, and the gap in the wardrobe if you rely on the reefed sail and it tears; thus effectively depriving you of two sails, not one.

Before the advent of the IOR, the RORC limited headsail size by controlling the horizontal distance between the tack and a perpendicular dropped from the clew. To get maximum area within this rule the clew had to be kept as low as possible. The IOR controls the distance from the clew perpendicular to the luff. Not only is this something which can be physically measured on the sail, but it allows the clew to be raised as high as you like without loss of area (the clew is brought aft as it is raised, along a line parallel with the luff, thus maintaining constant area; this line is technically known as the LP, or longest perpendicular, line). It is therefore tempting to recommend that a full size IOR genoa should have a clew high enough to enable the sail to clear the lifeline comfortably. Alas, although there would be no loss of area, efficiency would be impaired, so the clew still has to be low.

This is because it will take advantage of the quicker airflow over the hull and of the end plate effect which the deck has in restraining air escaping under the foot of the sail. Where regulations prevent a break in the lifeline to allow the genoa foot to be led outside the rail near the tack (the RORC, except as shown below, demands an unbroken lifeline at least 2 ft high all round the yacht), a low clewed genoa must be sheeted inside the rail when beating to windward. This means that it must be led between the main shrouds and the rail, which is often difficult. Nevertheless, maximum efficiency requires this, and it should be done by any dedicated owner. It is a good idea to angle the stanchions slightly outward in way of the shrouds (the RORC allows a maximum of 10°) to make room for the sail, which should be adequately protected from chafe by suitable patches each side of the foot where abrasion will occur. The RORC now permits overlapping pulpits so that a gap may exist between the lifeline and the pulpit. This allows a low-cut headsail to set without the difficulties described above.

The owner for whom a slight loss of efficiency is more than offset by greater convenience, will have his genoa cut high enough in the clew to avoid this problem. The sail will then pass over the rail well forward, and will set round the shrouds without any bother. He will also be able to close reach with his genoa, without having to re-reeve the sheet outside the rail. But he will lose out to his more painstaking rival, who puts efficiency before convenience. Incidentally, there should be a second chafing patch on the foot of the sail near the tack, where it rubs on the top rail when reaching.

Heavy Genoa (85 *to* 100 *per cent of cloth weight of working sails*)
This is a sail which will not normally be in the locker of a boat with a working or medium genoa. It requires a light genoa to complement it, and has a limited wind range from, say, force 4 to 5½, and then not on a boat which is tender. It is a full size sail and the only difference from a working genoa, besides the weight of canvas, is that the clew is cut a little higher, so that the foot is kept out of the water, and also so that the sail can clear the lifeline. This avoids having someone up to his knees in water every time a tack is made, and the sail has to be tucked between the rail and the shrouds.

Intermediate Genoa (85 *to* 100 *per cent of cloth weight of working sails*)
The intermediate genoa is the first change down when the boat begins to be overpowered by the full size working genoa. It represents a reduction in area of about 25 to 33 per cent of the larger sail, and it is tending to replace the working headsail more and more these days; its cloth weight is therefore more inclined to be 100 per cent of the standard than 85 per cent.

It should be shorter in the luff than the standard genoa, in order to keep the centre of effort low, and also shorter in the foot in order to reduce area. It should have an area about half-way between the genoa and the working headsail so that it makes a logical reduction to the total area carried as the wind reaches the point where it replaces the larger sail. As with a dinghy's heavy weather jib, the intermediate genoa should be cut very flat, with a fair amount of hollow in the leech to open the slot; the clew should also be higher than that of the genoa, with little or no round to the foot. These last two points are so that the sail will pick up less water as the boat heels under the influence of the strong wind and so you can see under it. When considering the length of foot for this sail, it should be remembered that it has to set properly. If it is to go adequately round the main shrouds, setting outside them so that it may be freed off on a reach, the foot must be long enough so that the clew does not bear hard against the shrouds and cause a kink in the lower leech; about 1·25 × J is the minimum which will do this. You may decide that you want to lead the sail inside the main shrouds, between them and the lowers. This means that the upper leech will have to clear the lower spreaders, and that the sheet will have to be re-rove outside the main shrouds when you free off to a reach, or it will bear against them and chafe, besides giving a wrong lead.

Light Genoa (4 *to* 6 *oz*)

A light genoa is essential for a boat which has a heavy, but not a medium genoa. There must be a full area headsail which can cater for wind strengths up to force 3, and the heavy genoa will not do this properly. The light genoa will be cut along the lines of the medium equivalent, with particular emphasis on plenty of round to the foot, in order to achieve maximum area. Draft will be full and forward, so that the leech does not have a belly, while the line of the leech itself can be nearly straight (i.e. without hollow), because the slot may be narrower in these weights of wind with little danger of choking.

Most boats up to 45 ft LWL will use a cloth of fixed weight, as indicated above, rather than one related to the standard weight, and the temptation to use it in winds stronger than those for which it was designed must be firmly resisted. If there is only a mile to go to the windward mark and the wind is increasing, it is sometimes impossible tactically to change sails. The owner in this position – perhaps with a rival just under his lee – must be prepared to see the sail ruined, possibly for all time. He should confess his sins to his Sail Maker as soon as possible, and be prepared to buy a new sail. Such is the price of racing. If, on the other hand, an owner can foresee that he will often need to hold on to the light genoa in winds of force 3½ and more, he should have it made of heavier canvas, and it then becomes a light-medium genoa. At all events, do not use it in strong winds and then blame the sail for being out of shape. Play fair with your Sail Maker.

General

You may well ask what the ideal working wardrobe should comprise. This depends on your pocket and your dedication. The aim is to have a sail which will respond to most conditions of wind and sea, and the minimum would appear to be a light genoa to cover all winds up to force 3, a working genoa from 100 per cent standard to take over above this, with an intermediate as next buy. On the other hand, you may prefer to have a light-medium genoa of 75 per cent standard to cover force 2½ to 4, with a ghoster below and an intermediate above; next buy is a heavy genoa to fill force 4 to 5. The variations are many and offer pleasant fireside speculation.

CHAPTER XI

Light and Heavy Weather Sails

Light Weather Sails

Cloth. There are those who believe that a light weather suit of sails, particularly for a dinghy, should be made of a light cloth, and there are those who say that it should be heavy. The former maintain that the merest zephyr will fill out a light cloth immediately, while the latter say that the heavier material is sufficiently stiff not to lose its aerofoil shape even when the wind has gone completely, and thus is ready to receive the first whisper of wind and turn it into power. There is merit in both schools of thought, and I would be loath to dissuade an owner from either proposal. On balance, I would advise that dinghies should use a light cloth if they really want a light weather suit of sails.

You will note that I specify dinghies. Ocean-racers are often prevented by their rules from having a special light weather mainsail (the IOR, for instance, has just such a prohibition) and, in any case, such a large sail could not be made of the 3 or 4 oz. material which I have in mind as the sort of sail which will respond quickly to the first puff of wind as it fills in. These larger boats will, of course, have their ghosting headsails designed to catch this nascent breeze, and I shall deal with these separately later.

Light weather sails should never be used in winds stronger than those for which they have been designed. It is no good asking your

Sail Maker to make you a suit of sails for force 0 to 2½, and then trying to use them in force 3. Not only will they be too full but, if they have indeed been made of a lighter cloth than normal for the type of boat, they will stretch out of shape never properly to recover. This latter effect can be minimized by making the sails with narrower panels than usual, thus cutting down the amount of bias available to pull out of shape.

Finally, bear in mind my earlier remarks about ultra-light weather sails losing more races than they win. It may well happen one day, in a near calm, that a boat with very full sails will trounce you. Her owner will doubtless extol the virtues of this suit, but remember that he has to take every advantage of such a rare occurrence, and that he does not tell you how many races it has lost for him.

When considering sails for light weather it is not enough to say that they should be fuller than usual. There are qualifications, particularly regarding the headsail, which can always be given extra fullness by easing the sheet, and the spinnaker which, as it increases in size at the head, increases its total weight aloft and thus its tendency to collapse in ghosting conditions. There is also a special art in setting and sheeting all sails in light airs, and I must repeat some of the factors about sails which make a boat go fast under these conditions. The same holds good for heavy weather as we shall see later.

Light Weather Mainsail

It is the very full mainsail which loses the race for you as the wind gets up beyond the strength for which it was designed. Many are the dinghy owners who choose a mainsail admirably suited to the force 1 wind prevailing at the start of a race, only to find themselves knocked down on the second beat to windward because the wind has increased. Unless you have a method of taking some of this fullness out of the sail, such as a bendy mast or an efficient slab reefing coupled with a Cunningham hole, it does not pay to own such a sail. I naturally except waters where ghosting conditions are the rule rather than otherwise, or where light airs are predictably constant, such as parts of the Mediterranean.

By its very fullness, an ultra-light weather mainsail must have a leech which returns sharply to windward so that it can rejoin the boom at the clew. This return means that the leech of the sail will be actively trying to thrust the boat astern as soon as the wind can get a grip on it. In very light airs the luff is not lifting and thus is contributing all its power, the bunt is not heeling the boat because the wind is not strong enough, and there is not enough force in the wind to cause the leech to do much harm. As soon as the wind increases to a certain critical point (which will vary according to the fullness of the sail), the luff may lose drive through lifting, the flow will move aft slightly under the action of the wind, thus aggravating the leech return, and the bunt of the sail will heel the boat; the leech itself will be trying to drive the boat astern (see figure 61). A flatter sail or use of a leech Cunningham would be much faster, and this usually occurs around force 2½ for the average very full mainsail.

Fig. 61. Showing how F_T for the after section of a mainsail with a bellied leech resolves with F_X facing aft.

Slab Reef. The boat which does not have a bendy mast can, as I indicated just now, employ a slab reef and a Cunningham hole to do the job of flattening the mainsail when required. A slab reef, also called a roach reef or a flattening reef, is one which runs along the foot of a mainsail, starting at the tack, curving up into the sail as it proceeds aft, and coming back to the boom at the clew. When it is pulled in it removes some of the cloth at the foot, thus flattening the sail as though it had less foot round cut into it in the first place. The reef can be effected by means of a continuous lacing line, but a simpler system employs the zip fastener. Providing a non-corroding zipper is used, such as nylon or one of the more modern plastics, it is a way of taking in a slab reef quickly; this in turn means that it will be used more often than the old-fashioned lacing system. It is important to use a zipper which has been tested and found serviceable, for the slider can also corrode or the whole thing may be found to be too weak. There are problems involved in enamelling or plating sliders, because their tolerances are often measured in thousandths of an inch. Incidentally, it is usually better to leave such a zipper open when you stow the sail in its bag, for closed teeth can disengage when the zipper is bent or twisted. It is also a good idea to follow Bruce Banks Sails practice of fitting a second slider at the outset to act as a spare should the first one break while sailing. Easier still is to pull down Cunningham holes above both tack and clew, leaving the spare cloth to flap idly over the boom.

A zipper can also be used up the luff of a mainsail, where the class rules permit (the IOR prohibits it), in a similar manner. While it will take out fullness from a better place for effective flattening of a mainsail, it should be remembered that zippers are by no means infallible, and it is easier to get at a jammed slider along the foot of a sail than half-way up the mast. I do not like luff zips.

Cunningham Hole. The Cunningham hole is a simpler device, which is possibly even more effective than a slab reef; it may be used in conjunction with the latter and can be most useful on its own. Invented by Briggs Cunningham in the 6 metre days, it is a method of putting more tension on the luff of a mainsail which is already out to its black bands, also on the leech and clew outhaul.

A light weather mainsail will usually be made rather longer in the luff than a medium weather sail for the same boat. This is because flow does not have to be induced by very much tension on the luff, since light winds will not blow aft the resulting fold near the bolt rope; the sail will rely more on the flow which the Sail Maker has built into it by means of broad seam and round to the luff. There comes a time, however, when the wind gets up stronger than anticipated, and the beautiful curve in the mainsail is pushed towards the leech. The owner would like to stretch the luff a little more, to draw the flow back towards the luff again, but the sail is already hard up against the black band. Cunningham's idea was to have an eye worked into the luff tabling, just up from the tack – about 6 in. on a dinghy and up to 1 ft on a medium-sized ocean-racer. A line is passed through this hole and tension applied downwards on the luff, thus stretching it more. The flow in the sail is therefore drawn forward, although small creases appear in the tack area as the sail bunches. This, however, is by far the lesser of two evils, and is easily outweighed by greater overall aerodynamic efficiency in the sail. A similar effect can be had by applying the same treatment to the leech which, if also drawn slightly aft, will flatten the whole foot area as well.

It is no good having a Cunningham hole if it is never used. Many a mainsail has one fitted, yet the owner does not have the tackle to enable him to adjust it quickly. If a lacing has to be rove between the Cunningham hole and the tack eye, and tension applied by drawing the two together and tying a knot, then it will seldom be

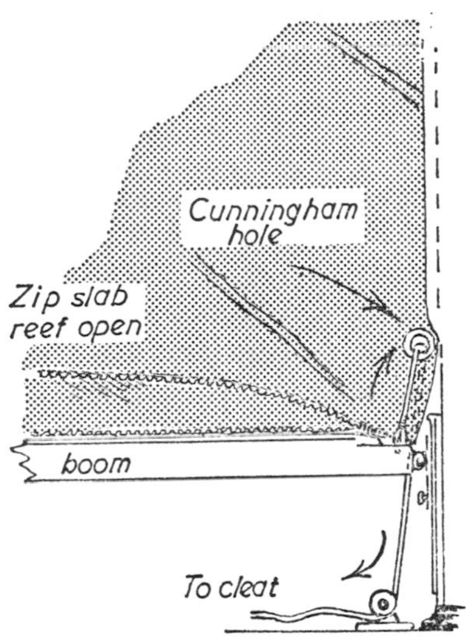

Fig. 62. The Cunningham Hole.
A line may be led from the tack, up through the Cunningham hole, and then down the other side via a suitable fairlead to a cleat.

done. A line should be led from the tack, through the Cunningham hole, and down to a sheave on deck, from where it can go to a convenient cleat. Similarly a permanent line should be rove through the leech Cunningham and taken via a ringslide to a cleat on the boom.

Some dinghy classes have developed the slab reef beyond the stage where it flattens a sail for heavier weather. A large shelf is built into the foot of the sail, and a zipper incorporated in order to close it off when required. The shelf is unzipped off the wind, to provide a really full sail for reaching and running, and closed for the windward leg, where a more conventional shape is needed. Many of the top 14 ft Internationals have it, but when I persuaded Robin Judah to try it on his Merlin Rocket in 1964, he soon gave it up; perhaps the short foot length of his sail did not give the flow a chance to develop. I did some wind tunnel tests on this idea in 1963, and releasing the shelf on a reach gave a 5 per cent increase in driving force over the sail with closed zipper, with little change in heeling force.

Quadrilaterals

The IOR requires headsails to be sheeted from only one point on the sail, and specifically excludes quadrilaterals or similar sails.

Ghoster (2 *to* 3 *oz*)

The ghoster is a headsail suitable up to and including force 2. It will take the boat to windward in these conditions, and should be made of a cloth slightly above the minimum available. It is cut in the same way as a light genoa for greatest area: low clew, maximum foot round and no hollow to the leech. It should have lightweight sheets tied to the clew (to avoid the weight of a shackle), and hanks or snap hooks should be double spaced. Strength of mind is needed to take the sail off as the wind gets above force 2.

Drifter (1 *to* 2 *oz*)

The drifter is virtually synonymous with a ghoster, but I have chosen to differentiate between the two for the purposes of this book. Let us say, then, that the drifter is the sail which indicates when the first puff of wind arrives, and then has to be changed immediately; it is suitable up to and including force 1. Anything above this will blow the very light cloth out of shape, so it is a sail of limited application to say the least.

As a good deal of its time will be spent hanging lifeless from its halyard, the drifter can be made with or without hanks or snaps according to preference. There is a strong case to be made for doing away with them, so that the light genoa can be hanked on to the stay, ready to go up at the first sign of a steady wind. This practice helps to encourage early removal of the drifter, thus prolonging its life.

The clew will usually be rather higher than that of a ghoster, so that the greatest area is kept fairly high, where the first whisper of breeze occurs. This, of course, means that the sheet fairlead must be further aft for correct trim. Sheets must be as light as possible, and may be single.

I generally try and discourage owners from ordering drifters, on the grounds that the sail would almost certainly be used in winds stronger than those for which it was designed; the truth of this assumption has been demonstrated to me many times both ashore and afloat. Perhaps a good solution is to have a drifter cut from heavier cloth – whereupon it becomes a ghoster – but it is necessary to remember that it will still have an upper limit of force 2.

Light Weather Dinghy Headsails (2–3½ *oz*)

The light weather dinghy headsail can afford to be cut rather flatter than one might believe suitable, since flow can always be achieved by easing the sheet; there should be little or no induced flow to leave a fold up the luff. It will, however, be used in winds above its designed range, particularly if it is a good looking sail, so it should be cut accordingly. You will note that I state categorically that it *will* be misused, not that it *might* be; this is as sure as tomorrow's sunrise, and the better the sail, the greater the likelihood of dawn coming up as usual. The sail should have maximum foot round, with little or no hollow to the leech. A window is not recommended, as it will almost certainly be stiffer than the rest of the sail and this, coupled with the danger of tight stitching around its edges, can give rise to creases. Very light wire luff clips, such as those marketed by Lewmar, are better than normal snaps or hanks because they are lighter and they allow a better airflow; they will be quite strong enough for the light winds the sail ought to encounter (and if they bend or break it will serve the owner right for using the sail in too strong a wind).

Storm Sails

Many rules, including both the RORC and the CCA, require a yacht to have storm canvas capable of taking her to windward. This means that a sloop or cutter should have a sail of reduced size to set on the mast (a yawl or ketch can sail to windward without the mainsail), and that all yachts should have a headsail which can safely be set in a storm.

Trysail (85 *to* 100 *per cent of cloth of working sails*)
A trysail is a most seamanlike storm sail, as it does away with the need for a boom, which can be a danger in a heavily rolling boat under storm conditions. In addition, the boom may be broken, yet the trysail can still be set. It may be of the same weight of cloth as the mainsail or, where this exceeds 9 ounces, it can be one weight lighter. This may sound odd for a storm sail, but polyester is so strong that there is plenty of margin in the standard weight. The only reason that the mainsail is not made lighter is that it would stretch out of shape, but a certain amount of stretch is acceptable in a trysail, which is not expected to enable the boat to tack in 90°; a lighter and softer cloth will be easier to handle (it is worth specifying softness to your Sail Maker for this reason), and will take up less space in the locker.

The sail should be cut so that the clew is lower than the tack, and the sail is then hoisted so that the clew comes above the level of the boom. It is a good idea to have a permanent strop on the tack, so that the correct height is automatically found, and so that it can be shackled straight on to the normal tack fitting without having to search round for a suitable length of strong lashing.

When the trysail is set, I prefer to see the boom lashed to its gallows and twin sheets led either side of it, so that they pull down and aft like a headsail's. Indeed, the sail is usually cut with a mitre, so that the cloths run at rightangles to the loose leech and foot for the same reasons as they do on a headsail. Some owners, however, prefer to leave the boom free, and to sheet the trysail to its end with a view to avoiding the need to tend sheets when tacking.

In area, the sail should be substantially smaller than the close-reefed mainsail. To avoid the use of battens, it should have a hollow to the leech and a straight foot. Terylene and Dacron are strong enough not to need roping all round except on the largest yachts. Luff slides may be used in the normal way, particularly if a second emergency track is available on the mast, as these are so much easier than the old-fashioned parrel beads. The eyelets for the slides should

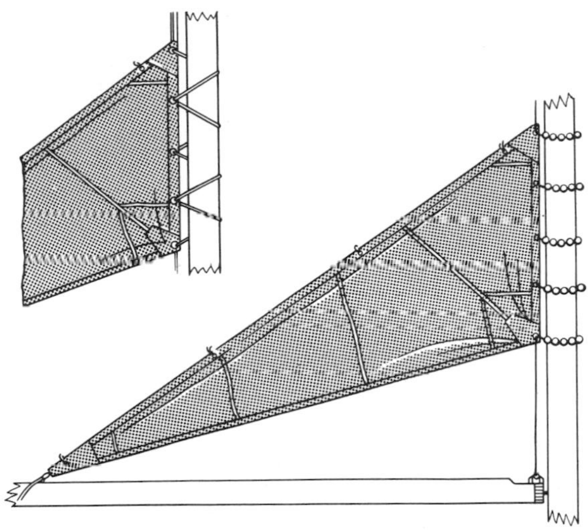

Fig. 63. Headsail acting as a trysail. The foot, reinforced with tape, becomes the luff and is fastened to the mast with parrel beads. See insert for jam-free method of lacing.

be large enough to allow a lacing to be passed through, should the track be unserviceable. A small headsail can always be made to serve as an emergency trysail, if eyelets are provided in the foot (which should be adequately strengthened with tape). The sail is bent to the mast with a lacing, and the sheet is made fast to the head, which has now become the clew.

I have always been surprised to see that more owners do not have their racing number put on the trysail. Most rules require an alternative means of displaying this information when the mainsail is not hoisted, and it strikes me that it is a simple way to do so on the trysail.

Swedish Mainsail (100 *per cent of cloth weight of working sails*)
Some people prefer to use a storm mainsail set on both mast and boom, as this is felt to give better control of the sail and does not involve separate sheets; in addition it will make the boat as close-winded as an ordinary mainsail. The Swedish mainsail answers this requirement.

It is a sail about three-quarters of the length of the ordinary mainsail on the luff and foot, and it loses more area by pronounced hollowing of the leech. The result is a sail about half as large as the full-sized mainsail, and which will sail as close to windward as the boat will lie under storm conditions. Needless to say, the hollow leech does away with the need for battens, which is all to the good, and there will be a ring at the top instead of a headboard. The sail should, of course, be cut flat for the strong winds it will encounter, and there is no reason why it should not have a reef if desired. Its main disadvantage lies in the fact that it has to be set on the boom, which may slam across the cockpit under certain conditions, or may

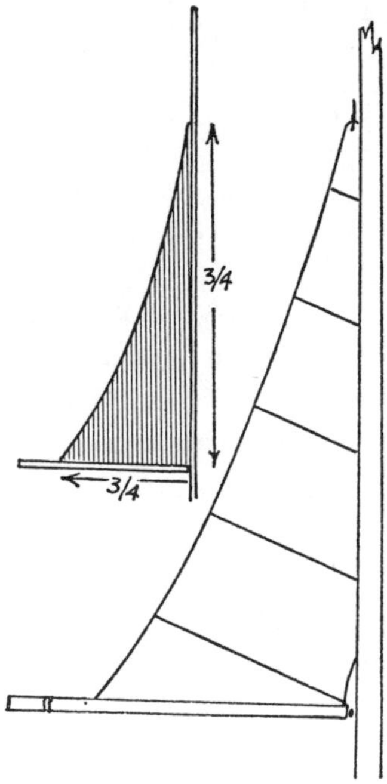

Fig. 64. Swedish mainsail. The cloths may have to be tripped round the curve of the leech to avoid too much bias at head and clew.

even be broken by the very weather which necessitates the setting of the sail. A slamming boom may be thought more acceptable than flogging trysail sheets of wire, particularly if the leech of the Swedish mainsail is made short enough to lift the boom well clear of heads in the cockpit.

Storm Jib or Storm Staysail (100 *per cent of cloth weight of working sails*)
The storm jib or staysail should be standard weight, as it should not be allowed to stretch unduly, or the boat may develop poor handling qualities. It should be about half the area of the working jib or staysail, or even less, and should have a high clew in order to keep the sail out of the water; this also helps to bring the sheet lead to the working headsail's fairlead. Some boats carry their storm jib on a small tack pendant to keep it well above the water, but this should not be overdone or the centre of effort will be too high.

Here again, Terylene and Dacron are so strong that a leech rope is not necessary unless the boat is large – say over 50 ft LWL. A roped leech will tend to curl and flog, to which storm jibs are prone anyway. I do not favour battens, such as are recommended by some Naval Architects, because they represent something else to break or work loose; it should be possible to cut the leech with sufficient hollow and skill so that it lies fairly quiet in the strongest winds. If it does not, then take it back to its maker for attention.

It is quite feasible to use a working jib or staysail as a storm sail, if a reef is employed. Points reefing is as good as anything for this purpose, as they tie firmly under the loose foot. Care should be taken that the result is a sail which responds to the requirements of high clew and sheet lead position.

CHAPTER XII

Reaching and Running Sails

Reaching Genoa (66 *per cent of cloth weight of working sails*)
A reaching genoa should normally be a weight lighter than the windward going genoa it replaces, assuming that the latter is not to the full standard weight. That is to say that a light genoa of 5 ounces will be replaced by a 4 ounce reacher; a medium genoa of 8 ounces will be replaced by a 5 or 6 ounce reacher, and a ghoster of 3 ounces will be replaced by a 2 ounce reacher. This, of course, is because a given wind has less apparent force on a reach than to windward. In addition, the sail is better if it is fairly full in the middle, which a light cloth will ensure. To this end it can be set flying, that is to say without snaps or hanks, as the sag in the luff will not be detrimental to performance.

The clew may be cut low (unless the sail is principally for light weather reaching when it should be higher clewed to catch the wind), because it will rise as the sheet is eased, and the fairlead should be further aft than the standard genoa position, or it may be sheeted to the end of the main boom with great advantage. This is a rich man's sail of limited application, for the average genoa will work nearly as well on a reach, whereas the reacher will be no good to windward, except in light weather, when it should not be sheeted too hard.

Genniker (2 *to* 3 *oz*)
The genniker (or spanker, or star-cut spinnaker) is, as its name

implies, a cross between a genoa and a spinnaker. The principal object is to gain area by setting a sail which measures under the spinnaker rules, but which can be used nearly as close to the wind as a genoa. It is primarily a racing sail, when it has to be set with a spinnaker pole, but it can do useful work while cruising when it can be tacked to the stemhead for close reaching without a spar. It is cut rather like a storm spinnaker, with full width foot tapering to the rule minimum 75 per cent at mid girth, with narrow shoulders from there up.

One of the main drawbacks of any spinnaker is that the very light cloth bellies easily, so that the sail tends to have a full leech when

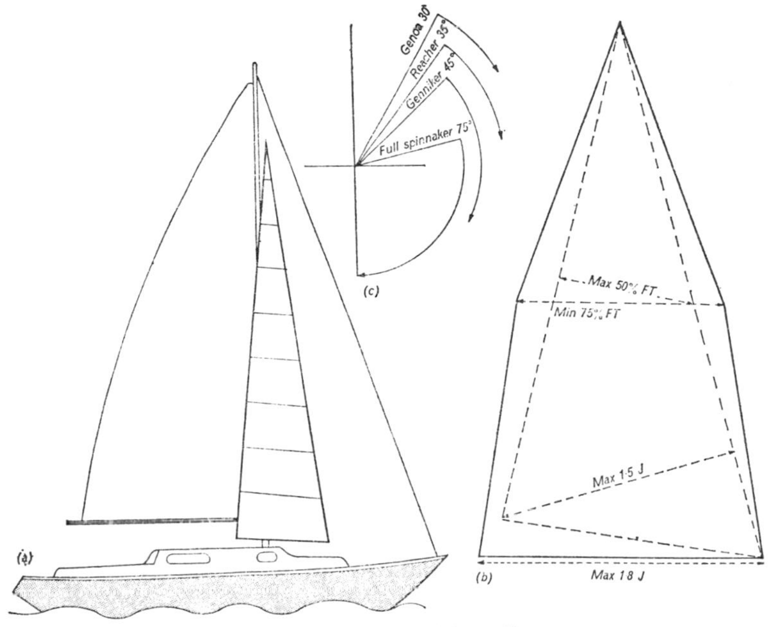

Fig. 65. Tallboy and Genniker.
A tallboy (a) should overlap the mast as much as the spreaders will allow; it will tack down somewhere between 30–40 per cent of the J measurement forward of the mast. A genniker, or spanker, (b) is a flat cut spinnaker, the genniker here is shown with a normal reaching genoa in broken outline superimposed. The series of arcs (c) suggests relative wind angles through which various headsails and spinnakers may be best used.

close reaching. To help overcome this in the genniker, the Sail Maker uses a moderately heavy cloth, which he lays so that minimum stretch occurs along all three unsupported edges – hence the star-cut pattern with its variations; see figure 65.

Besides close reaching in light to medium winds, the genniker can be used for broad reaching in a stiff breeze, and as a general purpose heavy weather spinnaker.

Tallboy (3 *to* 5 *oz*)

A tallboy, or slat sail, is a tall narrow headsail which is tacked down just in front of the mast, with the object of forming a more efficient slot off the wind; it can also be used when beating to windward providing the weather is very light. The sail should have a control luff (preferably sleeved over a wire, so that the luff can always be straight and tight whatever the tension on the sailcloth) and a bridle, or double span, at the tack to help position the sail correctly. The tack position can be critical, and it is usually best located at a point between 30 and 40 per cent along the foredeck, on the centreline for close reaching, and coming to windward and aft as the wind goes abaft the beam.

The object is to trim the tallboy fairly close to the mainsail, so that the airflow immediately to leeward of the mast is cleaned up in order to give more thrust. The sail is best used in the lighter wind ranges and where conditions are likely to be stable for some time; small boats (20 ft. LWL and under) may find that the presence of one or two hands on the foredeck, for what may turn out to be a lengthy period as the sail is trimmed, may harm performance more than the sail will eventually improve it.

A further use for the tallboy is in front of the mizzen of a yawl or ketch. This sail operates permanently in the dirty wind of the mainsail, and anything which can be done to clean up its airflow must enable it to produce greater thrust than it does at present. Used like this the tallboy ranks as a mizzen staysail.

Spinnaker-Staysail (1½ *to* 2 *oz*)

The spinnaker-staysail (also known as a saveall and even as a demi-bra at times) sets under the spinnaker on a reach, in order to fill a gap forward. It is usually made of Dacron or Terylene, but may be made of nylon if preferred. The former makes a slightly better sail as it stretches less than nylon, but the difference is marginal and not so important that it should prevent those owners' wives who wish for a coloured sail from having what they want (most Sail Makers stock coloured nylon but only white Terylene or Dacron); boats with a water-line above 45 ft may increase the weight of cloth by not more than double the above recommendation. The sail can tack to the stemhead, in which case its size will be limited by the same rules which govern a genoa, and it may hank to the forestay and carry about two thirds up it, thereby acting as a spinnaker net at the same time. Alternatively a second tack eye several feet up the luff can be tied to the weather pulpit rail by means of a short rope pendant; this will give it a rather less disturbed wind, and will see that it disturbs the spinnaker as little as possible in turn.

A spinnaker-staysail set in this manner ranks as a headsail, and the rules may have something to say about it. For instance, the IOR requires that no headsail shall have a mid-girth (measured between the mid-points of luff and leech) more than 50 per cent of the foot length. In addition, the J measurement shall be taken to the luff of any headsail set flying if this is forward of the forestay. The IOR, however, allows headsails to be tacked athwartships, and the IYRU makes specific exception to the spinnaker-staysail when it requires jib tacks to be fixed 'approximately in the centre-line of the yacht'. The meaning of all this is that the spinnaker-staysail may be tacked to the weather pulpit rail provided it is not forward of the forestay. There is an overall requirement in the IOR that no staysail or jib may be tacked so that its clew, if trimmed flat along the centre-line of the yacht, would fall abaft the LP line (normally a line parallel to the forestay, and $1 \cdot 5 \times J$ aft of it). The effect of this is that no staysail or jib clew should come aft of the largest genoa clew closehauled, no matter where the former sail is tacked in the foretriangle.

A better airflow is obtained if the luff is not allowed to get too near the spinnaker, so the halyard is best led to a point just over half-way up the mast, and the sail allowed to set flying without hanks. If no special halyard is available, it can certainly be hoisted flying on one of the normal headsail halyards; in any case, the head of the sail should preferably not go much higher than half-way up the mast, or it will interfere with the set of the spinnaker. The clew is usually drawn below the deckline on the sail plan, because it will rise as the sail fills on a reach.

Mizzen-Staysail (2 *to* 3 *oz*)
Much of what I have just said about spinnaker-staysails holds good for mizzen-staysails. Recommended cloth weight is rather heavier for the latter because its larger area means a greater total weight of wind in the sail at any one time, and this would tend to stretch it more; this in turn would belly the sail into a bag, with consequent danger of it approaching the mainsail and interfering with the air flow. Once more, yachts with a water-line over 45 ft should consider increasing cloth weight above my recommendation, but not more than twice the figure above.

The clew is drawn below and just short of the mizzen clew, so that it can sheet comfortably to the mizzen boom end or to the counter. It is set flying, with the tack to windward, and the luff wire should be cased with leather in way of the permanent main backstay, to guard against chafe.

The IOR formula requires mizzen-staysails to be three-cornered, tacked abaft the mainmast and secured to the railcap, deck or cabin top; it may be sheeted to the hull or to the mizzen boom but not to any other spar. There is no restriction on the number of mizzen-staysails carried, but not more than one may be set at the same time. It follows that mizzen spinnakers are permitted (they set, of course, without a pole). Only half the rated area of either the mizzen or the mizzen-staysail goes into the rating, but the formula requires that the larger of the two *rated* areas shall be used. Thus an enormous mizzen-staysail setting as a spinnaker from the mizzen masthead will be paid for in the rating.

Some heavy cruising yawls and ketches use the mizzen-staysail more as a working sail. In this case it will possibly be hanked to a removable stay, and made of a cloth between 75 per cent and 100 per cent of the standard for the working sails. In passing, it is interesting to note that one Italian name for this sail is *carbonera*, and this stems from the days of trading boats which were half coal-fired and half sailing vessels. The mizzen-staysail used to set over the smoke stack and quickly became dirty.

14. *Gitana IV* on the Fastnet 1965. We found that removing the mizzen under certain conditions made the boat less inclined to weather helm, and this increased her speed by a quarter of a knot or so. The spinnaker pole is at right angles to the wind and in the same plane as the after guy; the sheet is eased as much as possible so that the spinnaker is pulling well ahead. *Associated Newspapers Ltd.*

15. The genoa luff is all-important. Place a straight edge or rule along this Contessa 32's luff, and you will see that it has very little sag. Try the same on a photograph of your own boat and you may be persuaded to buy a hydraülic backstay ram.
Jeremy Rogers.

16. *Tempest* and *Cobra*. The two British entries which finished first and second in the IYRU two-man keel-boat trials at Medemblik, Holland. Note *Tempest*'s bendy mast and well setting mainsail. *Yachting World*.

17. A crew member standing in the slot will cause turbulence and loss of thrust. Note also the curl in the genoa leech; the lady is completing the task of lousing up the airstream. *Eileen Ramsay*.

18. *Above*. Osprey. The mainsail has either not been pulled to its boom band, is too long on the foot, or needs re-roping; at all events the cloth should have more tension on it along the boom. It might also have too much cloth bias at the lower leech. The headsail has too much foot round to stand on the wind. The luff seizings have moved down, so need regulating. *Yachts & Yachting*.

19. *Above left*. OK. This mast bends too much for the sail, particularly just below the mid point. The creases at the leech might be helpe by hollowing the leech very slightly between the battens, but the rules may prevent this. The top batten is a trifle stiff at its inner end. *Yachts & Yachting*.

20. *Below left*. Dart. Fullness in lower quarter of luff needs more broad seam to shape it. The window is set in a very curved part of the sail, and the lack of foot seam makes the creases worse. This sail may well have too much cloth bias at the lower leech. *Yachts & Yachting*.

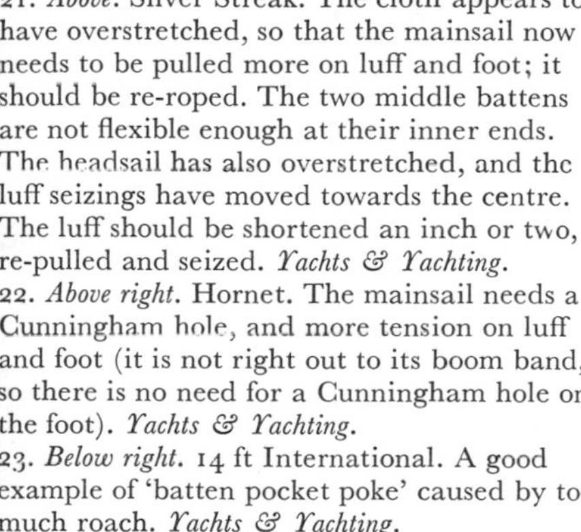

21. *Above*. Silver Streak. The cloth appears to have overstretched, so that the mainsail now needs to be pulled more on luff and foot; it should be re-roped. The two middle battens are not flexible enough at their inner ends. The headsail has also overstretched, and the luff seizings have moved towards the centre. The luff should be shortened an inch or two, re-pulled and seized. *Yachts & Yachting*.
22. *Above right*. Hornet. The mainsail needs a Cunningham hole, and more tension on luff and foot (it is not right out to its boom band, so there is no need for a Cunningham hole on the foot). *Yachts & Yachting*.
23. *Below right*. 14 ft International. A good example of 'batten pocket poke' caused by too much roach. *Yachts & Yachting*.

24. *Above*. Lazy E. Mainsail needs more tensic on luff and foot and might be better for re-roping. Headboard is either pulling away c is too tightly sewn – possibly both. Top batte is too stiff at inner end. Headsail is not pulled enough on the wire, and the clew eye has bee sewn too tightly. *Yachts & Yachting*.

25. *Above left*. Yachting World Solo. The batt are not in tight enough, in addition the cloth would appear to have overstretched. The sail could do with a decent clew patch, and may have been roped too tight near the clew. *Yachts & Yachting*.

26. *Below left*. G P 14 Footer. Mainsail needs more tension on luff and foot, and might be better for regulation of the roping. The heads luff appears to have moved on the wire, so th it is not pulled enough near the tack. *Yachts & Yachting*.

27. *Above*. Moth. This is a full sail made from light cloth. It would benefit from a Cunningham hole. The window has not been put in very well. *Yachts & Yachting*.
28. *Above right*. 505. The mainsail needs a Cunningham hole, and more tension on luff and foot. The cloth appears to have been overstretched, and may need re-roping. The cupped upper leech might be helped by slight hollowing of the leech between battens. *Yachts & Yachting*.
29. *Below right*. 12 ft National. Mainsail has too much roach to stand properly. A good example of 'batten pocket poke'. *Yachts & Yachting*.

30. *Tempest*. The boat is on a close reach, so the headsail luff is not as taut as desirable due to the slack rig. The curve is accentuated by the slight bend of the mast to windward, which opens the slot. *Yachting World*.

The Mule (66 *per cent of cloth weight of working sails*)
The mule, or main backstay sail, sets on the permanent main backstay of a yawl or ketch, and sheets to the head of the mizzen mast. Usually a fairly light weather sail, it is cut like a headsail, and has snaps for as far as the main backstay is single; if the latter divides near the deck, naturally the mule cannot hank to one of the lower legs only (or, indeed, be hoisted past the joint if it were). It is an effective means of increasing area on a close reach. Weight of canvas varies, according to the use expected of the sail, but an average is close to the large jib of a twin headsail rigged yacht. Fifty per cent of the area is included in the rating calculation, and its use rules out the carrying of a mizzen-staysail.

Downwind Sails
Downwind sails are mainly spinnakers, as far as we are concerned, but I have also added a few words on twin running sails as advice is sometimes required on their design.

Working Spinnaker (1½ *to* 2½ *oz*)
Dinghies and cruisers up to 25 ft water-line can use the lower end of the above range for their working spinnakers, boats over this size should go higher proportionately; standard cloths are usually produced in 1½ and 2 oz, and these will do for all but the heaviest yachts. As its name implies, this is a reaching and running sail for most weather conditions up to force 4. It should not, therefore, be extreme as regards fullness in the head (i.e. not too full, nor yet too flat) but should, of course, be to the maximum area allowed by the rules.

Light Spinnaker (½ *to* 1½ *oz*)
Normally, the light spinnaker for boats of all sizes should be made of the lightest nylon available on the market – providing the owner remembers this fact. Much so-called ½ oz spinnaker material is, in fact, rather heavier and usually comes out at about ¾ oz.

The light spinnaker will, of course, be used in light airs, so it should not be unduly small. On the other hand, a sail which has every inch of area crammed into the head will not set well, except with a force 2 wind dead aft: the sail will be too broad and full aloft to set on a reach, and there will be so much cloth in the head that even a lightweight nylon will produce a total weight aloft which is more than very light airs can blow out. The 12 metres found that their really large orbital spinnakers were of limited application, and some of their best sails were no more than moderately sized. Extra area can more efficiently be got into a light weather spinnaker by adding a skirt along the foot.

Heavy Spinnaker

Heavy spinnaker is usually a misnomer for a working spinnaker or, sometimes, a heavy weather spinnaker. Owing to its ambiguity, the name is best not used at all, particularly as no spinnaker should be heavy.

Heavy Weather or Storm Spinnaker (2 to 4 oz)

The demands of modern ocean-racing are such that a spinnaker must be used downwind whenever it is safe to do so. The heavy weather spinnaker is a common sail in the locker of the top offshore boats and, indeed, the top boats of any class where such a sail is permitted. It should normally be of 2½ to 3 oz for all cruisers of any size, the lighter material of 2 oz/yd^2 only being used by dinghies and those cruisers with a LWL of less than 20 ft; owners of yachts over 45 ft on the water-line should consider carefully whether or not to go heavier

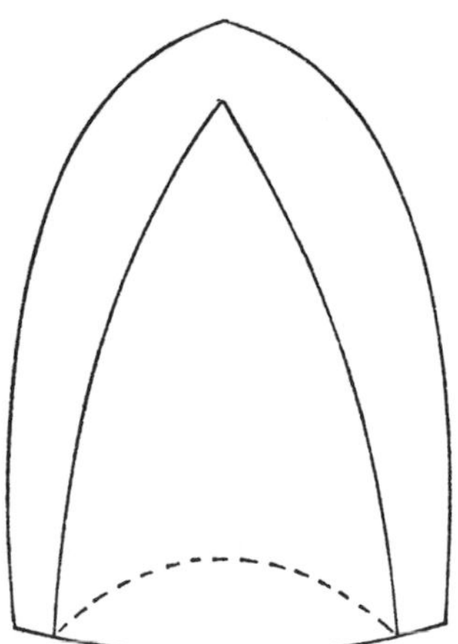

Fig. 66. Heavy weather or storm spinnaker compared with a standard spinnaker. The dotted line represents a possible further reduction in area if desired.

than 3 oz., and may well have the heaviest cloth recommended above, namely 4 oz. This is a marginal decision, however, and in 1963 I designed a storm spinnaker for Herr Burmester's KR yacht *Dorothee*. The sail measured 65′ 5″ on the luff and leech, and 36′ 0″ on the foot and widest part, yet we only used 3 oz nylon, admittedly of the reinforced ripstop variety.

A heavy weather spinnaker for a dinghy will be the same on the stays and foot as the working spinnaker. It will merely be of a heavier material and cut flat in the head to help control. This also suits the sail admirably as a reacher, and it can easily double the two jobs. The International keelboat day-racers, such as the Dragon and Soling, usually have such varying rules that it is not possible to generalize. All I can say is that, where little tolerance is allowed, cut as flat as possible and go up one in cloth weight; where the tolerance is great, reduce the size of a large sail (such as the Soling) and cut it flat.

So that the heavy weather spinnaker of an ocean-racer shall reach from the halyard sheave to the spinnaker pole, and so that it shall pass round the forestay, the luff/leech and foot should be within 10 per cent of the full-sized sail. The sail is cut narrow and flat in the head, so that area is lost aloft, where it is least wanted in a blow. If it is desired to reduce size even more, a segment can be cut out of the foot, which has the added advantage of improving forward visibility.

Reaching Spinnaker (*1½ to 2½ oz*)

Most modern working spinnakers are cut so that they are efficient both reaching and running, particularly if they have horizontal cloths. For offshore races, however, it may be advantageous to have a spinnaker cut especially for reaching purposes, in case conditions are such that a particular leg gives a wind just forward of the beam over a fairly long distance. Such a sail should be cut full-size, of the same weight of cloth as the working spinnaker, and fairly flat in the head. The star-cut, originally developed by Bruce Banks Sails, helps restrict distortion and cuts down unwanted leech curl.

Big Boy

When a boat is running with the wind within 30 degrees of dead aft, the spinnaker is squared well across to windward and there is an open space on the lee side of the foretriangle in front of the mainsail; the big boy fills that gap. The sail is basically a genoa set flying with its luff sagging to leeward so that the spinnaker sheet passes between it and the forestay. Although usually made of light nylon and acting as a second spinnaker, the sail rates as a headsail and is restricted to the maximum genoa size under the IOR (because the rule will not allow two spinnakers to be set at the same time); it is cut with a lot of hollow to its upper luff, so corresponding extra inches are added as round to the leech. To allow the luff to sag well away to leeward, the big boy is often not hoisted right to the masthead; the sheet may either be taken to the main boom end (within BAL) or direct to the hull, allowing the clew to fly well out to one side.

The big boy is not always greeted with enthusiasm by helmsmen (although it is usually popular with enthusiastic foredeck gangs), because it reduces forward visibility almost to zero but, besides adding to boat speed, it also improves downwind stability. In this connection, the sail often works better if the mainsail is hauled amidships or lowered altogether to give it unrestricted airflow (and the helmsman a glimpse of the horizon ahead).

Twin-running Sails (66 *per cent of cloth weight of working sails*)

Twin-running sails are an excellent method of making good time on passage sailing before a trade wind. They avoid the constant trim required of a spinnaker (and can be kept up in stronger winds) as the boat is being pulled rather than driven, and they can be quickly reefed by easing forward both clews at once.

A typical running sail has its clew rather higher than the average working jib or staysail, but careful drawing can often make the one double as the other, thus effecting a saving in the wardrobe. As they are downwind sails, they will usually be lighter than the standard weight for the boat but, here again, an effective compromise can often be reached and a heavier weight accepted for the running sails, so that they shall also serve as working jibs or staysails.

The tacks of the two sails should be between two and four feet abreast, at points about 20 per cent along the base of the foretriangle from the mast, although there is nothing to stop these figures being altered considerably; successful twins have been hanked together to the forestay, and at varying distances apart at most positions in the foretriangle. The tacks should ideally be raised from the deck by about three feet, because there will be virtually no wind lower down, and this will help them disengage the deck somewhat; it will also help the foot clear the lifelines if the clew is a little low. The sails may be hoisted from the normal headsail halyards and will, of course, be set flying if tacked back from the stay, so the luff should be suitably stout, preferably of 1 × 19 construction. The poles should be rather shorter than the perpendicular distance from the clew to the luff, so that some shape is given to the sails when they are braced aft.

On Wright Britton's 40-ft yawl *Delight*, both running sails were 400 sq. ft in area, and were fastened to a common forestay, which was fitted with a Wykeham-Martin roller furling gear. G. Colin Ratsey made these sails, which he christened Roller Wings, at New York in 1964, and suggested vents down the luff to help stability, which is often a problem with this rig. Whether the vents helped or not, Wright Britton reported the sails as a great success, being quickly set and furled.

Another boat which had twins on a common stay was *Beyond*, the 16-tonner which Tom and Ann Worth took round the world. These sails were cut particularly high in the clew, which was some 15 to 20 ft above deck, and had cloths running parallel to the leech. They set with their tacks on the stem head, hanked to the forestay. It is as well to specify this to your Sail Maker, if you propose it, so that he can stagger the hanks or snap hooks.

Sir Francis Chichester was another man who used twins tacked together at the stem head. He rigged *Gipsy Moth III* like this for the 1962 Transatlantic Race, and departed even further from tradition by adding a bonnet on the foot of each headsail, which was boomed out by a telescopic pole attached to the original clew. This meant that the sheets were attached some 5 or 6 ft below the pole, but the system worked well.

You obviously do not have to be orthodox, therefore, and there are many variations to the theme. Your Sail Maker is probably as good a man as any to advise you, if you cannot get hold of someone with first-hand experience of round the world trade wind sailing under twins.

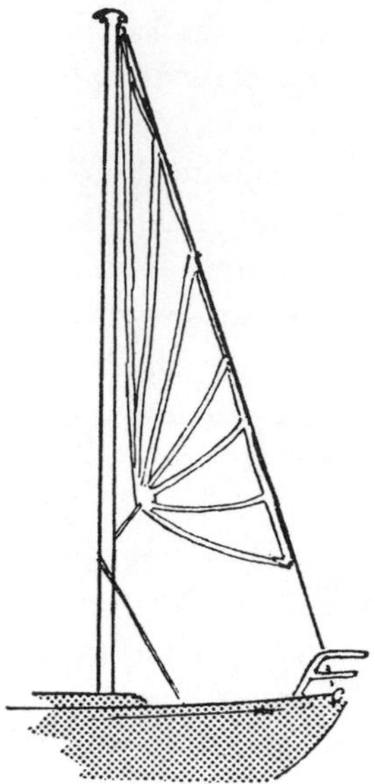

Fig. 67. Typical spinnaker net. The sheet is taken round the halyard and led forward to keep it clear of the after deck.

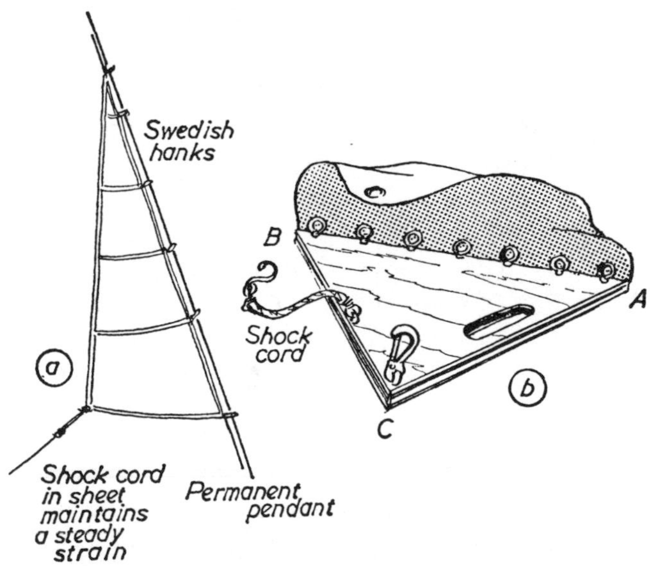

Fig. 68. The net board. (a) A simple spinnaker net. (b) The board on which it stows. It is about two feet in largest dimension.

Spinnaker Nets

The tendency for a spinnaker to wrap itself round the forestay under many conditions, makes it prudent to have some means of preventing this. The standard method is a net of webbing, hoisted on the jib halyard and hanked to the outermost stay. The three sides of the net form an outline not unlike that of a working headsail with a horizontal foot. Since the important part of the forestay to cover is the upper two-thirds, the head should be only two or three feet down from the halyard sheave, and the net should continue downwards to cover the danger area; there should be enough room underneath so that a man can walk upright on the foredeck. A single light 'sheet' may be led straight to a convenient point aft, or may double round its own halyard and back towards the bow. Hanks should be smooth so that they do not, themselves, offer possible snags to the spinnaker. A good type are the Swedish snaps or hanks, which operate pincer jaws by means of a central press button catch. The net should be fitted with a permanent tack pendant to ensure that it is hoisted to the correct height every time.

Net Board. One of the principal sources of bother with the conventional spinnaker net is its propensity for tangles. It is the kind of gear which gets put away in a hurry, and not looked at until it is wanted again. A net board can keep everything neat and tidy.

Referring to figure 68, when the net is lowered, the bottom end of the tack pendant is fastened to a snap hook at A, each Swedish hank is attached to its own eyelet or ring along the long edge A–B of the board, and the head eye is fastened to a second snap hook at B. The clew, or end of the shock cord sheet, goes on to snap hook C and the piece of shock cord already attached to the board is fastened across to hold the net in some control. The board can then either be dropped into a bag, or can have a shaped piece of canvas attached along side AB which folds over to corner C, and fastens with a suitable press stud, hook and eye, or lashing.

Zipped Net. An alternative system is to make use of the zip fastener. The net is made in conventional manner, and fastens to the forestay with a zipper. A second sleeve is provided with its own zipper and slider, to contain the net when it is not in use. This zipper should be the type where the slider comes off the bottom after it is closed, such as the Zip-R-Luff marketed by Ike Manchester of America, and sold in England by Bruce Banks.

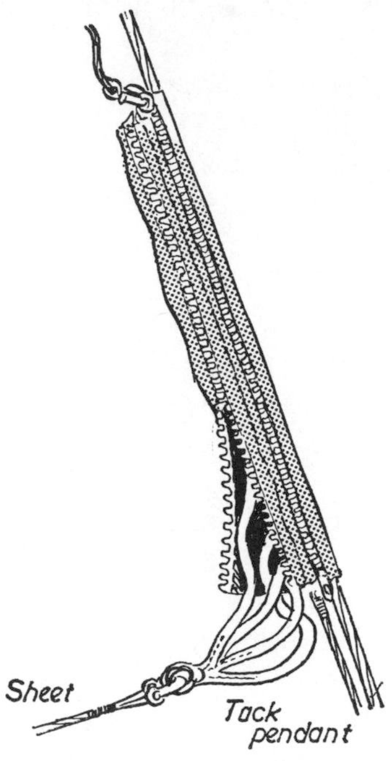

Fig. 69. Zipper stowed spinnaker net. The sketch shows the net zipped on to the forestay, and the stowage pocket just coming unzipped.

When the net is lowered, it is folded into the second sleeve and zipped up, with its sheet hanging out of the bottom. Stopping cotton is used to prevent the zipper of this sleeve coming apart after its slider has been taken off the bottom. To hoist, the net is hauled up in sausage form, the luff zipper closing over the forestay as usual (incidentally, no danger of the spinnaker fouling hanks here). The sheet is then pulled, the stopping cotton breaks and the two sides of the second zipper come apart to release the net, which cannot be in a tangle if it has been stowed properly. An alternative method of closing the second sleeve is to use Velcro, which is simple to do up and undo, and prevents the possibility of losing the slider.

Permanent Net. Both the previous systems are merely attempts to alleviate the evils inherent in a separate net; they do not get to the bottom of the trouble. The permanent net tries to solve the problem from a fresh angle. It has been used in America with success for some

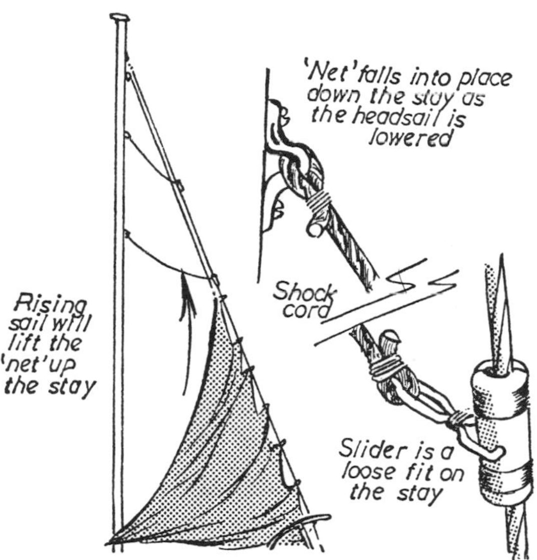

Fig. 70. Permanent spinnaker net.

years now, and consists of a series of lazy lines attached to the mast, which are free to slide up and down the forestay at their other ends.

When a headsail is hoisted, the rings are pushed up the stay by the head of the sail (a better job is made of it if the halyard has its own hank). If it is desired to keep the lazy lines from sliding too far down the stay when they are free to do so, they can be shortened if shock cord is used (3/16 or ¼ in. diam.), but care should be taken to see that it does not have to stretch more than about 30 per cent of its length when the highest headsail is hoisted.

CHAPTER XIII

Spinnakers in the Abstract

Origin

There has long been much discussion regarding the origin of the spinnaker, and many conflicting theories are suggested. To a certain extent, it depends on the exact interpretation you care to put upon the word. If by spinnaker you mean any sail thrust out to the side of a sailing-boat by means of a long pole, to help downwind speed, then it is virtually impossible to decide who started it all, and when it first occurred. Fishermen boomed out their masthead jibs when running before the wind for centuries. Before them, the square riggers used studding sails, set on spars thrust out as extensions to the yards.

There are grounds for believing that the word is a corruption of 'spin-maker' and there are those who maintain that it originally referred, in this context, to a triangular sail set between the end of the bowsprit and the dolphin striker in sailing men-of-war. This sail was also known as a 'Jimmy Green', and its purpose was to counteract weather helm by making the ship 'spin' to leeward.

If, however, you mean a sail specially made of light canvas, to be boomed out opposite the mainsail downwind by racing yachts, we can pinpoint the origin more accurately. On 5th June, 1865, two yachts were match racing off the Isle of Wight. On reaching the weather mark, Mr William Gordon's *Niobe* hoisted a huge jibheaded sail to her topmast head, boomed it out and drew rapidly away.

The racing spinnaker had been born.

Mr Gordon, need I add, owned a small sailmaking business in Southampton, just across from the Isle of Wight. History does not relate whether he prospered as a result of his invention, but he sold one to Mr Herbert Maudslay, owner of the *Sphinx*, for use in the following year, and there are those who trace the origin of the word spinnaker to this fact. Before we examine this supposition, however, let me return to the earlier use of the sail on board *Niobe*. The famous old British racing skipper Tom Diaper, in his memoirs written in 1939 and published in 1950, tells us that his grandfather was skipper of *Niobe* when she first used the new sail. His father, who took over as skipper on the old man's death, told him that when the sail was set, one of the hands said:

'Now that's the sail to make her spin.'

A 'gentleman' on board, Diaper continues, took the phrase and reversed it to *spin-maker*. This was shortened, in the same way that *pendant* becomes *pennant*, to *spin-aker* or *spinnaker*. The new sail was also known as a *niobe* for a short while.

In the following year Mr Herbert Maudslay, owner of the *Sphinx*, had his similar sail made, and it was first used in a match race of the Royal Victoria Yacht Club at Ryde off the Isle of Wight. The boat was known to the hands as the *Spinks*, and the locals called the sail a *spinker*, in the same way they had called it a *niobe* the year before. This became *spiniker* or *spinniker* and appears to have joined forces with the corrupt version of *spinmaker* to settle down as *spinaker* or *spinnaker*, both of which are correct usage.

The first recorded use of the word in print is in the British sporting weekly the *Field* of 18th August, 1866. Mr Dixon Kemp, compiler of the monumental *Manual of Yachting & Boat Sailing and Naval Architecture*, mentioned the *spinniker* in a description of a race on 15th August, 1866, in which he took part aboard the *Sphinx*. The form *spinnaker* appeared first in the *Yachting Magazine* for September 1866.

Authority is lent to this timing of the origin by Admiral Smyth's 744 page *Sailor's Word Book*. First published in London in 1867, it makes no mention of either *niobe* or *spinniker*, yet we have two instances of the latter appearing in print in 1866. This leads one to suppose that the word had not found common usage by the publication of the dictionary in the following year. It must therefore have only just started its life at this time.

In the years before the introduction of the spinnaker, a square sail and a square topsail, or raffee, were used. Sometimes a large jib was hoisted on a block half-way up the topmast, and was boomed out by the tack if the rules allowed it. These large jibs were not generally allowed, however, until 1865. In that year the Royal Thames Yacht Club rescinded the rule which read:

> ... but no jib to exceed 2 ft in the head, nor to be hoisted above the mainmast head (*i.e. from the topmast*), neither shall it be boomed out.

Development

Since then, of course, great strides have been made. Early spinnakers were asymmetrical and straight sided, mainly due to the influence of using large jibs for the task. These were cut of light cotton with the cloths running parallel to the leech; they were set inside the forestay. The fashion persisted until the late 1920s, when thought was given to making spinnakers symmetrical. The first such sails were made at Ratsey & Lapthorn's New York branch in 1927, and the first one in England was made by the same firm's Gosport branch, to the order of Mr Sven Salen, for his 6 metre *Maybe*.

Development of this kind usually starts in the smaller classes, because it is cheaper to experiment. 6 metres were small boats in those days, but before long most of the International classes were using spinnakers which had the same luff and leech, and which were wide enough to set round the forestay. The newly started International One Design class, however, thought the idea novel enough to include in their rules in 1936:

> ... spinnakers may be carried around the jibstay and sheets may be trimmed outside the shrouds.

The newer sails were made in two halves, joined vertically down the middle, with nearly straight stays and most of the shape built into the centre seam. Sail Makers laid the cloths parallel to the leeches, which gave an acute angled inverted V shape when seen from ahead or astern. The angle in the middle varied slightly, but it was not until M. Herbulot of France widened it so that the cloths struck the leeches at quite an appreciable angle, that any great change was achieved. By this time, however, development had advanced apace and the new cut only enjoyed a short vogue before it was superseded by further improvements.

Originally it was enough to control the lengths of the three sides of the spinnaker, but the new rounded sails had a good deal more area. The rule had to change if it was to remain a fair one. There are three basic types of spinnaker rule today.

One-design Rule

The first requires that the sail be symmetrical and made with straight seams, i.e. no broad seam is allowed. It so closely limits the maximum and minimum dimensions at several predetermined points (usually seven at least), and the tolerances are so small, that all spinnakers to a particular rule are the same shape if folded in half about their centre, when they are required to lie substantially flat on the floor. The only way a Sail Maker can influence the shape of such a sail is by laying the cloths at varying angles, which in turn affects the degree of localized stretch. The Dragon is an example of this rule.

Restricted Rule

The second classification is one where the length of the stays (luff and leech), the length of the foot and the maximum width of the sail at any point are all limited. This gives a maximum size for the sail, within which the shape may be varied at will. There is often also a minimum width at half height to prevent a spinnaker being cut so flat that it virtually becomes an oversize genoa which sneaks in under the spinnaker rule.

The RORC is a good example of this. There was no mention in their rules prior to 1937 of any limit on the spinnaker boom, although there were penalties if the luff or leech was more than 95 per cent of the leading edge of the foretriangle, the foot more than 1·33 ×J and the width at half height more than two-thirds of the permissible width of foot (or 0·88 ×J).

In 1937 the maximum foot was increased to 1·5 ×J and the width at half height to 1·25 ×J. This still produced a sail too narrow to set properly round the forestay. In 1948 a maximum foot and half height of 1·8 ×J was introduced in order to conform with the CCA rule, with a minimum half height width of 75 per cent of the foot;

this is now the IOR requirement. This sets comfortably round the forestay and gives a seamanlike sail which can be handled on the open water.

The IOR limits maximum spinnaker stays without penalty to $0{\cdot}95\sqrt{(I^2+J^2)}$. This is a tedious calculation which Southampton University kindly worked out for me on their computer in 1961 for all values of (I^2+J^2) from 750 to 5,000; this covers spinnaker stays from 25 to 67 ft and I have put the table at Appendix D. All you have to do is to add together the squares of the I and J measurements in feet and decimals of a foot, and then read off the maximum permissible stay length against the appropriate figure in the table.

In 1951 Ted Hood of America, in consultation with Ray Hunt, found that laying the cloths of a 210 Class spinnaker horizontally instead of in an inverted V, helped to broaden the shoulders, because the cloths could be more efficiently tapered at the stay ends in order to hold the shape of the upper half better. This was particularly useful with CCA and RORC spinnakers, and Carleton Mitchell used the first such sail to Bermuda in the following year.

Free Rule

This rule allows whatever sail the owner is courageous enough to set. It may sometimes (but not always) restrict the length of stays and foot, but allows the sail to be as wide as you like above the foot. The rule usually applies to the International classes, and results in sails of all shapes and sizes. In particular, the usual sail is one with a large width at half height.

The seams were laid in the conventional inverted V for many years, but Hard Sails of America turned their attention to the problem a few years after Ted Hood had introduced the horizontal cut. They came up with the spherical spinnaker (also called the orbital in Great Britain). This does away with the central seam, but flattens the middle portion of the sail by trimming off part of the cloths along their length near the middle. The sail can then be made a good deal wider at half height than at the foot, and virtually becomes the greater part of a sphere.

Other Rules

A few classes, particularly in America, permit the half height to be wider than the foot, without allowing complete freedom. If the limits are carefully set, the half height being about 130 to 140 per cent of the foot, a good sail with more natural shaping results.

A second type of rule for the more progressive is one which limits the total perimeter of the sail, measured along the luff, leech and foot, but allows complete freedom within this restriction. This results in all sorts of shapes and sizes, but encourages experiment and is easy to measure.

Cloth

Not until nylon was developed during the Second World War did spinnakers enjoy a change of material from the light cotton out of which they had been made since they started, with the possible exception of one or two silk sails which had been made in the 1930s. *Ranger* used a quadrilateral made of rayon in her 1937 defence of the America's Cup, but this material does not seem to have been used for spinnakers. The advent of Terylene in the 1950s got everybody excited, and for a short while it was thought to be superior to nylon. Spinnakers need to stretch a certain amount, however, and polyester does not have as much elasticity as nylon, which is still the best cloth for this type of sail. It has been shown repeatedly that a low degree of porosity is desirable in spinnaker material. If the cloth passes a lot of air, then it is obviously allowing the pressure to equalize on either side of the sail. Rather than drag the boat through the water and expend its energy in this way, air will choose the line of least resistance and leak pressure through a porous material. A cloth which has a lot of fillers in it will be non-porous to start with, but the chemicals will soon break up to leave the original loose weave; what we require is a tightly woven fine cloth with the minimum of finishing to render it air-tight.

Flow Design

The design of a spinnaker, like any other sail, can be divided into outline design and flow design. Outline design is the sphere of the Naval Architect, who is nearly always bound by rules, so that his influence on the shape of a particular spinnaker is only achieved through alteration of measurements of the yacht which govern the outline of the sail: usually the foretriangle measurements I and J.

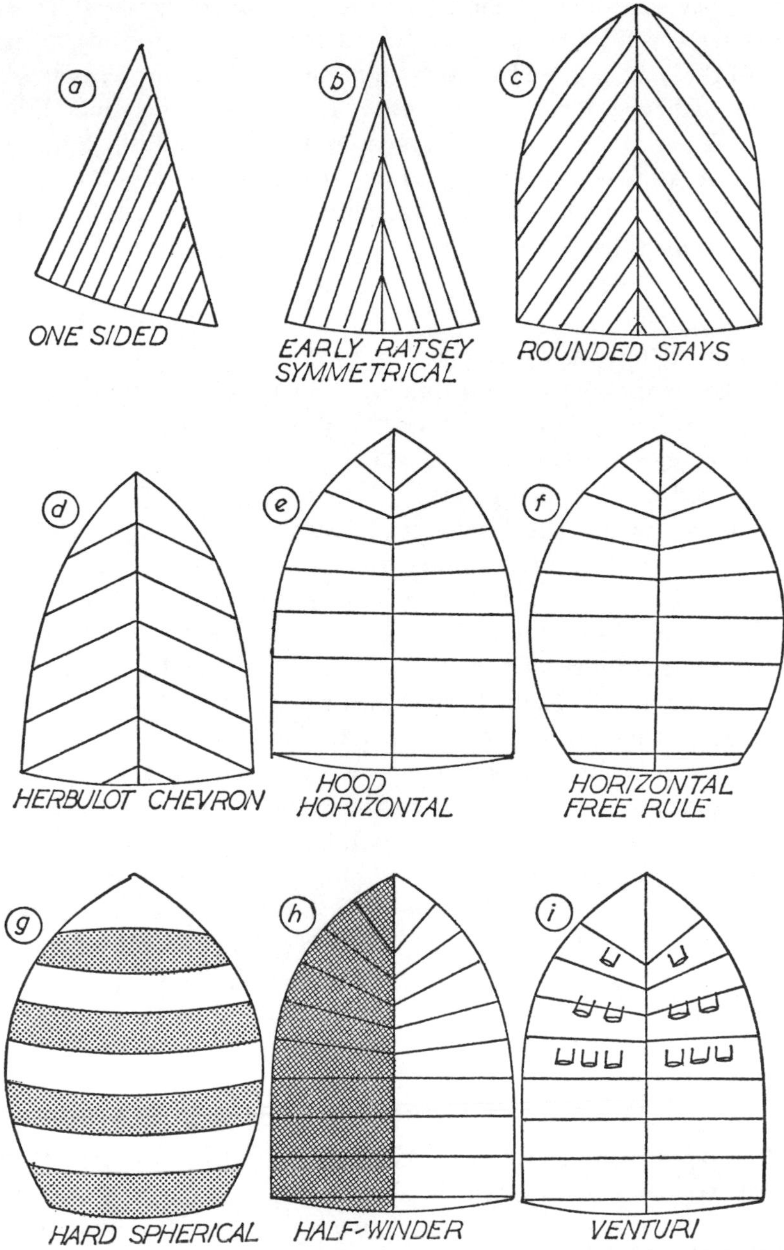

Fig. 71. Some different spinnaker cuts.

In considering flow design we have to understand what happens to the wind in the sail. On a reach it behaves very much as in a headsail, in that it flows across the sail from luff to leech. On a dead run it flows from the centre towards both sides, with a bleed downwards off the foot.

Figures 72 (*a*) and 72 (*b*) represent a flat and a full cut spinnaker on a close reach. The flat cut sail at 72(*a*) shows a fair airflow across

Fig. 72. Airflow round a spinnaker.

the sail, starting with a clean entry. The full cut sail would probably never set because of the angle at which the wind strikes the luff. Even if it did stand all right, the airflow over the sail would be turbulent, because it has first to curve to the right towards the sail, and then sharply to the left again; in addition, the leech returns to windward and offers the same disadvantages as a curling leech on a genoa.

Figures 72(*c*) and 72(*d*) show the same effect on a run. Figure 72(*c*) allows the air to reach the surface of the sail and then divide each way, thus spreading the stays and achieving maximum area presented to the wind. Figure 72(*d*) has a pocket of dead air in the depth of its centre, and the turbulence associated with this merely serves to disturb the free flow of air towards the stays; the sail will therefore be narrower in the head than 72(*c*).

It follows that old-fashioned ideas about very full cut spinnakers have to be re-examined and more flatness achieved, particularly in the head where the stays are most tender to a reaching wind. This calls for skill on the part of the Sail Maker, as he tries to keep the springy nylon from stretching into too much of a Roman nose. He achieves his aim by subtle manipulation of the cloth, and by tapering each seam with a mathematically calculated precision. Each Sail Maker has his own secrets in this respect and you can see more cloths in some spinnakers than in a patchwork quilt, with each one probably having a ¼ in. or so of broad seam carefully shaped at some point in its length. They all have their day, as a new vogue appears, but the horizontal cut sail takes a good deal of beating for all round use, as it offers advantages regarding reduction of bias stretch and presents suitable seams to taper, as we shall see shortly.

The drawings at figure 71 are the conventional way of showing a spinnaker graphically, that is to say seen from head-on. This method, however, cannot give any indication of the fullness of a particular sail, which must be presumed to bulge out of the paper towards the reader to an unknown degree. Short of a three-dimensional illustration, therefore, we have to turn elsewhere if we want to have a proper idea of the shape we are trying to imagine.

Since a spinnaker is usually symmetrical about its vertical line, a Sail Maker lays out the sail in two halves when cutting it. He therefore has to draw the left or right half of the sail full-size on the floor, and this is how we must envisage the sail on paper. It means a fresh mental approach to the problem, but the result is easier to envisage when this has been mastered.

Restricted Rule Spinnakers

Let us therefore examine a spinnaker to the maximum size under the IOR; figure 71 (*e*) shows such a sail in the conventional manner. In that drawing the leeches appear to be a good deal longer than the middle seam which bisects the sail vertically. In fact, however, they are shorter, as a glance at the correct drawing at figure 73 will show.

The central seam is sewn together, all the way up to the head, to give a three-dimensional shape. The dotted line represents a sail which is full in the head, and the broken line is a flat one. A medium sail lies somewhere between these two extremes, and will usually have an angle at the head of the half sail somewhere between 68° and 75°. For the IOR, our typical spinnaker will be rectangular from the foot up to a point about 55 to 60 per cent of the hoist (or stay, as it is known). This achieves full size in the lower half of the sail, and any

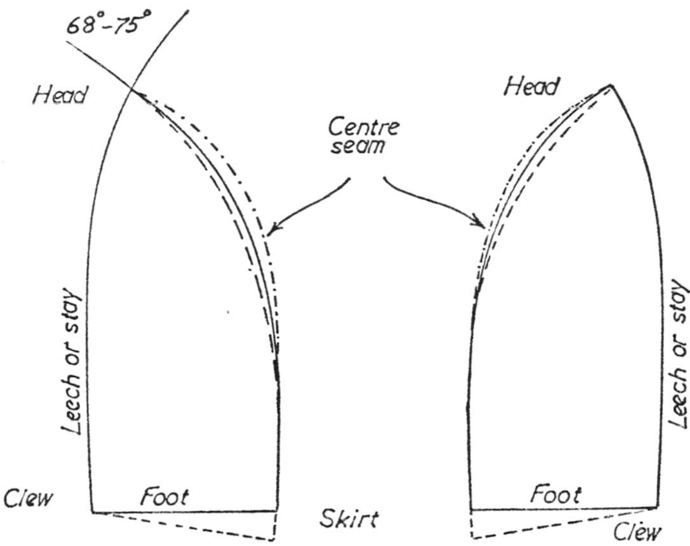

Fig. 79. Spinnaker laid out in two halves.

attempt to take it higher up must usually be at the expense of reaching properties. Spinnakers have been made where the curve in to the head does not start until nearly three-quarters of the way up the stays, but they will only set on a dead run, and then usually only in force 2 (which is enough to fill the sail, but not too much to cause it to oscillate).

The curve at the head is not the only way in which draft can be given to a spinnaker; as with fore and aft sails, the cloths can be tapered to increase or decrease the basic flow imparted by the outline shape. There are some classes which prohibit this tapering or broad seam in the interests of uniformity (the Dragon is an example), but they are getting sails which are not as efficient as they might be. The correct draft is further complicated by the fact that an efficient sail does not only depend on draft, but also on the area it offers to the wind when it is set. Thus a very full spinnaker, with a lot of area and draft in the head, will probably blow forward in the middle at the top and become narrow. This will certainly happen in light airs because there will not be enough wind to spread the sail properly; in heavy winds the top will most likely fill with too much air and this will become stagnant, destroying the smooth flow of air across the surface of the sail, thus promoting oscillation.

Nylon obeys the same laws as Terylene or Dacron in that it will distort its maximum if tension is applied on the 45° bias to the threadline. This becomes progressively less as the angle is reduced, although the light nature of the cloth means that there will always be a certain amount of give, even on the threadline itself. This inherent elasticity, which is more than that of the equivalent weight of polyester, means that the cloth should be woven with little or no twist in the thread if threadline stretch is to be kept as low as possible This in turn will mean slower weaving, and greater likelihood of thread breakage in the process, but it is the price which has to be paid for the best material.

Consequently, the Sail Maker has to make up his mind how he is going to lay out his panels for a particular spinnaker, what broad seam he is going to give them to achieve the shape he has in mind, and which seams will be tightened at the leech to compensate for the bias stretch he expects to encounter. The stresses in a spinnaker run throughout the sail, radiating from the corners so, no matter how the cloths are laid, bias stretch will result somewhere. The problem is greatest of course, with a large sail where the loads are considerable; the dinghy spinnaker gets away with it much better.

Broadly speaking, we want to keep stretch at the edges to the minimum so that the stays and foot will not be slack and inefficient, whereas we can accept a certain amount of stretch towards the middle of the sail. It is best, therefore, if the cloths are laid with the warp or the weft lying parallel to the stays. In figure 71(*b*) above, I have shown the old-fashioned double sided spinnaker, where the stays were straight; this sail could, and did, have the cloths running parallel to the stays. But leeches are not often straight these days and, as with the roach to the leech of a mainsail, the best way in which the Sail Maker can keep the threadline parallel to them is to lay the cloths at rightangles to the leeches, and concentrate on lining up the weft with the tension down the stays. The clew often forms a rightangle, so this means that the threadline will also be parallel to the foot.

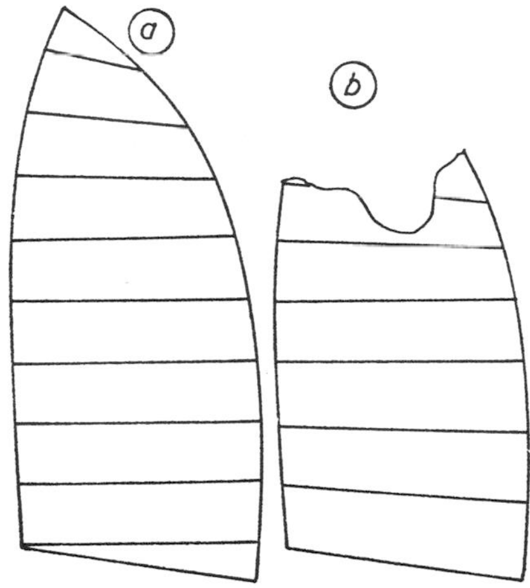

Fig. 74. Fitting a skirt to a spinnaker.
(a) A wedge added to the foot would bring too much bias.
(b) Cloths should be gradually tripped round to keep bias low.

Where a skirt, or additional piece is desired at the foot, the cloths will have to come off the threadline somewhere. If a piece were simply added on, as in the dotted line at figure 73, the selvedge could be allowed to run along the foot, but there would be a clash of stretch factors where the bias of the bottom wedge-shaped cloth was joined to the selvedge of the one above it. This would give rise to an ugly and inefficient ridge along the skirt. Accordingly we have to trip the cloths gradually round so that minimum bias is joined to minimum bias, until we have reached the threadline again (figure 74(*b*)). The slight bias at the clew can be accepted, as the wire or tape will hold it in check; indeed a little controlled bias is sometimes desirable to keep the stays from curling through tightness.

As we have seen above, some rules stipulate that the half sail shall 'lie substantially flat on the floor', and that all seams except the one down the middle, shall be straight. This precludes any further shape or fullness being added by the Sail Maker. On the other hand, many rules allow him to do this. Tapering the cloths at the end which lies in the body of the sail will have the effect of throwing fullness into each half and flattening the middle, which we have seen is what we are interested in doing. Alternatively one or two darts can be put into the sail at rightangles to the central seam, where they will have more effect due to their more efficient angle with the centre.

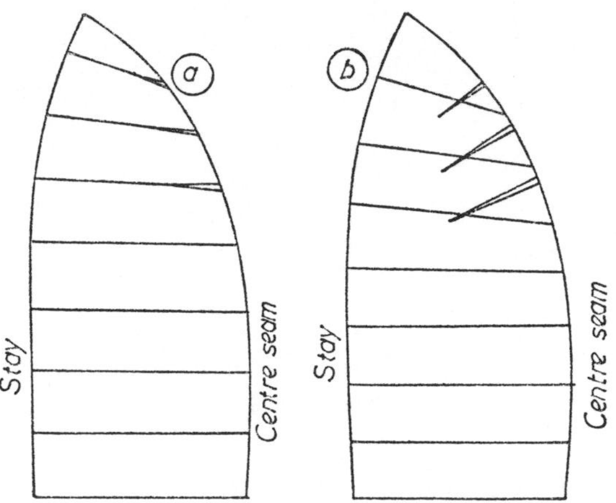

Fig. 75. Broad seam in spinnakers.
(a) Six inches taken out, along the natural lay of each of the top three cloths.
(b) The same amount of broad seam taken out in three darts at rightangles to the centre seam.

In figure 75(*a*) above the cloths have been tapered at the centre seam, but it will be seen that the resultant flattening will be achieved more at a slanted angle than might be fully efficient. If darts are put into the sail as in figure 75(*b*), they can be placed in the direction where they will do the most good. A combination of the two systems is sometimes the best solution The length and direction of the broad seam and /or darts, as well as the degree, are a matter for each Sail Maker to decide in the light of his experience and the type of sail which is required. He must remember, however, that the more broad seam he puts in, the more will the head of the sail be pulled over as the cloth is cut away.

A second point in theory of construction which might prove advantageous, but which has not been sufficiently put to the test, is to try and shift the centre of effort of an IOR spinnaker nearer to the

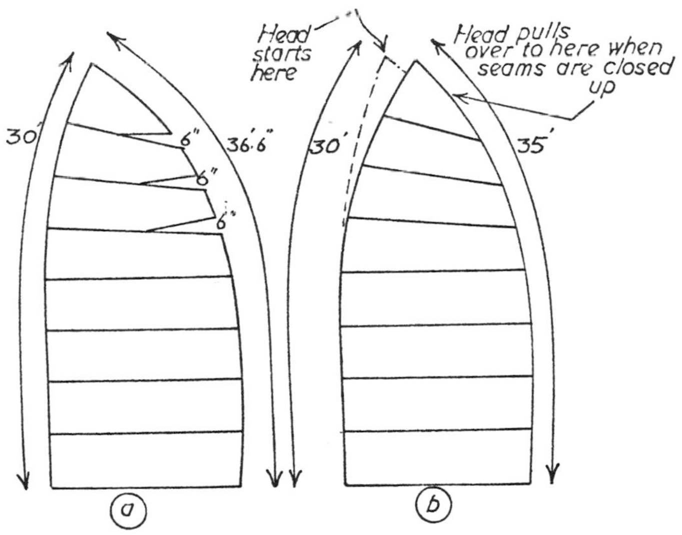

Fig. 76. How broad seam pulls the head of a spinnaker towards the centre seam.

outer end of the spinnaker pole. This can be done if a small amount of area is surrendered. It may well be shown that the sacrifice is worth it. To illustrate the idea, I have to revert to showing the full sail in frontal plan in figure 77.

If the sail is cut away at the shaded area, it will then move its clews from A to B. This will mean that the whole sail will shift further outboard on the pole, which will disengage it from the mainsail. The slight loss in area may be more than offset by a greater efficiency. This is a matter for trial and experiment, and is really a move towards the orbital spinnaker as we shall see below.

Area. The area of a restricted rule spinnaker can be taken as that of the full rectangle formed by the stays and the foot, minus 10 per cent for the area lost by the curve at the head.

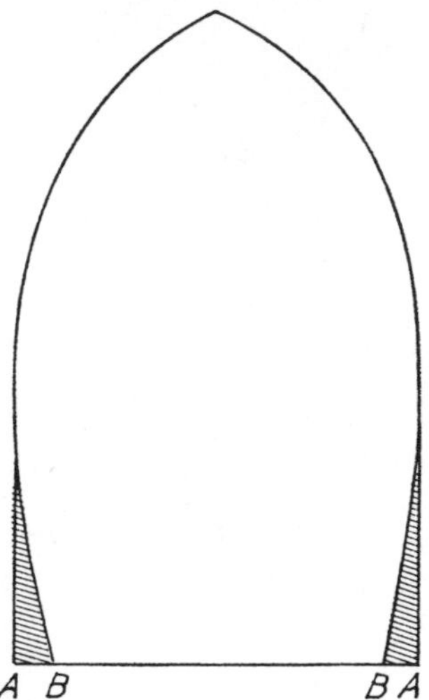

Fig. 77. Tapering a spinnaker at the clews in order to shift the centre of effort near to the outer end of the spinnaker pole.

Orbital Spinnakers

Orbital spinnakers are the result of the free rule, which does not limit the cross measurement of the sail above the foot. The rule sometimes restricts the length of the stays and the foot, but in any case a practical limit is imposed by the length of the sail which will set from the spinnaker halyard sheave without falling in the water in light airs, and by the width of foot which can conveniently be set on a particular pole. The effective limits for these two distances are approximately the same length as the I measurement for the stays, and two and a half times the spinnaker pole length for the foot (although dinghies can go up to about three times the spinnaker pole for the foot of a spinnaker, where the pole is not longer than about 5 ft). Once the foot is under control on the pole, however, the sail can widen out above it to achieve greater area, providing it is cut correctly. Hard Sails Inc. pioneered the way in 1955, and most free rule spinnakers have been cut that way ever since.

The centrefold of the half sail is approximately the arc of a circle, whose radius is found by an exact calculation which is the secret of each Sail Maker. Some modification may be made to this rule of thumb, such as flattening the curve at the head, but the sail is based on the circle conception.

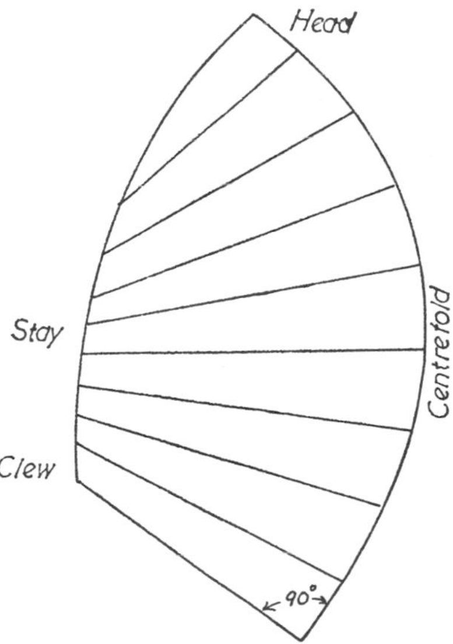

Fig. 78. Orbital spinnaker. The cloths strike the centrefold at right-angles and fold back upon themselves to form the other half of the sail. This results in excessive bias at the stays, which must be held in check by tightening the seams in a series of short 'nips'.

It is also usual to make orbital spinnakers with cloths running exactly horizontal in the middle of the sail, so that appropriate broad seam can be most efficiently incorporated. This means that the cloths strike the centrefold of the sail at rightangles, and therefore that the central seam is superfluous because the cloths can be folded back upon themselves during the cutting out stage, to form the other half of the sail. This in turn means that the angle formed by the foot and the centrefold of the sail in the middle of the foot must be a rightangle, if the foot is to be on the threadline. This is desirable, but not essential, if stretch is to be kept down.

In order that the rather wide and full sail shall not have too deep a horizontal section in the middle, a good deal of cloth has to be taken out of the panels in the form of broad seam, to flatten the sail in the right places. This, coupled with the natural wastage where two cloths overlap as they are tripped round at the head, makes this a rather more expensive cut than the conventional centre seam sail.

The disadvantage of this cut is that the cloths strike the stays at an angle, which is particularly marked at the head. This means that the luff and leech will be subjected to stretch at the head, where it is least wanted, and therefore steps have to be taken to tighten the necessary seams in order to control the situation. The result would

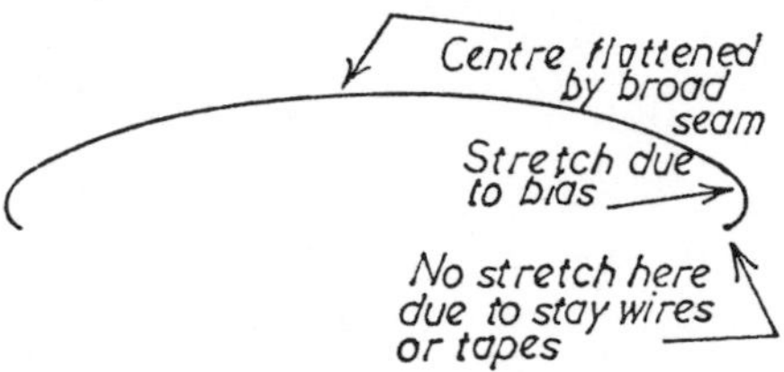

Fig. 79. Section through orbital spinnaker not tightened at the stays.

otherwise be curling leeches, for the very edge of the sail would not stretch where the wire or tape held it in check, but the cloth immediately inside it would stretch, to give a section as in figure 79.

Area. The area of an orbital spinnaker is hard to assess, as it depends so much on the mid-girth width. A rough guide is to take the area of the rectangle which would be formed by the stays and the foot, and then to add 10 per cent for the extra area (i.e. rather more than 20 per cent larger than the calculation for the restricted rule sail).

Combined Horizontal/Orbital Spinnakers

The horizontal cut has the disadvantage that the cloths strike the centre seam at an angle, thus presenting cloths which are not running in the right direction for broad seam to have its full effect. The orbital cut has the opposite disadvantage that the cloths strike the stays at a sharp angle, thus being open to excessive stretch. It would appear that the way is open to a compromise, employing the advantages of both systems and avoiding their drawbacks. This, in fact, is what has been done by several firms, with varying results.

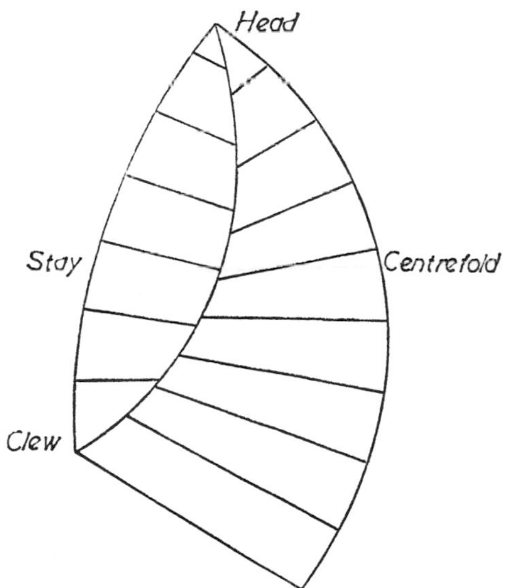

Fig. 80. Combination orbital and horizontal spinnaker. Cloths are laid at rightangles to both stays and centrefold, with a curved mitre at their join.

The middle portion of the sail is cut with cloths striking the centre line at rightangles, while separate pieces are added at the wings so that the cloths are at rightangles to the stays. Broad seam and tightening can be added as required. In theory this gives the best possibility of achieving the correct shape, and the American Roller spinnaker is among those based on this idea.

Cloth Weight

Once again I must emphasize the importance of a proper appreciation of the limitations of various cloth weights. It has taken a long time for a true realization of the part played by sails to become widespread; too often the spinnaker lags behind.

A heavy weather spinnaker may weigh three times as much per

square yard of cloth as a light weather sail, so the former should not be expected to fill in a force 1 wind. Perhaps more important, a light weather spinnaker should no more be used in a force 4 wind than should a light genoa; unlike the light genoa, which might only blow out of shape, the spinnaker will almost certainly burst. This is particularly true if it is used on a reach, where the relative wind is greater than on a run. Reference to the formula $W = 0{\cdot}004V^2A$ on page 35 will show that an apparent wind of 25 m.p.h. will exert an average pressure of 2·5 lbs per sq. ft on the effective sail area presented; this means over a ton in a sail of 900 sq. ft. A wind of 35 m.p.h. will produce the same weight in a sail half the size.

Gear

Spinnaker gear must be studied carefully if the foredeck gang is expected to put up fast times. The gear itself must be simple and strong, and must be partly tailored around the gybing technique. This in turn may be influenced by the preference of the owner and the hand in charge of the spinnaker, if the boat is lucky enough to have a permanent man.

Pole. The advantage of a double-ended pole is that it can be plugged in either end. Its disadvantage is that it cannot therefore have the ideal outer end fitting, which would make it too bulky to go into the spinnaker cup. The final selection will be influenced by the gybing technique and the rig, as we shall see later, because a single pole gybe on a cutter demands a double-ended pole, while a similar gybe on a sloop allows a single-ended pole to be used. At all events, take care to see that all end attachments are sufficiently robust for their task and simple to operate (they may have to work under pressure in the dark).

Hoisting. Spinnakers always used to be hoisted in stops, or straight from the deck if the weather was light. These are still good methods, and a stopped sail is often used in large yachts, particularly in heavy weather, as it keeps the sail under full control as it goes up. The modern tendency, however, is to hoist from some sort of special bag or turtle made for the purpose. I shall go more fully into various forms of spinnaker stowage in Chapter XV. It is enough here to say that some device is needed for stowing the spinnaker neatly, while at the same time having it ready to hoist at a moment's notice.

The secret in most systems is not to waste time while it is going up, but to haul away with a will. The sheet should be trimmed as the sail goes up, but not too much or too soon, or else the spinnaker will fill early and be hard to get up the final few feet.

Winches. Winches must not only be powerful enough for their task, but they must also be sited where they can be brought into use without interfering with the smooth running of the boat. Considerable thought is needed in this planning, which is closely linked with the system of gybing which it is proposed to adopt. Let me merely say here that winches should be powerful enough to wind the pole off the forestay in a stiff reaching wind, when the mechanical advantage

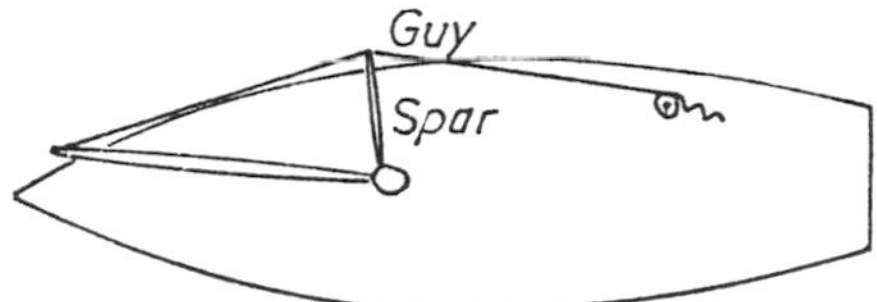

Fig. 81. Spinnaker guy bearing out spar.

is low due to the narrow angle of the guy. It is also useful if the spinnaker does not have to rely entirely on both genoa winches, as the leeward one may certainly be wanted while the spinnaker sheet is on it; this becomes progressively more important with size, and at 30 ft L W L and over it is essential to have a total of four sheet winches at least.

Sheets and Guys. On boats up to 24 ft L W L, both sheets and guys can be of three strand polyester rope. Above this size, if the boat is raced seriously, the spinnaker boom guy should be of wire with a rope tail, because the stretch in a rope will allow the pole to move forward too much under pressure – particularly on a reach when this movement is most likely to spoil the set of the sail. Generally speaking, the sheet should be led through a fairlead on the counter, but there is nothing to stop the guy leading farther forward. In boats where one rope doubles for guy and sheet, according to which side the pole is shipped, the guy will also lead to the counter. On larger yachts, which may use a sheet and a guy on each clew, the guy will probably lead somewhere amidships.

Bearing-out Spar. Many rules, including the IOR, allow a short spar to be used to bear out on the guy where it rubs the shrouds when reaching. This not only frees the guy from the effects of chafe, but also increases its mechanical advantage, and is thoroughly recommended.

CHAPTER XIV

Using a Spinnaker

When sailing dead before the wind, the object of a spinnaker is to present the greatest area of sail to undisturbed wind, so that maximum drag is achieved; the boat will thus be blown downwind. To do this, sufficient cloth must be in the sail in the first place, and it must be so shaped that the air flows outwards from the middle to spread the stays as far apart as possible. So we are not entirely concerned with drag pure and simple, even when the wind is right aft.

When sailing on a reach, the airflow round the spinnaker changes from one which blows into the middle and out of each side, to one which passes horizontally across the sail from luff to leech. The object here switches from the dead run case to one more allied to the function of a headsail: the airflow must be changed into forward thrust through the pressure differential pattern we examined in Chapter II. The spinnaker's principal advantage over a conventional headsail in these circumstances lies in its greater area. Although it is acting exactly like a headsail, it does not have the advantage of a headsail's straight luff, flat flow or straight leech; quite the contrary, it has a sagging luff, deep section and a leech which returns to windward to a marked degree when judged by headsail standards, even if the spinnaker is flat by its own criteria. We have to be more than ever on our guard, therefore, to see that the wind is not deflected too much into the lee of the mainsail, and that the component of the spinnaker's thrust is as forward acting as possible.

We should remember, therefore, in reading the rest of this chapter, that for most of the time a spinnaker is set we are dealing with the equivalent of a very large, full headsail which is set without the advantage of a straight luff. Only on limited occasions when the wind is within a 5° to 10° arc either side of dead astern are we concerned with drag as a prime requirement.

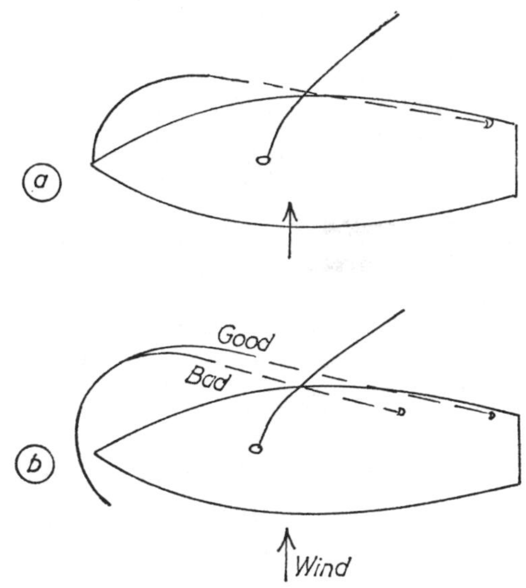

Fig. 82. Backwinding on a reach.
(a) A headsail will almost always give a less efficient airflow with the wind abeam and broader.
(b) The spinnaker should be sheeted to the counter to keep the slot as wide as possible.

The first consideration with using a spinnaker is often whether to use it at all. There are occasions, particularly on a close reach, when the sail will fill and draw, but when another sail would be more efficient. The governing factors are apparent wind angle and strength, and the type of sail which is available as an alternative. If the spinnaker is strapped alongside, so that there is almost as much thrust aft as forward, it will only serve to heel the boat and slow her down, possibly giving rise to a broach. On the other hand, it may be that the sail is contributing to forward speed, but only marginally. In this case it would possibly not pay to take off the sail in, say, a Soling where the alternative is a headsail which is less than a sixth of the size of the spinnaker, yet it might easily pay in one of the ocean-racing fleet, where the spinnaker is only two to two and a half times the size of the largest headsail.

As a rough guide we can make a quick rule of thumb, for use in medium winds, which says that a properly cut spinnaker can be carried with advantage in apparent winds five degrees forward of the beam, for each amount by which the spinnaker is larger than the headsail which would replace it. Thus, if the spinnaker to headsail ratio is six or seven to one (as large a difference as is usually met), the larger sail will pay dividends with the apparent wind up to 35° forward of the beam. As the wind strength increases, the headsail's advantage is correspondingly increased also. A star-cut genniker or spanker gains another 10° or 15°. A ratio of three or four to one brings the angle down to 15° or 20°, because anything further forward would mean that the moderately large headsail could drive her better.

Trim

'The most important single factor in proper spinnaker trim is the positioning of the spinnaker pole.'

This was said by Stephen van Dyck, spinnaker trimmer in *Constellation* for the 1964 America's Cup defence, writing in *Yachting World* back in July 1965. There are not many who would disagree with him.

Pole Angle. The object of trim is to get the spinnaker to spread as broad as possible, high and wide into air undisturbed by other sails or spars and rigging, and to develop maximum forward thrust. To achieve this the sail must be extended as far from the mast as possible across the direction of the apparent wind, when seen in plan view.

This means that the pole should normally be at rightangles to the apparent wind, as figure 83 will show. A vertical elevation of the pole under the same conditions shows that it should also be at right-angles to the mast to achieve the same effect in this plane.

In both cases the tack is then allowing the sail to stand as far as possible from the mast, in order to collect the most undisturbed air.

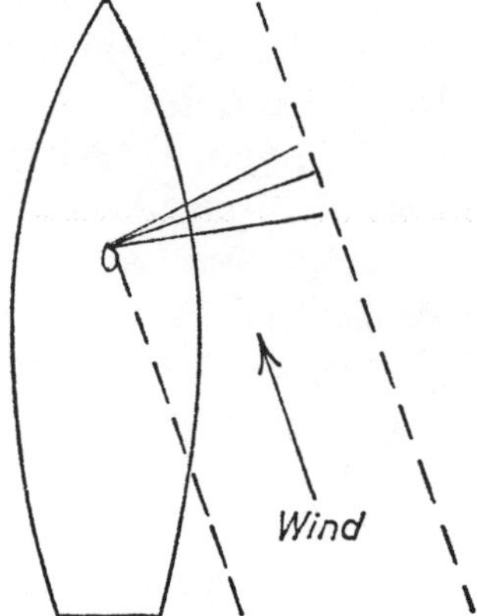

Fig. 83. Pole angle. Maximum distance in plan view across the wind from the mast.

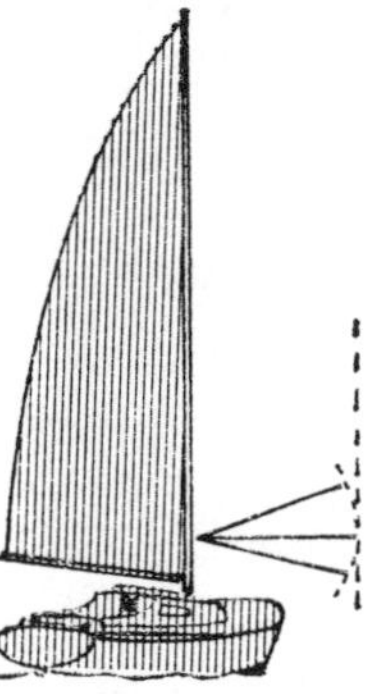

Fig. 84. Pole angle. Maximum distance in elevation across the wind from the mast.

Naturally, a small angle of difference from the optimum will not affect the issue very much, and other considerations of trim may require a slight deviation from 90°. As soon as the pole strays from the rightangle by more than about 15°, however, the percentage loss of tack offset goes up rapidly.

I recall racing a Dragon in Cowes Week one year. I was fortunate enough to have the spinnaker hand from the American yawl *Bolero* on board, while the latter was undergoing repairs after hitting an uncharted underwater obstruction. Needless to say, I gave him charge of the spinnaker, although he assured me that he had never been in a Dragon before. We were running eastwards up the Solent in perfect conditions lying third about twenty-five yards behind *Nortic*, where we had been keeping exact station for about five minutes.

'Give me an inch of pole,' called my spinnaker trimmer, and we gave him exactly that. Immediately the relative speeds changed and we slowly started to creep up on the boat ahead. I am afraid that I cannot recount a tale of crushing victory, for *Nortic* soon spotted us and restored the *status quo*, but the lesson was graphic.

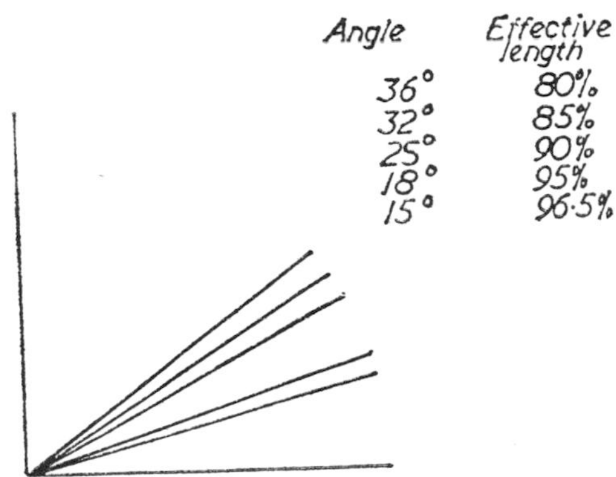

Angle
Effective length
36°
32°
25°
18°
15°
80%
85%
90%
95%
96·5%

Fig. 85. Pole angle. Percentage of effective length for different angles offset from rightangle.

The illustration at figure 85 shows how the effective length of the pole varies according to its angular displacement from the optimum. In fact, the effective length lessens by the cosine of the angle of displacement.

At 18° up or down from a rightangle, or aft or forward for that matter, the pole is 5 per cent in from its maximum; at 25° this increases to 10 per cent, and at 36° it is as much as 20 per cent. The moral of this is obviously not to let the pole be more than 10° to 15° off the rightangle at any time.

Pole Height. The height of the pole must also be settled. Basically, the aim is to see that the tack and clew of the spinnaker are the same height above the water; this will ensure that the sail, being symmetrical, is not twisted into a poor aerodynamic shape. The outer end of the pole must therefore be hoisted to the position where it is estimated that the tack will have to go to keep level with the clew; the inner end should then be raised to ensure that it is at rightangles to the mast, and the pole squared to the apparent wind. The sheet may then be adjusted until the luff is on the point of falling in (more on this later) and the tack and clew compared for height. Any difference should be adjusted by raising or lowering the pole bodily. If the tack is allowed to rise higher than the clew, the leech will tend to twist inwards, close the slot, and backwind the mainsail.

The spinnaker is now in basic trim, and fine adjustment must be made on the sheet.

Exceptions. There are, of course, exceptions to such a broad generalization. In light winds the pole should be squared aft an extra 10° or so, to prevent the upper part of the spinnaker from falling away too much. In heavy winds, the converse is the case, in order to reduce the tendency to roll and to aid in control: it may not always be possible to trim the sheet quickly enough to stop the sail falling in, so a little in hand will help here.

Similarly, the pole should be kept low in winds of force 2 or less, in order to straighten the luff and to reduce the amount of sail which has to be lifted before it fills. It may then be slowly raised as the sail fills and the free clew lifts. In these circumstances pole angle is important, in order to catch as much air as possible, but height of pole (and thus aerodynamic shape) takes second place to the importance of getting the sail to fill at all.

A final exception concerns the height of the inner end of the pole in large yachts when close reaching. If it is allowed to be lower than the outer end (which will be near the forestay), a reduction in strain will result, as the pole will be more nearly in the same plane as the afterguy. The topping lift will then only have to counterbalance the foreguy, and will not be fighting the afterguy as well.

Sheet. We have already seen that we want the spinnaker to develop as much forward thrust as possible (F_T spin, to revert to the symbols adopted in Chapter II). This means that the sail, regardless of the pole position, should be trimmed so that it presents its arc facing as fully forward as possible. To achieve this the clew should be abreast of the tack when reference is made across the boat [figure 86(*b*)].

Naturally, it is not possible to achieve this neck and neck situation when the boat is other than on a broad reach or run. A simple rule can be stated for sheet trim: ease the sheet until the luff starts to fall in at the head, then harden it so that the sail is just on the quiver. In very light winds it seems to pay to ease the sheet rather more than usual; in heavy winds it may be better to harden it a

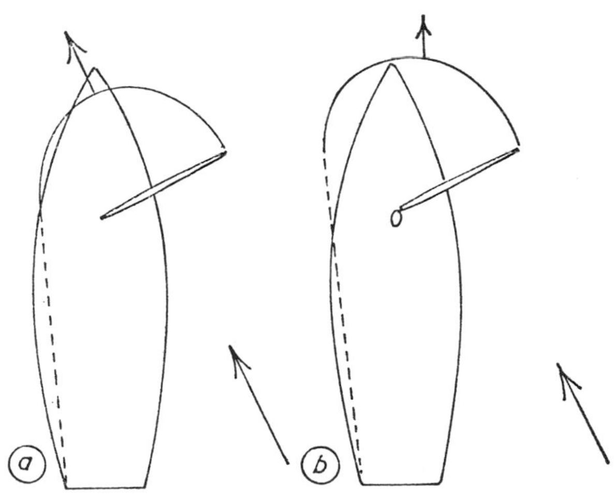

Fig. 86. Plan view of spinnaker trim.
(a) Sheeted too tightly; some thrust to leeward.
(b) Sheet eased until clew is level with tack. Total thrust from spinnaker is forward.

little more, so that sudden puffs do not cause the sail to fall in. This knife edge balance demands the utmost concentration and speed on the sheet. If the sail collapses in light winds it may take quite a long time to re-establish it.

Here let me say that Stephen van Dyck's dictum that there should be only one man in charge of trimming the spinnaker is worthy of more than the lip-service it all too often receives. A soviet of opinion is all very well, indeed it is to be encouraged for many a good suggestion will come of it, but there must be only one man who collates all the information, both visual and aural, together with the possible courses of action, and who then translates this into executive instructions to the crew.

Let me repeat here that the sheet should be led to the counter, in order to keep the leech of the spinnaker as far from the mainsail as possible. It pays to let the sheet pass over the outer end of the main boom on a broad reach, as this opens the slot still more, but take care not to let it ride too high or it will hook the mainsail to windward. Many boats have a travelling sheave under the main boom, so that the spinnaker sheet can be hauled out to the best position; this also helps to combat chafe.

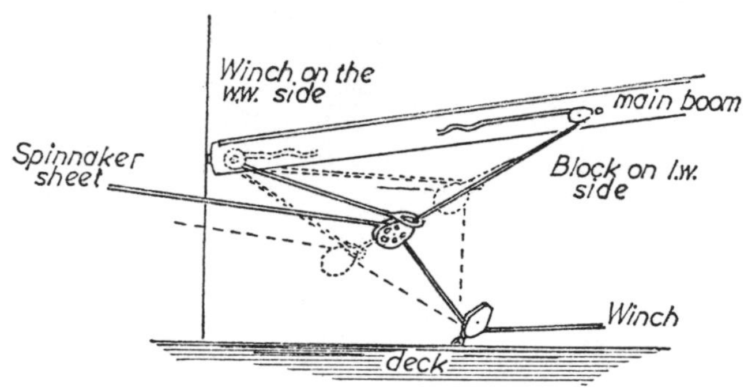

Fig. 87. Measures taken by *Windrose* in the 1960 transatlantic race, to prevent chafe on the spinnaker sheet against the main boom.

Corny Shields has written some wise words on spinnakers, not least of which is his generalization on trimming. He says, quite rightly, that it is in light to moderate weather that correct trimming pays the greatest dividends. When the wind is really blowing, your boat soon reaches her maximum hull speed, so the finer points are wasted. He goes on to say that a spinnaker should, however, be hoisted whenever practicable, because there are always lulls which would cause a drop below maximum speed without it. Both he and van Dyck are unanimous in recommending that the sheet be trimmed hard in hard weather because of the difficulty of reacting quickly enough in the gusts. In addition it can sometimes help to lessen rhythmic rolling if the sheet is hardened and led further forward in the boat, say to a strong point at the chain plates. I would like to add a warning here against strapping the sail too closely alongside, thus causing the boat to heel excessively to an inefficient underwater shape.

Halyards. In winds up to force 3, the spinnaker should be hoisted hard up. Above this, it may be eased at the head with advantage, particularly when reaching. The amount of drift varies with different boats, ranging from 6 to 12 in. on a dinghy, to 5 to 6 ft on the larger yachts, depending also on wind strength. This has the effect of disengaging the sail from the interference of the mainsail. An eye should be kept on the lower quarter of the sail, to see that it does not cause it to slope too much back towards the boat, thus burying her nose. Remember that, by virtue of two of its attachment points being at the stern and the masthead, a spinnaker has a natural tendency to push the bow down – despite what many people say to the contrary.

A slightly eased halyard will serve as a good indication of the direction of pull of the sail. If the head falls well off to leeward, the thrust is inefficient and you should start thinking in terms of a genoa if the spinnaker cannot be trimmed to better advantage. If the sail is pulling well forward, then you have done your job well. On occasions it can move out to windward, and this means that the sail is exposing more area to undisturbed wind, so it is also a good sign.

Gybing

I do not want to become too involved in spinnaker techniques, for the only way really to become proficient in handling them is to practise – first of all on a calm day, then in rougher weather, and finally in a good blow at night. Gybing, however, offers one of the more absorbing ways of losing or winning races, so a few words may be pertinent, particularly if an improved technique can save a sail being torn.

Single Pole (Single Ended)

Most boats up to 24 ft water-line length have only one spinnaker pole. The spinnaker will be small enough to allow one rope to double as both sheet and guy, and the pole will be either single- or double-ended. If the boat is a sloop, with a clear foretriangle through which the pole can dip while still attached to the mast, the pole may be single-ended, and gybing is a matter of allowing it to swing forward, unclipping it from the tack of the spinnaker, dipping it past the forestay and clipping on to the new tack. This technique can be used with any sized spinnaker, if the pole will pass through the foretriangle. The only difference made by size is that beyond a water-line length of about 24 ft, particularly if the boat is raced seriously, the guy needs to be made of wire for proper control. This means that each clew of the spinnaker has to have both a rope sheet and a wire guy attached to it, and one of them is 'lazy' while on the run (although it may be called into use to help relieve the strain during the actual gybing operation).

Single Pole (No Foredeck Hand)

I am indebted to *Yachts and Yachting* for their permission to republish an article and drawing published in November 1962, from material supplied by Jack Knights. This describes the O'Day spinnaker gybe system, which does away with the need for a foredeck hand.

'Primary object of the arrangement is to enable the gybing manoeuvre to be carried out – in moderate to fresh winds – entirely from the cockpit, so doing away with the need for a man on the foredeck to see to the unsnatching of the old guy and the snatching in of the new.

'The sketch [at figure 88] is fairly self-explanatory and shows the wire guy and rope sheet attached to either clew of the spinnaker. Wire rather than rope is used for the guy as this must have the minimum amount of stretch if the spinnaker boom end is to be positioned at all accurately when the sail is set on a reach. Often a rope tail is spliced to the wire to make for easier working round the winches when under load.

'At no time are the sheet, guy or clew of the spinnaker made fast to the outboard end of the spinnaker boom. The sheets are taken direct to their leads, but the guys are treated differently. Taking the starboard guy, it is led from the clew of the sail, through a very free-running lead in the outboard end of the spinnaker boom and then back down the starboard side outside the shrouds. The port guy is rove off the same way down the port side. When in use the spinnaker boom is positioned horizontally by a lift and downhaul which are not shown in the sketch for reasons of clarity.

'Two situations are shown in the drawing: the heavy line shows the sail set to port while the lighter line shows the state in mid-gybe, when the spinnaker is flying free from both sheets while the boom is being dipped under the forestay before being hauled out to the new clew.

'Once the guys have been snatched in their leads on the boom end, the boom set up on its lift and the sail hoisted, the appropriate clew is hauled to the boom end by taking up the slack in the wire guy it is

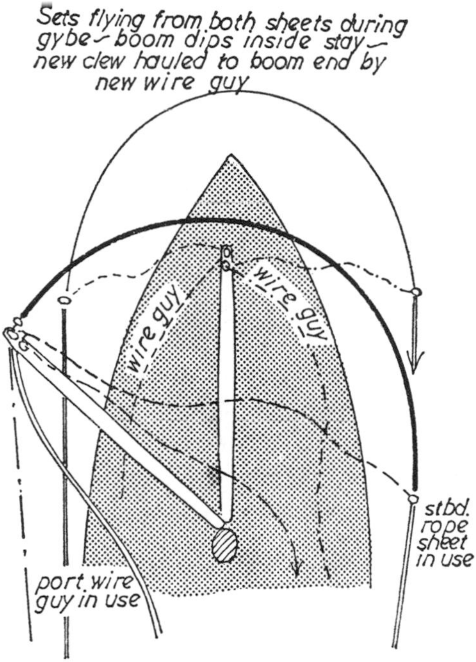

Fig. 88. The O'Day spinnaker gybe system.

intended to use – in the first situation shown, the port guy. The starboard guy, meanwhile, is allowed to hang quite slack and care taken to see that the weight of the wire in no way interferes with the setting of the sail (hence the disadvantage of using the system in light weather).

'When the moment comes to gybe, the sail is set flying from both sheets while the old guy is slacked away. Next the spinnaker boom lift is eased off so that the boom may be dipped inside the forestay (easing the lift tends to swing the boom towards the centreline). The slack in the new guy is then taken up and the boom raised on its lift. Finally the weight is taken off the rope sheet. All these separate actions must be worked in their proper sequence by the cockpit crew.

'It cannot be over-stressed that the teamwork has to be precise and that the set of the sail will be disturbed if the system is used in light weather. One last point, it is important of course, that the spinnaker boom can be dipped inside the forestay while the inboard end is still attached to the mast.'

Single Pole (Double-ended)

A cutter will have to unclip the spinnaker pole from the mast in order to pass it to the other side of the boat. This is more easily done if the pole is double-ended, so that it has what are virtually port and starboard ends. The pole has to be unclipped from both the sail and the mast, passed through the foretriangle, and reconnected on the other side. To effect this, the pole is usually allowed to swing forward, the tack let go, the pole unclipped from the mast and moved across the boat. The new outer end is then attached to the new tack, and the pole finally attached to the mast. It can become exciting in a blow if the sail takes charge near the end of the operation, just before the pole is reattached to the mast. A good deal can be done by the sheet hands to make things simpler, and it is often easier to keep the sail full all the time if the mainsail is trimmed amidships during the process.

Twin Poles

J. H. 'Chippy' Davie provided material for an article in *Yachting World* in March 1963, and I have been allowed by the editor to republish it here, together with the illustrations which accompanied it. The Editor has also kindly let me use the material which he wrote himself in the issue of August 1964. Both these authoritative articles are important and will be found useful.

'Skippers who wish to do well in present-day offshore racing are obliged to set a spinnaker as often as possible and for as long as possible. This being so, it is clear that the business of gybing the spinnaker smartly, without interrupting its driving power, is of the first importance. The diagrams at 89(*a*) and (*b*) demonstrate a new system of spinnaker control using two booms, which has been developed by J. H. 'Chippy' Davie of *Fenya* fame.

'Alternative arrangements are shown for boats of less than about 30 ft LWL which are unlikely to have more than two sheet winches [figure 89(*b*)]. For the arrangement on larger boats it is assumed that four winches would be available in the cockpit [figure 89(*a*)].

'The principles of operation are the same in both drawings but the system for smaller boats avoids the use of wire ropes, and arranges for the outhaul rope which holds the boom in position to be cleated to the inboard end of the boom, instead of the sheet being led back to the cockpit, as it is in larger boats. By using this system the sail can be gybed without it collapsing, without having to disconnect the spinnaker boom from the mast, without dipping the boom under the forestay and without anyone having to work forward of the mast.

'Referring to figure 89(*a*), the procedure for gybing is:

(1) Ease port foreguy.

(2) Top up port boom.

(3) Take load on port wire sheet (boom will swing into position).

(4) Gybe main boom.

(5) Take load on starboard rope sheet and ease starboard wire (starboard boom is now free to haul inboard).

(6) Ease starboard boom topping lift and haul boom inboard with starboard foreguy. The gybe has now been completed without interfering with the sail itself in any way.

'In figure 89(*b*) there is no wire sheet and the gybe is as follows:

(1) Ease port foreguy.

(2) Top up port boom.

(3) Haul in spinnaker outhaul and cleat to boom (boom swings into position).

(4) Gybe main boom.

(5) Take load on starboard guy and ease starboard outhaul (boom now free to swing inboard).

(6) Ease starboard topping lift and haul boom inboard with starboard foreguy.

'The advantages of the system are obvious. There will be no question of the foredeck hand having to fight to get the boom under control, and reconnected to the sail. The difficult part is done, as it were, by remote control. One man would stand at the mast to work the topping lifts and, in small boats, the outhauls, while all the rest of the work is done from the cockpit.

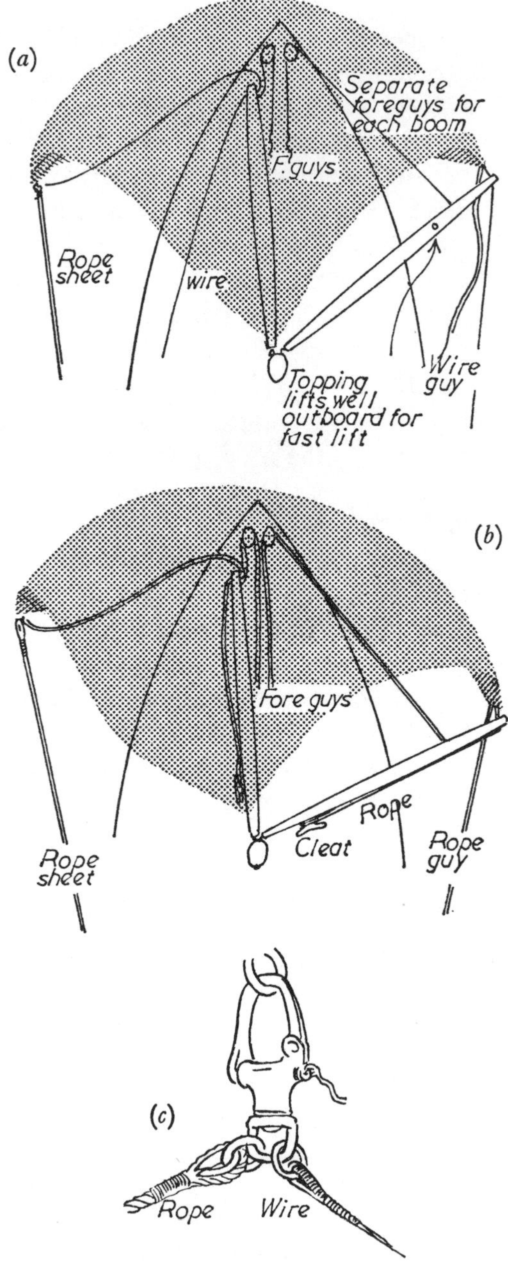

Fig. 89. The 'Chippy' Davie spinnaker gybe system. Diagram (a) shows how the gear is arranged in boats longer than 30 ft L W L, while (b) shows the arrangement for small boats where the gear is subjected to less loading. (c) shows the clew arrangement for large boats.

'Developments of this kind can be regarded as a natural extension of the trend which concentrates more and more activity in the cockpit and less and less on the foredeck. Among other things it should enable spinnakers to be handled with somewhat greater confidence at night, when gybes often tend to get out of hand, and practised crews should be able to make very fast changeovers while racing round the buoys.'

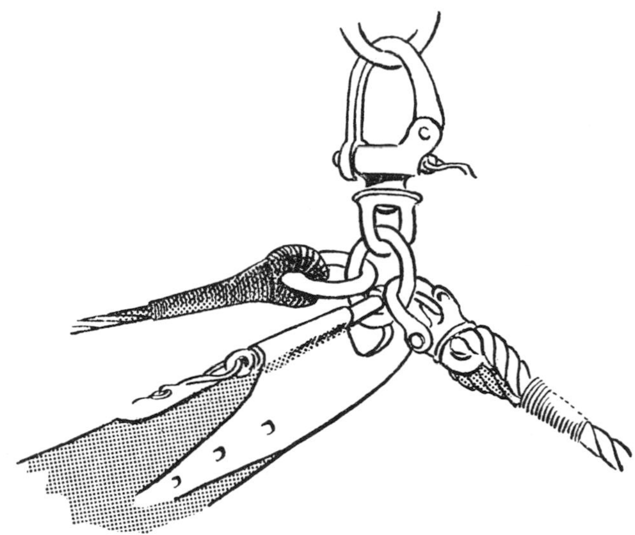

Fig. 90. Outer end of port boom showing a chafe-free answer for all but ghosting conditions. Outer end of boom should have plunger uppermost, but inner end is best if hook is face down.

Simplified Twin Poles

The Editor of *Yachting World* followed this up the next year.

'Both the (above) systems rely on the guy running through the boom end or through a special fitting on the end. Still another development has been seen in America where the outhauls disappear into a bushed hole at the outboard end of the boom. Thus the outer end is merely a tube with a soft mouth.

'However, all these methods need some extra equipment and the American one has the disadvantage that the boom is no longer double-ended. For a sloop without an inner forestay this is no great disadvantage because the pole can be dipped under the jibstay if necessary (a 12 metre idea), but for a cutter or a sloop with an inner forestay, a double-ended boom is essential if the traditional spinnaker gybing method is also to be possible.

'The advantage of the sequence of events illustrated here is that although a second boom is needed, either boom can be used by itself if it should be necessary through loss or damage. It is not necessary to have the complication of twin sheets and guys which only work satisfactorily when there is a pair of winches available, both port and starboard, and room for the two men to work them. Furthermore, no outhaul is needed on the boom itself so that it can be raised or lowered without the complications associated with outhauls led to the mast.

'The sequence as shown starting on a broad reach on port tack is to rig the starboard spinnaker boom on the mast with its forward end shipped on deck, or better still, in the pulpit. When the helmsman is ready to start gybing, the man in the cockpit slacks away the spinnaker sheet and the man on the foredeck takes hold of the slack starboard foreguy. The sheet is slacked to a marked position on the winch at the point where the man forward can reach the clew comfortably and snap it on to the starboard (unloaded) boom. The moment the clew is secure the cockpit man can winch back a little and the mainsheet can be brought in and gybed across. It is best if the helmsman handles the main. While this is taking place the foredeck man hauls on the port foreguy and the cockpit man slacks away on the port side on what was the guy and is about to become the sheet. Again at a marked position the operation is halted and the foredeck man discovers he can unhook the boom from the ring. He stops hauling on the port foreguy and the gybe is complete. All that is necessary is for the foredeck man to top the new spinnaker boom and stow the old one and the cockpit crew to adjust the sheet and guy.

'The secret is to have the exact position for sheet and guy marked clearly and boldly for the man in the cockpit, and a refinement is to have the foreguys also marked at a convenient place, so that the foredeck man can make fast quickly at a point where the boom will be horizontal when the load comes on the foreguy. A further refinement is to have the topping lifts similarly marked so that as the weight comes out of the sail the boom will drop to a convenient height. For a

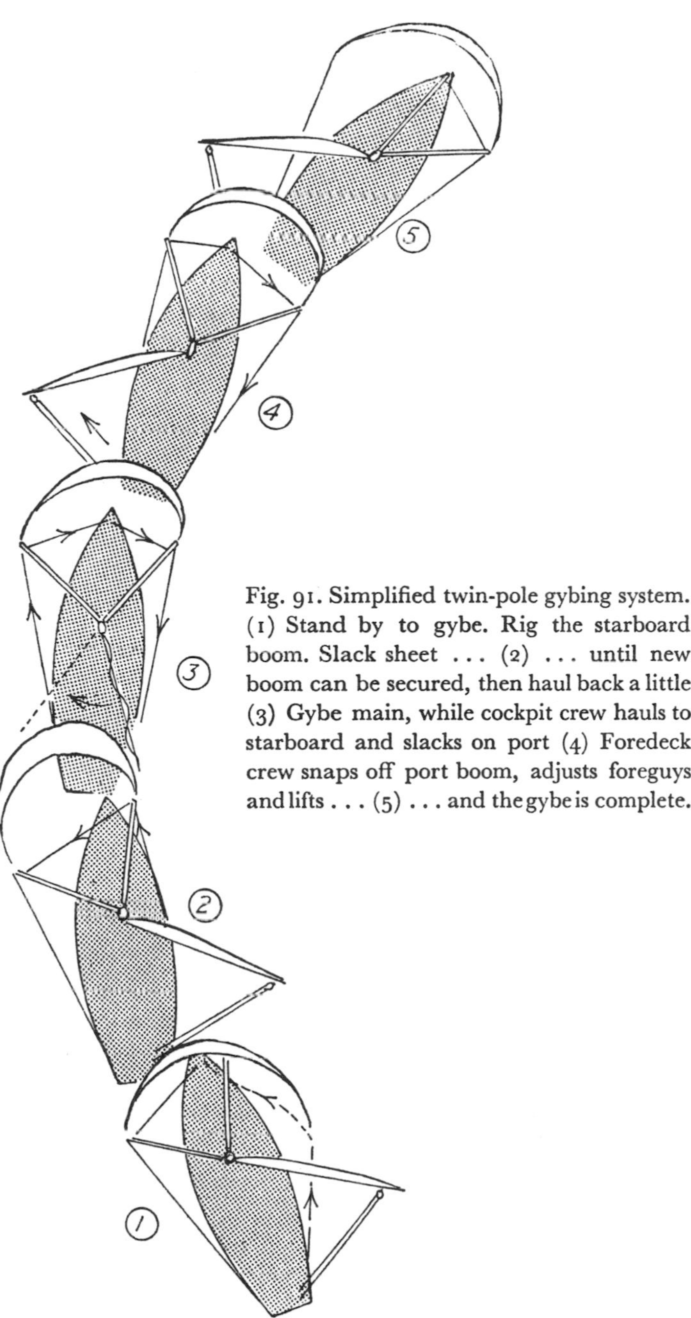

Fig. 91. Simplified twin-pole gybing system. (1) Stand by to gybe. Rig the starboard boom. Slack sheet ... (2) ... until new boom can be secured, then haul back a little (3) Gybe main, while cockpit crew hauls to starboard and slacks on port (4) Foredeck crew snaps off port boom, adjusts foreguys and lifts ... (5) ... and the gybe is complete.

foolproof gybe it is better to have the forward ends of the spinnaker booms too low rather than too high and to keep control of them, because there is always a faint risk that if the cockpit crew are over-eager the end of the spinnaker boom that has just been unhooked can be poked through the sail.'

Lowering a Spinnaker

The best way to lower a spinnaker is to allow the pole to go forward so that a hand can reach the tack, at the same time the clew of the sail should be brought to a position under the main boom so that it can be taken in hand easily. The tack is then freed, thus allowing the sail to blow freely to leeward without any weight in it. The sail is then gathered in along the foot and pulled down, while a hand lowers away on the halyard as fast as the crew can receive it.

The effect of the IOR on sailplans has been to increase mast height and thus the luff/foot ratio and the overall size of spinnakers, to a point where they are sometimes becoming unwieldy for the size of crew available. Predictably, spinnaker chutes have moved into the smaller keelboats, but they are not really practicable above about half-tonner size due to difficulties of installation and loading; in strong winds hoisting becomes a matter of stopping the sail, as suggested on p. 204, but lowering such a large area with a restricted crew remains a problem. Some boats let go the tack or even the whole guy from the pole end, at the same time as the sheet, while a grabline, previously rigged to the clew from a point by the lee shrouds, is used to haul the clew inboard. A more recent development is to adapt something of the chute idea by having a recovery line attached to the middle of the spinnaker; both tack and clew are allowed to fly and the sail collapses about its mid-point as the halyard is slacked away. Lowering is then a matter of co-ordinating hauling on the recovery line and easing the halyard.

CHAPTER XV

Care and Maintenance

Laying-up

You will only get the best use from your sails if you lay them up for the off-season period carefully. Briefly, they should be repaired, cleaned and stored, in that order. A Sail Maker will usually reverse the first two, because he has clean premises in which to do his repairs and he wants to keep them that way; the amateur sailmaker will probably get some dirt on to the sail he is repairing unless it is done in the drawing-room.

Stitching. Chafe is the bugbear of synthetics, so look at all stitching. You may only find one or two stitches gone, but this would spread rapidly the following year, so stop the rot immediately. In bad cases a chafing patch may be needed. The points to watch are where the mainsail bears on shrouds or lee runners, the leech of the mainsail if the topping lift has been allowed to rub against it, headsail leeches and clews in way of shrouds, jumper stays, spreaders and sundry projections on the mast, such as the spinnaker track, as the sail comes about. Batten pockets tend to go at both ends: at the leech it is the stitches where the batten end stretches the hole as it is pushed home; at the inner end it is the padding effect caused by the extra thickness of the elastic in the end which makes the batten chafe through the cloth. Take care not to sew in the leech line as you repair leech tablings and batten pockets. See that the protectors on the ends of full-length pockets are doing their job properly. Finally, do not forget the spinnaker, particularly if the head swivel is shackled on, thus giving it play to work from side to side and attack the stitching around it; check the clew rings and look also at the foot tape where it bears against the forestay from time to time. Try to establish the reason for any chafe you find, and see whether you can eliminate the cause, perhaps by re-siting a mast cleat or other projection.

Fittings. Check on the rope around the *headboard* and *clew eye.* This can sometimes start to pull away, and should be resewn by hand. Remove the hide casing, if fitted, and pass the needle between each lay of the rope, using four parts of waxed thread; the hide casing can be softened for easy sewing by soaking it in water for half an hour or so. On a grooved luff mainsail, the cloth between the rope and the headboard may show signs of chafe. A patch would make the sail too thick to pass in the groove, so about all that can be done is to sew by hand four or five rows of stitching up and down the affected part, to give it more strength; the finished job should be beaten as flat as possible. *Cringles* and *eyelets* should be examined for distortion. See that all *slides* are at an even distance from the bolt rope and that seizings, as on *snap hooks* or *piston hanks,* are firm. Check the latter to see that they are good and tight (or they may jam on the way up or down the stay) and apply not more than two drops of oil on the piston. Where slides are shackled to the sail, see that the bolt rope is cased with hide or cloth to minimize chafe. All *lashings* and *lacings* should be properly whipped at the ends, and do not forget the *reef points* under this heading. If your *battens* are wooden, they should be rubbed down with sandpaper, and given a couple of coats of varnish. Split a short length of PVC tubing and fasten it to the inner end of a full-length batten if you do not have external protectors; tape the ends of thin battens to help stop them splitting. You should also look at your *sheets* and *halyards* while you are about it, for you will get chafe where the same part of a rope or wire always bears on a sheave. Switch them end for end to change the point of stress, renew whippings and throw away suspect wire and shackles. You will probably do these two items at the same time as the rest of the running and standing rigging. Have a really close look at all *luff wires.* Stainless steel does not always live up to its name and, while it will not necessarily rust, it reacts chemically with polyester to produce a discoloration of the cloth which is hard to remove even if it is harmless. Galvanized wire will rust or corrode away unless it has been properly protected. Most Sail Makers in Europe use PVC-coated galvanized wire for temperate climates. Pay particular attention to the tack, for this is where the wire gets wettest and where the PVC coating has been disturbed in making the tack eye. Pull spinnakers out by their clews from the head, and compare the length of the *stays*. If a sail is symmetrical and the wires differ in length, one of them is probably broken and its repair is a job for the Sail Maker.

Fillers. The chemicals which are put into some synthetic cloths will eventually work their way out of the weave, to the detriment of the performance of the sail. As these fillers have been forced under pressure into the material between heated rollers, they cannot be put back again once the cloth has been made into a sail. There is nothing, therefore, which anyone can do – professional or amateur – to restore the filling to a Terylene or Dacron sail.

Cleaning

A dinghy mainsail once came into the sail loft where I was working with a letter from an irate owner complaining about the set of the sail. When we put it on the test spar, it looked like a badly-made accordion; the owner was right, it certainly did not set well. We knew that it could only have been made to look like that with some very harsh maltreatment, so I wrote to the owner and suggested that he might have boiled it in a machine, or put it through a rotary ironer. It transpired that he had done both, so there *are* those who will do the strangest things to a sail and expect it to stand up to it.

Sails small enough to go comfortably into the bath – anything up to 120 sq. ft – may be washed that way. If the sail is too big for the bath, find a stretch of clean concrete or tarmac where you can spread the sail and hose it down. If you use the garage apron, be sure first that it is clear of oil. Use a scrubbing brush – Sail Makers often use an industrial rotary scrubber – and any mild household detergent. Stubborn stains may be attacked with a proprietary brand of chemical cleanser, without harm to the cloth. Remember to rinse the sail in fresh water afterwards to remove any trace of a 'high-water mark'. Terylene and Dacron are resistent to chemicals, and I am indebted to Imperial Chemical Industries Ltd for the detailed instructions about removal of different stains, which will be found at Appendix E.

Ironing. Ironing synthetic sails, as I implied just now, is not recommended. There are, however, people who do so, and who do so successfully. If you are tempted to follow their example, be prepared for isolated patches of the sail to be overheated. This will cause localized fusing of the filaments and distortion of the cloth which can never be cured. In addition, a heat of 160 °F causes shrinkage, so you must be careful even if you are satisfied that you will not overheat the cloth. I would be failing in my duty if I did not strongly advise against ironing. If, despite this warning, you are determined on this course of action, use a heat controlled iron on the coolest setting. Switch the iron off before using it, and do not leave it in contact with one part of the sail for more than one or two seconds. The safest treatment for sails which are badly creased is to wash them and then spread them in the open air to dry. If you are going to hang them up to dry, never hang them by the leech; hoist by the head and then hold the other end up by the tack, so that the strain comes on the luff wire or rope.

If you are going to ask your Sail Maker to do any or all of these tasks, do it early in the slack season so that he can fit it into his quiet period. You will acquire merit, and get better attention and service.

Mildew. While mildew cannot attack synthetic cloth itself, it can form on any dirt or moisture left on a sail, as indeed it can on a moist piece of glass. This will leave an unsightly stain which it is difficult to remove, although a weak solution of bleach will do a fair job.

Storage. Sails should be stored loosely flaked in a clean, dry attic or garage, so that air can circulate freely; the truly conscientious will turn them over once or twice during the winter. These conditions, however, are the ideal ones and I am aware that they hardly ever occur. The main thing to remember is no damp and no creases, therefore any dry place will do, and the sails may be stored in their bags if the latter are big enough to avoid having to cram the sails into them. Dinghy sails can often be stored rolled round the main boom and hoisted on to the rafters of the garage. At all events, avoid folding or bunching the sails too tightly, and do not put heavy weights on top of them. Avoid creasing windows.

Fitting-out

If you have done all that you should have done at the end of the season, your sail problems regarding fitting-out should be minimal. If you did not do a thorough job of laying-up, get out your sails as soon as you can and go through the items listed at the beginning of this chapter. In any event, put a second drop or two of oil on all hanks, snap-hooks and shackles, and a light coating of grease on slides if they are not nylon or nylon coated. You then need only to check that mildew has not managed to start, and that the sails have not been eaten by rats or mice (whether they actually eat the cloth, or merely use it to make their nests, they seem to have a liking for synthetics, and the result is the same whatever they do with it), and you are nearly ready to go.

Rigging. I say nearly, because you should first check that your rigging is properly cleaned down and free from chafe-promoting stray barbs of broken strands. A newly launched boat in particular will have dirty wires, and light alloy spars have an amazing propensity for picking up dirt as well. A clean rag on wires, with some petrol or gasoline for bad patches, and a Brillo pad and warm water for metal spars, will work wonders in a short time. Be careful if your spars have a protective coating: Brillo may take some of it off so only use a clean rag soaked in fuel in this case.

Decks. Do not forget to see that your decks are clean as well, because the sails will spend a certain amount of their time lying on them.

Spars. The grooves of wooden spars in particular should be inspected for splinters or other snags; some alloy spars can also become rough in the groove if they are not anodized and salt is allowed to gather. A fine sandpaper or emery cloth followed by a light coating of paraffin wax should be used in both cases. See that screws holding tracks to spars are fully home and secure, so that their heads will not catch on the slides; check the easy operation of any second track reserved for a trysail, and also the gate if one is used.

Breaking-in New Sails

Gone are the days of slow stretching of new sails. Dacron or Terylene comes out to its marks almost immediately, and new synthetic sails can be used without any preliminaries. Ideally, it is best to sail on a broad reach in light winds for about half an hour while the canvas settles down, but you can race as soon as you bend the new sails if it is essential (it never should be, for it only needs a start to the day's sailing thirty minutes earlier than usual). You should not criticize new sails for faults, however, until they have been used in something stronger than light airs for three or four hours. Leeches of headsails, in particular, may judder a bit until the mitre has stretched out to allow the clew to draw back and down, thus putting more tension on leech and foot.

I would advise against reefing a new sail in its first four or five hours of sailing.

Care in Use

There are some general points which apply to the use of both new and old sails, if they are to give long service. The overriding precept is to use your sails with care. There naturally comes a time in every

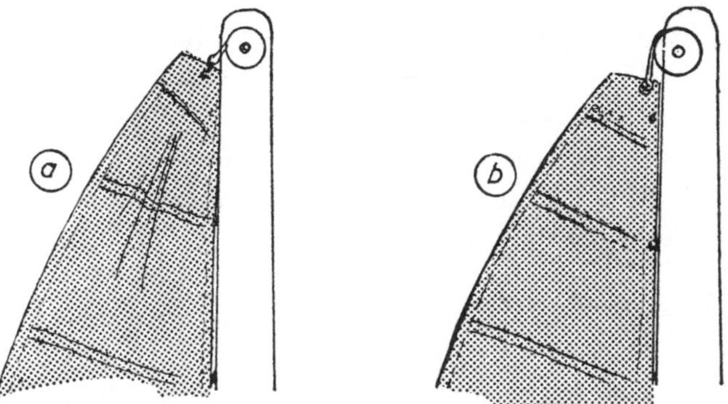

Fig. 92. Headboard crease, emanating from bad halyard lead. (a) Creased. (b) Wider sheave gives fair lead.

boat when consideration for the equipment has to take second place, and your sails should stand up to limited misuse from time to time, but they will react unfavourably to prolonged or repeated mishandling, so watch the following points.

Bending the Mainsail. I have already gone fully into the question of setting and sheeting sails from the trim point of view. The only aspects which concern us here are those which apply to the proper setting of the sail at rest. The main halyard should lead off the sheave fairly on to the head; the most common fault is for the lead to be too close to the mast, which will cause the headboard to pull over towards the mast thus creasing the upper part of the sail.

The tack-pin should ensure that the foot rope runs in a straight line all the way. If the boom is not a roller reefing one, the tack-pin will normally be between $1\frac{1}{4}$ and $1\frac{3}{4}$ in. away from the mast, and the Sail Maker will allow for this; if it is any different, he should be told to an accuracy of half an inch. The clew should also leave the foot rope in a straight line, and it is best to have a slide fitted at the clew eye, unless it fastens to a proper clew outhaul slide. A grooved foot should have a lashing round the boom at the clew when it is hauled out, to take some of the weight transmitted through the leech. This will help prevent the sail pulling out of the groove, or the groove itself splitting if it is of wood. This clew lashing should be tight enough to cause the clew eye to lie over sideways slightly with the sail at rest, because the strain along the leech will soon pull it upright when you start sailing.

Bending the Headsail. The tack of a headsail should ensure a straight luff, so it should not be too far from the foot of the stay concerned. If the sail is set on a tack span, have a snap hook or hank near the tack of the sail to prevent it sagging away from the stay; similarly there should always be one near the head. It is good to have a snap or hank on any head pendant, to stop it winding around the stay before the tension is fully on it. If you are bothered with the bottom hank riding down over a turnbuckle or swaging when the headsail is lowered, try putting a small disc or ball of wood or plastic round the stay immediately above the offending fitting, so that it acts as a buffer to the lowest snap hook or hank. A boom staysail foot should obey the same rules as a mainsail as regards tack and clew fittings.

Hoisting Sail. Always take the weight of the boom when hoisting the mainsail, either by holding it up or by taking up the slack on the topping lift. A sail which is flogging head to wind and trying to pull up the weight of the boom by its leech will soon stretch the leech and become inefficient.

Chafe. I have already said enough to make the reader aware that stitching sits on top of synthetic sailcloth, so chafe is a bugbear. Lee runners should always be allowed to go right forward, and should be lashed there if necessary. Anti-chafe measures at the ends of spreaders are worth their weight in gold, the topping lift should be removed on long voyages, and the spinnaker foot should never be allowed to bear against the forestay for any length of time. There are many anti-chafe precautions which can be taken, and they are more important to the Terylene or Dacron boat than they were in the days of hand-sewn cotton. Sheets and guys should not be forgotten, particularly where they bear against the boom or shrouds.

Minor Repairs. Minor repairs should be attended to right away, particularly those resulting from snagged sails or chafed stitching. A job which would take half an hour can quickly get beyond the resources of the crew if the sail is used without repair, even if it is only a few hasty stitches or a piece of sticky tape. Adhesive backed spinnaker repair tape can be obtained from most Sail Makers, and no yacht should be without a roll or two, especially as it will hold on a mainsail for a surprising length of time as well. Ordinary sticking plaster from the first-aid box is better than nothing. Immediate steps should, of course, be taken to locate the cause of a snagged sail, in order to eliminate it if possible.

Use of Leech Lines. The correct use of leech lines is so rare that they should be abolished. They are a tacit confession of failure by the Sail Maker, for their role is to steady a drumming leech, which should be corrected permanently in the sail loft. The right way to use one is to pull gently on it until the vibration partly settles down, and then to make it fast. If the line is pulled until the drumming stops completely, it will almost certainly cause the leech to curl to windward. This is the worst possible leech shape, and there are enough troubles with sails without producing any more deliberately. It is far better to have a slight vibration and a free run-off for the wind, than a quiet leech which is hooked. The best job the leech line does is not to the efficiency of the sail, which is not seriously impaired by so-called motorboating, but to the morale of the helmsman. If you find it hard to tie off the line when it has been pulled to steady a leech, try sewing a button in a handy place so that the line can be wound round it. At all other times the line should be left completely free.

Tied Reefing. Not only is it important to reef a sail properly to get the best out of it, but also so that the set of the sail shall not be permanently ruined by uneven stresses along the foot. Take care that the tack cringle is lashed firmly so that it is in line with the new foot of the sail. The reef ear-ring on the leech of the sail should be pulled out hard, so that the foot is well spread; it must of course be tied down securely. Individual reef points should be tied with the same tension throughout, so that the sail sets well; a continuous lacing should not have any hitches at each reef eyelet, or it will not be able to render and thus equalize the strain along the foot. It is preferable to tie under the foot rope, but a grooved boom effectively prevents this; in this case the line has to be passed right round the boom. Jiffy reefing, as described on p. 106, makes the operation easier, and thus reduces the chances that the sail will be damaged in the process.

Roller Reefing. Roller reefing is the modern way to reduce sail, and full advantage should be taken of its speed and the lesser strain it puts on the crew. Illingworth loops as described on page 106 make it possible for a hand to haul aft on the leech with a boathook as the sail is rolled down; this ensures a much neater and more efficient reef. If the boat has a gooseneck travel, the boom may be wound from the bottom to the top of the travel without the need to touch the halyard or topping lift; the halyard is then eased until the boom is at the bottom of the travel again, and the process repeated.

Lowering Sail

There is no excuse for pulling a sail down by its leech. This is sheer laziness and will ruin a good sail in short time.

Stowing Sails

The dinghy man will always remove his sails from the boat after sailing, and so will the small keelboat one-design owner. For best results the sails should be hosed down with fresh water to remove salt, then dried and carefully rolled or folded so that multiple marble crazing does not occur in the cloth. A sail of under 5 or 6 oz. weight which is rammed into a bag, be it twice as large as necessary, will undoubtedly crease after a time. Besides causing breakdown of the chemical fillers in the cloth (this danger recedes as sail cloth improves in quality, thus doing away with the need to add too many chemicals in the finishing stage), creasing will tend to settle in one particular place; if that place should happen to be the leech of the sail, it will seriously interfere with the set. There comes a time when the leech has places on it which sit at rightangles to the main plane of the sail, due solely to repeated casual creasing in the same spot. Even ironing, which no true Sail Maker would ever recommend to an amateur, will not remove this sort of stubborn fold, and the only remedy is to trim off the offending cloth.

Folding a Mainsail. A mainsail which is taken off the boom may either be folded with the folds running vertically or horizontally. If the same folds are always taken, they will soon become creases, so different points should be chosen each time. It is not a bad idea to fold horizontally and vertically alternately.

Bear in mind that a horizontal crease will disturb the airflow less than a vertical one, but the former method causes sharp bends at

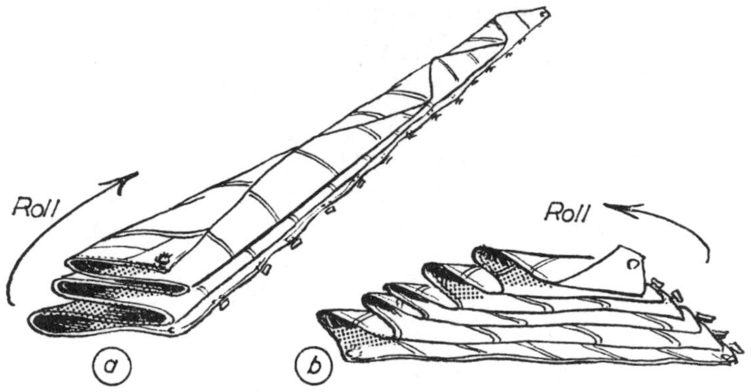

Fig. 93. Folding a mainsail.
(a) The creases will be vertical.
(b) The creases will be horizontal.

the leech itself. A better system is to roll the sail round the boom, thereby eliminating all creases.

Folding a Headsail. A headsail up to about 100 sq. ft can be stowed without folds at all. The luff wire should be rolled from the head towards the tack, thus making a tube stretching towards the clew. This is then stowed in its turn by rolling from the tack to the clew. If care is taken, any window can be arranged so that it does not have to be bent too sharply.

Stowing on the Boom. A sail stowed on the boom should be bunched down, with the foot of the sail pulled out and wrapped round the

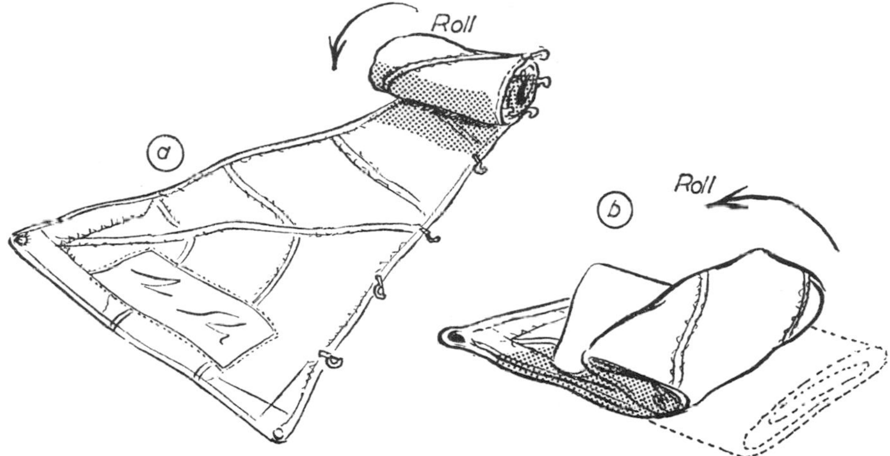

Fig. 94. Folding, or rolling, a headsail.
(a) The roll is started from the head, down the luff wire.
(b) The completed roll. It is then rolled again from luff to clew.

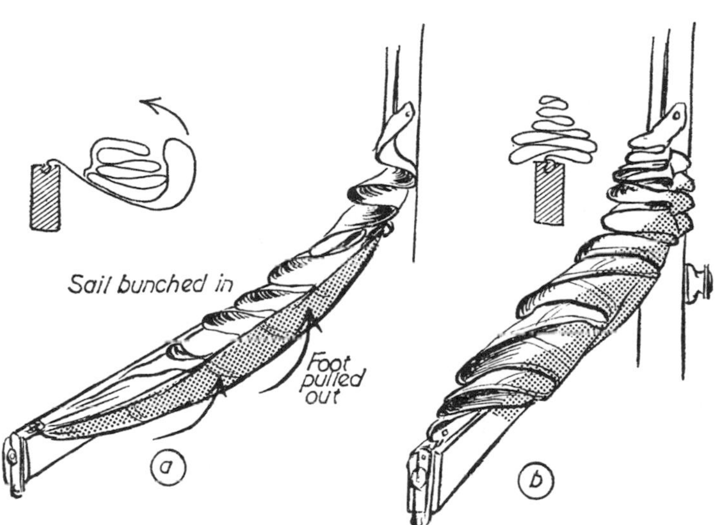

Fig. 95. Stowing a mainsail.
(a) Bunched, with the foot of the sail pulled out and over to make a neat final stow.
(b) Flaked neatly from side to side on top of the boom.

main bunt of the sail; pull well aft as you bunch down, or the result will be too bulky forward. This method has the disadvantage that the same part of the sail is always on the outside – namely the bottom 2 or 3 ft. If a cover is not used, the exposed bottom portion will eventually be subject to weakening from sunlight or industrial smoke. It is possible to ring the changes somewhat by flaking the sail carefully from side to side as it is lowered, and leaving it balanced on top of the boom.

Battens should preferably be removed, but they may be left in their pockets if they are carefully ranged along the length of the boom. Ease the clew outhaul, not so much to compensate for shrinkage which is non-existent with synthetic rope (though it will help the footrope to retain some of its springiness), but to encourage proper setting up of the foot tension next time out.

Sail Tiers. Conventional sail tiers should be of adequate length, and should be prepared before lowering a mainsail with slides on its foot. They are passed between the footrope of the sail and the boom, but you should not forget to tie the ends loosely together, in case they work free and go overboard before the sail is lowered.

Furling Gear

Mainsail. The normal sail tier is a simple and effective way of lashing the mainsail to the boom when in port; a through-mast roller reefing gear makes a quicker and easier job. The Americans, in the person of Ralph Wiley, introduced the shock cord system to the yachting public in November 1951, through the medium of Ham de Fontaine's column in the magazine *Yachting*.

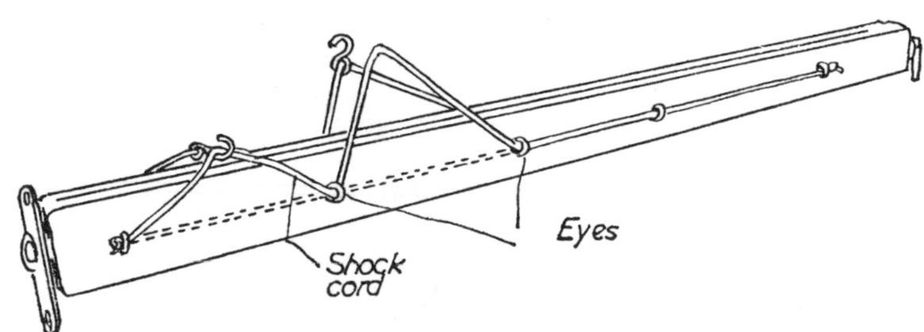

Fig. 96. Shock cord furling, as invented by Ralph Wiley of the USA, and published in *Yachting* in November 1951.

Basically the original conception was to have a length of shock cord stretched down one side of a rectangular boom under light tension. It was held fast at intervals of every 4 to 5 ft, and hooks were provided on the opposite side of the boom exactly half-way between these anchorages.

When the sail was stowed on the boom, the shock cord was taken across the top and hooked on the other side, thus forming a zigzag of restraining elastic.

It has since been found that a better job can be made if a length of shock cord just under double the length of the boom is taken, and formed into a loop. A stout eye or snap hook is attached to each end so that the loop may stretch double under the boom. A hook is attached about every four to five feet to one side of the loop, and the two sides are seized together midway between each hook. When the sail has been furled and stowed on the boom, simply take one length of shock cord either side of the boom and hook together on top.

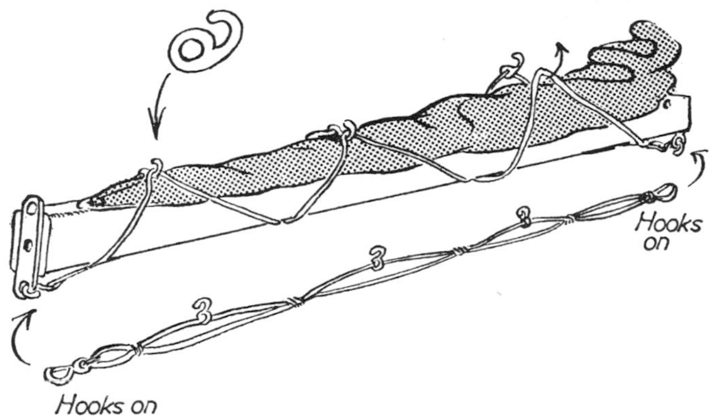

Fig. 97. Shock cord furling adapted to any boom, and made detachable.

This system has the advantage that it can be removed while not in use, thus prolonging the life of the shock cord, and also getting it out of the way if a reef has to be rolled down. For those who want to have it permanently rigged on a roller boom, grooves can be cut in a wooden boom, so that the shock cord and hooks are recessed. Metal booms should use a system which can be removed easily, such as the double length method described above.

Wykeham-Martin. Major Wykeham-Martin has given his name to the system of rolling a headsail round its own luff wire which he pioneered. It works on the principle of a swivelling drum at the tack and another swivel at the head. The drum has a length of cord or wire, depending on the size of sail, and pulling the cord rotates the drum, and the luff wire of the headsail attached to it. The sail is thus quickly rolled out of the way.

The snags are that the headsail cannot be hanked to a stay, and that a special luff wire (preferably of 1 × 19 construction) must be foreseen to avoid twist, so any old headsail cannot suddenly be adapted to the system. In addition it leaves the same part of the sail constantly exposed to the elements if it is left rolled while the boat is at her moorings. Terylene and Dacron are susceptible to the effects of prolonged weather of any description, and sunlight in particular, so weakness will result at the exposed places, as it will with nylon.

For a long time the use of the roller headsail was confined to the cruising man but, such is its efficiency, many classes like the Dragon and the 14 ft International have evolved more sophisticated versions of the principle, in order to be able to furl the headsail rapidly when the spinnaker is hoisted.

The Wykeham-Martin gear was not sufficiently robust to be used regularly for reducing sail in strong winds. Modern refinements of the system are specifically designed for this purpose and represent an efficient method of reefing a headsail in a hurry on even fairly large yachts, as well as handing it quickly when the spinnaker is hoisted.

Sail Covers

Sails which are left on their spars will deteriorate if they are not covered. Not only will they get dirty, but industrial smoke and sunlight both attack synthetic cloth and stitching. In 1965, the owner of the veteran sloop *Cynthia*, built at Falmouth in 1910, brought her six-year-old Terylene mainsail into the loft just after the Round the Island race. It had blown fairly hard at the start of the race and a number of boats had been dismasted, including I may say, the one I was in; *Cynthia* had torn her 11 oz. mainsail along the foot and the question was could it be repaired? It soon transpired that the cloth and stitching were rotten for the whole of the bottom 2 ft 6 in. of the sail, where it was always flaked on the outside of their boomtop stow without a cover; the rest of the sail was in good heart. We cut a

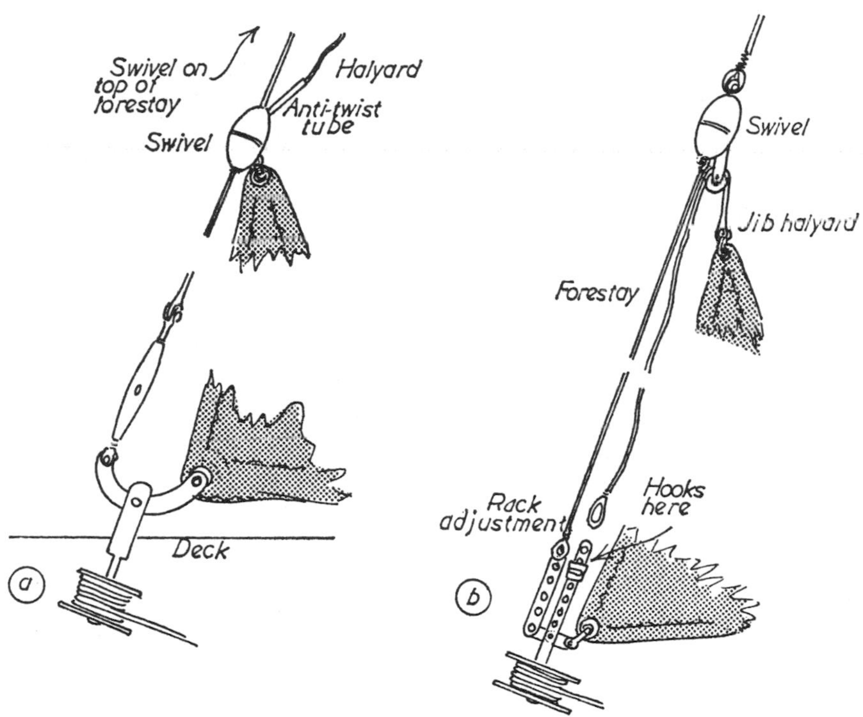

Fig. 98. Headsail roller furling.

(a) The Raubritter type of Dragon foresail furling gear. A simple system in which the head of the foresail is attached to a swivel running on the forestay. The working end of the halyard is taken down the mast internally as usual.

(b) The Borreson type in which a halyard tail is clipped to the working wire foresail halyard. This is taken through a sheave attached to the upper swivel and then back down the luff as in the Firefly. More complicated than the Raubritter type.

parallel piece 3 ft deep off along the foot, thus also shortening the foot length by 11 in., and the owner had her re-rated forthwith. Despite the fact that we had cut out a good deal of the broad seam originally put into the sail, the result was good enough for *Cynthia* to win the Albert Gold Bowl at Ryde the following Saturday. None of this would have been necessary, however, if a good cover had been used regularly.

To be good, a cover should be water- and light-proof, yet should allow the sail to breathe to avoid condensation. This means that it should not be too tight fitting underneath. There are several synthetic materials which are good for this purpose. The cover should go right round the mast at the forward end, with a tight collar at the top. A lacing is probably best for the attachment at the mast, as it can be got really tight; shock cord and hooks are the quickest way along the underside of the cover. The inconvenience of catching ropes and clothing on hooks if they are placed on the outside, should be weighed against the way they will scratch the boom if placed inside. I prefer the former, but there is not a great deal in it, particularly if the cover is nice and free hanging underneath the boom.

Bagging Sails. Large sails taken off the spars or stays usually have to be stowed in bags. Synthetic sails do not like being crammed into too small a compass, so see that the bags are plenty big enough, and that they have enough room in the locker. It is no good having a big bag, which then has to be jammed into a small sail bin. If you have a boat where the ability to roll or fold your sails, as compared with putting them into bags, is marginal, the most important sail to preserve is the light genoa. The cloth will be anything from 3 to 6 ounces and this is a range which will crease more readily than a heavy one and yet not be light enough to blow out again. Accordingly fold your light genoa if you can, even if you do not bother with the other sails.

Stopping Headsails. Headsails should be put in stops by holding the head and pulling the luff and leech out straight, side by side. The rest of the sail may be taken at the fold thus produced and rolled towards the leech (which should be kept close alongside the luff). An elastic band is then looped over each hank or snap hook, round the rolled sail and over the hank again; the size of band will be found by trial and error, but don't go too small or narrow except possibly near the head. Work along the sail by sections, from hank to hank towards the tack, and take care to see that the clew sticks out ready to receive the sheets. If you use stopping cotton instead of elastic, put only one turn near the head, but up to five or six at the clew, which should ideally have a stop each side of it.

Stopping Spinnakers. A spinnaker can be quickly stopped by using elastic bands and a short length of plastic drainpipe. The diameter

31. Flying Dutchman. A full mainsail suitable only for very light weather. The deep belly aft would knock the boat down in anything above force 2. Note how the leech is 'closed'.

FD
K 93

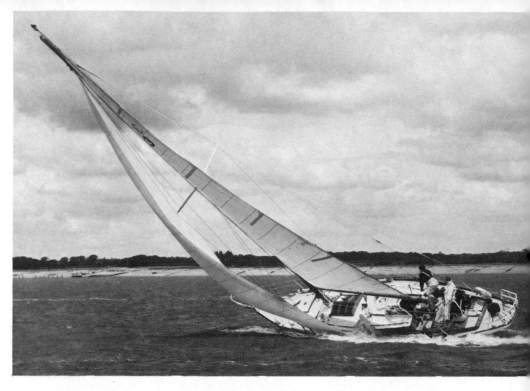

32. Ruination of a light genoa. This headsail is being used in winds too strong for it, and is showing a typical belly and curling leech as the light cloth stretches under pressure. Two hands in the cockpit are winching in the sheet by brute force in a vain attempt to flatten the sail, whose foot is already bearing hard against the lower shrouds. The boat is heeling so much that the hand sent to rig the boom vang can do nothing but hold on tight, up to his knees in water. *Beken.*

33. A clear deck is helpful for quick sail changes. *Flycatcher* houses twin spinnaker poles in troughs alongside the coachroof. *Author.*

34. The Spee Squeezer in action. The bell mouth is being pulled down, carrying the nylon sleeve with it to furl the sail. *Roger Smith.*

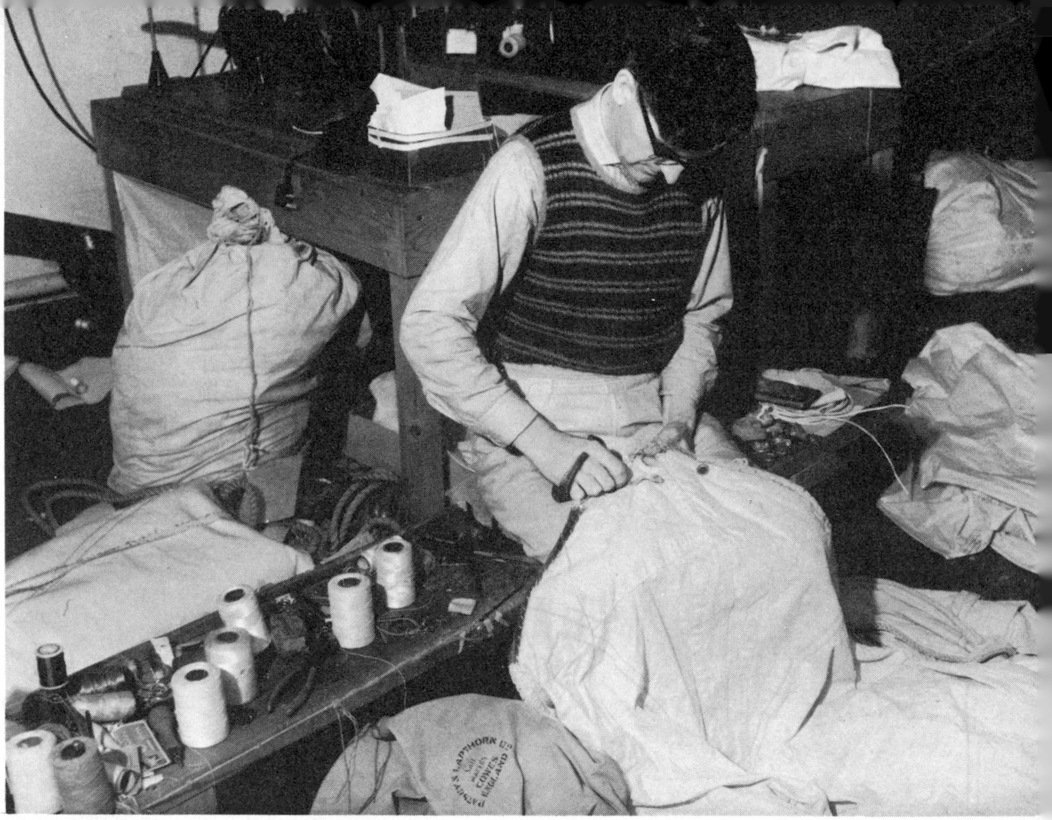

35. The Sailmaker on his bench. *Beken.*

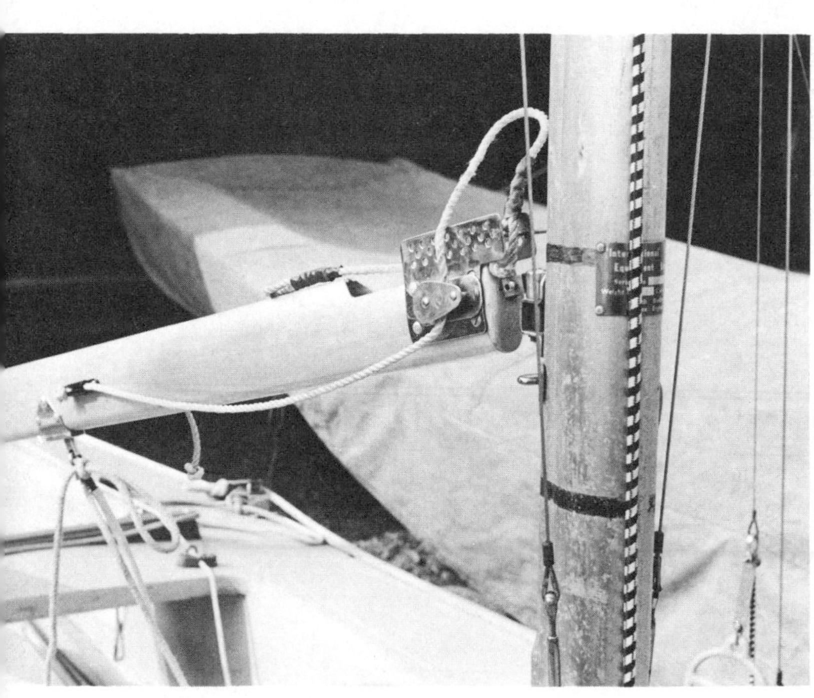

36. A complex fitting with multi-point tack pin adjustment and permanent Cunningham line. *Author.*

37. A bearing-out spar in use to prevent the spinnaker guy from chafing on the weather shrouds. *Author*.

38. There were enough tracks and controls on *Pen Duick VI* to satisfy the most ardent model railway enthusiast – or the keenest sail trimmer. *Author*.

39. *Golliwogg*. The wire or tape on the luff of this spinnaker is shorter than the cloth. Note the small wrinkles in the light coloured part of the sail at the edge as well as the general curling of the luff. The wire or tape should be eased. *Morris Rosenfeld.*

40. *Your* spinnaker, the narrow gutted sail which you cursed becomes *his* spinnaker, a high bosomed bursting beauty when seen from ahead. *Beken.*

41. The simple spinnaker chute of the Quarter-Tonner *Quarto*. Note the feed-rings attached to the hatch tops. *Author.*

42. Open air test rig. The girts from the head are evidence of an attempt to get too much cloth into the upper half of the sail. The creases at the starboard clew would disappear with a more correct sheet lead. *Beken.*

43. Comparison of two sailcloths of similar weight, showing cover factor. *Yachting World.*

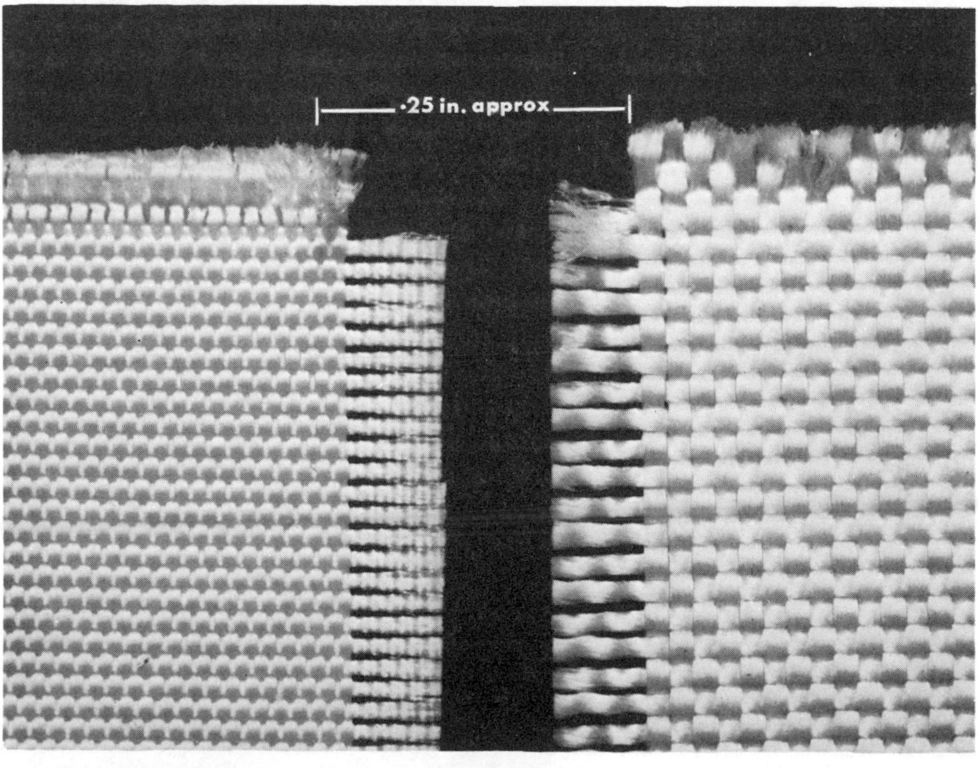

·25 in. approx

of the pipe should be about one inch for every ten feet of height of spinnaker or I measurement (a fruit tin, with both ends neatly removed and all sharp edges taken off, will do for experimental purposes). The bands are first put onto the drainpipe, and the head of the sail is then fed into one end. Taking care to see that the luff and leech are kept straight and side by side, the sail is pulled through the drainpipe while elastic bands are slipped off at approximately three foot intervals (see figure 99). If stopping cotton has to be used without the help of a piece of pipe, the head of the sail should be made fast and the luff and leech pulled out so that they are free from tangles. The sail should then be gathered together from each side, starting at the head, so that it is flaked not rolled towards each stay. A single

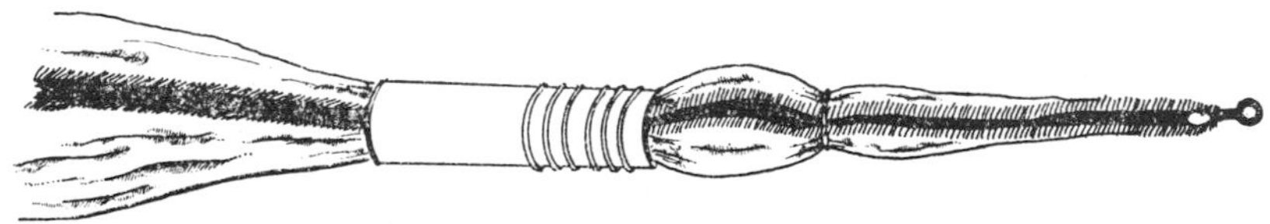

Fig. 99. Stopping a spinnaker with elastic bands and plastic drain pipe.

turn of stopping cotton is then made fast about 3 or 4 ft down from the head. This process is repeated every 3 or 4 ft, making sure that the cloth is pulled towards the foot each time to avoid bunching. The turns of stopping cotton should be increased towards the clews, where greater pressure will be available to break them out, but should never be more than single at the head. Even then the top two or three stops are best broken out by hand as the sail is hoisted, particularly in light weather. As the stopping reaches the foot, the clews can be divided so that two legs are formed. This will enable the tack and clew to be separated during the hoisting process, without the sail being broken out.

Zipper Spinnaker Stowage. A similar method of furling the sail is employed with the zipper stowage system, except that the 'sausage' is maintained by joining the two sides of a zip-fastener down the middle. This zipper is sewn down the middle of the sail, just far enough apart (between 6 and 18 in., according to the size of sail) to allow the sail to be gathered together, and then for the two sides of the zipper to be joined to hold it all together. A slider is started at the head and closed towards the foot, where it comes right off the zipper. The closure is maintained by an elastic band or a short length of stopping cotton. When the sail is to be broken out, having first been

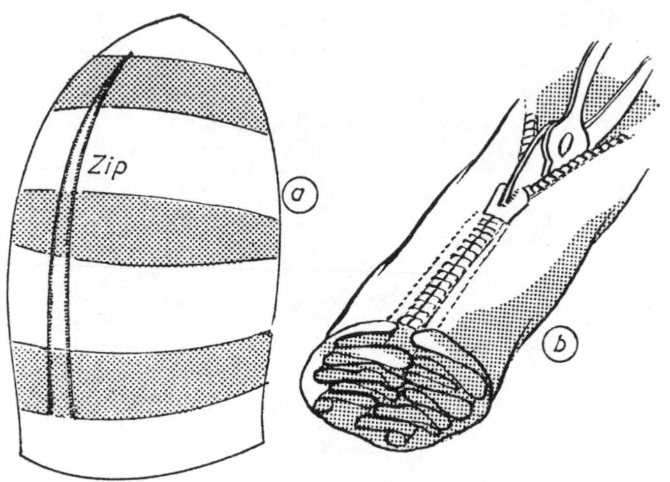

Fig. 100. Zipper spinnaker stowage (not often used).
(a) The sail set, showing the two sides of the zipper facing outwards.
(b) A section through the rolled and zipped sail.

hoisted as a 'sausage', the sheet is pulled, and this breaks the stopping, allowing the two sides of the zipper to peel apart unhindered by the slider. It is cumbersome and rather heavy in light weather.

Velcro Spinnaker Stowage. A lighter and quicker form of fastener which achieves the same results as a zipper, is Velcro. Instead of a zipper, appropriate widths of the two matching sides of Velcro are sewn up the centre of the sail, thus achieving the same result. It is much lighter, jam free and not subject to corrosion; it has no moving parts. It is not, however, always easy to pull apart in light winds, so it should be considerably narrower in the head than at the bottom. There is, of course, always the danger that it will catch up on itself while the sail is set.

Spinnaker Turtle. The spinnaker turtle is reported by Corny Shields and Ham de Fontaine to have been invented by Philip Benson of Marblehead. It is certainly a wonderful idea, and must have saved more time for harassed crews all over the world than almost any other single gadget. There are many variations on the theme, from the converted plastic trash bucket to the specially tailored knapsack with press-stud fasteners and shock cord all over it. They all achieve the same end: a spinnaker which is neatly stowed into small compass, with its stays checked for twists, and with head, tack and clew protruding ready for attachment to their various fittings.

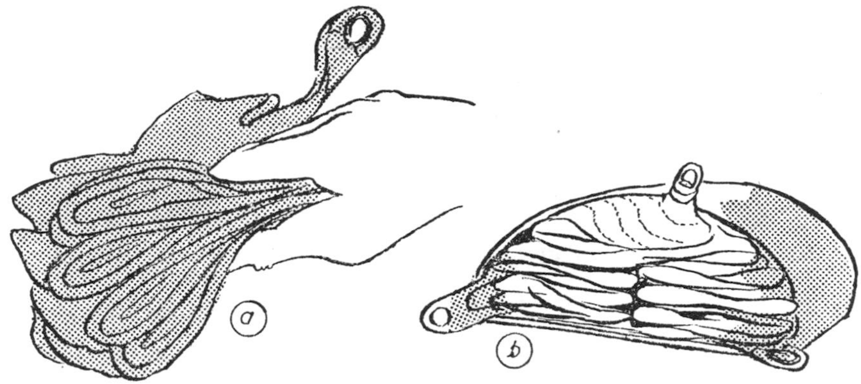

Fig. 101. Spinnaker turtle.
(a) The spinnaker is carefully flaked in to the hand along each stay, to avoid tangles.
(b) The whole sail is thrust into the turtle, leaving the head and both clews correctly disposed ready for attaching to their respective lines.

A spinnaker up to about 30 ft on the stays can be bagged into a turtle by one person. Starting at either clew, the stay is traced along its length, and flaked back and forth into one hand. This process is taken past the head and down to the other clew, so that both stays are then securely held in a bunch in one hand. The main bunt of the sail is then thrust into the turtle, preferably with the foot going in at the bottom, although this is not essential. Finally, the stays are pushed in last, with the head and clews carefully protruding in the middle and either side respectively.

The same result can be achieved by starting at the head and working down both stays simultaneously. The object in both cases is to see that the stays are free from twists and turns, and that they go into the bag last with the head and clews where they can be hooked on, to come cleanly away when hoisting sail. A larger spinnaker will take two people to bag, because the whole length of the stays cannot be held in one hand. If the sail has to be packed in a real hurry, hold the three corners and ram the rest of it into the turtle willy nilly; nine times out of ten it will come out right. In light winds, small sails can be launched direct from the arms of a crewman stationed to leeward.

Spee Squeezer. This is a nylon sleeve with a hard bell mouth. The spinnaker is encased in the sleeve and the head is hoisted to the masthead trailing a long sausage under it. To break out the sail, the bell mouth is hauled aloft compressing the sleeve so that the spinnaker is released; it is on an endless line so that it may be hauled down again to furl the sail when desired. Its disadvantage is that the bell mouth and sleeve remain aloft while the spinnaker is set, but it certainly makes setting and lowering easy for the shorthanded cruising man.

CHAPTER XVI

Repairs

Equipment

Every yacht's crew should have the ability to undertake the sail repairs which may become necessary during its voyage. This will vary from the emergency taping of a spinnaker rip on a Soling, to fitting a new clew cringle, or repairing a torn seam, on a trans-atlantic crossing. The rest of this chapter gives the necessary basic information, but practice is important and the amateur should take the opportunity to try his hand from time to time on a piece of old Terylene or Dacron cloth and a short length of rope.

Sewing Machine. It is usually only the largest yachts which have room for a sewing machine on board. If a seam should go from end to end, however, a machine can quickly repay the stowage space it occupies. What would be a long chore by hand, can be repaired in minutes with a machine. It should preferably have the ability to sew a cross-stitch, or zigzag as it is also called.

Machine Thread. The best thread for sewing synthetic sailcloth is synthetic, both for machine and hand work. Machine thread is finer than hand-seaming twine, and it comes in many styles and weights. Two weights, a light and a heavy, are enough for the best equipped boat. The light machine thread would be used with a sewing machine for all sails up to a cloth weight of about 4 ounces; the heavier thread would be used on the machine above this weight. Either thread can also be used for any light hand-sewing which might be needed, say, on a spinnaker.

Hand Twine. In England Terylene hand twine is graded by breaking strain, and is graduated in even pounds from 2 to 8. A comprehensive table is given at Appendix F, showing which weight of twine and which size needle should be used for most cloth weights. However, the average boat will not normally carry a full range of twines, and you will want to know the minimum which will see you through. The answer is to have two: one fairly light and one reasonably heavy. A rough guide to the proper twine to use with a particular cloth is to halve the cloth weight in ounces to find the breaking strain of the twine in pounds. Thus a 4-oz. cloth should be sewn with a 2-lb. twine. Therefore, you should have available at least one twine for the working canvas and one for lighter headsails, in addition to the machine thread for hand-sewing spinnakers and ghosters. If you are working on parts of the sail which have three or four thicknesses, such as the head, tack and clew patches, or on the rope, or on a worked eye, you should ideally use a size heavier twine. The twine should be waxed before use, not only for added protection but so that it will lie together and not unravel and snag in use. If beeswax is not available, a candle will do; even soap will help hold the twine together for easier sewing. But most hand twine is pre-waxed these days.

Needles. Sailmakers' needles are graded to conform with the standard Wire Gauge. Sizes most commonly in use in the loft range from number 13, which is used for the heaviest work connected with a sail of about 13 or 14 oz. cloth, to number 19 which is used for hand work on dinghy sails. Most Sail Makers have larger needles, in case they have to rope a really heavy cotton sail for a schooner, but 13 to 19 are the commonest in use. The larger the needle, the easier it is to thread and hold, so the temptation is to employ too big a needle for each job. But the larger the needle, the larger the hole it makes in the canvas, sometimes to the detriment of the task. The table at Appendix F gives the ideal size of needle and twine for each particular task. As with twine, however, you will want to know which three or four needle sizes will suffice for most jobs. If you have numbers 18, 16 and 13 on board, plus an ordinary domestic needle, you should get by on most occasions. It is a useful dodge to blunt the point of any needle which is used for roping, so that it passes between the lay of the rope more easily.

Sewing Palm. A sewing palm is not difficult to get used to, and should form part of the kit of every yacht. It takes practice to become really proficient, however, so do not wait until a repair is required before you try it out. There is a minor difference between a roping palm and a seaming palm, but only in the needleguard and the thumb piece. The roping palm has larger indentations in the needle guard which is deeper set, because a roping needle is usually one or two sizes larger than the sewing needle for a given sail; it also has a raised portion round the thumb, designed to allow the thread to be wrapped round it and pulled tight at each stitch. A roping palm is not really suitable for the amateur, because the deep-set needle guard means that it may be difficult to hold the shorter needles when they are back against it.

Other Equipment. Serving mallets, stitch irons and the like are not necessary unless you intend shipping as sailmaker on a schooner (in which case you will need more training than can be learned from this book). A sharp knife is essential, and a short school ruler will often be found useful. It may be as well to have the cutters, punches and dies for two or three sizes of rings, together with the necessary brass rings and turnovers, if it is thought that this sort of work will be undertaken. There are many sizes and they are heavy and bulky, so specialist advice should be sought before purchase. A bench-hook takes up little room and can help with hand-sewing. The hook goes into one end of the work, and it is tied by a line away to one side. One hand then tensions the cloth against the pull of the bench-hook while the other does the sewing. A marlin spike is a usual item on board most boats, and an extra big one is useful as a fid for reaming eyes and cringles. The whole collection should go into a convenient hold-all after anything metal has been lightly greased to prevent rust. The hold-all makes an admirable item on which to get some practice sewing, if it is made by yourself.

Types of Stitch

Machine Sewing. A zigzag stitch is usually best for machining sails, and there should not be too much tension. This is so that there shall be room for a certain amount of movement without stressing the thread. This is not to say that a straight stitch is no good at all – it is certainly better than nothing, and may even be best on spinnakers. Be sure that the thread tension is the same on both sides, so that the interlocking part of the stitch is in the middle of the cloth and not lying exposed on one side. You will need a certain amount of room round the machine in order to work on a large sail; one of the governing factors will be whether the sail will manoeuvre under the arm of the machine, or whether there is too much cloth to go through. Try to keep the work spread flat, but without tension. It helps considerably to tack or pin the work before sewing.

Hand-sewing. The twine should normally be used doubled or even quadrupled, because this will mean fewer stitches for a given strength factor. This advice extends especially to working eyes, which should have well-spaced stitches using at least four parts of twine. The fewer stitches, the less likelihood of wrinkles being caused. To wax the twine, draw it across the beeswax block so that it cuts into the surface; four passes should be enough to do the job properly. Most hand-sewing should aim at five to six stitches per inch, and the following three basic stitches should prove enough for most tasks:

(i) *Round Stitch*. If the edge of a sail has to be sewn, as when a turned tabling is joined at the very leech or when the outer end of a batten pocket is sewn to the sail, the round stitch is used. It will usually be found best to sew from left to right, pushing the needle up and away from you. As with most other stitching, a start is made leaving an inch of the end of the doubled twine protruding from the work. This should then be laid along the cloth in the direction of sewing, and the first five or six stitches should be made

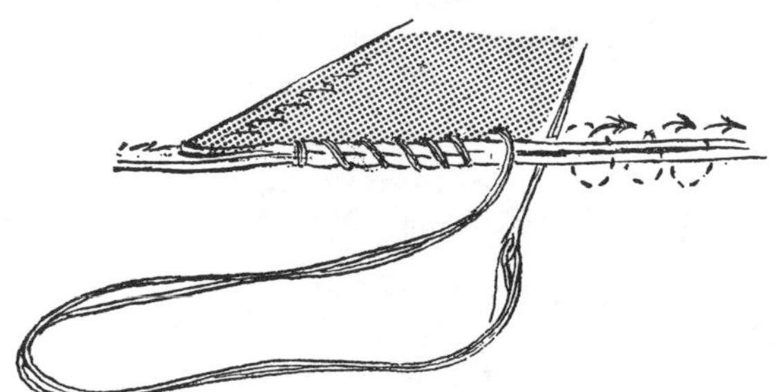

Fig. 102. Round stitch. Used when the very edge of the sail has to be sewn.

round it, to form a solid anchor. This is then a simple matter of up through, round and over, and up through again, taking care to keep the stitching even. It is finished off by passing the needle under the last few stitches and then taking a final tuck into the canvas.

(ii) *Flat Seaming Stitch.* If a seam or patch is involved, or the inner edge of a tabling for that matter, it will not be possible to push the needle repeatedly up through the work. It must therefore be pushed down through, and then up again all in one movement. This is the flat seaming stitch, also known as the tabling stitch.

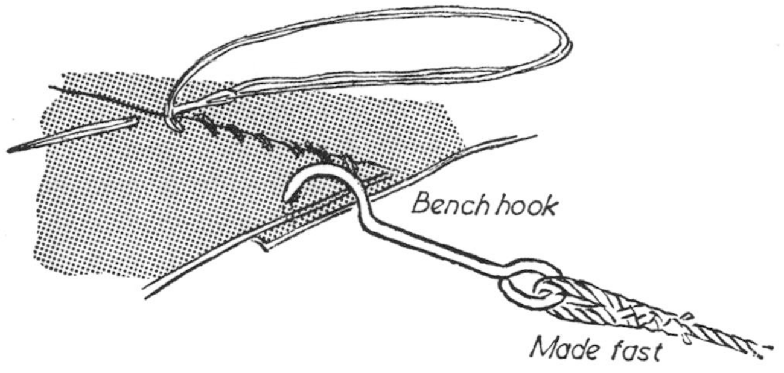

Fig. 103. Flat seaming stitch. Hold the two parts of the work together with the left hand, and pull to the left to steady the work against the tension of the bench hook.

It will be easiest to work from right to left, pushing the needle towards the body as it enters the canvas. See that the needle emerges at a uniform distance both along and across the work, and do not pull the stitching too tight, or it will pucker. A bench-hook, attached away to the right, will allow the left hand to hold the work together and pull it to the left while stitching with the other hand, thus ensuring steadiness. Often the seam to be sewn will be in the middle of the sail, and this means that a bight of the sail must be doubled towards you over your knee while sewing. This being so, care must be taken to 'skin' so as not to catch the bottom layer in what the sailmaker knows as 'catching a crab'.

(iii) *Sailmaker's Darn.* This stitch is useful for gathering the two sides of a tear, either temporarily or as a permanent repair, and is the same as the domestic herringbone stitch. This is one of the few occasions when the doubled twine can be knotted at its end to form a stopper at the beginning of the work, which is sometimes rather looser than other sewing. Stitching is from left to right, and the start is made by pushing upwards through the far side of the tear. The needle is then brought back over the tear and passed down through the near side, to be brought up on the *left* side of the stitch thus formed.

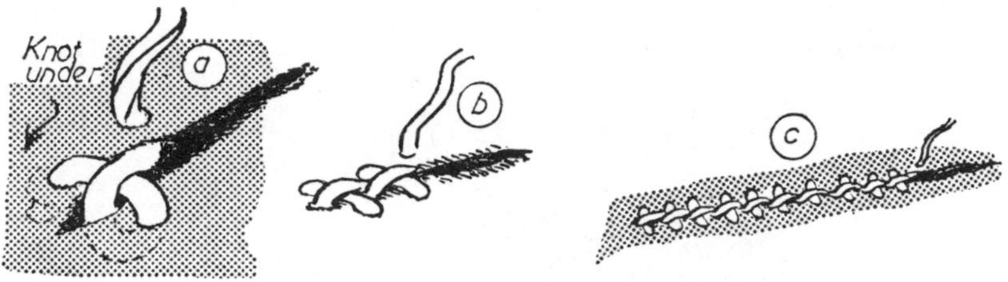

Fig. 104. Sailmaker's darn. Used for mending a tear.

After crossing over the top of this stitch, the process of sewing up through the far side is repeated. Each stitch should not be pulled tighter than is necessary to hold the two sides of the tear together. This is not to say that they should be slack, for their very job is to draw two pieces of canvas towards each other. The twine is usually tied off in a half-hitch and tucked under, to finish the job.

Practical Work

Roping. Twists must be eliminated from the rope before it is sewn to a sail, so that it lies naturally. Repair work usually involves putting a short length back on the sail, so it will probably already be attached for most of its length. If, however, a complete new rope has to be put on, it should be carefully checked for twists and then held out taut while a pencil line is marked along it as a reference while sewing. Rope has a tendency to shorten up during sewing so, if a specified length is to be sewn to a sail, it should be struck up at intervals of about 1 ft, so that the length is shared evenly and the rope is not sewn on tight at any particular point. It is an interesting fact that most hand-sewn rope will lose some of its length during the sewing; an exception is some soft spun rope. If a sail has 25 ft of rope sewn to the luff and the rope is then taken off, it will be found to measure about 6 to 9 in. short. It is for this reason that a sail cannot have its rope taken off during adjustment, and then the same rope put back – there would not be enough. If for some reason the same rope has to be used, it is best to use a fairly light twine and not pull the stitches too tight in order to reduce shrinkage. Conversely, if a sail is roped too slackly and stretches too easily on the spars, it can be made tighter by sewing over the roping a second time and pulling each stitch tight.

The actual process of roping can be fairly quickly assimilated as far as the beginner is concerned, for he will not normally be required to rope a sail from top to bottom, but rather to renew a short length

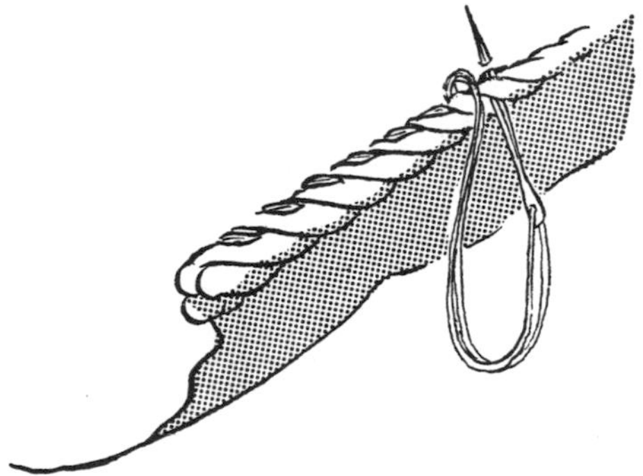

Fig. 105. Hand roping.

which has pulled away. The finer craft of full-scale roping takes a good deal of practice to learn, because consistency is important if wrinkles are not to appear from a rope-bound sail. The edge of the sail should be towards you, over your knees, and the rope laid just under the edge, which is then turned up through 90° for convenience of sewing. A bench-hook, tied away to your right, is useful for steadying the job. Start at the left and, pushing away from you, pass the needle between the strands of the rope and then through the edge of the sail, in what is virtually the same movement as the round stitch described above. It will make things easier if the point of the needle is dulled first, to stop it going too readily into the actual rope itself. Pull the stitch tight and bring it back over the top towards you, and repeat the process between the next two strands. It is important not to sew through a strand thus weakening it and causing irregularities in the lay of the rope. It is also important to pull each stitch with the same tension. You will find that you will have to make a conscious effort to use up all the sail before the next set of match marks is reached, and it is usual for the beginner to reach the rope mark before the one on the sail. Practise on a spare length for an hour or so before tackling any important job.

Worked Eye. A hand-worked eye has two or three times the strength of one stamped in with a hand punch. If the eye is going to be subject to chafe on its inner surface, a liner or turnover should be clenched over the stitching as a protection. First, the brass ring is laid at the desired place, and its inner and outer circumferences

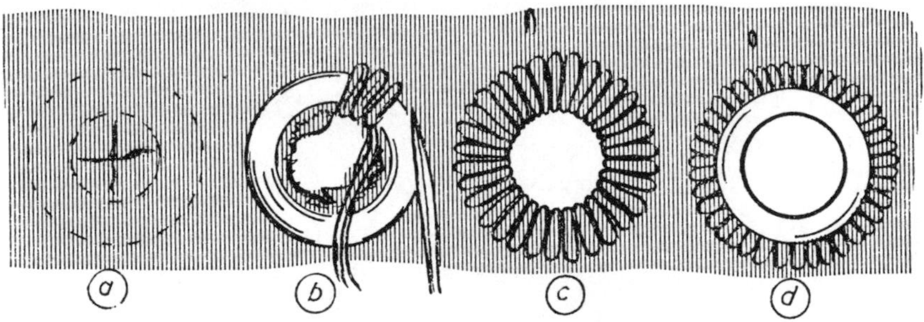

Fig. 106. A hand worked eye.
(a) The outside and inside circumferences of the metal ring are marked in pencil. The centre is cut out or cut in a cruciform.
(b) The ring is sewn round, the centre being seamed with a fid from time to time.
(c) The final stitch is pushed through the cloth away from the eye.
(d) A brassy is punched into the eye to protect the stitching from chafe.

traced on the sail in pencil. Part of the inner circle is then cut out, either using a special circular cutter rather smaller in diameter than the ring, or else a cross shaped cut may be made in the sail. If the full inner diameter is cut away, the final job will not be strong enough. The brass ring is then laid on the cut-out, and the needle passed down through the canvas outside the ring at any point on the outer circle marked in pencil, usually on the side away from the worker. The twine is pulled through downwards, leaving a tail to be sewn over by the first four or five stitches as a stopper, and the needle then brought up through the cut-out and centre of the ring. It is then passed over the top of the ring and down through the pencil line again, moving slightly round the circle each time, for the process to be repeated. Ideally, a fid or tapered spike, should be reamed through the partly worked ring at regular intervals during sewing, in order to keep the canvas spread and the stitches even. Each stitch should be pulled really tight, and a bench hook may be useful when working a large eye. The hook is tied away to the right and, after each stitch, the twine is laid across the left knee, which is then used as a lever to pull away to the left and tension the stitch. Modern practice is to use four parts of twine, spacing the stitches rather wider apart than used to be customary, in order to reduce the risk of wrinkles. The brassy is then punched into the sewn ring to protect the stitching against the chafe of shackles etc., and the job is done. Modern machinery can punch in stainless steel eyes with almost the same security as those sewn by hand.

Cringle. It is sometimes necessary to work a cringle in a sail, either for an external tack eye or for a reef cringle. This is a rope loop attached to two small eyes on the edge of a sail, and it usually has a metal thimble wedged into it to protect it from chafe. A single strand of rope should be unlaid, without disturbing the twist too much, to a length equal to about 3½ times the circumference of the final cringle. The correct estimation of this length becomes important when a thimble of given size has to be forced into the finished cringle, and this only comes with practice. Put one end of the strand through one of the eyes and see that its ends are in the ratio of 2 : 1 [figure 107(*a*)]. These ends should then be twisted together in the same lay and direction as the original rope.

The longer end is then passed through the second eye [figure 107 (*b*)] and twisted back along the length of the partly formed cringle to form a three-strand rope once more. You should be careful to have enough of each end of the single strand left over at either end, to pass it through the eye and then to tuck it into the three strands of the cringle in the same way as a splice [figure 107 (*c*)]. The thimble is inserted by reaming out the diameter of the cringle with a fid or large spike, and then hammering in the thimble before the diameter can shrink back to its normal size once more.

Patches. A clean cut of about an inch in length may be sewn together with a sailmaker's darn, providing the cloth is in good heart; anything larger should have a patch. The tear should be trimmed square with the warp and weft, and a patch cut in similar cloth (with its warp and weft lined up with those of the sail) plenty big enough to overlap the squared off hole. If the two threadlines are not lined up, uneven stretching may result, causing wrinkles. Many authorities advise turning the edges of the patch under, but synthetic

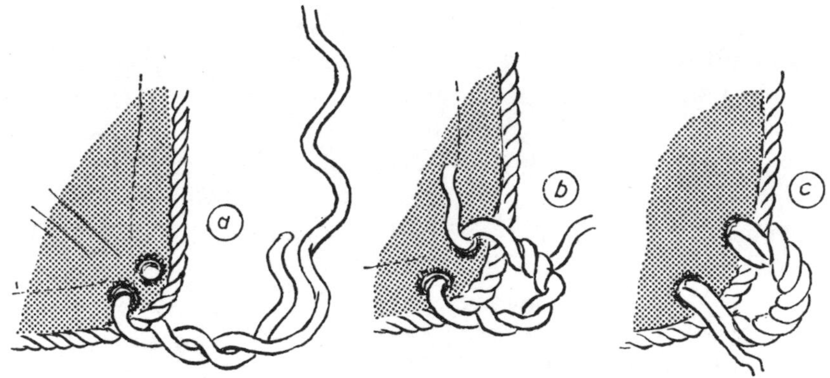

Fig. 107. A rope cringle.
(a) The two ends are twisted together in the ratio 2:1.
(b) The long end is further twisted into the original lay to form a three-stranded loop.
(c) Both short ends are now spliced into the cringle.

cloth can be sealed at the edges if it is cut out with a fine electric soldering-iron: the heat will melt the threads to cut out the patch, while at the same time causing them to fuse together so that they do not fray. The tear in the sail may be trimmed in a similar manner. Of course, if you are on board and do not have a heated iron, the edges of the tear and the patch will have to be turned under to avoid fraying. In any case, the patch should be put on slack, or it may tend to gather the sail into small puckers. It may help to keep the whole thing in shape if any trimming of the tear is left until after the patch is put on one side. The two sides of the tear can be stitched together temporarily as further assistance; use of repair tape or sticking plaster will also speed things up and go towards seeing that the sail is not distorted while the patch is applied properly. At all events, the patch should be pinned, stuck or tacked in place, and then sewn round from right to left with the needle being pushed into the canvas towards you, in the flat seaming stitch described above. When the patch is in place, turn the work over and proceed to square off the tear if this has not already been done. Mitre-cut into the corners and turn the edges under, so that they lie between the new patch and the original sail. Sew round again from the second side and the job is complete.

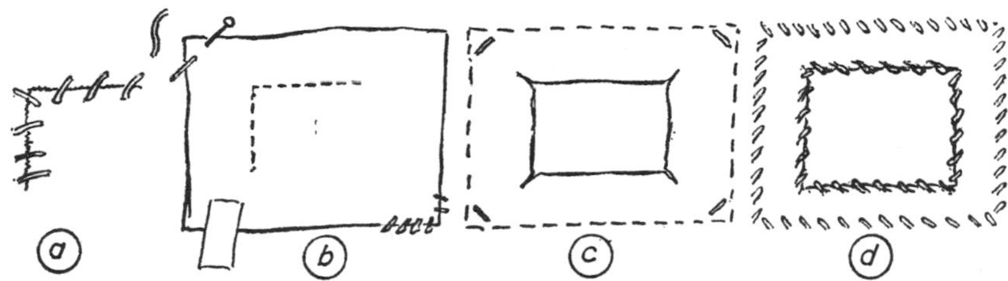

Fig. 108. A hand patch.
(a) The tear is cobbled together.
(b) A sealed patch, plenty large enough, is pinned, stuck or tacked at the corners. Warp and weft should line up with the sail.
(c) Sail is turned over, tear is trimmed square which is mitre-cut into its corners.
(d) Edges are turned under, and patch is sewn round again using flat seaming stitch.

Darning. Darning should be restricted to very small cuts and holes no bigger than the end of a cigarette, and should never be used where the canvas is known to be weak. Use a double, or even quadruple, seaming twine, and pass the needle under and over the first layer of stitching you put in, in the usual domestic manner.

Repair Tape. An excellent repair tape is available from most Sail Makers for repairing spinnakers. It comes in a variety of colours, so a multi-hued spinnaker need not be disfigured. The tape is self-adhesive, with a waxed paper backing which has first to be removed. It is about 2 in. wide, and usually comes in rolls of 25 ft so that quite long tears can be most effectively mended. It will hold in place for a long time, indeed will certainly last a season's normal use, so it tends to make the lucky owner rather lazy regarding his repairs. In addition it will hold on Terylene or Dacron sails quite well, so do not hesitate to use it if you cannot patch a mainsail. Insulating tape from the engine kit and sticking plaster from the the first aid box both offer an emergency alternative.

Sailmaker's Whipping. An ordinary whipping will quickly come undone in the normal wear and tear of working the ship, thus promoting frayed ropes ends; the sailmaker's whipping is much more resistant. Thread a fine needle with seaming twine so that two parts are put on at one time. Most sailmakers will scorn to knot the end, preferring to leave a small tail exposed to be sewn over at the

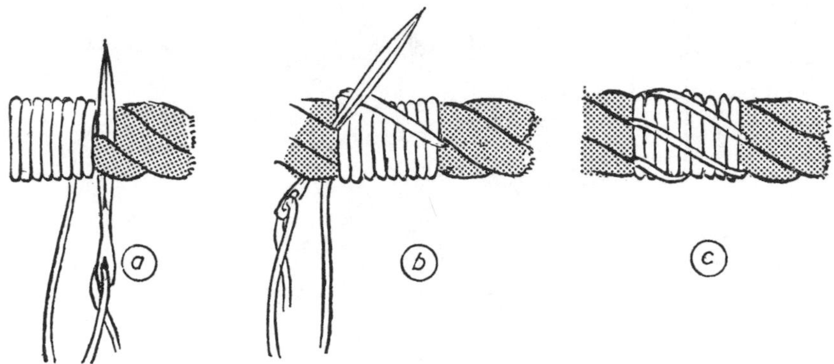

Fig. 109. Sailmaker's whipping.
(a) The end is whipped as usual. The twine is then passed between the lay of the rope by the needle.
(b) The twine is then laid along the whipping in one of the grooves formed by the lay of the rope.
(c) This is repeated until all three grooves are filled; the end is fastened off.

start to make an anchor; but you and I are not shipping as sail-makers, and we wish to know the simplest secure system, so we start with a knot. Wax the twine and then sew through the rope so that a firm start can be made. Whip in the usual way, then sew between the strands of the rope and out the other side. Lead the twine back over the whipping along the line of the lay of the rope and then sew again between the lay at the other end of the whipping. Lead the twine back over the whipping, again along the lay, and repeat once more until three passes have been made. Sew through the rope to finish off securely.

CHAPTER XVII

Faults and Creases

A Sail Maker sees more bad sails set up in his loft than good ones. If his production is anything more than a few sails a week, he does not have the time or manpower to test every sail he makes, so he does not see the hundreds which go out to all parts of the world which are satisfactory All too rarely does he get a letter back from the satisfied owner. He does, however, hear the complaints, although here again he sometimes does not hear straight away. The average Sail Maker considers that he has to make a dozen winners to wipe out the effect of one bad sail caused by its dissatisfied owner complaining in the clubhouse. To this end he usually has an alteration service designed to bring speedy attention to a faulty product, so that the disgruntled owner realizes that he gets the best and quickest remedy.

A sail will often only show its faults when set on the boat, with its attendant mainsail or headsail, and using its normal spars. Sometimes the faults will not appear unless the boat is actually sailing. It is therefore important for a Sail Maker to be a practising helmsman, and to be able to go afloat to examine his products. Often he can decide on remedial measures on the spot. At other times he can determine what is wrong, but needs a closer examination before making up his mind what he will do to cure it. He will then take the sail back to the loft for further attention on a test rig.

Test rigs can either take the form of a mast and forestay rigged on land in the open, where the wind is not disturbed by buildings and trees, or else the sails can be set up horizontally in the loft. In the latter case, a series of different sized tracks may run along a wall, with a gooseneck fitting on to which a boom can be fitted, again with a number of different sized tracks on it. This, of course, is so that various types and sizes of slide can be accommodated. A groove will also be needed, and this can often be made, as Bruce Banks has done, with a slot large enough to take most types of slide, thus doing away with the need for a multitude of different tracks. Smaller mainsails, used perhaps on bendy spars, will be set on a horizontally rigged grooved mast and boom, arranged so that they can be bent at will in the right place.

A headsail can be set up horizontally by fastening it at the tack and pulling out the head on a tackle to stretch the luff taut; the clew can then be pulled out on one side. In both cases, mainsail and headsail will take up their designed shape under the influence of gravity.

When a sail is set up like this in a loft, the Sail Maker can walk all round it. He can then examine at close quarters those parts of the sail which are suspected of giving trouble; he can also try pinching and pulling the cloth with his hands, to see what effect tightening a seam or pleating the luff or foot will have. I do not say that an indoor horizontal rig will always provide the answer, but it is an invaluable adjunct to the Sail Maker's armoury in the fight against sail faults.

Many sails are returned to their makers for attention because of faults which are imagined or induced by their owners. On the other hand, a sail is like a suit of clothes and has to be individually tailored to the boat on which it will be used, if it is to give of its best. Something 'off the peg' will very often set well, but as class competition becomes hotter special needs require special attention, and it is often necessary for minor alterations to ensure a perfect fit. It is important to give the Sail Maker the chance to make those alterations, because he cannot do anything if he does not know about it, and a poor-looking sail may only need a few touches here and there to turn it into a potential winner. It is equally important to give a sail a fair trial. By this I mean that it should not be condemned too quickly, nor should it be refused a second chance after alteration. A first class example of hasty criticism, was the way some of the 12 metre sails for the British America's Cup challengers were assessed in 1964. Sails were taken aboard the two yachts *Sovereign* and *Kurrewa V*, tried for one or two races in the presence of the Sail Maker concerned, and sent back to the loft for immediate alteration. They were never given a chance to settle down, and some genoas were altered six and seven times in a period of as many weeks. In the end, the records of the sails were so heavily amended that it was impossible to know the precise effect of what had been done to the sail, which might very well have been better for a little more sailing and a little less cutting. On the other hand I have known sails brought into the loft by very angry owners, when it has been most difficult to persuade them to give another chance to what they considered a hopeless case. In most instances the problem has been cured, and in several the sail has proved to be a favourite thereafter. In some, I regret to report, the owner has been too stubborn to try again, so both sides are the loser.

It is, of course, important to be frank with your Sail Maker, and not to expect the impossible. He cannot cut a sail if he is not given all the pertinent facts, nor will it set well if it is hoisted badly, used under different conditions from those given to the Sail Maker (different spars or winds), or maltreated in use.

You would be surprised at the number of sails returned under complaint by owners who have only themselves to blame. A Sail Maker quickly learns to spot this sort of thing, although he is not always able to accuse the owner outright for fear of giving offence and acquiring bad publicity. It is a cross which has to be borne, but not borne willingly.

Mainsail Faults

The principal faults which affect mainsails, in order of frequency, are as follows:

1. Leeches: slack (motor-boating or falling away) or tight.
2. Creases: wrinkles, pleats and hard spots.
3. Fullness: too flat or too full; fullness in the wrong place; backwinding.
4. Size: too small or too large.

Mainsail Leeches

Motor-boating. If the leech is slack at its extreme edge only, that is to say at the tabling, it will vibrate for its last two or three inches. This is known as motor-boating because of the noise it makes. The cause is often to be found in the way the tabling is put on: it is probably a little on the slack side and needs removing and shortening slightly. Care should be taken not to overdo it, or the reverse will occur and the leech will curl. This in itself may also cause the same effect, as the part of the sail which sits tight up to windward will vibrate in the airflow. If the tabling is not a turned one, but has been merely rolled over, the fault may be in the way the cloths are joined together at the very leech: they may have been allowed to wander apart at the leech end of the seam, thus slackening the edge of the sail. In addition a cupped leech may give the same effect, and this fault is treated separately below.

It is also possible for a leech line to be the cause of the trouble, not because it is too loose, but because its weight and bulk cause a disturbance to the airflow. This is particularly true if the leech tabling is narrow and thus gives little room for the line to pass along it, because the cloth will then strain at the stitching and cause wrinkles which in turn will cause the airflow to vibrate the slight extra weight of the leech line. It is also possible that a slightly rounded curve to the leech between the battens will flutter in the wind, so the sail should preferably be straight between batten pockets as in figure 110.

The foregoing are all the responsibility of the Sail Maker, but there are two more possible reasons for motor-boating, both of which occur as the direct result of mishandling by the owner. First, the leech may become creased parallel to its length, thus causing a short length to sit up at an angle to the main plane of the sail. The cure is either to try and smooth out the crease (which is not easy), or to cut off the offending cloth if this is feasible.

The second fault in the power of the owner to avoid is local stretching of the cloth. This is most likely to occur through hauling the sail down by the leech. This cardinal sin is so frequently committed, even by the top helmsmen, that it is hard on the nerves of a Sail Maker to attend the dinghy park as the boats come ashore at the end of a day's racing.

Most of these faults show on the horizontal test rig, but there are some which do not, and the proper course is to take the offending sail on to the water. Sometimes an intelligent guess can be made, based on probabilities, but no Sail Maker likes to have to do this.

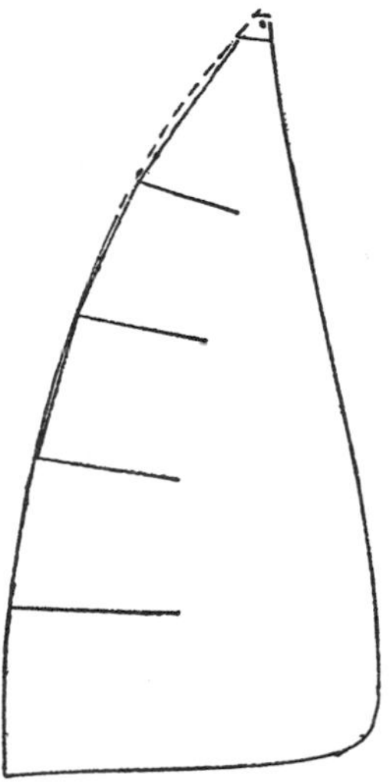

Fig. 110. Leech flutter (1). The dotted line shows the conventional curve to the leech, which should be trimmed to the straight line to avoid this form of flutter.

Fig. 111. Leech flutter (2). A section through a sail with a creased leech tabling, showing how it stands up to windward under tension.

Fig. 112. Leech flutter (3). A section through a sail with a cupped leech, which has gone slightly slack just inside the leech tabling.

Cupped Leech. A cupped leach is one which has a good flow to within 6 or 8 in. of the tabling, then falls away to leeward in a slight pocket which returns to the correct position at the tabling. This is caused either by the cloth at the cup being too much on the bias, and thus stretching, but not doing so at the very edge due to the extra resistance offered by the doubled cloth at the tabling, or else it is the reaction caused by pressures set up by the battens. The tendency is for the leech half-way between the battens to move towards the luff, whereas the battens are pushing their part of the sail towards the rear.

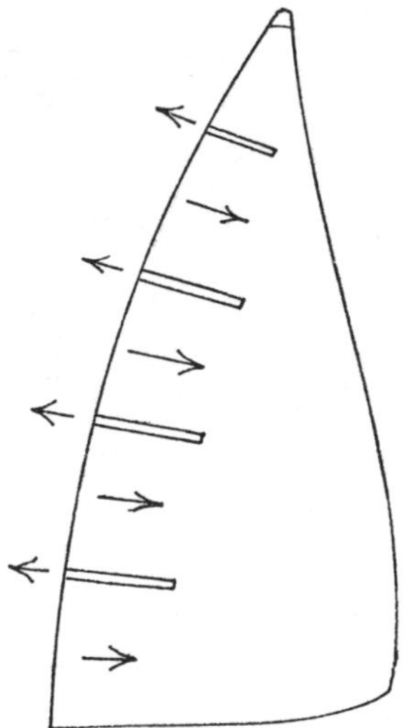

Fig. 113. Local pressures in a mainsail leech (1). Action and reaction set up by the presence of battens in a leech.

The cure in the case of the first reason lies in the cut of the sail, but this cannot be altered once the sail has been made. Either a narrower tabling should be fitted, or else a few seams tightened inside the tabling, just enough to take up the slack; this will mean tightening about an $\frac{1}{8}$ in. for a distance into the sail equal to the amount of the cup, say 6 or 8 in. The answer to the second again lies in the cut of the sail, but a cure can sometimes be effected if the leech is very slightly hollowed between the battens, say a $\frac{1}{4}$ in. on a dinghy, up to 1 in. on a large ocean-racer. Then, when tension is applied down the leech of the sail, there will be a tendency for the hollow part between the battens to pull outwards.

Leech Falling Away. If the whole leech of the sail, or even part of it, falls away, then there are again several possible reasons. All of them promote a slackness right down the leech, well into the sail, and not just at the tabling. It is necessary to find the cause of the slackness in each particular case.

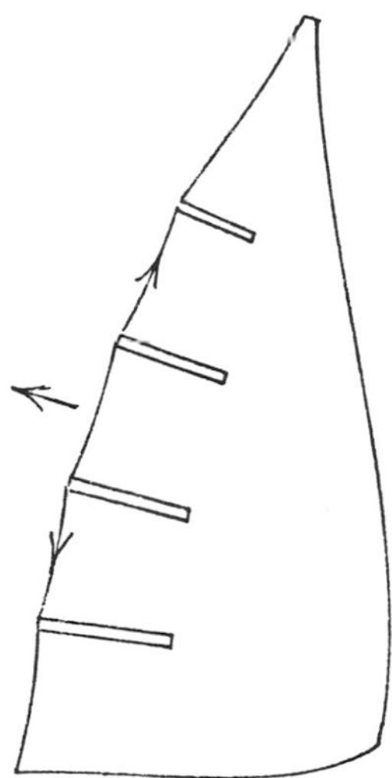

Fig. 114. Local pressures in a leech (2). If the leech is very slightly hollowed between each batten, a reaction outwards will be caused midway between the battens, helping to overcome leech flutter.

1. *Halyard.* If the halyard is not pulled right up, the luff will not be set up hard and the flow will not be drawn forward; this means that the leech will have a hard line along the inner ends of the battens, which will fall away. The same thing can be caused to a lesser extent by not pulling the foot out hard. The cure may not always be easy, because the sail may already be out to its marks, or the halyard purchase may be insufficient. A quick check can be made by pulling down on the Cunningham hole if one is fitted, or on the lowest slide eyelet, which should show whether there is any slack in the luff. I went on board a large sloop some time ago, where the mainsail luff was over 65 ft long and the owner was complaining of a slack leech. A quick tug at the luff rope showed that the sail was not pulled up sufficiently. I pointed this out, and

that there were 2 or 3 ft of track still clear at the head, but he would not believe that his halyard winch (which he had selected himself, and not through a Naval Architect) was not man enough for the task. Because the winch could not get any more tension on the luff, the owner claimed that the sail was hauled up properly. Unfortunately there was no downhaul to the boom, so that could not be used. I rigged a four part purchase handy billy on the bottom slide eyelet and pulled it down over a foot with little effort. The crease at the leech disappeared instantly.

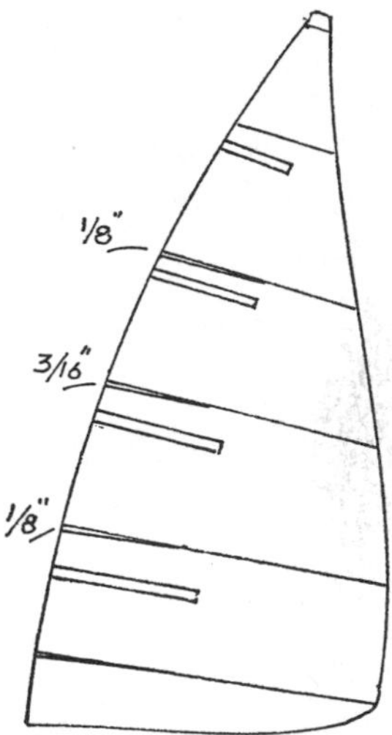

Fig. 115. Tightening a mainsail leech. Usually one seam is tightened between each pair of battens where the leech is slack; the seam is tightened in the order of $\frac{1}{8}''$ or $\frac{3}{10}''$ from the very edge in as far as the end of the battens.

2. *Stretched Leech.* The Sail Maker cannot always lay the blame for slack leeches at the owner's door. The second most common cause is that the cloth has stretched too much for some way inside the leech of the sail – usually at least in to the ends of the batten pockets. This can be caused by one of two things: either the cloths have been laid at such an angle that the pull comes too much on the bias and so distorts the cloth, or else too light a cloth has been used to make the sail, and it has not been able to stand up to the

forces imposed upon it. Both these reasons are the fault of the Sail Maker (for even if he is given strict instructions to make a sail from a cloth which he considers too light, he should inform the customer of the dangers). The cure lies in ripping open some of the seams at the leech, and tightening them by increasing the overlap of one cloth upon the other, in a tapering nip, going at least in to the ends of the batten pockets. The number and distribution of seams, and the exact amount of tightening (in the order of $\frac{1}{8}$ in. or so per seam) will depend on the gravity of the trouble; they are decided by the Sail Maker as a result of observation.

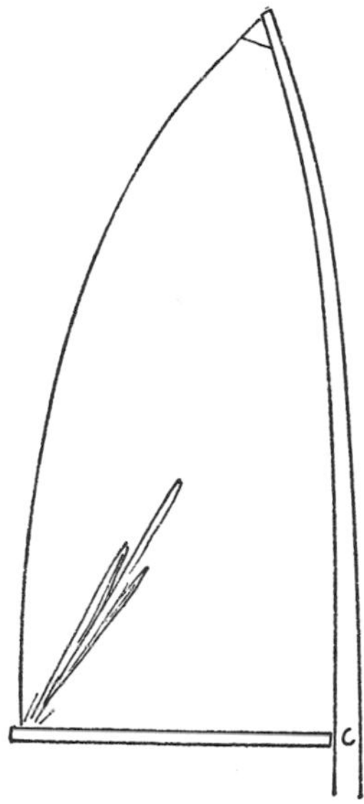

Fig. 116. Crease from mainsail clew caused by too much mast bend aloft.

3. *Bendy Mast.* The third reason for a generally slack leech is a mast which bends aft at the head more than the Sail Maker was informed, or for which he did not make proper allowance. If not enough round has been built into the top of the luff, and the masthead comes aft, the sail will be held on a line from the clew to just below the head (at the point of maximum forward curvature), yet the head itself will come aft, thus slackening the leech. The cure is either to stiffen up the masthead, or cut more round

into the upper luff – an alteration which is not possible without shortening the luff and leech slightly as will be seen in Appendix H.

4. *Roach.* The final reason for a completely slack leech is a roach which is too large. If the Sail Maker puts on too much, he is asking for trouble, and the only certain cure is to remove the extra inches. A stop-gap palliative can be provided by tightening some seams at the leech, but this may lead to the whole leech being closed rather than open. This, coupled with the typical ridge along the inner ends of the battens, will stop a boat more quickly than almost anything bar an anchor.

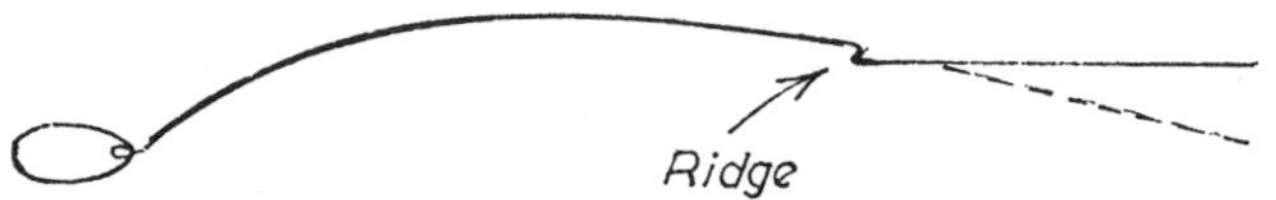

Fig. 117. Excessive roach. Note how the batten end causes a ridge to windward. and the whole batten area falls off to leeward. The dotted line shows the possible result if some leech seams are repeatedly tightened as the only cure. Imagine the airflow over this section!

Tight Leech. A tight leech to a mainsail stops a boat even more effectively than a slack one, because of the rear component of the wind force which is generated, and the energy dissipated in disturbing the airflow unnecessarily. The only possible exception to this is an extremely full mainsail under ghosting conditions, because the forces involved are so low that only that portion of thrust which is generated at the powerful forward part of the sail has any effect. Tight leeches can be subdivided in the same way as slack ones:

1. *Leech Tabling.* If the tabling has been put on tight, it will draw the after end of the sail together and will feel drum hard to the touch when the sail is sheeted home on the wind. The cure is to ease the tabling in the sail loft, which may involve adding a few inches of new tabling and sharing it out evenly.

2. *Whole Leech.* Here again the Sail Maker is at fault. If he has either laid his cloths without any bias on the leech so that it has no give, or if he has tightened one or two seams in the wrong place, the whole leech area at the battens will hold too far to windward.

The wind will not get a free run off, and the boat will slow appreciably. The cure lies in easing some seams in the sail loft.

3. *Too Full.* A very full mainsail must, of necessity, fall well away to leeward from the luff to achieve its fullness. The sail eventually has to return to the boom, and this means that the leech has all the characteristics of a tight one. The solution is not to use such a sail in anything other than drifting conditions, or it will knock the boat down and hold her back. Failing this, the after end of the sail may be flattened by tightening some seams inside the tabling as described on page 273 under the heading *Too Full Aft.*

Mainsail Creases

I have put creases second in order of frequency of mainsail faults, because I am not counting those creases we have just dealt with under slack and tight leeches. I am more concerned here with smaller creases emanating from various points on the sail for no apparent reason. It will be found in general that most faults with a sail will lead to creases of one sort or another, and we shall overlap slightly here on what I have just written and what is to come.

Clew. Creases at the clew form the most widespread complaint with Terylene or Dacron mainsails. A hard line from the clew to the inner end of the bottom batten is often a sign of a slack leech in the lower half of the sail, and the cure lies in one of the solutions I have put forward above: hoisting harder, tightening one or two of the lower leech seams, or reducing the leech round. It may, however, stem from a tight leech, in which case the kink will be to windward and not to leeward, and the solution is to ease a seam or two. Equally, the sail may be too full along the foot in the clew area, in other words the fullness has been taken too far aft. If some of the foot round is rubbed away from the after part of the sail, the leech will be flattened at the clew and the sail thus drawn up to windward to take away the crease.

On the other hand the leech itself may be good, and yet the clew area may have creases radiating from it. This is an unfortunate failing of synthetics, and one for which there is no immediate solution. Its origin lies in the hardness of the cloth, which will not give like cotton when it is confined or crimped up as when sewing an eye. These radiating creases, therefore, originate from the clew eye itself, and there is little that can be done, save perhaps fitting a heavier clew patch, to try and alleviate the trouble. The eye should have been worked with fewer stitches, and perhaps not pulled quite so tight as they were. As cloth becomes softer, this danger recedes.

There is also the crease which runs from the clew towards a point about half or three-quarters of the way up the luff, and having no

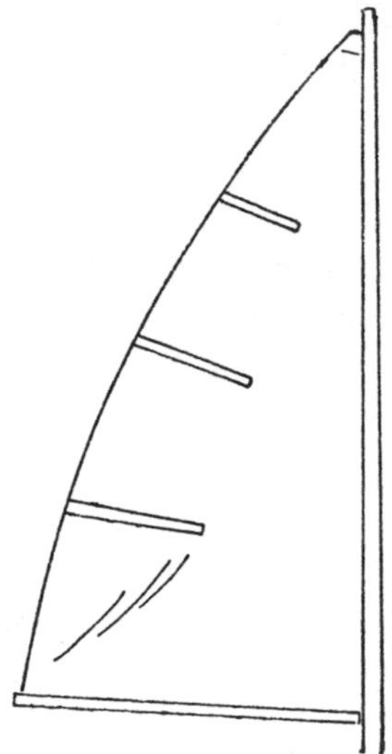

Fig. 118. Crease from mainsail clew.
Possible cures are: 1. Haul sail up harder. 2. Ease or tighten a seam between the clew and the bottom batten. 3. Reduce foot round near the clew. 4. Reduce leech round.

relation to the batten pockets. This is usually the result of a sail which does not have enough round to the luff for the amount that the mast bends. The cure is either drastic surgery to the sail to increase its luff round (a difficult and costly business), or else stiffening the mast so that it does not bend so much, perhaps by tightening the jumper stays.

Head. Creases from the head are usually caused by the way the headboard is sewn into the sail. Too many, or too tight stitches can cause this, as can an irregularly shaped headboard, or faulty cutting of the cloth at the head. The cure lies with the Sail Maker, and is not always easy. It explains why headboards are put in in a variety of ways these days: plastic boards riveted either side of the sail on the outside; plastic boards sewn into a pocket at the head, without any stitching going through the board; or metal boards with the minimum of stitching. Check also that the halyard leads fairly off the sheave and does not pull the headboard over towards the mast as shown in figure 92(a).

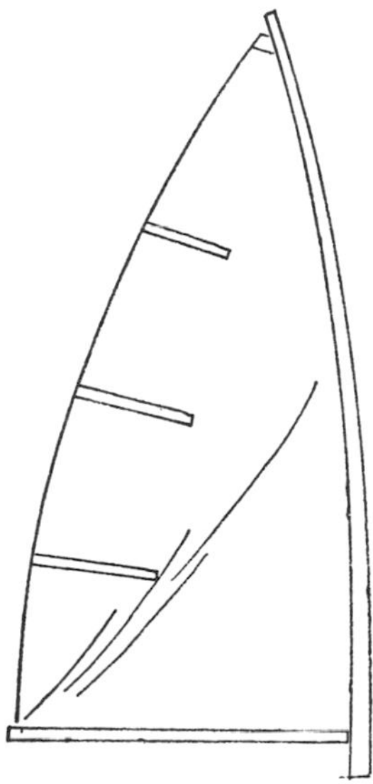

Fig. 119. Excessive mast bend. The crease may run from the clew the whole way to the mast.

Tack. If creases run from the tack they may be caused by a badly sewn tack eye, as with the clew. This is not usual, however, as a mainsail is under sufficient tension on both luff and foot to eliminate most wrinkles of this origin. A more likely cause is that the sail has not been cut back at the tack by the right amount to lead straight to the tack pin, which is why the distance from the pin to the aft face of the mast is so important to the Sail Maker; alternatively the tack pin may be out of horizontal line with the foot of the sail, which is thus being pulled out of its true direction. Another reason can be the cut of the sail itself, for which there is often no cure, unless the fault is that there is too much round to the lower luff, in which case the sail can be flattened. This is a fairly common fault with fully battened mainsails, which need fullness in this area yet cannot accept very much round due to the way the battens restrict the movement of the cloth. A crease which runs more as a fold along the length of the luff or foot is the result of too much tension on the halyard or outhaul. It is manifestation of the flow in a sail, and a good breeze will soon blow it into shape – as, if you are lucky, it may with many other creases mentioned in this chapter, so do not rush into remedial action until you have given the sail a good chance to settle down.

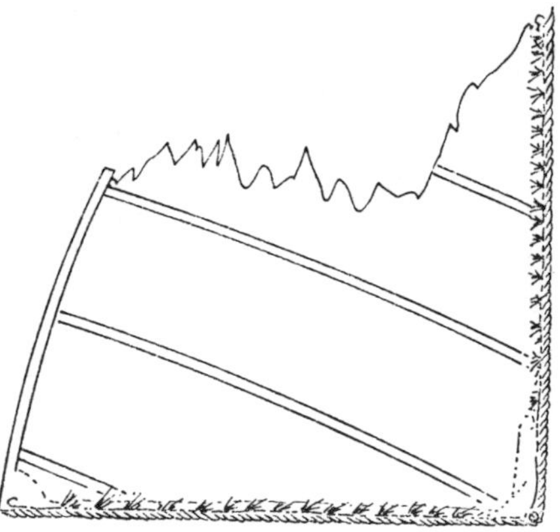

Fig. 120. Creases at the rope.

At the Rope. A multitude of small creases emanating from the rope, usually inclined towards the other roped edge and running most of the way along their own edge, is a sign that the sail has not been hauled up or out hard enough. If it is already at its marks, Cunningham holes should be fitted as an immediate measure; the sail can be shortened slightly if a permanent cure is sought.

On the other hand, the rope may have been sewn too tight all along its length, and will not allow the cloth to stretch as it should. Re-roping is the only cure. It may, however, only be tight at one spot, in which event 'crow's-nest' creases will be evident over a short distance, say 6 to 12 in., of its length. It may be that the roping is tight at this particular spot, or that the rope has been allowed to twist as it was put on. Again, re-roping is the cure, and it is normally a job for the Sail Maker.

Hard Spots. A hard spot can be caused in a sail if the cloths are not overlapped exactly parallel with one another (allowing for any broad seam involved). If one cloth is pulled over or eased away from the other, local areas of tightness or slackness will be caused, and the cure is to rip the seam and re-sew it. Similar puckers can come from racing numbers, insignia or windows which are not lying exactly flat when they are sewn, or sometimes if they are sewn on with too small a stitch or too tight a tension on the sewing machine.

Mainsail Fullness

Fullness is a question of relativity. What one man may consider full, is medium for the next; one helmsman may want more fullness from a heavy weather sail than the next. The only way to be fair to a Sail Maker when specifying fullness is to refer as a yardstick to another suit of similar sails he has made himself.

Too Flat. A mainsail which is too flat is difficult to cure without major re-cutting. More cloth has to be found from somewhere to give the extra flow, and it cannot satisfactorily be put in one long strip up the luff. There are two ways in which the job can be done properly. The first, and easiest, involves moving the headboard slightly over towards the leech to allow the luff to be re-rubbed with more round. This is not always practicable, because it means reducing the length of the luff and leech slightly.

The second method is more complex, and involves taking the sail to pieces. The rope has to be taken off the luff and from around the tack, and then the seam which usually strikes the tack must be ripped from end to end, so that the sail is in two halves. A new cloth is inserted in the resulting gap, the headboard and batten pockets must be dropped, and the luff rubbed fuller. The new cloth should be well crumpled before going in, otherwise it may sew tight on to the old cloths. If there is a row of reef points crossing the ripped seam the result may be slightly bizarre, but this must be accepted. This method may bring trouble from the phenomenon of the vanishing rope which I mentioned on page 250. When the luff rope comes to be sewn back on to the sail, it will almost certainly be found to be too short; depending on the deficiency, the sail may have to be re-roped

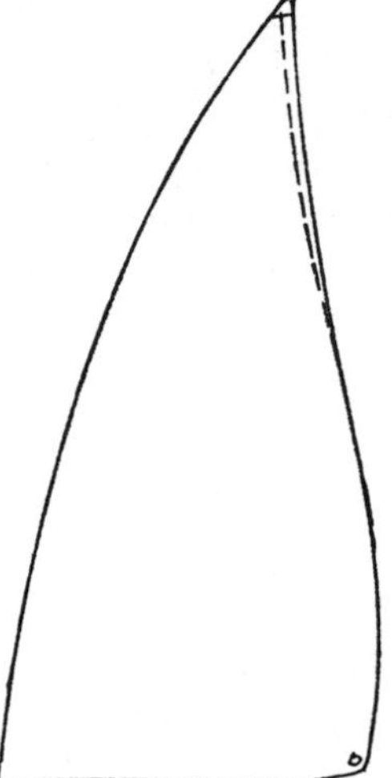

Fig. 121. Increasing mainsail luff round (1).

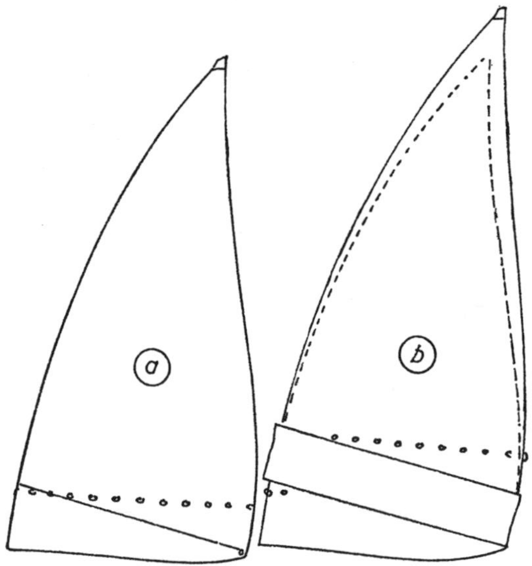

Fig. 122. Increasing mainsail luff round (2).
(a) The sail is separated into two halves at the tack seam.
(b) A new cloth is inserted at the tack. The dashed line shows the old size.

all round. It is also sometimes possible to rip the luff end only of a few seams, and to build in more broad seam. This, of course, shortens the luff by the amount of extra broad seam (not normally significant) but cannot, by itself, produce extra fullness if the cloth is not there in the first place.

A third, do-it-yourself, possibility exists for dinghies, which has an air of desperation about it. I do not recommend it unless all else has failed and you are prepared to see the worst come to the worst. The boat can be laid over on her side with the mainsail hoisted, and wet sand shovelled into the sail. If this is left for several days some stretching will certainly occur, even if it is in the wrong place. It has been done successfully, however, but do not do it to your best sail. It is not good sailmaking to say the least.

Too Full Forward. A sail which is too full forward can easily be flattened by pleating along the luff or foot, as appropriate. This does not harm the aerodynamic qualities of the sail, and has the advantage that it can always be released again with no more harm than a row or two of stitch holes.

Too Full Aft. If the mainsail is too full aft, the boat will go badly, except in light winds. The cause of this trouble lies in one of three factors: the cloth is poor; the sail was made that way; or it has been used in winds too strong for it. Whatever the reason, there is not a great deal which can be done without considerable re-cutting, if the problem is serious. We know, however, that more tension on the luff pulls the flow forward, so the first step is to do this. Either pull harder on the halyard, or fit a Cunningham hole and pull down on it. If the sail will not stretch more on the luff, it can be re-roped with a slacker rope, at the same time possibly dropping the headboard so that it stays within the black bands when fully stretched. The final measure is to rip apart several cloths and re-design the broad seam in the sail, removing any tightening at the leech and increasing it forward. This, however, is a costly remedy for what may be a bad sail not worth further expense. First-aid along these lines can be administered, however, by tightening some seams along the point of greatest fullness at the roach. This should not be carried right to the tabling, or the whole leech will come up to windward, whereas if it is stopped about 6 to 12 in. short, it will be the equivalent of easing some seams at the leech, thus freeing the whole area. An additional remedy is to pleat out some of the foot round towards the clew; this must not be overdone, however, or a hard spot will result.

Fig. 123. Mainsail too full aft.
Seams may be tightened near the leech to flatten the section along the dotted line.

Backwinding. I have separated backwinding from a sail which is simply too full because, while the mainsail may indeed be too full, the fault is often to be found in the headsail. If the headsail leech curls to windward, or if there is not enough hollow in it to allow free passage to the airflow, the wind will be deflected into the lee of the mainsail. The best cut mainsail will backwind in these circumstances, so the two sails should be examined in conjunction. I shall deal with headsail leeches later in this chapter.

Mainsail Size

A sail which is too small or too large has to be altered by the Sail Maker. Sometimes the owner of an ocean-racer would rather alter his black bands to conform with the sizes as found, rather than risk deforming his favourite sail through surgery. It is, of course, easier to reduce a sail than to make it larger, but I go more fully into this question towards the end of this chapter. Let me just say here that it is very seldom that a mainsail is as much under size as some owners think. A Sail Maker is used to working in his material, and knows how much to allow for stretch, so it is rare that he makes such a large allowance that the sail is as much as 1 per cent short of its marks. Yet most Sail Makers have had complaints of this nature from time to time. They mainly stem from incorrect measurement. Many a sail has been condemned as too small because it fails to show the full luff length when spread on the lawn. It must be set under normal halyard tension on its spars before a fair assessment can be made. I grant you that a sail which is roped tightly will be under size, and will never get out to its marks, but re-roping should not only solve the problem, but make the sail set in the way it was intended.

It is, of course, more common for a sail to be under or over the cross measurements in a closely controlled class. In this case inches, and even parts of inches, count, and the Sail Maker is often at fault. This mostly concerns the dinghy classes, although keelboats like the Dragon also bring their problems. In defence of the Sail Maker, I would mention that he is working to fine tolerances. The rules will outlaw any sail which is the smallest fraction of an inch over the maximum; the owner will sometimes refuse any sail which is more than half an inch under, because he is losing area. Add to this that different measurers in different clubs can get the same sail to produce many different answers for the same measurement, and you have a nice problem in compromise. I remember one owner calling at the loft in Cowes with a 5–0–5 mainsail which he said his Measurer made two inches under on the half height; he felt that this was losing too much area. I measured the sail in his presence, and made it half an inch under. He went off a happy man, but returned next day, saying that his Measurer would not believe my figures. We measured it again, with the same result. This happened no less than four times, when finally the owner telephoned to say that the club Measurer had decided that he was not getting very accurate figures spreading the sail on an uneven lawn, so he had taken it to a gymnasium and that he now agreed my figure. Mark you, not many Measurers have the perfect facilities of a sail loft for their difficult task, and full allowance must be made for this. Which is why the average Sail Maker errs slightly on the small side when he is making a sail to a specific rule.

Headsail Faults

The headsail is prone to similar faults to the mainsail, with the addition of a slack foot. Once again I have listed them in the order which I have found most frequent. It may well be that other Sail Makers find a different frequency, but there is nothing significant in it, and I only mention it for the sake of interest.

1. Leeches: slack or tight.
2. Fullness: Too full aft; too full forward; flow too high; too flat. I refer here, principally to headsails with luff wires, not tapes.

3. Foot: slack or tight.
4. Creases: wrinkles, pleats and hardspots.
5. Size: too small or too large.

Headsail Leeches

Slack Leech. A slack leech is a sign that the wind is escaping from the aft end of the headsail, and is thus not a particularly bad fault. The sight and sound of it, however, have a poor effect on morale, so it should be attended to if for no other reason. Check first that the sheet lead is not too far aft, then the leech line may be gently tightened so as to alleviate the flutter to a more acceptable movement, but it should never be tightened so that the leech curls. The real remedy lies in the sail loft, where a few seams and/or the tabling should be tightened $\frac{1}{8}$ in. or so each. On the other hand, the leech may show fair on the test rig, but there may not be enough hollow to it, and it can then be hollowed some more. See also my remarks about mainsail as regards *creased*, *cupped* and *stretched* leeches. The most common single fault with a headsail is the cupped leech, and it requires the most delicate attention. If the worst comes to the worst, increase the hollow to cut away the stretched portion of cloth, but care must be taken not to set the new leech too much on the bias as a result.

Tight Leech. A tight leech on a headsail is one of the worst faults which can occur. Not only does it affect the flow over the headsail, but it also badly disturbs the air over the lee side of the mainsail, thus causing a major breakdown in thrust. After checking that the sheet lead is not too far forward, this important part of the sail should have immediate expert attention from the Sail Maker. The individual breakdown of the reasons for a tight headsail leech is exactly the same as that for the mainsail as shown on page 266. An additional remedy available to the headsail once again is to hollow the leech further, thus cutting away the offending cloth. If it does nothing else, it will make the Sail Maker take off the leech tabling and put it back on again, with the chance that he will tension it better the second time.

Headsail Fullness

Too Full Aft. The flow in a headsail should be more forward than a mainsail. It will move aft for the same reasons as in a mainsail, and the corrective measures are the same. Where the mainsail is pulled harder on the halyard, the headsail is pulled more on the wire. This means that the luff seizings and hanks have to be cut away, the luff shortened slightly if there is not already some excess wire available, and the luff of the sail stretched more along its wire, to draw the flow forward.

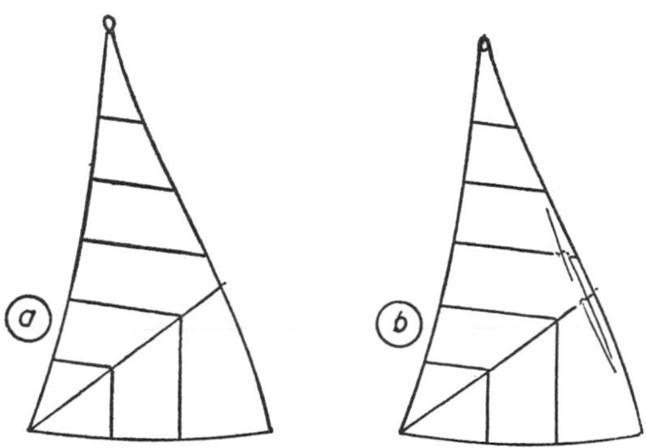

Fig. 124. Headsail luff fullness.
(a) The head eye usually runs out of the sail.
(b) The sail can be pulled more on the wire and the head eye worked into the sail, thus inducing more flow in the luff. If head eye does not run out to start with, the luff of the sail must be shortened first to allow it to be pulled more on the original wire.

This will not always work completely satisfactorily, but it is surprising what a new lease of life it can give to a sail which has been blown out of shape by heavy winds, providing the cloth was initially a good one. Ghosters and drifters are constantly being subjected to wind strengths far in excess of those for which they were designed ('The wind got up, but she was going so well that I didn't want to change to the genoa.'); even these can be helped a lot by pulling more on the wire if the maltreatment has not gone on too long.

Too Full Forward. If the headsail is too full forward, it may be because it is, indeed, cut too full, but it may also be because the stay sags too much. In either event the luff should have some cloth removed, and this can be done by pleating. An alternative reason is that the sail may be pulled too much on the wire; it should be eased back a ¼ in. or so (rather more in large boats), until the sail takes up a better shape. Remember though that a heavy weather headsail will need to be pulled rather more than one for light weather, so it should have a deep fold down the luff in light airs; this will blow aft in strong winds. It is only the light weather headsail which should have a smooth curve preset to the one third position in conditions of little or no wind.

Flow Too High. After a certain amount of use a headsail may end up with its flow too high (or, indeed, too low or just badly spread over the luff). This will almost certainly be because the luff of the sail is seized at intervals to the luff wire, and these seizings have moved on the wire, causing the sail to be stretched more at one point than at another. The solution is to set up the headsail in a horizontal position, by making fast the head and pulling out the tack on a handy billy until the luff wire is taut. It should then be possible to see small irregularities in the luff tabling around the seizings where these have ridden up or down from their original positions. If you are lucky, you may be able to force these errant seizings back to their proper places by pushing and pulling with your hands. It is then only a question of seeing that the tension is evenly shared out along the luff wire, and the flow will immediately improve. On the other hand, if the seizings are loose enough for you to move them by hand, they will almost certainly move again, and you should renew the seizings, taking care not to pass the needle through the protective covering on the wire.

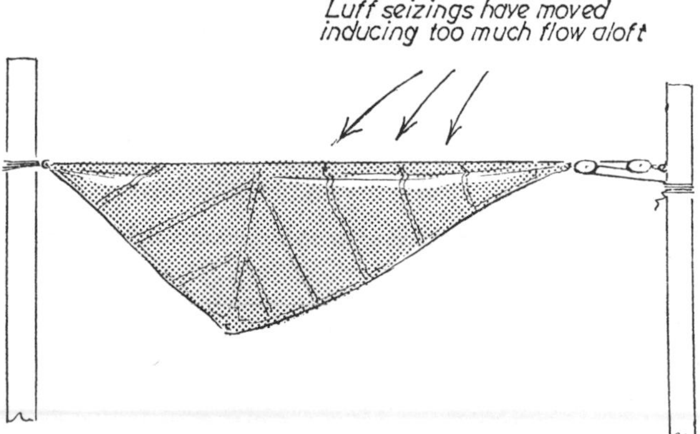

Fig. 125. Setting up a headsail.

Too Flat. The rear half of a headsail should always be pretty flat so, if the sail is said to be too flat, it usually means that there is not enough flow forward. This can usually be cured by pulling the cloth more on the wire, to induce a fold in the cloth up the luff, from where it will be blown back into the sail when the wind acts on it. In extreme cases the sail may have to be taken to pieces and some broad seam put into the mitre, but this should not normally be necessary.

Headsail Foot

Slack Foot. Apart from a sheet lead which is too far forward, a slack headsail foot is usually the result of too much round being built on to the foot in an attempt to gain free area. A conservative guide to the correct amount of foot round is 1 in. for every 3 ft of foot length. Foot round, however, not only represents free area, but it also keeps a

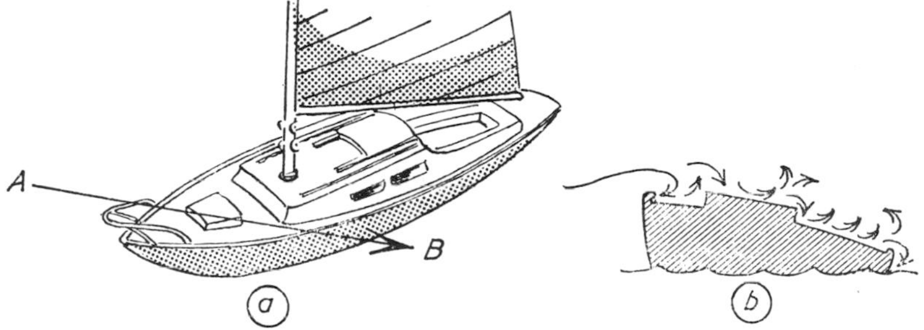

Fig. 126. Airflow over the deck.
(a) Wind direction is from A to B.
(b) Section through deck at A-B.

genoa or genoa staysail near the deck. This prevents too much wind escaping under the foot. There is also the school which suggests that the airflow is faster over the deck because of the greater distance it has to travel; this may well be true, but it must also be a most disturbed region due to the poor streamline shape of a canted deck [figure 126(*b*)].

A slack foot can also be caused by the cloths lying too much on the bias, and thus stretching. The remedy in both the above cases lies in tightening a few seams into the sail for about 5 per cent of the foot length; i.e. a genoa 20 ft on the foot should be tightened into the sail about 1 ft, a working jib with a foot of 10 ft should go in 6 in. and a dinghy jib of 5 ft length should be tightened in to 3 in.

Tight Foot. It is rare to have a tight foot to a headsail, and not particularly detrimental to performance; in fact it can be advantageous in reaching conditions, and I have sometimes wondered why a drawstring along the foot tabling has not been tried more often, with a view to tightening the foot off the wind. If the foot is, in fact, too tight for windward work, one or two seams should be carefully eased an $\frac{1}{8}$ in. or so. Before doing so, however, check that the tightness is not caused by the sheet lead being too far aft.

Headsail Creases

General creases occur in a headsail for more or less the same reasons as they do in a mainsail, and my previous remarks concerning the latter should be observed where they apply.

Tack. Probably the most common crease in a headsail is the one which runs up from the tack. This is caused by the shape of the tack eye, which is usually worked into the sail so that the foot shall be as low as possible, and the tension which is always on it due to the luff being stretched on the wire.

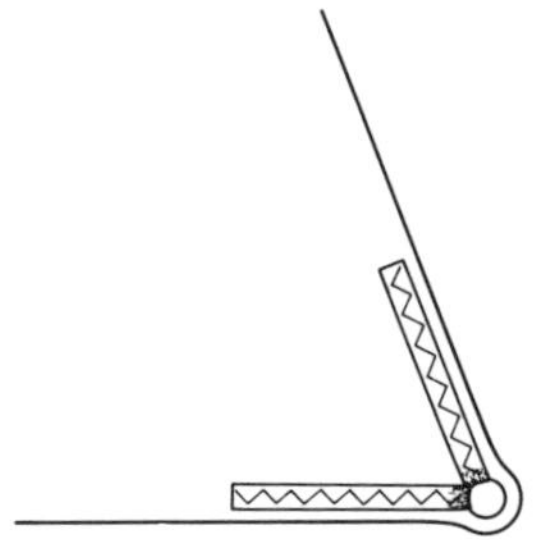

Fig. 127. Headsail tack creases. One or two lengths of synthetic tape should be sewn through the tack eye and then along the direction of tension. Use large stitches with heavy seaming twine.

The cloth has to be shaped round the eye at the bottom of the wire, which is then sewn into the sail. The sail is next pulled on the wire so that the canvas is stretched from the small arrows. Sewing the shaped sail tightly to the tack eye can cause wrinkles on its own; when the cloth is subjected to tension in addition, the risk is greater. Apart from letting the tack eye run right out of the sail, so that it does not have to be shaped, the cure for this fault is not easy. If a tack board is allowed, a small piece of Perspex can be slipped under the tack patch, and this should do the trick. Not many rules allow this, however. A second possibility is to sew a length of webbing through the eye and up into the sail, so that some of the stresses can be absorbed. This should be taken 6 to 18 in. into the sail and sewn with broad stitches, care being taken to see that there is room in the eye for the tack shackle or pin.

Clew. All the stresses of the sail concentrate at the clew when hard on the wind. It is natural that a certain amount of creasing should be set up in this area. The clew eye itself may encourage this, in the same way that any eye will do so; the stainless steel D-ring type clew, with tapes radiating into the sail will do a great deal to spread the load, as will a large and heavy clew patch with plenty of underpatching

Head Eye. The head eye usually runs out, so is not so prone to creases. Where they occur, they most likely originate from the small eye worked at the head so that the sail may be pulled on the wire. A length of webbing tape is the best hope of success.

Piston Hank or Snap Hook Eyelets. Piston hank or snap hook eyelets can cause creases if the hank itself is seized so tightly that it folds the eyelet over against the luff wire; this is aggravated if there is too much distance between the eyelet and the wire. In addition, the sail may have moved on the wire through the seizings pulling up or down, as explained on pages 277 and 278; this occurs if the headsail is lowered by pulling too hard on the cloth and not on the wire. The answer is to regulate the cloth on the wire as described above.

Hard Spots. Treatment for hard spots in a headsail is exactly the same as for a mainsail; see page 271.

Tight Mitre. A tight mitre is sometimes evident in light winds. This results from shaping of the mitre seam, and will almost certainly blow out in stronger winds, to leave a nice flat leech. If the crease persists, and cannot be cured by pulling more on the wire as described on page 279, the seam must be eased slightly in the middle.

Sails

Headsail Size

A wire luff headsail lies on the ground the same way that it is made. By this I mean that there is no rope to gather it up so that it looks short, and there is little broad seam to the average headsail so it will lie fairly flat. There is thus little scope for error or misinterpretation of the facts, so that relatively few headsails are found to be the wrong size.

The principal source of misinterpretation is on the luff, particularly where the sail is not seized to the luff wire but is left to 'float' and find its own level. We have already seen that a headsail is made short in the luff, so that it can be stretched on the wire to induce flow in the luff. If the wire is loose inside the luff tabling and the sail is laid on the ground, it will appear short unless the wire is pulled straight (thus stretching the cloth). A sail which is seized at regular intervals to its luff wire will show clearly if the wire is not straight, because it will lie in slight twists under the tension of the already stretched cloth. In either case a firm pull is required, particularly if the cloth is fairly heavy. The same applies to a taped luff.

Spinnaker Faults

Spinnakers are not such special sails that diagnosis and treatment of their troubles merit a special chapter to themselves, even though I have accorded that honour to making and setting them. They suffer the same sort of faults as mainsails and headsails, but to a lesser extent because the springy nature of their canvas tends to allow creases to dissipate throughout the sail. I propose to deal here only with those faults which are peculiar to spinnakers.

Narrow Head. The most common fault from which nearly every spinnaker suffers is that it is too narrow in the head. The cure for this is to get off your boat and on to somebody else's, where you will find that his high shouldered, bursting beauty which you were admiring from afar, looks just as narrow gutted from close behind as your own sail now looks broad in the head.

The two photographs in plate 40 were taken in 1965 in the Ratsey & Lapthorn wind tunnel at Cowes, and are of the same spinnaker within seconds of each other. If, in fact, your particular spinnaker is narrow in the head, there is little the Sail Maker can do about it. You should resign yourself to the fact, and take what profit you can: it

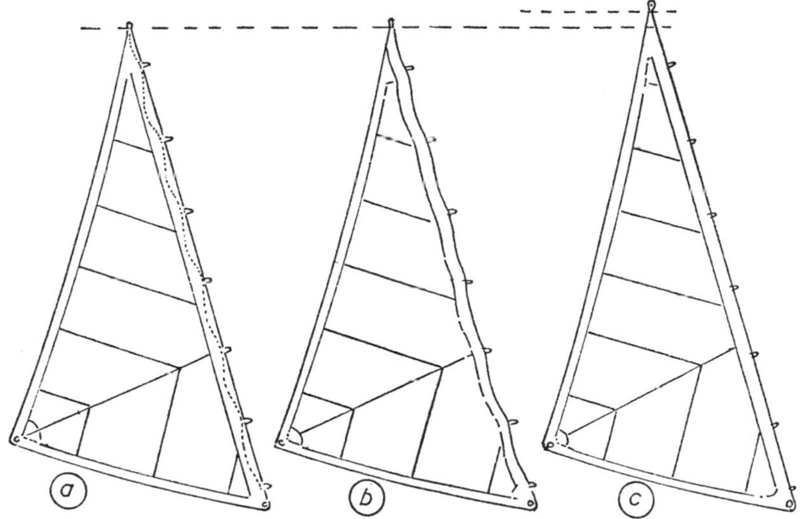

Fig. 128. Headsail luff measurement.
(a) Luff is not pulled enough to stretch the cloth, and the luff wire is loose inside the tabling (except where it is seized by the snaps or hanks). Sail appears short but dotted line shows wire.
(b) Similar to (a), but luff is seized to luff wire, so easily shows the kinks.
(c) Both (a) and (b) correctly stretched out to straighten wire and achieve full length, thus inducing flow in the luff.

will knock the boat down less in a strong beam wind; it will probably be flatter aloft, and so you can use it with the wind well forward; there is not so much weight of canvas aloft, and therefore less total weight to lift if conditions are very light.

Tight Stays. Many spinnakers suffer from tight stays. They curl in, particularly near the head, and make the sail a poor performer on a reach because the luff collapses before it should.

This is caused either by the wires being too short for the sail (which has been caused in its turn by the sail stretching and the wires staying their original length), or by the tapes on the luff and leech being too short, as a result of being sewn on too tight or possibly even shrinking. The cure is to ease the wires or tapes, taking care that they do not exceed the maximum allowed by the particular rule

Fig. 129. Curling spinnaker leeches.
(a) Tight stays or leeches cause turbulence.
(b) Straight stays allow better flow.

under which the sail is measured. If they do, then the sail will have to be shortened by the appropriate amount.

Head Creases. Two major creases radiating down from the head for about one fifth of the way into the spinnaker are a sign that the head is too full or the sail has been badly designed. The Sail Maker has tried to fit too much cloth into the top of the sail, and it will not stand unless the wind is dead aft. Either the sail must be made narrower aloft, or else the head seams should be completely unmade and tightened considerably more – probably a little of both. This is not an easy fault to cure without cutting away a good deal of cloth.

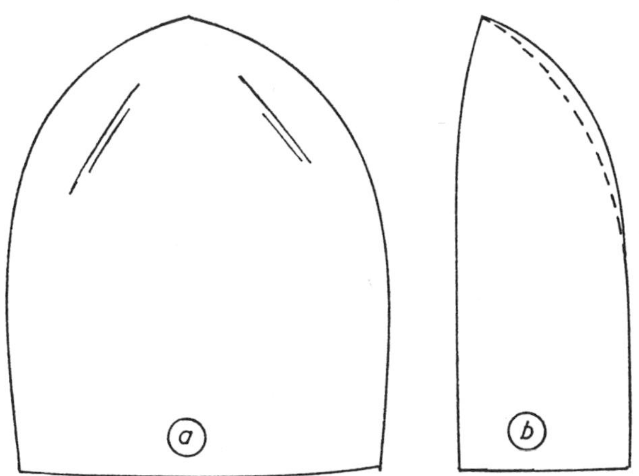

Fig. 130. Spinnaker girts from the head.
(a) View from the front.
(b) Dotted line on the half sail shows normal outline. The full line shows too much cloth in the head.

Loose Foot. A spinnaker which has too large a skirt on the foot will set badly in that area on almost all points of sailing. The solution is to remove the offending extra cloth, and/or to tighten the foot by inserting some vertical darts in the bottom cloth as shown in figure 131.

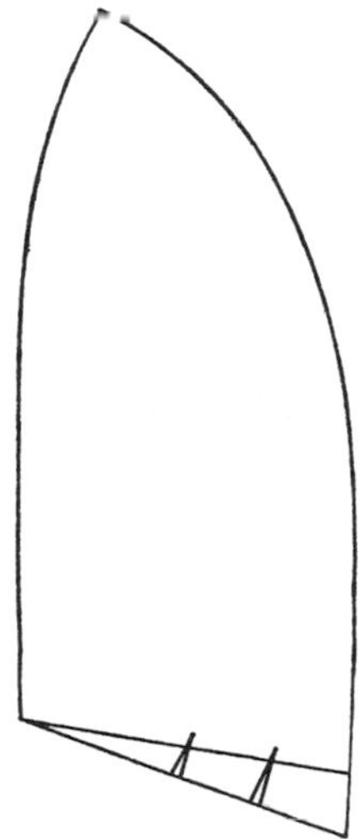

Fig. 131. Slack spinnaker foot.
Slackness is sometimes caused by too deep a skirt. Remove the wedge at the foot, or tighten the foot by means of vertical darts.

CHAPTER XVIII

Alterations to Size

Any major alteration to the size of a sail must change the relative position of any shaping which was built in when it was first made. There is therefore more than an outside risk that it will be spoiled for all time. Nevertheless, it is sometimes important to make these changes, and they can often be done successfully.

Naturally there are limits to what can be done, depending on the original cut of the sail, and I am assuming conventionally laid cloths in this chapter. Even so, most Sail Makers will be reluctant to give a firm opinion as to whether a particular change can be made, before they have had a chance to see the sail in question spread on the loft floor. There are sometimes snags which only reveal themselves when the twine is stretched round the sail to the new sizes, such as an awkwardly placed batten pocket, a row of reefing eyelets, or a window in the wrong place.

I have given most of the effective ways of reducing or enlarging sails in some detail in Appendix H, together with sketches. I would like here to run through some of the broad principles.

The most important single point to remember when deciding on a re-cut, is the bias of the cloth. We have been all through the reasons for containing the bias angle on the leech of most sails to within about 5°, so I will not repeat them here.

Reducing Mainsails. Let me illustrate the point in a simple way.

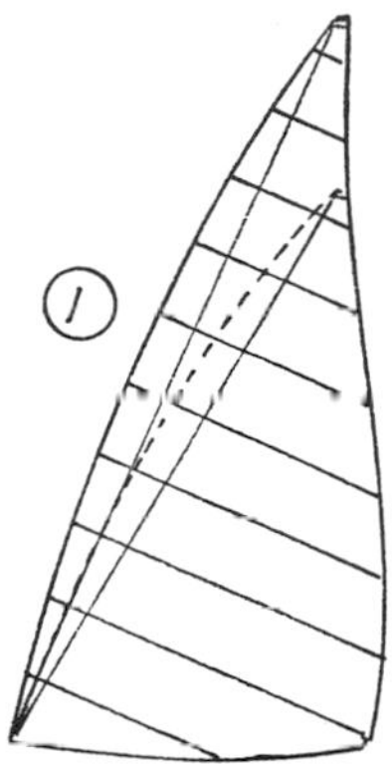

Fig. 132. Reducing a mainsail (1)
Note how the reduction of the sail to the dotted size puts the cloth on the bias to the straight line joining clew to head.

Let us assume that it is desired to reduce the mainsail in figure 132 from a luff of 25 ft to one of 20 ft, leaving the foot as it is. If the head is dropped 5 ft, the measurements will be right, but the bias at the upper leech will be excessive, and the leech will fall to leeward.

If, however, we cut the sail as shown in figure 133, the leech will be undisturbed and should set properly in use. Agreed, we shall have to re-rope the whole sail, and we shall be cutting away a good deal of broad seam at the luff and foot – although some shape can be given to the new sail through luff and foot round. If we wanted to, we could add 3 or 4 in. to the length of the luff, and then rip the seam at the new tack in to 2 or 3 ft, in order to taper the two sides of that seam by the 3 or 4 in. we had allowed. The headboard, racing number and all batten pockets would have to be re-positioned whichever method were used.

The above is not to say that a limited amount of extra bias cannot be accepted on a cut down sail, particularly if it is only going to be used for cruising or passage making. The Sail Maker can compensate for a certain degree of extra stretch by tightening the appropriate seams, but the owner should be prepared for the worst. I can assure you that the Sail Maker will do the job in the easiest way he can, for his own convenience, because these jobs are often a nuisance which he wants out of the way as soon as possible. There is little merit or money, but plenty of potential odium in them.

When indicating to your Sail Maker the sizes to which you require the sail remade, you should try and give him an indication of how much to take off. It is far better to ask for 9 in. off the foot, than to offer a sail with an indeterminate foot length, and instructions to cut it to suit black bands of 9 ft 3 in. The Sail Maker will not know how much to allow for the tack fitting, or what length the sail produces when it is set on the boom in its present state, particularly if he did

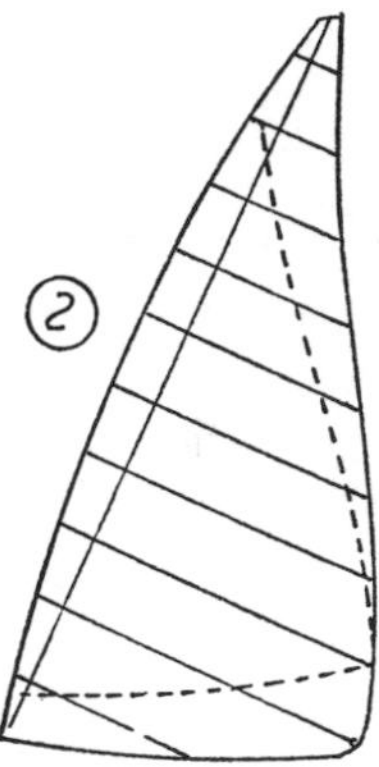

Fig. 133. Reducing a mainsail (2).
By cutting the sail in at the luff, leech bias can be contained. Note that the tack is still on a seam, so tack seam can be built into the sail.

not make it in the first place. The stretched length he finds in the loft may be anything up to 3 or 4 in. different from the one actually measured on board.

Enlarging Mainsails. To enlarge a mainsail is a more difficult task. It is not a practical proposition to add a strip of cloth along the dimension which it is desired to increase, because conflicting cloth bias will result. Moreover, due to the way the cloths are laid, it is not possible to add to the foot length without putting a short length on to each cloth all the way up the leech – not a feasible solution. This restricts us to the luff and leech, and these can be lengthened if the sail is split in two, usually at the tack cloth, and a new cloth added. The leech of the top portion will have to be faired into the line of the new leech, depending on how high the luff is to go (it will be rare that it is exactly a cloth width); alternatively a part cloth can be inserted to make the exact extra length required [figure 134(*c*)].

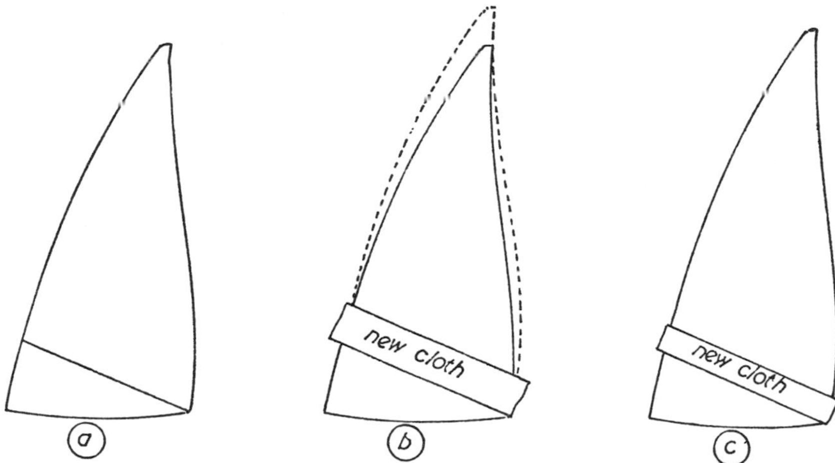

Fig. 134. Enlarging a mainsail.
(a) The sail is taken apart at the tack seam.
(b) If a full cloth is inserted, the headboard must be dropped the appropriate amount.
(c) A part cloth can be inserted to enlarge the sail by exactly the right amount, but the look is not so good.

Reducing Headsails. A good many of the foregoing remarks about reducing mainsails apply to headsails, with the added complication that many of the latter have mitres. Any new clew should come on the line of the mitre, although there have been instances where it has been allowed to go above or below it with a fair degree of success. A new sail has the mitre in the clew for good reasons of stress, however, and I would not like to have to guarantee a sail where it started above or below that point.

A good method of deciding whether a certain headsail can be cut in a particular way is to draw it to scale and put in the mitre – this usually bisects the clew angle. Next, use tracing paper to draw the reduced sail to the same scale, and then manoeuvre it on top of the first drawing. You will soon see whether you can get it to lie so that leech bias is within limits, and so that the clew comes on the old mitre.

If the sail can be cut in at the luff, without disturbing the clew at all, there will be every chance of complete success.

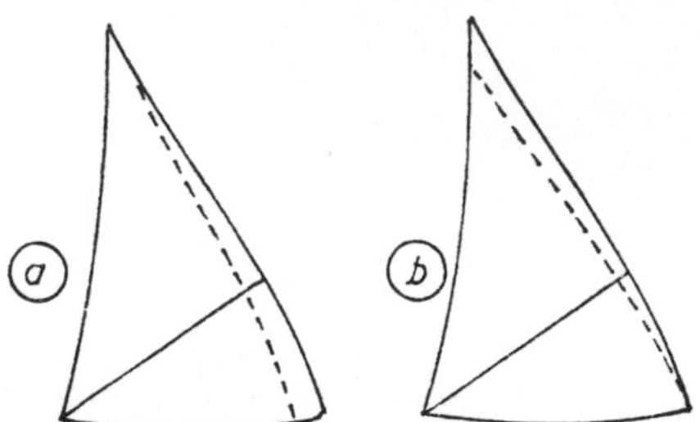

Fig. 135. Reducing a headsail.
(a) Shorten foot.
(b) Shorten luff and leech.
Both alterations leave the leech undisturbed.

Care should be observed with regard to the way the clew will be raised or lowered by this method of cutting. In figure 135(*a*), the clew will be lower when set on the original stay, while figure 135(*b*) will make it come higher.

Enlarging Headsails. As with a mainsail, a mitre-cut headsail has to be ripped apart if it is to be made larger.

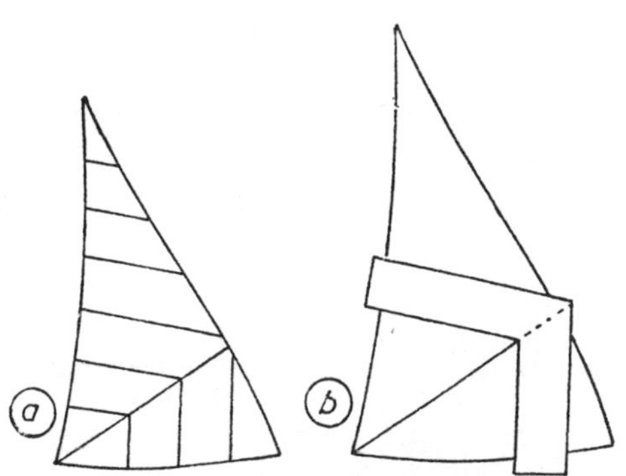

Fig. 136. Enlarging a mitre-cut headsail.
The sail has to be taken apart and new cloths inserted. Only if a seam ends at the luff near the mitre will this be successful.

To achieve anything like a reasonable sail, a seam has to strike the luff at or near the point where the mitre meets it. Then new cloths, or part cloths, are inserted above and below the mitre to enlarge the sail. It should be noted that the result will be a sail with similar

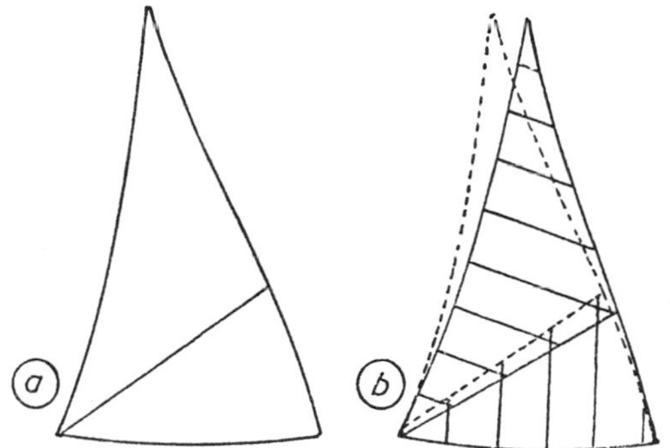

Fig. 137. Altering the shape of a mitre-cut headsail.

proportions to the old one. If it is desired to change these, either the sail should be cut as we have already discussed, or else the mitre can be ripped and the clew angle changed, as shown in detail in Appendix H. Horizontal cut headsails enlarge like mainsails.

Reducing Spinnakers. I am not concerned at the moment with alterations to the head of a spinnaker to make it fuller aloft or to make it

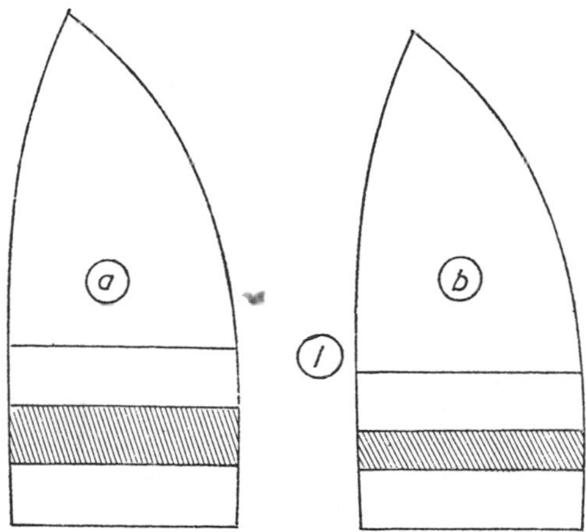

Fig. 138. Reducing a spinnaker's stays.

go better on a reach, for we have already discussed this earlier. I now want to consider how a spinnaker can be reduced in maximum width or stay length, for instance to eliminate any penalty it might carry, or to convert a second-hand sail to a slightly smaller boat.

If it is made symmetrically, with a seam running vertically and many more running horizontally, a spinnaker offers a comparatively easy problem. To reduce the stay length, the first seam above the foot is ripped all along, the appropriate amount is cut from the sail and the wires shortened equally, and the two halves sewn together again. There is normally no broad seam in the lower half of a spinnaker, which is a simple rectangle, so there is no danger of disturbing the set of the sail. Doing the job this way means that the clews and foot do not have to be remade, thus making a quicker task.

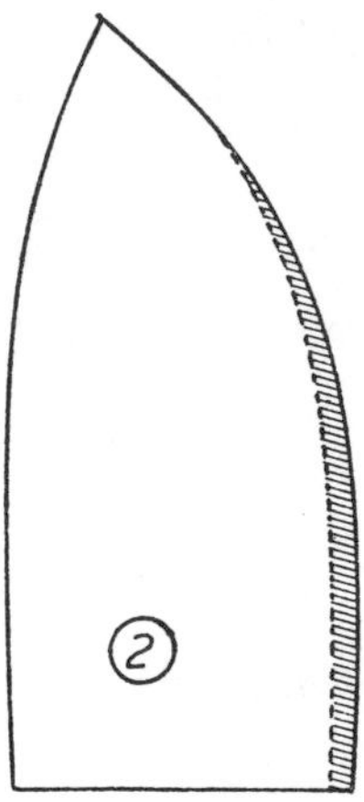

Fig. 139. Reducing the width of a spinnaker.

To reduce the sail in width, it is spread in half as usual, the racing number is lifted, and a slice is cut down the middle. The vertical seam is then remade and the number put back. Once again the head and clews are undisturbed, but this time a certain amount of broad seam may be removed. Depending on how much narrower the sail has to be made, so the reduction will have to carry higher into the head where broad seam is involved. With a reasonable reduction in width there is not usually any problem.

Enlarging Spinnakers. A similar approach can be made when enlarging a spinnaker. It is easy to add a cloth or cloths in order to make the sail longer in the stays. A horizontal seam is ripped as described above, and the new cloth added to make the required extra length. A thin tapering cloth can also be added down the middle in order to make the sail wider. The result is neither aesthetically pleasing nor very good sailmaking, but it seems to work for small increases, and is a good deal quicker (and cheaper) than fitting lots of short lengths to each cloth.

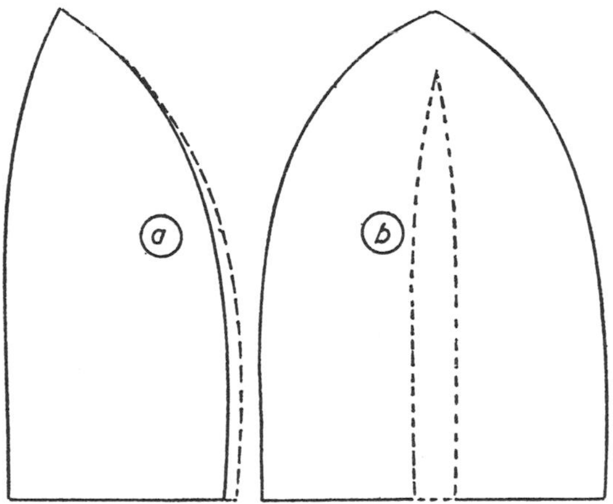

Fig. 140. Enlarging a spinnaker.
A vertical slice is inserted down the middle, tapering to a point near the head.

Spinnakers of Other Cuts. The above suggestions for reducing and enlarging spinnakers hold good for horizontally cut sails, with a vertical central seam. Other cuts will present different, and often more difficult, problems. The orbital cut, which has horizontal panels but no centre seam, will allow small alterations to length of stays, but any change in width will either entail manufacture of a seam down the middle, or else attention to the problem at both stays. This in turn means that the clews and wires or tapes will have to be remade, and possibly the head as well. On balance, if a sail of special cut has to be altered, it is probably best to put aside all thoughts of keeping the shaping, and to cut it boldly as though it were a horizontal sail. This will mean manufacturing extra seams across the line of the cloths, and they will be unsightly and somewhat inefficient. It is surprising, however, what can be absorbed by the elastic nature of nylon, and this sort of alteration can often make a good cruising sail.

Altering a Mainsail from Slides to Grooves. A frequent request to the Sail Maker is to alter a mainsail from slides to grooves. This entails rather more than might at first appear: the luff rope must be removed from the top of the headboard and left with the bare end at the top so that it can be fed into the groove.

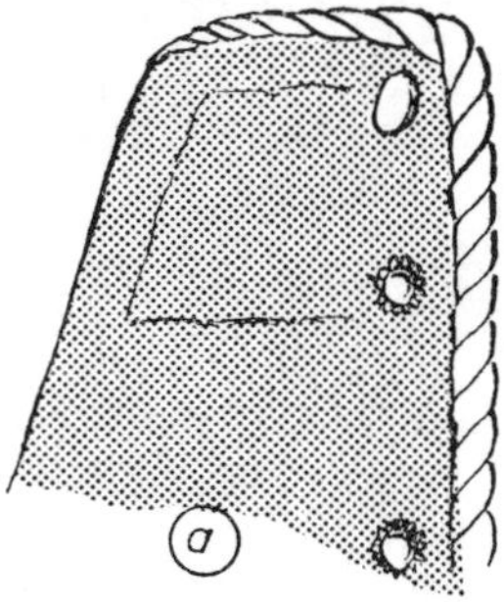

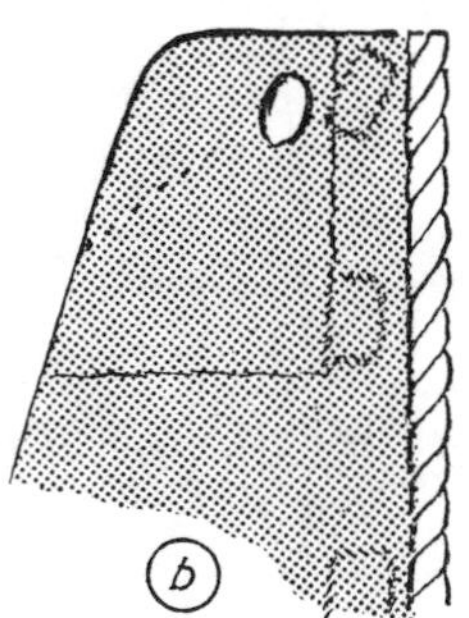

Fig. 141. Altering a headboard from slides to grooves.
(a) The luff rope is usually carried round the top of the headboard.
(b) The headboard must be made narrower, so that there is room for the mast groove. The rope must be stopped at the top, and the holes patched.

In addition, the headboard will have to be reduced in size, so that there is a narrow space between the board and the luff rope; this is to allow room for the jaws of the groove. It is not practicable nor strong enough to add a small extra strip at this point.

Similar treatment will have to be given to the clew. It is a matter of luck whether there will be enough room between the clew eye and the rope, for the former to clear the upper edge of the boom.

The slide holes all have to be carefully patched, taking care to see that the result is not too bulky to run in the groove.

Altering a Mainsail from Grooves to Slides. The opposite of the last alteration is to change a mainsail from grooves to slides. A quick job can be done by simply punching or working eyelets along the luff and foot. This means that the eyelet at the headboard will have to be placed within the short distance between the board and the rope, for it would be too far away from the rope if it were placed through the board itself.

The danger with this quick modification is that the rope will pull away, due to the slightly weaker construction having to withstand

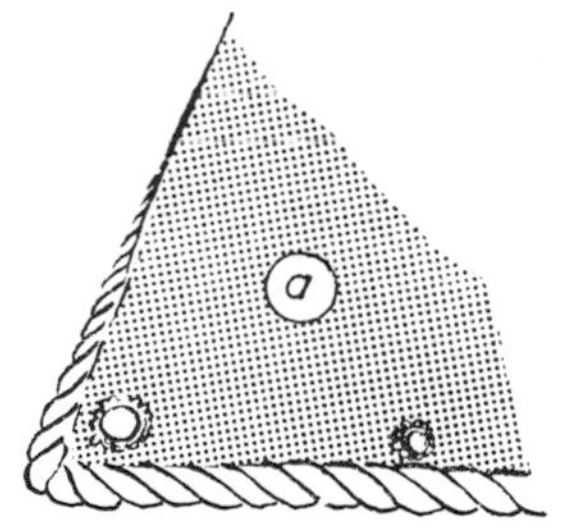

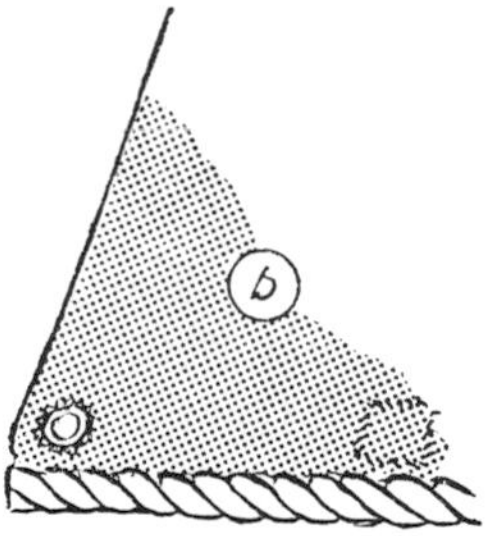

Fig. 142. Altering a clew from slides to grooves.
(a) The foot rope is usually taken round the clew.
(b) The rope must be stopped at the leech, and the slide holes patched. It is to be hoped that there will be enough room for the boom groove between the clew eye and the rope.

all the stresses localized at one slide eyelet. If the sail were made for slides from scratch, the rope would normally be taken a short way round the headboard and clew eye for added strength [see figures 141(*a*) and 142(*a*)].

The proper way to alter the sail is either to rub away a little cloth at the headboard, or to fit a larger board, so that the rope is hard up against the front of the board, thus allowing the slide seizing to pass through the board itself as it should; similar treatment is preferable at the clew. However, a sail cast off by a modern boat with grooved spars is often bought as a cheap way of providing a new sail for an older sister with tracks on mast and boom. In this case it may not be worth spending too much on alterations, and the former method is a serviceable solution, providing the boat is not going offshore where a rip at the headboard might prove embarrassing.

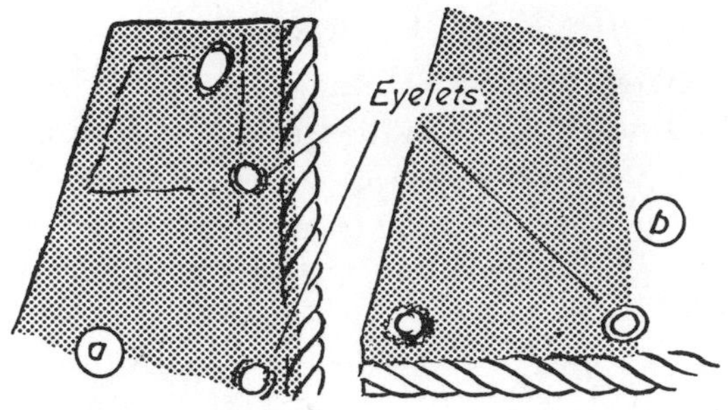

Fig. 143. Altering head and clew from grooves to slides. Eyelets may be punched or worked into the sail close to the rope, which will not run round the headboard or the clew.

General

Each requirement to alter the size of a sail presents a different problem, and there are often many different ways of going about it. As I said earlier, do not expect your Sail Maker to commit himself until he has had the sail on the floor, together with the new measurements. As a rule, small reductions in mainsails and headsails, and almost all reductions in spinnakers, are easy and cheap enough. The dinghy owner should remember, however, that there are some reductions which are too small: for instance it will not often be possible to reduce the foot length of a mainsail by less than 1 in., because anything smaller would cut through the centre of the clew eye. Large reductions in mainsails and headsails may or may not be easy, and only a full examination of the individual case can tell. Almost all attempts to increase the size of a sail are complicated, and possibly not worth the expense, except increasing the length of spinnaker stays. The Sail Maker will find it hard to estimate the cost of any change in size because, even after he has spread the sail and decided what method to use, he never knows what he is going to run into half-way through the job.

CHAPTER XIX

Design and Rating

A popular fallacy among those who write about yachts, but who only know about them from the point of view of the user, is that Naval Architects do not realize that the true centre of effort of a sail plan usually starts forward of the geometrical centre of effort, and then moves about as the wind changes. Nothing could be further from the truth.

Apart from the fact that they read books like anybody else, Naval Architects are usually practical sailing men with a great deal of experience of yachting in all its forms. Men like Uffa Fox, the Stephens brothers, and John Illingworth sailed the Atlantic more times than most of us have crossed the English Channel or Long Island Sound. The next generation of designers is combining the same path of practical experience with the fresh outlook of youth and the benefits of modern technology.

Speaking of the IOR formula for a minute (and other similar handicap rules), a designer's task is to integrate the hull he has in mind with the minimum total sail area necessary to give the boat a reasonable performance in light winds; fresh wind performance follows provided he keeps his ballast ratio sensible. He will have to adapt and compromise here and there, so that the resulting combination rates well under the rule, and is efficient over a wide range of wind and sea conditions. An inch or two improvement in the beam may have to be paid for on the sail plan; a gain in sail area may be at the expense of a compensating loss on the ballast ratio.

Rig

John Illingworth tells us in *Offshore* that he once looked into the problem of selecting a rig to the RORC rule for a light displacement ocean-racer of LWL 29 ft 8 in. He drew sail plans to the same area for a ketch, a yawl, a sloop and a cutter, and his judgement is that there would not be much in it as regards the advantages and disadvantages of each rig.

This is a measure of how far the Naval Architect is able to extract the maximum from the rule, when it is carefully considered in relation to the requirement. Naturally one rule will favour a particular type of boat rather more than another, but the foregoing is also a pat on the back for the rule-makers (those much maligned men), in as much as they had produced a formula which did not put the emphasis on one rig to the virtual exclusion of all others. Thus, the man who likes to play about with a multitude of sails can have a yawl or cutter and know that, other things being equal, he should be able to compete with the man who likes the simplicity of a sloop.

For offshore racing in English waters I am a cutter man myself, with the sloop for round the buoys. There is no knowing, however, what strange impulses drive a yachtsman towards a preference for one rig over another, so I shall not stick my neck out by making a recommendation. You pay your money and take your choice. On the other hand, there are some points regarding outline design of sails which are valid regardless of rig, and it might be interesting to examine a few of them. Besides the offshore fleet, these will also apply to the restricted and one-design classes such as the Soling, Dragon, Bembridge Redwing, Merlin Rocket and the like.

Luff/Foot Ratio

The ratio of the luff of a sail to its foot is sometimes incorrectly called the aspect ratio. Tony Marchaj in his book, *Sailing Theory and Practice*, correctly defines aspect ratio as the ratio of the height of the sail to its mean width. Worked out mathematically, so as to allow for leech round, this is represented by the formula which gives us:

$$AR = \frac{L^2}{SA} \ : 1$$

where AR = aspect ratio, L = luff in feet, and SA = sail area in square feet.

On the other hand, a simple relation of the length of luff to the length of foot is more readily grasped by the average man, and this is what I propose to use in this book. Note that this will give a value of just over half the mathematical aspect ratio. I shall use this relation of luff/foot for mainsails, headsails and spinnakers.

Beating to windward is the most inefficient point of sailing as far as making ground towards one's objective is concerned. On all other points of sailing one is heading towards one's immediate goal. In addition it is the condition where races are often won and lost, so the close-hauled situation is the one we should seek to improve, at the expense of reaching and running if necessary.

Mainsails

A mainsail produces less induced drag per square foot of area as its luff/foot ratio increases, though the relative disturbance caused by the mast increases, and some say that an elliptical form is theoretically desirable. There are, however, practical reasons at present why a permanently bent mast is not used on anything other than an extreme boat, such as some 30 sq. metres (the IOR forbids them), so we have to rule out the ellipse. The elliptical theory, however, may help to explain the undoubted efficiency of the headsail in its own right, due to its luff being slanted towards the rear. We have already seen on pages 28 and 103 the main reasons for a headsail's efficiency. Its slanting luff is a possible extra advantage, but more from the effect which sweep-back has on efficient loading than from its resulting similarity to an ellipse.

There are, however, practical limitations on the maximum value of the luff/foot ratio which can be used, particularly as the boat gets larger. These are almost all connected with problems of staying the mast, and also the attendant increases in hull size and weight to avoid excessive heeling with a tall rig, if a reasonable area is to be maintained. Marchaj gives this limit as 2 to 2·2 : 1 (his actual figures are an *aspect ratio* of 4 to 4·5 : 1), but there are plenty of yachts which exceed this figure. The 30 sq. metre in its heyday went as far as 3·5:1, a Dragon is about 2·7:1 and the Soling is nearly 3:1. Speaking of the ocean-racing fleet, John Illingworth gives his opinion of the upper limit as 3·2:1 for straight spars but, while I am inclined to agree with this figure for the so-called 'tea-time' sailors, I would think it rather high for an offshore boat and prefer 3:1 as a limit, unless the ratio is high due to a shortened foot length rather than an abnormally tall mast (such as when a rating is lowered by cutting the E measurement); the higher ratio may then be accepted. (Sparkman and Stephens' 1971 design for Mr Edward Heath's second *Morning Cloud* had a mainsail luff/foot ratio as high as 3·6:1.) I am, of course, referring here to keelboats, and not those smaller craft like catamarans and 10 sq. metre canoes which do not have the same staying and stability problems – although, let me hasten to add, that I realize that they certainly have their own particular brand of them!

Headsails

The optimum luff/foot ratio of a headsail is not normally a factor which influences the size of the sail significantly. This will be governed largely by the foretriangle within which the sail must be set, and the rules it must obey in doing so.

Where either an offshore racer to the IOR, or a new class of boat is being considered, the question of masthead or seven-eighths rig is more likely to be dictated by considerations of slot effect rather than headsail luff/foot ratio. The base of the foretriangle will then establish the luff/foot ratio for the offshore racer, because the sail may not have a longer perpendicular from the clew to the luff (LP) than 1·5 × J without penalty. Under this rule of measurement, therefore, a maximum size headsail will be a genoa of relatively low luff/foot ratio. Another way of looking at it is that the maximum luff of the headsail is fixed by the length of the forestay. To achieve a sail of 3:1 would mean having a foot shorter than the rules would allow, so free area is being needlessly sacrificed in a search for aerodynamic efficiency.

The Naval Architect, however, may vary the foot length of the headsail of a new class boat at will, but he is more likely to draw it so that the leech will coincide with the line of maximum camber of the mainsail.

An offshore racer's I measurement is more likely to be dictated, therefore, by the luff/foot ratio of the mainsail (which will determine the height of the mast), and the need for a masthead rig for full slot effect. The J measurement can be influenced by the luff/foot ratio desired for the headsail, but it is more likely to depend on the need for a suitably shaped spinnaker. We shall examine this factor shortly.

Only where a Naval Architect is designing a new class of boat and making up his own rules, therefore, is the luff/foot ratio of the headsail likely to be of more than academic interest.

In practice a headsail which has a ratio of about 2 to 2·5:1 seems about right. This is produced under the IOR by a foretriangle I:J ratio of 3 to 3·75:1.

A further point which has to be considered when deciding the J measurement of a boat to the IOR, is the sheeting base of the genoa. Ideally this sail should be sheeted at an angle of about 15° to the central line, with a fairlead somewhat in from the toe-rail, although an even narrower angle can be accepted in light airs and smooth water, as discussed on p. 127 under Barber Haulers. The same general effect holds good for a cutter, but the jib will, of course, be high cut to clear the staysail as discussed earlier in this book. This means that it will sheet right aft, but it should be cut low enough to bring this position sensibly forward if the stern narrows unduly, as with a double-ender.

Spinnakers

The foretriangle does, however, often affect the size of the spinnaker. There is no doubt that a spinnaker with a luff/foot ratio which approaches even 2:1 is a narrow-gutted affair which will not set very well in practice. Experience has shown that a ratio of somewhere between 1·6 and 1·8:1 will give a reasonably proportioned spinnaker. A low figure of 1·4:1, while giving a sail which sets well, does not have a big enough proportion of its area aloft where the wind will do most good. When we turn to orbital spinnakers, the ratio goes down again, not because the height needs to be less, but because the width can be more without infringing the rule. A Soling orbital spinnaker is about 1·3:1, while one for a 12 metre or a 14 ft International can be as low as 1:1 – and these measurements compare the luff to the foot of the sail only, not to the half-height width, which greatly exceeds the foot, thus reducing the effective ratio to considerably less than 1 : 1.

Let us turn now to the specific case of the IOR spinnaker, which is limited in width to 1·8 × J all the way from foot to head. We find that a foretriangle ratio of 3 : 1 (i.e. I:J) will give a spinnaker luff/foot ratio of $0{\cdot}95\sqrt{3^2 + 1^2}:1{\cdot}8$, which is 1·74:1, or the top end of our ideal range. Where the I:J ratio is increased beyond 3:1 the spinnaker rapidly becomes too narrow, unless some penalty is taken on the width of the sail. 3:1, as we have seen, is also the low end of the I:J range for a well-shaped genoa.

Proportion of Foretriangle to Total Area

We have seen that a headsail is a highly efficient sail in its own right, partly because it carries the main driving force of the combined aerofoil, and partly because there is no mast in front of it to disturb the airflow.

It is interesting to note how the foretriangle's share of the total sail area has changed over recent years. When John Illingworth first wrote *Offshore* in 1949, he suggested that the foretriangle should represent somewhere between 40 and 45 per cent of the total area of the mainsail and foretriangle combined. An increasing tendency towards masthead rig, coupled with a general awakening to the efficiency of the genoa, caused David Cheverton to suggest in 1967, when this book was first published, that the figure had by then risen to 55 per cent. The change to the International Offshore Rule caused further rethinking, because the effect on rating of the split of area behind and in front of the mast had once again to be reassessed against its efficiency and its cost. The result has been a further increase in the foretriangle, until the point has now been reached where it is more than half as big again as the mainsail. Sparkman and Stephens' design for the second *Morning Cloud* had a foretriangle of just over 61 per cent of the total area. Camper and Nicholson's then went as high as 63 per cent, while Angus Primrose and Fred Parker fixed the level at 60 per cent in *Langston Lady* and *Mystere* respectively, both designed for the first full IOR year.

These high foretriangle proportions are caused more by a reduction in the size of the mainsail than an increase in the headsail. If we take the second *Morning Cloud* as an example, we find that her vital statistics were P = 45·04 ft (13·60m), E = 12·4 ft (3·80m), I = 51·04 ft (15·55m) and J = 17·44 ft (5·30m), giving areas of 280 sq. ft (25·85m²) for the mainsail and 445 sq. ft (41·20m²) for the foretriangle. This is a mainsail luff/foot ratio of 3·6:1, and I:J ratio of 3:1 and a foretriangle percentage of 61·5. If the foot of the mainsail were increased by 2 ft 7 ins. (0·70m) to 15·0 ft (4·50m) so that the luff/foot ratio were now to become 3:1, the mainsail area increases to 338 sq. ft (30·60m²) thus reducing the percentage of the same foretriangle from 61·5 to 57·3. We can thus deduce that foretriangles have increased in proportion largely because mainsails have decreased by virtue of shortening the foot measurement. The fact that this is being done despite a penalty on high aspect ratio mainsails, is a tribute to the efficiency of the masthead genoa.

To summarize, a mainsail luff/foot ratio of 3·5:1 and an I:J ratio of 3:1 are by no means incompatible with a 60 per cent foretriangle proportion as defined above.

Rating

When cruising yachts of different size and shape race together they have to be handicapped with the object that all shall have an equal chance of winning. The two clubs which cover most of the world with their rules are the Royal Ocean Racing Club and the Cruising Club of America, and they have sensibly combined their different formulae for handicapping into the International Offshore Rule. In addition to this rating rule, there are many, more parochial, rules which have come into being due to the rather complicated nature of measuring a yacht under the more senior clubs. All aim at encouraging a seaworthy boat, with a sensible rig, and at penalizing extremes which might lead to an unsafe vessel. Most of them have been going long enough to ensure that any attempt to gain unfair advantage through possible loop-holes attracts a sufficient penalty to make it not worth while, but within the rules there is usually plenty of scope for intelligent experiment. This is really the sphere of the Naval Architect, but it may be interesting to examine superficially one or two of the more usual questions which are put to the Sail Maker in the course of his work.

Headsail Penalty. Perhaps one of the most common questions a Sail Maker is asked is whether it pays to take a penalty on a headsail. While it is convenient to use the phrase, it is in fact really a misconception to talk about a headsail *penalty*. The IOR fixes a lower limit to headsail size and 1·5 × J is used as the LP even if the largest sail is smaller than this; the rating then pays in proportion as the headsail gets bigger.

The following factors should be remembered when considering a headsail penalty for a particular boat:

1 The penalty operates all the time, even when overlapping sails are not being used (in heavy weather, or downwind).
2 While it is possible to take a penalty only on headsails, addition of a similar penalty on the spinnaker and its pole (through adopting an oversize J measurement) will not escalate the rating too sharply, and will allow advantage to be taken of greater sail area off the wind as well as to windward.
3 There are occasions, particularly offshore, when a boat carrying a penalty is able to complete a race before an adverse change in the weather. It is no good having a lower rating than a penalized sister ship, if the latter is snug in port saving her time while you are jilling about looking for wind half a day short of the finishing line.
4 The IOR penalizes oversized genoas rather more heavily than did the old RORC rule.
5 A no-penalty genoa under the IOR is already about 6 or 7 per cent larger than it used to be under the RORC rating rule.

Close analysis of the rule and improved sailcloth and sailmaking have revealed the efficiency of the modern genoa. It is therefore worth considering the LP as a variable up to a value of about 1·65 × J, particularly where a boat is an indifferent performer in light winds. This is also a simple and relatively cheap way to raise the rating to reach, say, a fixed Half-Ton or One-Ton level.

When I was racing in *Gitana IV* during the 1965 Fastnet we had a huge quadrilateral which not only carried the quad penalty (quadrilaterals were allowed, but penalized, by the RORC in those days), but had a foot in excess of 1·5 × J as well. We were fortunate in that race because we were able to make good use of the sail, but there were plenty of times when we were under jib and staysail, or spinnaker, yet we still had to carry the crushing penalty bestowed by the quad (our time correction factor was greater than 1·1 so, as the *Yachting*

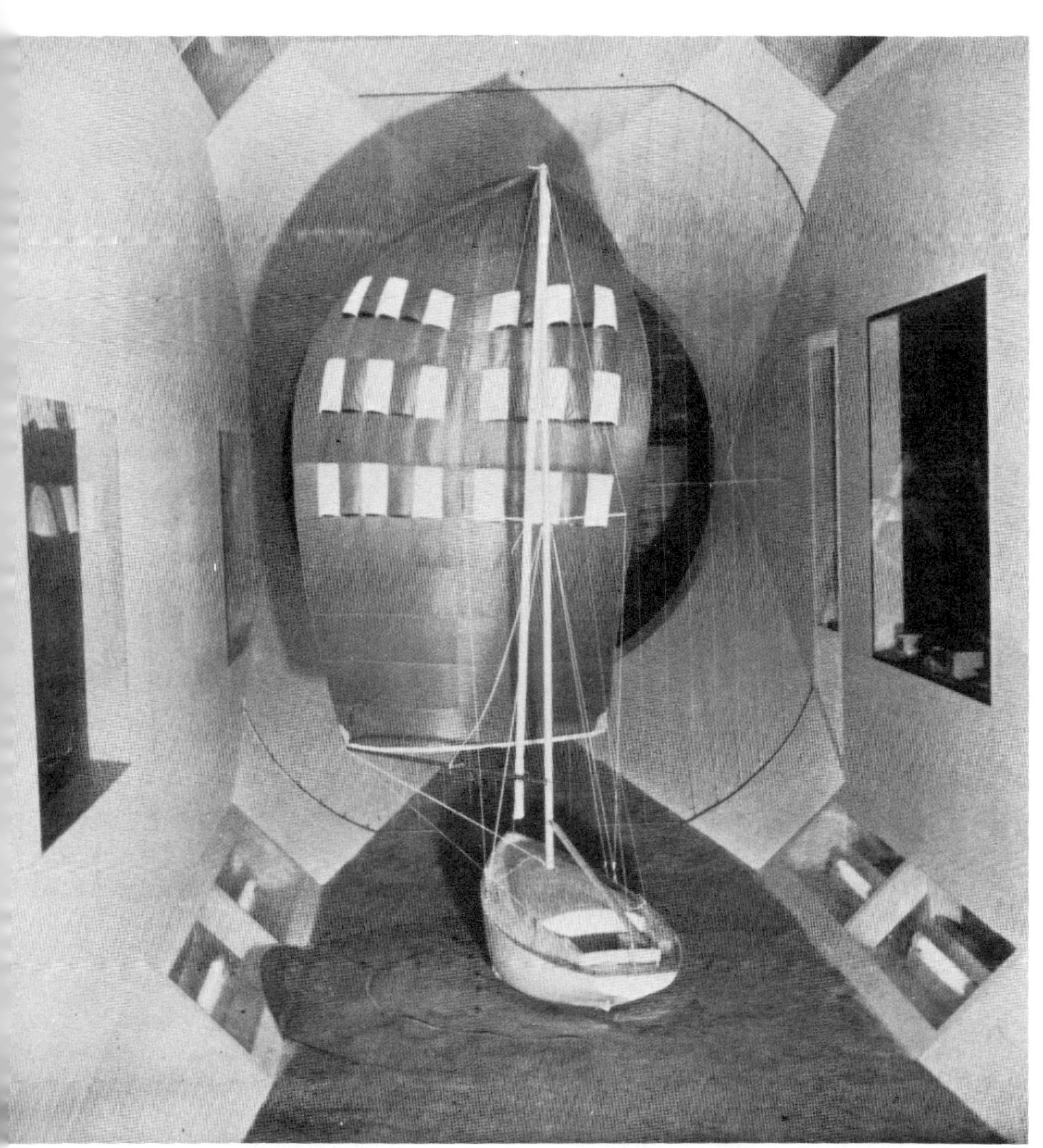

44. A venturi spinnaker under test in the wind tunnel. *Beken.*

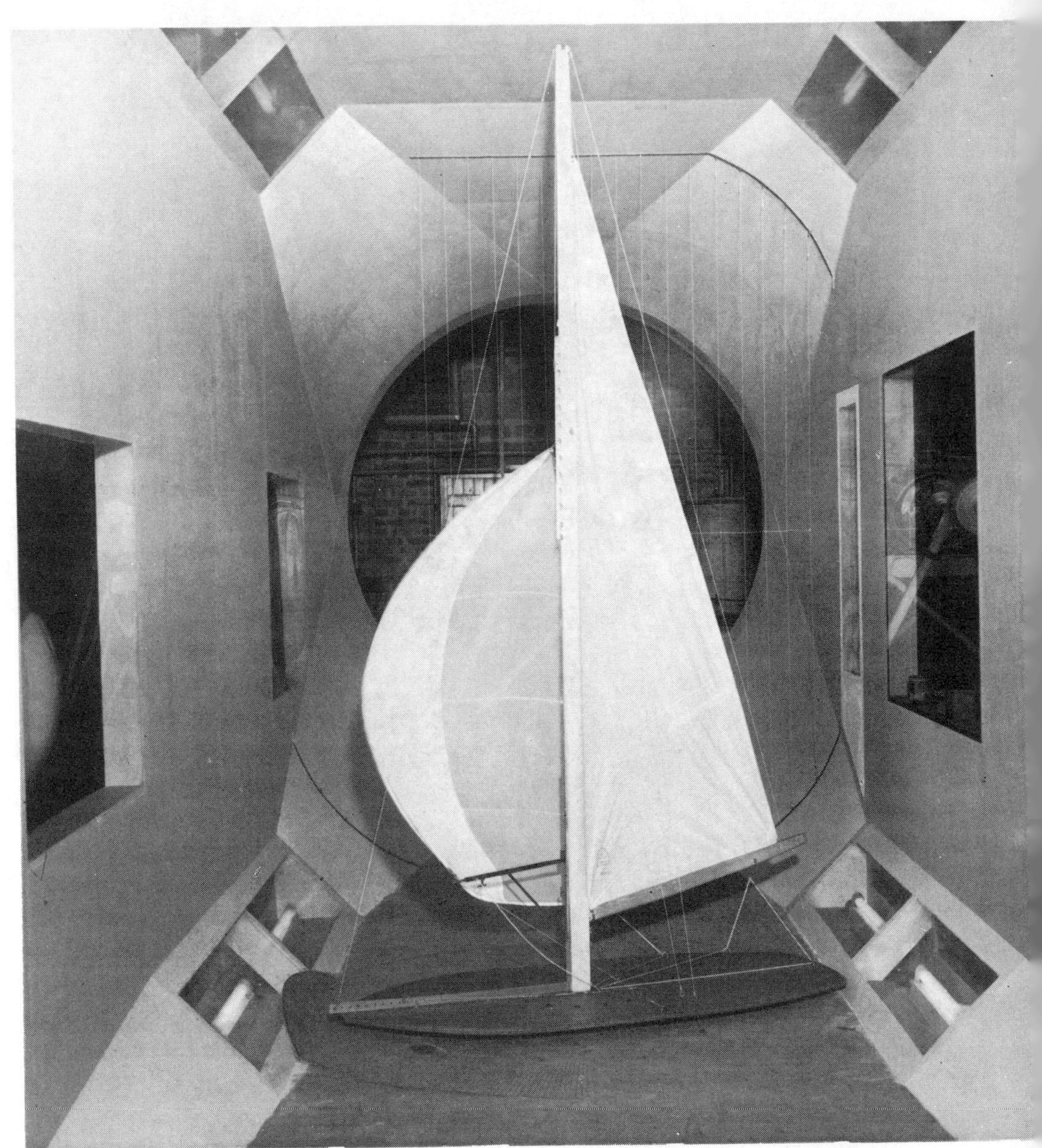

45. The half-winder in the wind tunnel clearly shows its principle. *Beken.*

46. The 4,000 square foot spinnaker shown being cut out in plate 2 being tested from a British Road Services crane. *Beken.*

47. Wind tunnel model. The author calibrating a scale model of the Ratsey & Lapthorn wind tunnel to test general flow characteristics before starting work on the full size tunnel. *Beken.*

48. A 14 ft International mainsail. Shelf unzipped, giving more flow over the boom. *Author*

49. A $\frac{1}{3}$rd scale 14 ft International mainsail in wind tunnel. Shelf zipped up, flattening the foot. *Beken.*

50. The author sailing Frank May's *Sunrise* (K 545), and sitting out rather lazily. B. Byham's *Sombrero* (K 844) has a bendy mast which is not taking all the fullness out of her mainsail in the light wind prevailing. *Castle Studios.*

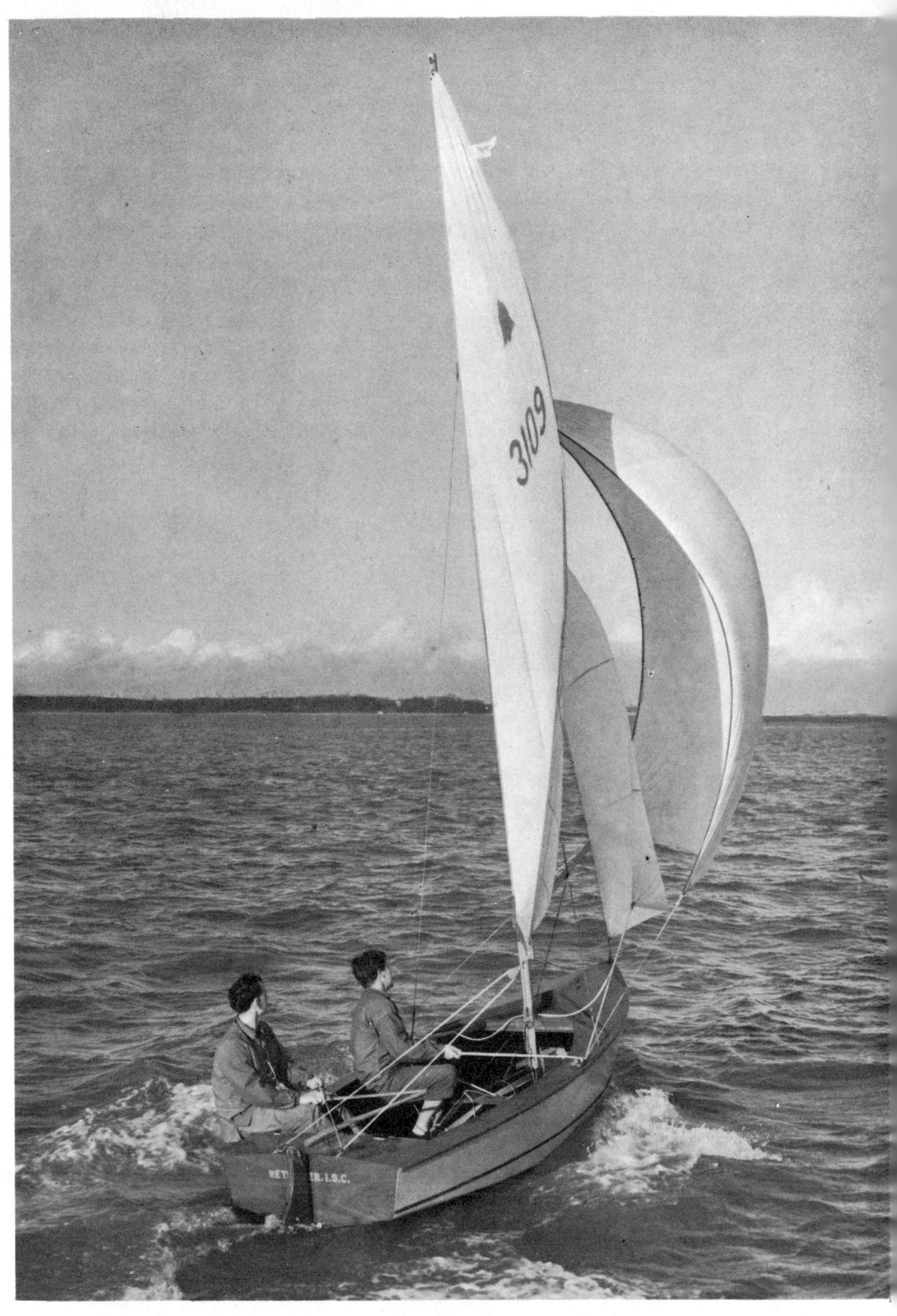

51 G P 14 Footer. The author tending headsail and spinnaker sheets on routine development trials in the early days of the G P 14 ft spinnaker. *Beken.*

52. An umbrella sail. I implied at the beginning of the book that old fashioned ideas and sails would not figure in these pages. I could not resist this horizontal sail, photographed in 1895. This boat will never capsize. *Beken.*

53. The launching chute of a modern dinghy cleans up the spinnaker (while Brand X does the same job for the jib?). *Author.*

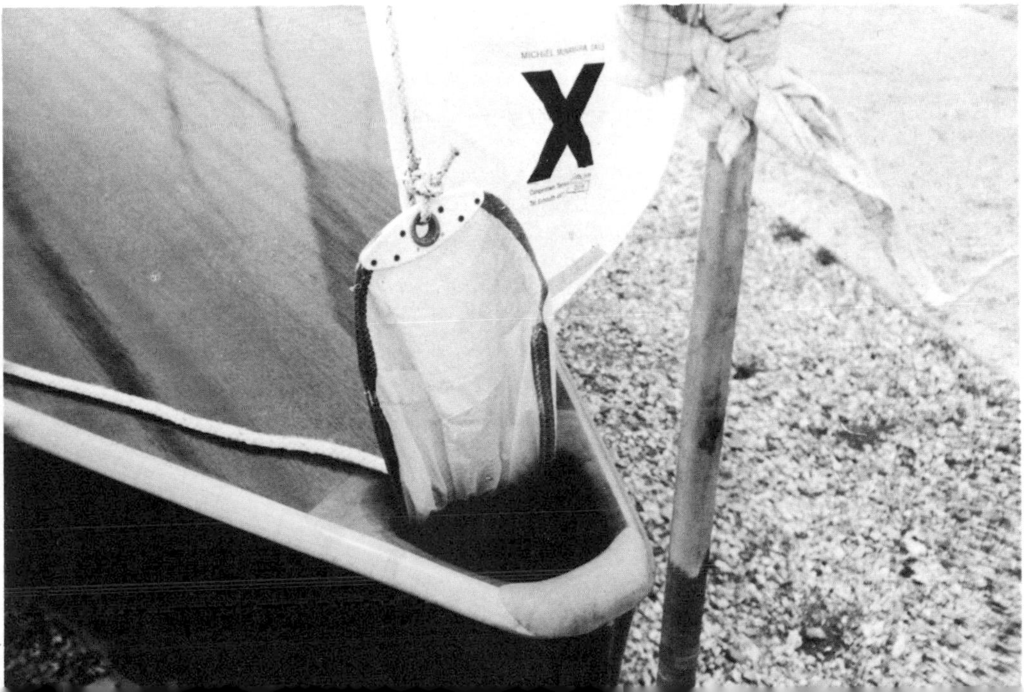

54. *Lady Helmsman.* The rig, designed by Austin Farrar, consists of a comparatively full-section wing mast and a fully battened Terylene mainsail. *J. B. Moore.*

World put it, we were giving ourselves time!). Incidentally, we only took 3 days, 9 hours and 40 minutes, which was a new elapsed time record. Not many yachts have finished the course in under four days, *American Eagle*, the modified 12-metre, beating our record in 1971. If the boat goes well under normal canvas in all but the lightest winds, therefore, it is probably not worth taking a penalty to improve performance in the few races which are completed in light airs. If, however, she is a poor performer up to and including force 3, she might well profit from the increased area on more occasions, and thus sail to a higher rating. A final decision should really be taken with the advice of a Naval Architect who has experience of sailing in the boat concerned, but this is not always possible. If the experiment is tried and proves a failure, the larger headsail can probably be cut down, so all is not lost; on balance, therefore, if the boat needs more canvas in light to medium winds, give it to her and see what happens.

Lowering the Rating. Most owners at some time or other have worked out that they would have won a coveted cup if only their rating had been just a little lower. The problem is to reduce the rating but to

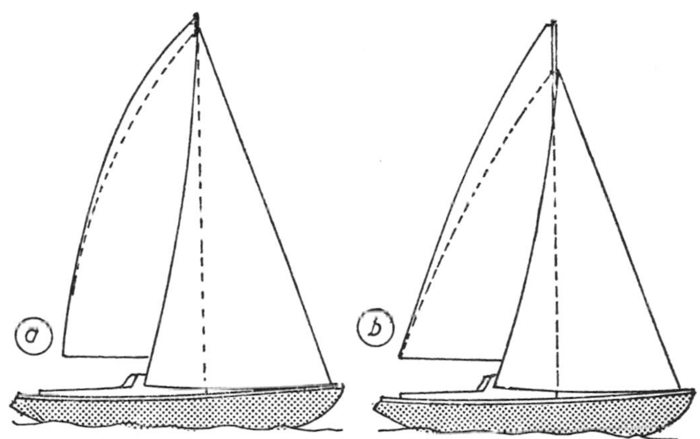

Fig. 144. Lowering the rating.
(a) If this mainsail is reduced to the dotted position, the whole of it will then be covered by the slot effect of the genoa, i.e. the part cut away will be a low efficiency area.
(b) If this mainsail is reduced to the dotted position, the boat is transformed to masthead rig with full slot effect. Once again, the part cut away is a low efficiency area.

keep the speed. This, of course, is not always possible, but it can sometimes be done without interfering too seriously with performance, by a reduction in the size of the mainsail. There are plenty of other ways in which it can be achieved, but I am only considering sails. If the boat carries excess weather helm, it is possible to reduce the rating and make her go faster if the foot of the mainsail is shortened; this will reduce the weather helm, thus increasing speed with the wind forward of the beam, and lower her handicap. Another useful reduction can sometimes be effected on the luff. If the sail is made shorter on the luff, it will then be more completely covered by the headsail, with resulting improved efficiency. Care should be taken not to reduce the mainsail below the minimum rated area as represented by $0{\cdot}094 \times IC^2$. If the boat has a seven-eighths rig, chopping the mast off at the forestay will transform her to masthead, reduce the rating and quite possibly improve her windward performance, due to greater aerodynamic efficiency. This sort of alteration is a much more major affair, and it would be most unwise to undertake it without expert advice; for one thing, the mast will need different staying arrangements as a result.

Raising the Rating. It is sometimes desirable to increase a rating by a small amount, perhaps to move from the top of one class to the bottom of the next, or else to sail to the maximum rating permitted by certain regulations, such as the One Ton Cup. There are, of course, many ways of getting a higher rating, but if it is to be achieved by means of sails (which has the advantage that it can be undone again quickly), a short answer may be to take a penalty on the J measurement, or to add a short bowsprit if headsail overlap would otherwise be too large. This gives both a larger genoa and spinnaker and thus ensures that advantage can be taken of the penalty on and off the wind. But the quantity SPIN in the IOR formula must be borne in mind. This is a spinnaker area which is used as the total rated sail area if found to be larger than the latter, thereby setting a maximum size to the spinnaker without further penalty.

Sail Area/Rating. Owners naturally want some idea of how much a particular sail change will affect their rating. Measurement under the IOR is so complicated, however, that a straightforward answer is not always possible, although a qualified Measurer can often give a fairly close estimate. Figures for an average yacht will give sufficient indication for this book, and I am indebted to Langston Marine Limited for the graph and sailplan of the 26 ft LOA sloop *Mystere* at Appendix I. She is a fairly typical small, modern yacht and I designed the taller rig shown on the sailplan. This was originally for the light winds of the Swiss lakes, but it has proved to be popular elsewhere. The graph shows the effect on the rating of alterations to some of the sail dimensions.

The complexity of the IOR rating calculation is such that it is tedious to do the sums by hand to turn a set of measurements into a rating. It is equally tedious to work out what changes are required in variables such as sails to effect a particular change in the rating. Gone are the days when an owner could do his own calculations fairly quickly on the back of an envelope, and nowadays we have to resort to expert help for comprehensive reliability.

Using their own computer, South Coast Rod Rigging specialise in these calculations and have evolved a system whereby the hull factors are reduced to two quantities which are constants, as long as there is no change in the hull or loading. The effect of sail alterations can thus be quickly evaluated and the machine takes care of the pitfalls which lie in wait for the unwary, such as minimum mainsail size, upper and lower black band limits and maximum spinnaker area without further penalty. Finally, the print-out presents a 'figure of merit' (total area/RSAT), which is useful when comparing proposed alternatives. It is claimed that there are not many ratings where they are unable to suggest relatively simple alterations to improve the figure; even batten length or headboard size penalties are fairly common. The modest charges make this a Best Buy for the racing man who wants to see that he is not being unnecessarily handicapped.

CHAPTER XX

Adding to the Wardrobe

The Sail Plan

Before an intelligent assessment of a boat's sail requirements can be made, a sail plan is desirable. Dinghies and small one-design keel-boats present no problem as their wardrobe is usually limited to a number of standard sails, so the owner does not need to spend hours poring over a plan. The larger classes, however, have a wider choice, and a pictorial display is helpful. I do not want to convey the impression that it is not possible to order a sail without a plan, but it will be difficult to make alterations to rig or rating, or to experiment with, say, twin running sails, without one. It will not even be possible to order a mainsail unless certain specific measurements are known. The Sail Maker has to know what is physically possible within the confines of the yacht's spars and rigging. This is in addition to limits imposed by rules and rating, which we shall examine shortly.

If the owner does not already possess a sail plan, it is quite possible that the Sail Maker does, especially if he has made for the boat before. If he has not got one, he may know where to find it; Sail Makers generally get on well with one another, and they sometimes call on each other for rare plans, for they usually pride themselves on not having to bother a customer with such details. A Norwegian owner might write to say that the 6 metre which his father built in 1936 needs new sails. The office immediately goes into action to trace the original plan, either in the firm's records or perhaps from the builder (whose name is found in *Lloyd's Register*, and not by worrying the customer). The quotation is sent off with a friendly reference to her last suit, or a request to know whether she still has the roller reefing which the record shows was incorporated in 1947.

It may be, however, that no plan of a boat exists, and that sails are required. In this case the Sail Maker will normally visit the boat to take what measurements he requires, providing the vessel is reasonably accessible and the order warrants the trip. It would be unreasonable to expect him to make a 250-mile journey to measure up for just a small staysail. For the benefit of the owner without a sail plan who is remote from civilization, yet who requires a new sail, I have drawn up a guide to measuring in Appendix J. This is a comprehensive recommendation, to cover a full plan for a yawl or ketch. If just a mainsail is required, it is obviously not necessary to provide all the detail included in the Appendix, for this also covers the foretriangle, mizzen, and general hull shape. Remember, however, that it is important to know the sheer line of the deck for the leech of the genoa, and mast rake is often vital to the mainsail.

Measuring is not a hard task, but it is one which demands methodical care and good notes. It is not, as might be supposed, essential to climb to the top of the mast, because these distances can be taken by shackling a measuring-tape on to the appropriate halyard and hauling it aloft. The principal points to remember are that you can never take too many measurements for a particular job, and that you should state quite clearly what the distances you find represent. In other words, tell the Sail Maker that you hoisted a steel or a linen tape on the main halyard in a 15 m.p.h. wind (a graduated wire is preferable for all measurements taken aloft where the distance is more than about 35 ft; this is because it will be blown out of the straight line less than a tape-measure); that the shackle and splice at the end of the halyard took up about 5 in.; that the boom measurement is from tack eye to clew eye, and not from aft of the mast to the very end of the boom (or vice versa). Above all do not make any allowance for clearance, say between the halyard sheave and the head of the mainsail or between the clew and the outhaul eye for a lashing, without telling the Sail Maker. It is also wise to tell him that you have not deducted anything. He will then make these allowances in the light of his experience, and they are more likely to be right than yours.

I once had a long correspondence with a Belgian who not only made these deductions without telling us, but who also took off some more, to allow for the stretch of the cloth. He sent a sketch of his boat, with measurements marked on the spars as being those found by means of a tape-measure along the lines I have just suggested. We made the sail to stretch to sizes slightly less than the distances he had given, so that there would be 3 or 4 in. between the clew and the outhaul eye for a lashing, and rather more between the head and the sheave for a halyard splice and shackle. The result was a sail which was over 3 ft short on a luff of about 35 ft, and 1 ft 6 in. short on a foot of some 14 ft. Yet the owner had clearly marked his distances as being between the clew eye and the mast, and between the sheave and the tack. Of course, there was a double error in this case, because he had also tried to teach us our business with respect to making the allowance for cloth stretch and induced flow, again without telling us.

Care should be taken in measuring, not only to avoid the wrong rope (topping lift for main halyard), but also to ensure that the halyard is hoisted hard up and made fast securely, so that it does not creep down between two different measurements. It is best to fit a rope downhaul on the halyard alongside the wire or tape, otherwise you may find it difficult to pull down afterwards.

Before I leave measuring, I must just repeat that one of the most important measurements for a mainsail is the distance from the aft face of the mast to the tack-pin; you should also remember to state whether your foot measurement includes this distance or if it has been deducted. Without these details the Sail Maker will not know how much to cut away at the tack so that the sail leads fairly to the pin.

Rules

It may seem obvious to say that all owners should be familiar with the rules governing their class. On the other hand some classes, and I am thinking here mainly of restricted classes and the IOR, have necessarily got such complicated rules that they are difficult to have at one's fingertips. However, the sail locker is something over which the owner has direct control and which he can vary with the years (unlike the hull, once it has been made), so it is important to have an understanding of those rules for your particular class which relate to sails.

Most rules change from time to time, but those dealing with sails are not so fluid that the average man cannot keep up to date with his own particular class. It is a rather different story for the Sail Maker, who has to stay abreast of a whole cabinet full of various rules, some of which he may not need for years on end. Class secretaries would be doing a service to their members if they would remember to circulate Sail Makers, whenever there is an alteration which affects the rig of the boat for which they are responsible. If you are the owner of a rare class of boat, therefore, you should check with your Sail Maker to see that he has all the latest amendments before he makes you a sail.

In this connection, do not forget that the IYRU rules also have something to say with regard to sails. Most of it concerns the Sail Maker and Boatbuilder, being about such matters as sail numbers and their positioning, makers' marks, forestay position, etc. However, there is a certain amount about changing sails, sheeting them to spars, and outriggers, which concerns the owner.

The first principle to absorb when interpreting rules is that they mean what they say. This may sound self-evident, but it is sometimes possible to guess at what a rule is designed to achieve, yet it may not put it into the right words. For instance, if a rule says: 'The jib shall not exceed the following measurements when new: luff 20 ft, leech 18 ft 6 in., foot 6 ft 3 in.,' then the sail may be made smaller on any or all of the three measurements. It may also stretch over the maximum as soon as it is no longer new, so there is very little control in this rule. On the other hand, a rule which says that the luff length shall be 20 ft, with a tolerance of 3 in., will limit that measurement to somewhere between 19 ft 9 in. and 20 ft 3 in. One which gives a *maximum* luff length of 20 ft, with the same tolerance of 3 in., will limit it to between 19 ft 9 in. and 20 ft, because the tolerance can only be downwards due to the overriding word *maximum*.

In addition to this, different rules may measure the luff between different points as follows:

(i) Outside points of head and tack eyes.
(ii) Bearing surfaces of head and tack eyes.
(iii) Centres of head and tack eyes.

(iv) Points where the leech and foot of the sail meet the luff wire.
(v) Apex points where the leech and foot would strike the luff wire if they were projected.

I recall attending the Prince of Wales' Cup Week at Falmouth in 1960, where I altered a mainsail for Sam Waters to make it suitable for very heavy weather. This entailed cutting off a parallel piece about 3 or 4 ft deep along the foot, so that it became the equivalent of a heavily reefed sail. In its turn this involved removing the bottom batten pocket altogether. The unfortunate owner was subsequently disqualified when he used the sail, because it did not conform to the rule which said that four battens should be placed 'within 5 in. above or below the respective points on the sail which divide the leech into five equal parts'. The fact that he would have been allowed to remove a batten from a full-size mainsail and then roll it down to the same size as his altered sail, made no difference to the literal interpretation of the rules as they then stood. They have since been altered to read that the number of batten pockets shall be 'no more than four, dividing the leech into equal parts, in number one more than the number of batten pockets'.

Equally, just because the rules do not specifically prohibit something, it does not mean to say that it is allowed. A good example of what I mean occurred in a class which now numbers over 20,000 boats. The class rules had a clause which prevented sails being other than according to the plan. With the laudable intention of stopping the rich man having too many gadgets like zippers and specially shaped sails at extra cost, this was interpreted literally so that these devices were ruled out. Unfortunately this also ruled out a simple extra like a Cunningham hole, so an owner was unable to have one sail to cope with a wide wind range, and had to buy one for light to medium conditions and another for heavy weather. Which shows that it is hard to legislate for every contingency.

Ordering New Sails

Now that we have gone thoroughly into the various factors which affect the size and shape of sails on the average yacht, we can consider the sort of information which the Sail Maker requires from an owner when he orders a new sail.

There is no mystique about ordering sails. Sail Makers are in business to make sails, and they will all give careful attention to the smallest order. The larger firms sometimes have to combat the impression that a sail for a small child's dinghy is beneath their dignity. Nothing could be further from the truth, and they give this as much attention as they do a schooner. Do not be afraid, therefore, to approach any Sail Maker with your request, no matter how small.

You must first, of course, choose your Sail Maker. I am naturally prejudiced, but I would be the last person to try and persuade anyone to leave a Sail Maker he has known for a long time. If there is no reason to leave, stay with him; you know each other's foibles and weaknesses by now and the devil you know is better than the one you don't. If you do not already have a Sail Maker, the choice can often be made by means of discussion with other owners in your club, or else by comparing known prices and quality. Try writing to several different firms; you can sometimes tell quite a lot from the way your letter is answered, besides getting a direct comparison of prices for the particular sails you want. You should remember that, as with a tailor, you usually get what you pay for, and a little extra expense at the start may save you renewal costs too early on. On the other hand, it may well be that a particular firm has a reputation for making the best sails for your class of boat. In this case you must decide whether the reputation is deserved, or whether the top helmsmen in your class would win with whatever sails they used, so perhaps you could try elsewhere at a cheaper price. Sometimes a firm may produce a sail which is an excellent shape, but does not last a long time. It may be that you are one of those who are content with a sail which will win races for half a season, and must then be put aside for another new one of the same calibre. There are plenty of helmsmen in this bracket, and the Dragon is an example of a class where headsails in particular are renewed more than once a season by many of the top owners.

Having selected a Sail Maker, you can place yourself entirely in his hands as I have already implied. He is accustomed to interpreting owners' requirements, and will request all the answers he needs in order to make the sail you want. But if you have read this book as far as this, you are obviously interested enough in what sort of sail you are going to get to be more than a 'Yes-man' and 'No-man' to your Sail Maker. You will probably have your own ideas as to the type of sail you require, and you should put them to him. In this case you should state the sort of sail you want, the conditions for which you require it, and any other factors bearing upon the problem, such as crew weight, spar bend, sheet winches, and so on. Do not try and tell him how to make the sail but if, for instance, you have firm ideas on the amount of fullness you want, try and relate them to an existing suit of similar sails made by the same firm; this will give the Sail Maker a direct yardstick by which to judge your idea of a full sail, which may be different from those of his last customer.

A standard boat with one-design sails will have no need of more than a bare statement that a particular sail is required, coupled with instructions as to whether it should be full or flat. A Dragon mainsail has the same dimensions the world over, so does a 470, Tempest or a Finn. On the other hand a 5·5 metre, most ocean-racers, a Flying Dutchman genoa or a 14 ft International all have individual requirements. If you cannot supply a copy of the sail plan, the boat's certificate should give a great deal of the information required. Many Sail Makers have special forms for some of the more popular restricted classes, in order to make things easier. The following are some of the basic details without most of which sails cannot be made.

Mainsail

1. *Cloth Weight.* This is sometimes governed by class rules. See page 57 for suggested weights.

2. *Length of Luff, Leech and Foot.* Luff and foot will usually be the black band distances; say if they are not. The leech is the one which is sometimes forgotten, but it may be important if the boom has a high cabin top to clear.

3. Distance from the aft face of the mast to the tack-pin. This is variously known as the *knock-back*, the *cut-away*, the *tack back* or the *tack off* distance. It will usually be between 1¼ and 1¾ in. for boats which do not have a roller-reefing gear, and that is the amount which most Sail Makers will allow unless they are warned differently. The distance, of course, has to be subtracted by the Sail Maker from the length of the foot as given on the boat's certificate, so that the clew shall not extend beyond the black band by that

amount. A roller gear will usually have a ***knock back*** of anything from 4 to 9 in., depending on the particular gear.

4. Details of the *mast ramp* (also known as the *mast batten*), if any. This is the ramp on which a luff track is sometimes built up near the lower end, so that it leads fair to the tack when the latter is back 6 in. or so (knock back) to accommodate a roller-reefing gear. If the luff fits in a groove, the distance above the tack where the *groove entry* starts should be substituted.

5. *Roller Reef.* If a roller boom is fitted, the Sail Maker must know so that he can tape the lower luff instead of roping it. This will prevent a build-up of rope at the tack as the sail is rolled on to the boom. In addition, he must know the distance from the aft face of the mast to the tack-pin, and the ramp details, if any, as in paragraphs 3 and 4 above. Finally, you should state if you want a row of emergency reef eyelets in the deep reef position as a precaution against gear failure.

6. *Points or Lacing Reefs.* If individual points, or a continuous lacing reef is required, the appropriate type should be specified. The Sail Maker should also be told the spacing needed between each reef, or the distance from the outer black band on the boom to the reef cleats, so that he can fit the reefs at the right height for proper purchase to be put on the reef ear-ring at the leech. If there are no reef cleats on the boom he should be told, so that he knows that he has a free hand over spacing between reefs.

7. *Slides or Grooves.* You would be surprised at the number of owners who specify slides for their mainsail, and completely overlook the fact that they have a grooved boom. State, therefore, how the sail attaches to both the mast *and* the boom. If slides are involved, try and send a sample which fits, as this is the surest way of avoiding errors; send one for luff and foot if they are different. Do not simply say 'one-inch slides', because this could mean four different sizes, as explained on page 392 of Appendix J.

8. *Rules.* Do not assume that the Sail Maker is conversant with the rules of your class unless he tells you that he is. This is especially important where the rules have recently been changed. Remind him of any sail insignia required, and be prepared to send a full-size tracing if your class is not a well-known one. State the rule on battens if there is any danger of misinterpretation.

9. *Spar Bend.* If you have a bendy mast or boom, the Sail Maker should be told the maximum bend by means of offsets taken as suggested on page 109.

10. *Racing Number and Name.* A note of the racing number will avoid another letter later on. If you give the name of the boat, the Sail Maker will be able to put it on your sail bags.

11. *Extras.* There are many extras, ranging from slab reefs to spare battens and windows. You will speed delivery if you remember to include them all at the beginning. It is best if a copy of all correspondence is kept for reference.

Headsail

12. *Cloth Weight, Luff, Leech and Foot, Rules and Boat's Name* are all the same as for the mainsail.

13. *Winches.* Say if your sheet winches are particularly powerful.

14. *Hanks or Snap Hooks.* Specify the type of hank or snaps you want if it is not the standard gunmetal pattern. Also give the lowest point on the luff at which the bottom hank can go without fouling turnbuckles or other equipment.

15. *Forestay Sag.* State the amount of sag in the stay on which the sail will be set.

16. *Extras.* Individual bag colours or stripes are especially important for headsails in these days of constantly changing crews. You are more likely to get the correct headsail hoisted on the stay if you ask for the bag with two red stripes as opposed to, say, the No. 2 jib. Indeed, some designers include this sort of thing as part of their standard specification to the Sail Maker, and add identifying patches on the sails to match the bag, with a further tag such as a black circle to pick out the tack. Ask for some offcuts to be put in as repair material. It is a good idea to specify tan thread for white sails, so that a broken stitch can be quickly spotted. Finally, do not forget that a No. 1 jib may mean the storm jib (i.e. the smallest sail) to some people, the genoa (i.e. the largest sail) to others, and the working foresail to yet others; make sure that you and the Sail Maker are talking about the same sail.

Spinnaker

17. *Cloth.* Not only weight but also colour enters into it here. I

have already discussed cloth weight for spinnakers, and touched on colour. There is no foundation for the belief that one colour attracts wind more readily than another, so the only operational factor which can affect the choice is the question of contrast. It is a good idea to have stripes of contrasting colours in the head, so that the luff can be more readily detected at night to prevent it collapsing. It is also a good idea to avoid those colours which are glaring to look at for too long on a sunny day. Otherwise the question of colour can be, and very often is, handed over to the distaff side of the boat for a decision. I would never dispute such a course.

18. *Sizes.* Spinnakers are often one-design, even for those boats which may vary their fore and aft sails, such as the Merlin Rocket. You may be able to specify reaching, running or heavy weather, but sometimes not even that latitude is allowed. If you are buying a spinnaker for an ocean-racer you should either give the maximum stays and width (from the boat's certificate), or else the I and J measurements. The Sail Maker will work out the rest from these data, which are all he needs to know.

Delivery

Some Sail Makers are poor at keeping delivery promises. You should always try and order well in advance, not only to ensure that you get your sails on time, but also to take advantage of off-season discounts. Allow for two or three weeks' delay in any target date you give, and you should not often be disappointed.

Second-hand Sails

Before buying a second-hand sail, it is wise to ask yourself why it is for sale. I stated earlier in this chapter that some of the top helmsmen in various classes replace their sails with almost monotonous regularity. You may have thought that this sort of thing is only practised by the very wealthy, but you would be wrong. Imagine the scene at any clubhouse as the dinghies come ashore after an afternoon's exhilarating racing. The local expert has won again, and a beginner profits from the great man's resulting good humour to offer his congratulations.

'I say, well done,' he murmurs, as he casts an appreciative eye over the winner's shining hull. 'You certainly left us standing today. Who made your sails?'

The hero throws out the name of his Sail Maker, and modestly passes the credit for his win to his jib.

'It certainly is a beauty,' says the star-struck beginner. 'I wish I had one half as good.'

'D'you want it?' asks the expert, knowing full well that he has thrashed the stuffing out of it for three months, and that the flow has started to move to the leech.

The upshot is that he sells it for half-price to the tyro, who proceeds to venerate it beyond its deserts, and the expert goes off and gets a new one – with the drive where it should be, further forward.

I am not saying that all experts, or indeed many, do this sort of thing, or that all second-hand sails are blown out. There are many occasions when they can be a useful addition to the locker, so let us examine some of the points to watch when buying.

First and foremost, will it fit your boat exactly as it stands? If it will not, you may end by paying alteration charges which will bring the total cost nearly to that of a new sail. Although the sail may be cheap, you will have to pay labour charges at current rates.

Secondly, you should bend the sail on your boat, to see whether it sets well; take it afloat for a proper trial. If all goes well with this test, examine it carefully along the lines of the points I have listed for a winter overhaul. I will summarize them briefly here:

1. Chafe in way of runners, shrouds and spreaders.
2. Rotten stitching caused by weakening in sunlight.
3. Conditions of bolt rope, with special reference to chafe at the slides and the rope pulling away from the headboard.
4. Wires, with special attention to where eye splices have disturbed the protective covering. Check spinnaker wires by comparing lengths.
5. Creased leeches.
6. Distortion of the thimbles.
7. Condition of seizings.
8. Do pleats, or a row of empty stitch holes, betray alterations, particularly at the leech, which might suggest a poor shape?

Finally, if you are determined on a sail which will have to be altered, do not take the vendor's word that it is a simple alteration – nor the evidence of this book. Offer to buy it, subject to a Sail Maker of your own choice agreeing to make the alterations for a reasonable sum.

CHAPTER XXI

The Future

The main factors which contribute to a yacht's performance are the helmsman, the crew, the hull (and its equipment), the sails, and luck. Estimates of the proportion contributed by the sails vary between 25 and 75 per cent but, for the sake of argument, we can say that each of the first four ingredients contributes 25 per cent to the recipe, with luck thrown in as an extra for seasoning. I cannot then be accused of bias.

Speaking broadly again, the hull with its fittings costs somewhere between 75 and 90 per cent of the total outlay, and the sails are responsible for the rest.

It is heartening for the Sail Maker to note that a general awakening to the importance of sails has taken place. For too long owners were content to make the inevitable economy cuts at the expense of the sail locker. What is the use of spending a year's salary on a boat, only to cut down at the last minute on the very item which is going to make her go? This is surely spoiling the ship for a ha'porth of tar.

Never forget that your sails are your power plant.

We are indebted in part to the spur of international competition for this general awareness. It is fair to say that the British received a rude awakening over the two America's Cup defeats of 1958 and 1964. Almost everything and everybody was vaguely blamed without deep analysis for *Sceptre*'s failure against *Columbia*, but people really started scratching their heads after *Sovereign* was equally soundly thrashed by *Constellation*.

The whole of the British yacht-racing fraternity was examined both publicly and privately. Nothing escaped criticism. As part of this examination, the Sail Maker had to bear his share. Moreover, the analysis went further into the question, and took a hard look at the raw materials of the business, including the thread with which the sails were made, and the shape of the needles used to do it.

Sailcloth

The Sail Makers, of course, did not like to think that the whole responsibility was theirs, and I am not going to be drawn into a fruitless argument about what part should be borne by lack of competition, by the hull, the spars or the crew. There is no doubt, however, that the quality of our sailcloth needed to be improved in common with everything else. It is good to note that energetic and far-reaching steps had results – in the Admiral's Cup at least.

I have already written something about cloth in Chapter III, and it only remains for me to emphasize here what I said there. Sails can only be as good as their cloth will let them, and we can expect that improvement will be best advanced by better weaving and finishing techniques.

We must not, however, assume that the answer lay solely in better canvas. The cloth produced by long-established weavers could not have been all that bad, as indeed the sails made by our Sail Makers could not have been all that bad, when the British team could win the Admiral's Cup for the first two seasons it was up for competition among teams of yachts from all over the world. It is not feasible that weavers who have been in the business for over 150 years should fail to produce a good cloth, just as it is not feasible that equally senior Sail Makers should fail to produce good sails. The spur of the Admiral's Cup shows that international competition is still the best incentive for improvement.

The Wind Tunnel

A primitive apparatus for measuring lateral, forward and downward components of wind-pressure on model sails at predetermined angles of attack and heel, was constructed and used by Mr Linton Hope of Great Britain around 1911 or 1912. At the request of the editor of the *Field*, a series of experiments was carried out to test the relative efficiency of a gunter lug sail, a gaff sail together with its jackyarder, and a high-peaked gaff sail; all had the same area of 500 sq. in., the same flow and the same centre of effort. It is interesting to note that they came out in the above order of efficiency, with the gunter lug, which most nearly approached the Bermudian sail in outline shape, ahead of both the others.

This early apparatus was mounted in the open, and relied on Nature for its airflow. In 1915 at the Massachusetts Institute of Technology in America, H. A. Everett and C. H. Peabody read a paper on 'Wind Tunnel Experiments with Yacht Sails', and Harold Larner and H. F. Hewins conducted a study into the efficiency of the Bermudian rig. Manfred Currey did a lot of wind tunnel work in Germany before the publication of his remarkable book in 1928. Sir Richard Fairey, of the aviation company which bears his name, conducted experiments at his factory's wind tunnel at Hayes, Middlesex, before the Second World War, but his results have never been published. This roll-call of early pioneers in yacht research would not be complete without the name of Professor Davidson, of *Gimcrack* fame, being mentioned.

All of this experiment is of value, even if it has since been proved that some of it is of limited application, in that it helps to establish the basic problems which are to be solved.

It was not until the late 1950s that a real start was made on the problem in Great Britain. T. Tanner, of Southampton University, had done some earlier personal work on the subject and, when the Red Duster 12 metre syndicate financed a research programme, he was the obvious man to do the work. There were at that time three wind tunnels in England especially designed for evaluating sails. The Amateur Yacht Research Society had built an open-air low-speed tunnel at Hythe in Kent, Messrs Ratsey & Lapthorn Ltd had a medium-speed tunnel at their loft at Cowes, and Southampton University had a similar one at Southampton. All these were capable of improving sail design and flow, with Southampton's rather more sophisticated instrumentation in the best position to provide the answers. Tony Marchaj's *Sailing Theory and Practice* is an excellent book on the theoretical side of sails, largely as a result of his experience in the University wind tunnel. I commend it to those who would seek a more intimate knowledge of this subject than I have been able to convey in Chapter II.

I do not believe that enough has been made of wind tunnels, for it is to science that we must now look if the marginal improvements still possible are to be achieved. At Ratsey's we never seemed to be able to devote the entire energies of one or two executives solely to the wind tunnel for the length of time it would take to mount a really effective investigation. I undertook one or two superficial studies connected with spinnakers and porosity in 1962, a trial on adding a shelf to the foot of a 14 ft International mainsail in 1963, and a slightly more detailed analysis of the ideal flow in the upper half of a 12 metre mainsail at the time of the *Sovereign* and *Kurrewa V* era, together with some tuft tests, but this is about all that was done in the first five years of the tunnel, which has now been regretfully dismantled to make room for more prosaic equipment. Part of the trouble was lack of funds. A Sail Maker's budget is not sufficient to finance a large research programme, and it always seemed a pity to me that the second post-war America's Cup challenge, which cannot have cost less than £200,000, did not make fuller use of the facilities available. I realize that Southampton University were financed in a research programme, but most of this was paid for by the Red Duster syndicate, which never built a challenger.

Wind Tunnel Requirement

The wind tunnel requirement can be divided into two basic elements. First, what outline shape should a suit of sails be (outline design), and secondly what flow should it have (flow design). Because he is nearly always presented with an outline shape by the Naval Architect, the Sail Maker is by nature more interested in flow design. You may think it is time that he took a greater interest in outline design, but this would be like presenting a Boat Builder with the overall length, beam and draft of the hull and telling him to draw up the lines himself.

Investigations by technical research teams have initially tended to concentrate their efforts principally on outline design. Many sail-testing programmes carried out by aerodynamicists have tried to determine the wind forces acting on a particular boat, and thereby to arrive at the vessel's optimum speed under certain conditions. This requires an exact replica of the hull, rigging and sails, together with a fair representation of both wind and water. At scales below about one tenth, this becomes almost impossible, the stitching and thread of the sails alone can never be reproduced accurately, except in metal; but rigid sails only hold good for the one set of conditions which induce their shape in the full-sized suit of sails. Further difficulties are added by scale effect, and the high tunnel wind-speeds needed if the tests are to be conducted at the same Reynolds number as that prevailing in the full-scale conditions it is hoped to represent. Winds in the order of 100 m.p.h. are demanded, and these once again require metal sails if distortion is to be avoided.

However, the Sail Maker's requirement is not to find out how fast a particular boat will go. It is usually to put the fastest suit of sails on to an existing boat to a given sail plan (outline design) and conditions. In other words, if he wants the boat to go faster, he has to try to make better sails than ones whose characteristics are already known through experience.

His aim is therefore clear: how to improve on a known factor.

Viewed in this light, the problem becomes simpler. If he were to scale down a known suit of sails and take readings in the tunnel, he could then use these as a yardstick against which readings from experimental sails may be measured. He can reasonably trust that errors due to scale effect, stitching, hull and rigging would be the same, or nearly the same, for both models. Provided that the shape and flow of the sails is truly representational, and that both suits are to the same scale and are set on the same rig under the same conditions, their comparative thrusts should also be representational.

Venturis

The venturi spinnaker is the result of an idea pioneered by M. Lemoigne of France, as a result of his work with vented parachutes, and developed by Ratsey & Lapthorn Inc., of New York. Based on the principle that thrust is deflected downwards by the vents, thus imparting lift to the spinnaker, these sails have been tried in varying sizes since 1961. There is little doubt that they set better than normal spinnakers in very light conditions, but whether they impart extra drive in the process is more doubtful. There are no data as to whether they actually lift the boat by their upwards thrust. I did some wind tunnel experiments with a venturi spinnaker and the results were inconclusive tending, if anything, to show that there was little or no gain in thrust. The principal point in favour of the venturi is that it may prove better on a close reach, because some of the air at the head bleeds off, thus reducing knock-down effect. There is also some increase in stability downwind.

Mainsails have also been made with vents in them, and the fact that they are not now in universal use would indicate that results have not been satisfactory, despite glowing initial reports from those most closely involved.

Vents are a nuisance in a sail, because they catch in spreaders, cleats and any other handy projection, often with disastrous results for all, except the Sail Maker who has to make a new one. I believe, however, that we have not heard the last of them, and suggest that research has so far been misdirected. A vent does not, in itself, promote thrust. Indeed, the opposite is the case, because it allows air to leak from one side of the sail to the other, thus tending to lower the pressure to windward and raise it to leeward. They can certainly be made to encourage the airflow into particular channels, however, and restricted use of them to this end could well pay dividends. I say restricted use, because nearly all venturi sails so far produced – mainsails and spinnakers alike – have had, in my opinion, too many vents. With pressure almost completely equalized on either side, the sail will be robbed of thrust.

The sort of thing I have in mind is one or two suitably placed vents near the leeches of spinnakers to help spread the sail so that maximum area is projected; similar treatment in a mainsail or headsail, to delay separation of the streamlines from the lee side of the sail; a vent near the head of a spinnaker to help lift the sail, and to bleed off some of the wind to lessen knock-down effect.

The Half-winder

While still sailmaking I was responsible for the half-winder. This is a reaching spinnaker which has part or all of the rear half, or leech area, made of mesh, in order that the sail shall not develop a rearward component of thrust; in addition, the wind is allowed to escape to leeward rather than backwind the lee of the mainsail. Here again, I overdid it. Half the sail developed practically no thrust (as intended) so the leech on that side would not spread. The sail, therefore, collapsed sooner than a conventional spinnaker as the wind went ahead. There is room, however, for development here: again, the top of a reaching spinnaker might have porous mesh incorporated

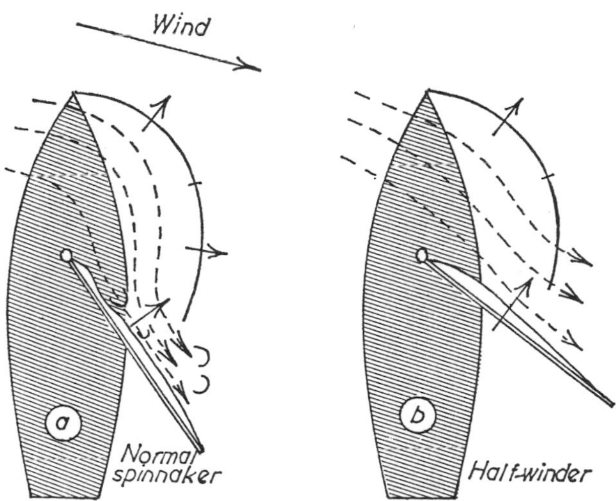

Fig. 145. The half-winder principle.

to allow air to bleed off; restricted use of mesh might be beneficial to the leech of a reaching spinnaker; there may be reaching headsails which could profit from allowing some air at the leech to seep from windward to leeward to minimize their heeling effect without loss of thrust.

Wing Sails

The affinity of sails and aircraft wings has been argued for a long time. Whatever views may be held, there is no doubt that a double-sided sail, with a section like an aircraft wing, will make a hull sail very well. One of the major problems to be overcome is that a symmetrical section is inefficient. This means that some system of changing the section on tacking is necessary, so that the windward side is flatter than the leeward side. This sometimes means an articulated leading edge, or mast, or else a complicated internal system of cranks and levers, which adds to complexity and weight. Another drawback is that the resulting 'sail' is often not transportable, and takes a long time to set up or dismantle.

Considerable progress of this nature has been made by Austin Farrar in the development of sails for C class catamarans. *Lady Helmsman*, the successful 1966 defender of what has come to be known as the Little America's Cup, had a wing section mast pivoting at the leading edge, with a conventional fully battened leech. At first it was thought that a fine section to the wing was necessary but, although this resulted in a very close-winded sail, the streamlines broke away quickly as soon as the angle of attack increased beyond fine limits. Tom Tanner, of the Southampton University Yacht Research Group, suggested that a blunter leading edge would give better results, and this proved to be the case.

It was originally intended to have a loose-footed sail, with a wishbone holding the clew out and down, in order to remove all twist from the head. This it achieved so well that Reg. White, the helmsman, complained that it was virtually impossible to control the sail in a fresh breeze. He could not feather the top of the sail while maintaining drive in the lower part. The wishbone was accordingly discarded for a more conventional boom. With its wide mainsheet traveller across both hulls, this was nearly as efficient at removing twist as the wishbone, but allowed controlled development of it if required.

A refinement adopted on *Lady Helmsman*'s sails was the use of windows to allow tell-tales to be seen to leeward. We have seen that maintenance of laminar flow to leeward is important; at catamaran speeds it becomes vital. The leeward tell-tale soon shows when the airflow to leeward is not smoothly along the sail, and therefore something has to be done to restore the situation.

A symmetrical wing, with a leading edge which will incline toward the apparent wind, thus reducing the local angle of attack, is a good theoretical construction. Something can be done along these lines to improve airflow over a normal sail, if a pear-shaped mast rotates sharply toward the wind. It will not be long before wing-shaped masts become more common, even if they are only 6 in. or so in chord, and not the rather more unwieldy size used on *Lady Helmsman*. One of the problems to be overcome is the windage caused by the mast which makes the boat unstable at moorings or in the dinghy park.

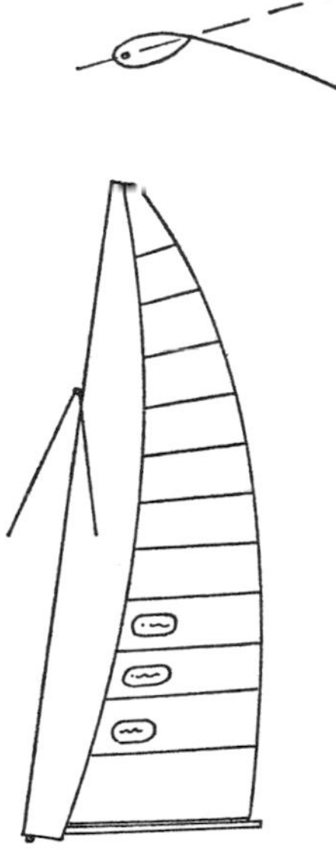

Fig. 146. Wing sail with fully battened leech, as developed for C class catamarans by Austin Farrar. Plan view shows symmetrical wing section mast, pivoting at leading edge. Side elevation. Note luff/foot ratio of about 3:1 when wing is included.

Experiments have been going on for a long time with wing sails proper, and one day somebody will produce a workable system which can be rigged and stowed easily. Until then it must remain the sphere of a few dedicated enthusiasts, who may nevertheless sail a good deal faster than their more conservative friends.

Horizontal Sails

The fact that some boats are more stable lying on their sides than upright is well known to many. It would appear logical, therefore, to develop a sail which starts life in the horizontal position. As long ago as 1895 an umbrella sail was tried, and my photograph shows this in action. The idea, of course, is to convert the wind's energy into two components as usual, but in this case one is forward and the second has a vertical or righting moment. The Amateur Yacht

Research Society has put forward an ingenious idea for using a modified glider as a kite to tow a boat, either to windward or downwind. This is another adaptation of the horizontal sail idea, and the future may hold something in store for us along these lines.

Windmill

H. M. Barkla, of Scotland, has proposed some interesting lines of thought for the future. At present, he says, effort has been concentrated on driving a hull supported in water, through the water by means of wind power. But what of the opposite state, where a hull supported in the air is driven through the air by means of water power? If a yacht can beat to windward, down current, faster than the current, surely suggests Barkla, an airship hanging a vertical hydrofoil in the water could be made to 'tack' up water, down wind faster than the wind. An alternative method of drive would be a water-propeller.

Perhaps this is not possible due to the relative viscosity of the two fluids under consideration (water and air), but there is certainly room for development of the windmill which drives a water-propeller. The late Lord Brabazon of Tara fitted a Bembridge Redwing with just such a system, and he sailed straight into the eye of the wind. He did not make such good speed to windward, however, as conventional Redwings cross-tacking. This was an excellent boat to use for the experiment, because their rules allow 200 sq. ft of sail area disposed exactly how the owner likes; there could be no question, therefore, that either system was being favoured. This was some time ago, and there is no doubt that speeds could be improved nowadays, especially if some form of hydrofoil were incorporated into the hull to lessen drag.

Conventional Sails

I cannot leave you with all these rather outlandish ideas as the last impression of this book. For the immediate foreseeable future conventional sails will continue to serve as they have in the past. They will only serve as well as you let them, so take care of them. They are made of a delicate fabric, which does not like mistreatment. They are the soul of the boat, and the motive power. Look after them and they will look after you.

APPENDIX A

Chart of equivalent cloth weights

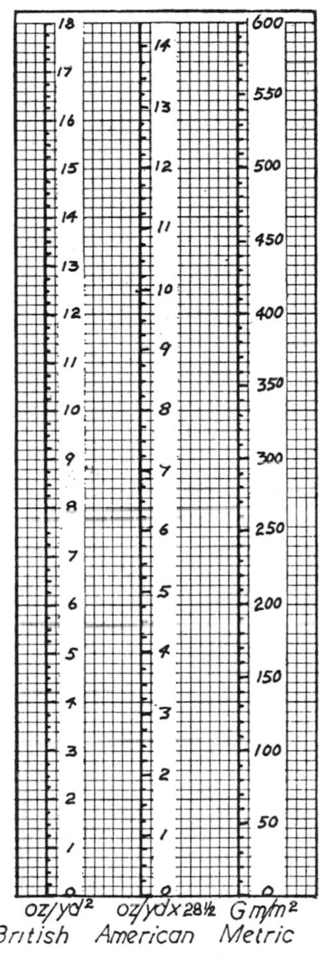

APPENDIX B

Approximate yardage of 36" cloth used in making various types of sail

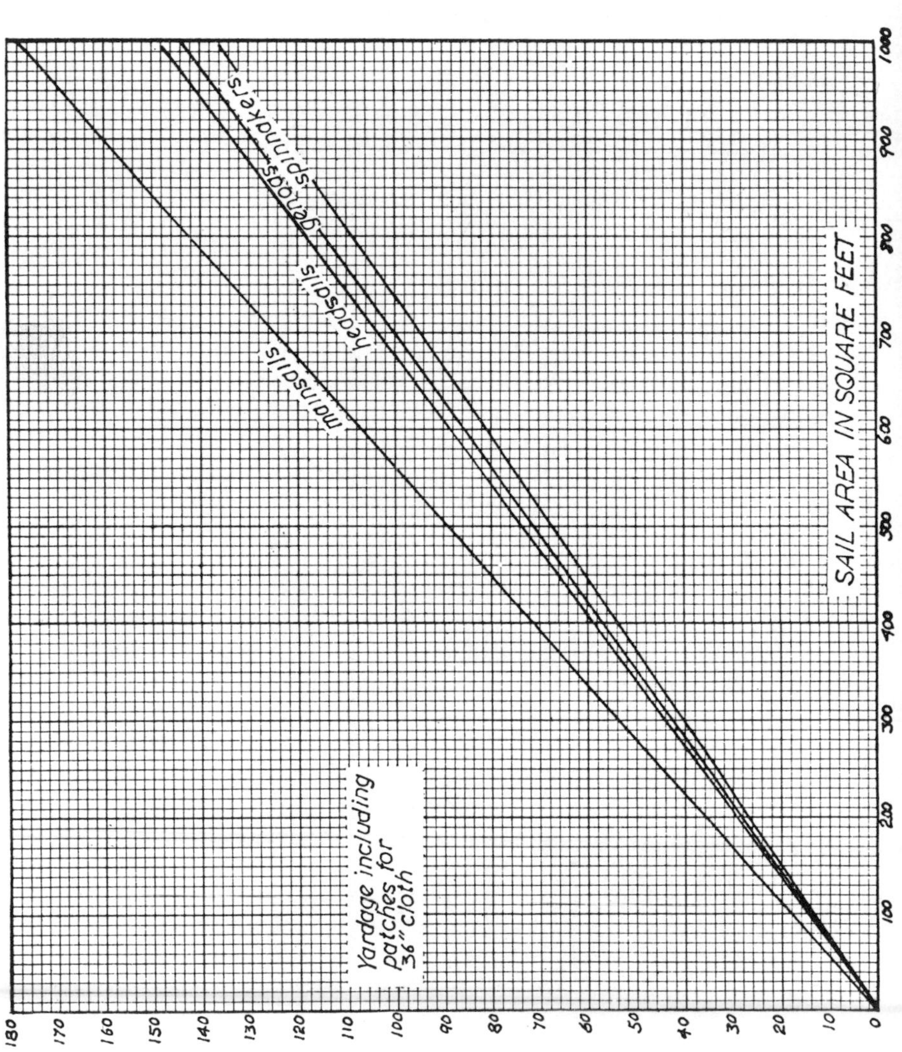

APPENDIX C

Headboard and batten limits under IOR formula

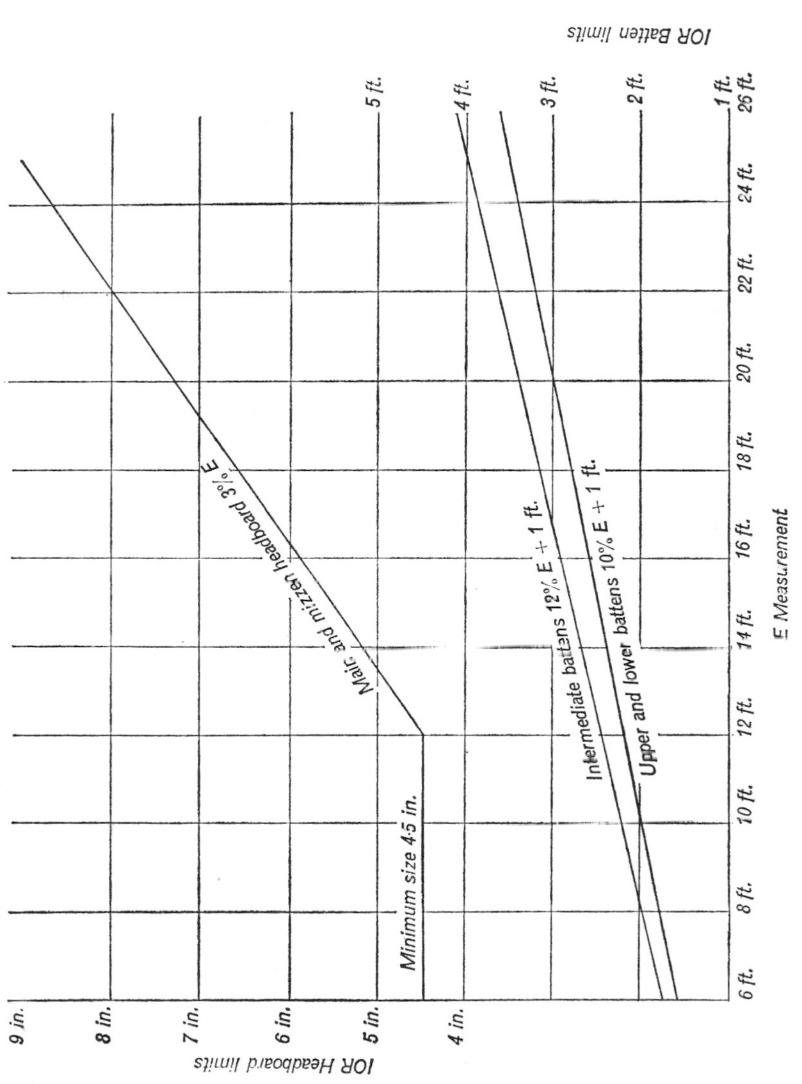

APPENDIX D

Spinnaker stay lengths for given $(I^2 + J^2)$ to the IOR

Method of Use

Determine the I and J measurements in feet and decimals of a foot to two places of decimals. Square them and add the two answers together. Read off maximum spinnaker stays in feet and decimals of a foot against the result.

Example

I = 31 ft 4 ins. J = 10 ft 7 in.

$31{\cdot}33^2 = 981{\cdot}5$

$10{\cdot}58^2 = 111{\cdot}9$

$I^2 + J^2 = 1093{\cdot}4$

Reading from table, against 1090, fourth column:

Stays = 31·408 ft = 31 ft 5 in.

Table to Calculate Maximum IOR Spinnaker Stay Length

(Units are feet and decimals of a foot)

	0 5	1 6	2 7	3 8	4 9
+700	+25·135	+25·153	+25·171	+25·188	+25·206
+705	+25·224	+25·242	+25·260	+25·278	+25·296
+710	+25·314	+25·331	+25·349	+25·367	+25·385
+715	+25·403	+25·420	+25·438	+25·456	+25·473
+720	+25·491	+25·509	+25·527	+25·544	+25·562
+725	+25·580	+25·597	+25·615	+25·632	+25·650
+730	+25·668	+25·685	+25·703	+25·720	+25·738
+735	+25·755	+25·773	+25·790	+25·808	+25·825
+740	+25·843	+25·860	+25·878	+25·895	+25·913
+745	+25·930	+25·947	+25·965	+25·982	+25·999

Spinnaker Stay Lengths for given $(I^2 + J^2)$ *to the IOR*—continued

(Units are feet and decimals of a foot)—*continued*

	0	**1**	**2**	**3**	**4**
	5	**6**	**7**	**8**	**9**
+750	+26·017	+26·034	+26·051	+26·069	+26·086
+755	+26·103	+26·121	+26·138	+26·155	+26·172
+760	+26·190	+26·207	+26·224	+26·241	+26·259
+765	+26·276	+26·293	+26·310	+26·327	+26·344
+770	+26·361	+26·379	+26·396	+26·413	+26·430
+775	+26·447	+26·464	+26·481	+26·498	+26·515
+780	+26·532	+26·549	+26·566	+26·583	+26·600
+785	+26·617	+26·634	+26·651	+26·668	+26·685
+790	+26·702	+26·718	+26·735	+26·752	+26·769
+795	+26·786	+26·803	+26·820	+26·836	+26·853
+800	+26·870	+26·887	+26·904	+26·920	+26·937
+805	+26·954	+26·971	+26·987	+27·004	+27·021
+810	+27·037	+27·054	+27·071	+27·087	+27·104
+815	+27·121	+27·137	+27·154	+27·171	+27·187
+820	+27·204	+27·220	+27·237	+27·254	+27·270
+825	+27·287	+27·303	+27·320	+27·336	+27·353
+830	+27·369	+27·386	+27·402	+27·419	+27·435
+835	+27·452	+27·468	+27·484	+27·501	+27·517
+840	+27·534	+27·550	+27·566	+27·583	+27·599
+845	+27·615	+27·632	+27·648	+27·664	+27·681
+850	+27·697	+27·713	+27·730	+27·746	+27·762
+855	+27·778	+27·795	+27·811	+27·827	+27·843
+860	+27·859	+27·876	+27·892	+27·908	+27·924
+865	+27·940	+27·956	+27·973	+27·989	+28·005
+870	+28·021	+28·037	+28·053	+28·069	+28·085
+875	+28·101	+28·117	+28·133	+28·150	+28·166
+880	+28·182	+28·198	+28·214	+28·230	+28·246
+885	+28·262	+28·277	+28·293	+28·309	+28·325
+890	+28·341	+28·357	+28·373	+28·389	+28·405
+895	+28·421	+28·437	+28·452	+28·468	+28·484
+900	+28·500	+28·516	+28·532	+28·547	+28·563
+905	+28·579	+28·595	+28·611	+28·626	+28·642
+910	+28·658	+28·674	+28·689	+28·705	+28·721
+915	+28·737	+28·752	+28·768	+28·784	+28·799
+920	+28·815	+28·831	+28·846	+28·862	+28·877

Appendix D

Spinnaker Stay Lengths for given (I^2 + J^2) to the IOR—continued

(Units are feet and decimals of a foot)—*continued*

	0 **5**	**1** **6**	**2** **7**	**3** **8**	**4** **9**
+925	+28·893	+28·909	+28·924	+28·940	+28·956
+930	+28·971	+28·987	+29·002	+29·018	+29·033
+935	+29·049	+29·064	+29·080	+29·095	+29·111
+940	+29·126	+29·142	+29·157	+29·173	+29·188
+945	+29·204	+29·219	+29·235	+29·250	+29·266
+950	+29·281	+29·296	+29·312	+29·327	+29·343
+955	+29·358	+29·373	+29·389	+29·404	+29·419
+960	+29·435	+29·450	+29·465	+29·481	+29·496
+965	+29·511	+29·527	+29·542	+29·557	+29·572
+970	+29·588	+29·603	+29·618	+29·633	+29·649
+975	+29·664	+29·679	+29·694	+29·709	+29·725
+980	+29·740	+29·755	+29·770	+29·785	+29·800
+985	+29·815	+29·831	+29·846	+29·861	+29·876
+990	+29·891	+29·906	+29·921	+29·936	+29·951
+995	+29·966	+29·981	+29·997	+30·012	+30·027
+1000	+30·042	+30·057	+30·072	+30·087	+30·102
+1005	+30·117	+30·132	+30·147	+30·162	+30·177
+1010	+30·191	+30·206	+30·221	+30·236	+30·251
+1015	+30·266	+30·281	+30·296	+30·311	+30·326
+1020	+30·341	+30·355	+30·370	+30·385	+30·400
+1025	+30·415	+30·430	+30·444	+30·459	+30·474
+1030	+30·489	+30·504	+30·519	+30·533	+30·548
+1035	+30·563	+30·578	+30·592	+30·607	+30·622
+1040	+30·637	+30·651	+30·666	+30·681	+30·695
+1045	+30·710	+30·725	+30·740	+30·754	+30·769
+1050	+30·784	+30·798	+30·813	+30·827	+30·842
+1055	+30·857	+30·871	+30·886	+30·901	+30·915
+1060	+30·930	+30·944	+30·959	+30·973	+30·988
+1065	+31·003	+31·017	+31·032	+31·046	+31·061
+1070	+31·075	+31·090	+31·104	+31·119	+31·133
+1075	+31·148	+31·162	+31·177	+31·191	+31·206
+1080	+31·220	+31·235	+31·249	+31·264	+31·278
+1085	+31·292	+31·307	+31·321	+31·336	+31·350
+1090	+31·364	+31·379	+31·393	+31·408	+31·422
+1095	+31·436	+31·451	+31·465	+31·479	+31·494

Spinnaker Stay Lengths for given ($I^2 + J^2$) *to the IOR*—continued

(Units are feet and decimals of a foot)—*continued*

	0	1	2	3	4
	5	6	7	8	9
+1100	+31·508	+31·522	+31·537	+31·551	+31·565
+1105	+31·579	+31·594	+31·608	+31·622	+31·637
+1110	+31·651	+31·665	+31·679	+31·694	+31·708
+1115	+31·722	+31·736	+31·750	+31·765	+31·779
+1120	+31·793	+31·807	+31·821	+31·836	+31·850
+1125	+31·864	+31·878	+31·892	+31·906	+31·921
+1130	+31·935	+31·949	+31·963	+31·977	+31·991
+1135	+32·005	+32·019	+32·033	+32·048	+32·062
+1140	+32·076	+32·090	+32·104	+32·118	+32·132
+1145	+32·146	+32·160	+32·174	+32·188	+32·202
+1150	+32·216	+32·230	+32·244	+32·258	+32·272
+1155	+32·286	+32·300	+32·314	+32·328	+32·342
+1160	+32·356	+32·370	+32·384	+32·398	+32·412
+1165	+32·425	+32·439	+32·453	+32·467	+32·481
+1170	+32·495	+32·509	+32·523	+32·537	+32·550
+1175	+32·564	+32·578	+32·592	+32·606	+32·620
+1180	+32·634	+32·647	+32·661	+32·675	+32·689
+1185	+32·703	+32·716	+32·730	+32·744	+32·758
+1190	+32·772	+32·785	+32·799	+32·813	+32·827
+1195	+32·840	+32·854	+32·868	+32·882	+32·895
+1200	+32·909	+32·923	+32·936	+32·950	+32·964
+1205	+32·977	+32·991	+33·005	+33·018	+33·032
+1210	+33·046	+33·059	+33·073	+33·087	+33·100
+1215	+33·114	+33·128	+33·141	+33·155	+33·168
+1220	+33·182	+33·196	+33·209	+33·223	+33·236
+1225	+33·250	+33·264	+33·277	+33·291	+33·304
+1230	+33·318	+33·331	+33·345	+33·358	+33·372
+1235	+33·385	+33·399	+33·412	+33·426	+33·439
+1240	+33·453	+33·466	+33·480	+33·493	+33·507
+1245	+33·520	+33·534	+33·547	+33·561	+33·574
+1250	+33·588	+33·601	+33·614	+33·628	+33·641
+1255	+33·655	+33·668	+33·681	+33·695	+33·708
+1260	+33·722	+33·735	+33·748	+33·762	+33·775
+1265	+33 788	+33·802	+33·815	+33·829	+33·842
+1270	+33·855	+33·869	+33·882	+33·895	+33·908

Appendix D

Spinnaker Stay Lengths for given $(I^2 + J^2)$ *to the IOR*—continued

(Units are feet and decimals of a foot)—*continued*

	0	1	2	3	4
	5	**6**	**7**	**8**	**9**
+1275	+33·922	+33·935	+33·948	+33·962	+33·975
+1280	+33·988	+34·002	+34·015	+34·028	+34·041
+1285	+34·055	+34·068	+34·081	+34·094	+34·108
+1290	+34·121	+34·134	+34·147	+34·160	+34·174
+1295	+34·187	+34·200	+34·213	+34·226	+34·240
+1300	+34·253	+34·266	+34·279	+34·292	+34·305
+1305	+34·319	+34·332	+34·345	+34·358	+34·371
+1310	+34·384	+34·397	+34·410	+34·424	+34·437
+1315	+34·450	+34·463	+34·476	+34·489	+34·502
+1320	+34·515	+34·528	+34·541	+34·554	+34·567
+1325	+34·581	+34·594	+34·607	+34·620	+34·633
+1330	+34·646	+34·659	+34·672	+34·685	+34·698
+1335	+34·711	+34·724	+34·737	+34·750	+34·763
+1340	+34·776	+34·789	+34·802	+34·815	+34·828
+1345	+34·841	+34·853	+34·866	+34·879	+34·892
+1350	+34·905	+34·918	+34·931	+34·944	+34·957
+1355	+34·970	+34·983	+34·996	+35·008	+35·021
+1360	+35·034	+35·047	+35·060	+35·073	+35·086
+1365	+35·099	+35·111	+35·124	+35·137	+35·150
+1370	+35·163	+35·176	+35·188	+35·201	+35·214
+1375	+35·227	+35·240	+35·253	+35·265	+35·278
+1380	+35·291	+35·304	+35·316	+35·329	+35·342
+1385	+35·355	+35·368	+35·380	+35·393	+35·406
+1390	+35·419	+35·431	+35·444	+35·457	+35·469
+1395	+35·482	+35·495	+35·508	+35·520	+35·533
+1400	+35·546	+35·558	+35·571	+35·584	+35·596
+1405	+35·609	+35·622	+35·634	+35·647	+35·660
+1410	+35·672	+35·685	+35·698	+35·710	+35·723
+1415	+35·736	+35·748	+35·761	+35·774	+35·786
+1420	+35·799	+35·811	+35·824	+35·837	+35·849
+1425	+35·862	+35·874	+35·887	+35·899	+35·912
+1430	+35·925	+35·937	+35·950	+35·962	+35·975
+1435	+35·987	+36·000	+36·012	+36·025	+36·037
+1440	+36·050	+36·062	+36·075	+36·087	+36·100
+1445	+36·112	+36·125	+36·137	+36·150	+36·162

Spinnaker Stay Lengths for given ($I^2 + J^2$) *to the IOR*—continued

(Units are feet and decimals of a foot)—*continued*

	0 5	1 6	2 7	3 8	4 9
+1450	+36·175	+36·187	+36·200	+36·212	+36·225
+1455	+36·237	+36·250	+36·262	+36·275	+36·287
+1460	+36·299	+36·312	+36·324	+36·337	+36·349
+1465	+36·362	+36·374	+36·386	+36·399	+36·411
+1470	+36·424	+36·436	+36·448	+36·461	+36·473
+1475	+36·485	+36·498	+36·510	+36·523	+36·535
+1480	+36·547	+36·560	+36·572	+36·584	+36·597
+1485	+36·609	+36·621	+36·634	+36·646	+36·658
+1490	+36·670	+36·683	+36·695	+36·707	+36·720
+1495	+36·732	+36·744	+36·757	+36·769	+36·781
+1500	+36·793	+36·806	+36·818	+36·830	+36·842
+1505	+36·855	+36·867	+36·879	+36·891	+36·904
+1510	+36·916	+36·928	+36·940	+36·952	+36·965
+1515	+36·977	+36·989	+37·001	+37·013	+37·026
+1520	+37·038	+37·050	+37·062	+37·074	+37·087
+1525	+37·099	+37·111	+37·123	+37·135	+37·147
+1530	+37·159	+37·172	+37·184	+37·196	+37·208
+1535	+37·220	+37·232	+37·244	+37·256	+37·269
+1540	+37·281	+37·293	+37·305	+37·317	+37·329
+1545	+37·341	+37·353	+37·365	+37·377	+37·389
+1550	+37·402	+37·414	+37·426	+37·438	+37·450
+1555	+37·462	+37·474	+37·486	+37·498	+37·510
+1560	+37·522	+37·534	+37·546	+37·558	+37·570
+1565	+37·582	+37·594	+37·606	+37·618	+37·630
+1570	+37·642	+37·654	+37·666	+37·678	+37·690
+1575	+37·702	+37·714	+37·726	+37·738	+37·750
+1580	+37·762	+37·774	+37·786	+37·798	+37·810
+1585	+37·821	+37·833	+37·845	+37·857	+37·869
+1590	+37·881	+37·893	+37·905	+37·917	+37·929
+1595	+37·941	+37·952	+37·964	+37·976	+37·988
+1600	+38·000	+38·012	+38·024	+38·036	+38·047
+1605	+38·059	+38·071	+38·083	+38·095	+38·107
+1610	+38·119	+38·130	+38·142	+38·154	+38·166
+1615	+38·178	+38·190	+38·201	+38·213	+38·225
+1620	+38·237	+38·249	+38·260	+38·272	+38·284

Appendix D

Spinnaker Stay Lengths for given ($I^2 + J^2$) to the IOR—continued

(Units are feet and decimals of a foot)—*continued*

	0 5	1 6	2 7	3 8	4 9
+1625	+38·296	+38·308	+38·319	+38·331	+38·343
+1630	+38·355	+38·366	+38·378	+38·390	+38·402
+1635	+38·413	+38·425	+38·437	+38·449	+38·460
+1640	+38·472	+38·484	+38·496	+38·507	+38·519
+1645	+38·531	+38·542	+38·554	+38·566	+38·577
+1650	+38·589	+38·601	+38·613	+38·624	+38·636
+1655	+38·648	+38·659	+38·671	+38·683	+38·694
+1660	+38·706	+38·718	+38·729	+38·741	+38·753
+1665	+38·764	+38·776	+38·787	+38·799	+38·811
+1670	+38·822	+38·834	+38·846	+38·857	+38·869
+1675	+38·880	+38·892	+38·904	+38·915	+38·927
+1680	+38·938	+38·950	+38·962	+38·973	+38·985
+1685	+38·996	+39·008	+39·019	+39·031	+39·043
+1690	+39·054	+39·066	+39·077	+39·089	+39·100
+1695	+39·112	+39·123	+39·135	+39·146	+39·158
+1700	+39·170	+39·181	+39·193	+39·204	+39·216
+1705	+39·227	+39·239	+39·250	+39·262	+39·273
+1710	+39·285	+39·296	+39·308	+39·319	+39·330
+1715	+39·342	+39·353	+39·365	+39·376	+39·388
+1720	+39·399	+39·411	+39·422	+39·434	+39·445
+1725	+39·456	+39·468	+39·479	+39·491	+39·502
+1730	+39·514	+39·525	+39·536	+39·548	+39·559
+1735	+39·571	+39·582	+39·593	+39·605	+39·616
+1740	+39·628	+39·639	+39·650	+39·662	+39·673
+1745	+39·685	+39·696	+39·707	+39·719	+39·730
+1750	+39·741	+39·753	+39·764	+39·775	+39·787
+1755	+39·798	+39·809	+39·821	+39·832	+39·843
+1760	+39·855	+39·866	+39·877	+39·889	+39·900
+1765	+39·911	+39·923	+39·934	+39·945	+39·957
+1770	+39·968	+39·979	+39·990	+40·002	+40·013
+1775	+40·024	+40·035	+40·047	+40·058	+40·069
+1780	+40·081	+40·092	+40·103	+40·114	+40·126
+1785	+40·137	+40·148	+40·159	+40·171	+40·182
+1790	+40·193	+40·204	+40·215	+40·227	+40·238
+1795	+40·249	+40·260	+40·271	+40·283	+40·294

Spinnaker Stay Lengths for given $(I^2 + J^2)$ *to the IOR*—continued

(Units are feet and decimals of a foot)—*continued*

	0 **5**	**1** **6**	**2** **7**	**3** **8**	**4** **9**
+1800	+40·305	+40·316	+40·327	+40·339	+40·350
+1805	+40·361	+40·372	+40·383	+40·395	+40·406
+1810	+40·417	+40·428	+40·439	+40·450	+40·462
+1815	+40·473	+40·484	+40·495	+40·506	+40·517
+1820	+40·528	+40·540	+40·551	+40·562	+40·573
+1825	+40·584	+40·595	+40·606	+40·617	+40·628
+1830	+40·640	+40·651	+40·662	+40·673	+40·684
+1835	+40·695	+40·706	+40·717	+40·728	+40·739
+1840	+40·750	+40·762	+40·773	+40·784	+40·795
+1845	+40·806	+40·817	+40·828	+40·839	+40·850
+1850	+40·861	+40·872	+40·883	+40·894	+40·905
+1855	+40·916	+40·927	+40·938	+40·949	+40·960
+1860	+40·971	+40·982	+40·993	+41·004	+41·015
+1865	+41·026	+41·037	+41·048	+41·059	+41·070
+1870	+41·081	+41·092	+41·103	+41·114	+41·125
+1875	+41·136	+41·147	+41·158	+41·169	+41·180
+1880	+41·191	+41·202	+41·213	+41·224	+41·235
+1885	+41·246	+41·257	+41·268	+41·279	+41·289
+1890	+41·300	+41·311	+41·322	+41·333	+41·344
+1895	+41·355	+41·366	+41·377	+41·388	+41·399
+1900	+41·410	+41·420	+41·431	+41·442	+41·453
+1905	+41·464	+41·475	+41·486	+41·497	+41·507
+1910	+41·518	+41·529	+41·540	+41·551	+41·562
+1915	+41·573	+41·584	+41·594	+41·605	+41·616
+1920	+41·627	+41·638	+41·649	+41·659	+41·670
+1925	+41·681	+41·692	+41·703	+41·714	+41·724
+1930	+41·735	+41·746	+41·757	+41·768	+41·778
+1935	+41·789	+41·800	+41·811	+41·822	+41·832
+1940	+41·843	+41·854	+41·865	+41·875	+41·886
+1945	+41·897	+41·908	+41·919	+41·929	+41·940
+1950	+41·951	+41·962	+41·972	+41·983	+41·994
+1955	+42·005	+42·015	+42·026	+42·037	+42·048
+1960	+42·058	+42·069	+42·080	+42·090	+42·101
+1965	+42·112	+42·123	+42·133	+42·144	+42·155
+1970	+42·165	+42·176	+42·187	+42·198	+42·208

Appendix D

Spinnaker Stay Lengths for given ($I^2 + J^2$) *to the IOR*—continued

(Units are feet and decimals of a foot)—*continued*

	0 5	1 6	2 7	3 8	4 9
+1975	+42·219	+42·230	+42·240	+42·251	+42·262
+1980	+42·272	+42·283	+42·294	+42·304	+42·315
+1985	+42·326	+42·336	+42·347	+42·358	+42·368
+1990	+42·379	+42·390	+42·400	+42·411	+42·422
+1995	+42·432	+42·443	+42·453	+42·464	+42·475
+2000	+42·485	+42·496	+42·507	+42·517	+42·528
+2005	+42·538	+42·549	+42·560	+42·570	+42·581
+2010	+42·591	+42·602	+42·613	+42·623	+42·634
+2015	+42·644	+42·655	+42·665	+42·676	+42·687
+2020	+42·697	+42·708	+42·718	+42·729	+42·739
+2025	+42·750	+42·761	+42·771	+42·782	+42·792
+2030	+42·803	+42·813	+42·824	+42·834	+42·845
+2035	+42·855	+42·866	+42·876	+42·887	+42·898
+2040	+42·908	+42·919	+42·929	+42·940	+42·950
+2045	+42·961	+42·971	+42·982	+42·992	+43·003
+2050	+43·013	+43·024	+43·034	+43·045	+43·055
+2055	+43·066	+43·076	+43·086	+43·097	+43·107
+2060	+43·118	+43·128	+43·139	+43·149	+43·160
+2065	+43·170	+43·181	+43·191	+43·202	+43·212
+2070	+43·222	+43·233	+43·243	+43·254	+43·264
+2075	+43·275	+43·285	+43·295	+43·306	+43·316
+2080	+43·327	+43·337	+43·347	+43·358	+43·368
+2085	+43·379	+43·389	+43·400	+43·410	+43·420
+2090	+43·431	+43·441	+43·451	+43·462	+43·472
+2095	+43·483	+43·493	+43·503	+43·514	+43·524
+2100	+43·534	+43·545	+43·555	+43·566	+43·576
+2105	+43·586	+43·597	+43·607	+43·617	+43·628
+2110	+43·638	+43·648	+43·659	+43·669	+43·679
+2115	+43·690	+43·700	+43·710	+43·721	+43·731
+2120	+43·741	+43·752	+43·762	+43·772	+43·783
+2125	+43·793	+43·803	+43·813	+43·824	+43·834
+2130	+43·844	+43·855	+43·865	+43·875	+43·885
+2135	+43·896	+43·906	+45·916	+43·927	+43·937
+2140	+43·947	+43·958	+43·968	+43·978	+43·988
+2145	+43·998	+44·009	+44·019	+44·029	+44·039

Spinnaker Stay Lengths for given (I^2 + J^2) to the IOR—continued

(Units are feet and decimals of a foot)—*continued*

	0 5	1 6	2 7	3 8	4 9
+2150	+44·050	+44·060	+44·070	+44·080	+44·091
+2155	+44·101	+44·111	+44·121	+44·132	+44·142
+2160	+44·152	+44·162	+44·172	+44·183	+44·193
+2165	+44·203	+44·213	+44·223	+44·234	+44·244
+2170	+44·254	+44·264	+44·274	+44·285	+44·295
+2175	+44·305	+44·315	+44·325	+44·336	+44·346
+2180	+44·356	+44·366	+44·376	+44·386	+44·397
+2185	+44·407	+44·417	+44·427	+44·437	+44·447
+2190	+44·458	+44·468	+44·478	+44·488	+44·498
+2195	+44·508	+44·518	+44·529	+44·539	+44·549
+2200	+44·559	+44·569	+44·579	+44·589	+44·599
+2205	+44·610	+44·620	+44·630	+44·640	+44·650
+2210	+44·660	+44·670	+44·680	+44·690	+44·701
+2215	+44·711	+44·721	+44·731	+44·741	+44·751
+2220	+44·761	+44·771	+44·781	+44·791	+44·801
+2225	+44·811	+44·821	+44·832	+44·842	+44·852
+2230	+44·862	+44·872	+44·882	+44·892	+44·902
+2235	+44·912	+44·922	+44·932	+44·942	+44·952
+2240	+44·962	+44·972	+44·982	+44·992	+45·002
+2245	+45·012	+45·022	+45·032	+45·042	+45·052
+2250	+45·062	+45·072	+45·082	+45·092	+45·102
+2255	+45·112	+45·122	+45·132	+45·142	+45·152
+2260	+45·162	+45·172	+45·182	+45·192	+45·202
+2265	+45·212	+45·222	+45·232	+45·242	+45·252
+2270	+45·262	+45·272	+45·282	+45·292	+45·302
+2275	+45·312	+45·322	+45·332	+45·342	+45·352
+2280	+45·362	+45·372	+45·382	+45·392	+45·402
+2285	+45·412	+45·422	+45·431	+45·441	+45·451
+2290	+45·461	+45·471	+45·481	+45·491	+45·501
+2295	+45·511	+45·521	+45·531	+45·541	+45·550
+2300	+45·560	+45·570	+45·580	+45·590	+45·600
+2305	+45·610	+45·620	+45·630	+45·640	+45·649
+2310	+45·659	+45·669	+45·679	+45·689	+45·699
+2315	+45·709	+45·719	+45·728	+45·738	+45·748
+2320	+45·758	+45·768	+45·778	+45·788	+45·797

Spinnaker Stay Lengths for given ($I^2 + J^2$) *to the IOR*—continued

(Units are feet and decimals of a foot)—*continued*

	0 **5**	**1** **6**	**2** **7**	**3** **8**	**4** **9**
+2325	+45·807	+45·817	+45·827	+45·837	+45·847
+2330	+45·857	+45·866	+45·876	+45·886	+45·896
+2335	+45·906	+45·916	+45·925	+45·935	+45·945
+2340	+45·955	+45·965	+45·975	+45·984	+45·994
+2345	+46·004	+46·014	+46·024	+46·033	+46·043
+2350	+46·053	+46·063	+46·073	+46·082	+46·092
+2355	+46·102	+46·112	+46·121	+46·131	+46·141
+2360	+46·151	+46·161	+46·170	+46·180	+46·190
+2365	+46·200	+46·209	+46·219	+46·229	+46·239
+2370	+46·249	+46·258	+46·269	+46·278	+46·288
+2375	+46·297	+46·307	+46·317	+46·327	+46·336
+2380	+46·346	+46·356	+46·365	+46·375	+46·385
+2385	+46·395	+46·404	+46·414	+46·424	+46·434
+2390	+46·443	+46·453	+46·463	+46·472	+46·482
+2395	+46·492	+46·502	+46·511	+46·521	+46·531
+2400	+46·540	+46·550	+46·560	+46·569	+46·579
+2405	+46·589	+46·598	+46·608	+46·618	+46·627
+2410	+46·637	+46·647	+46·657	+46·666	+46·676
+2415	+46·686	+46·695	+46·705	+46·715	+46·724
+2420	+46·734	+46·743	+46·753	+46·763	+46·772
+2425	+46·782	+46·792	+46·801	+46·811	+46·821
+2430	+46·830	+46·840	+46·850	+46·859	+46·869
+2435	+46·878	+46·888	+46·898	+46·907	+46·917
+2440	+46·927	+46·936	+46·946	+46·955	+46·965
+2445	+46·975	+46·984	+46·994	+47·003	+47·013
+2450	+47·023	+47·032	+47·042	+47·051	+47·061
+2455	+47·071	+47·080	+47·090	+47·099	+47·109
+2460	+47·118	+47·128	+47·138	+47·147	+47·157
+2465	+47·166	+47·176	+47·185	+47·195	+47·205
+2470	+47·214	+47·224	+47·233	+47·243	+47·252
+2475	+47·262	+47·271	+47·281	+47·291	+47·300
+2480	+47·310	+47·319	+47·329	+47·338	+47·348
+2485	+47·357	+47·367	+47·376	+47·386	+47·395
+2490	+47·405	+47·414	+47·424	+47·433	+47·443
+2495	+47·452	+47·462	+47·471	+47·481	+47·490

Spinnaker Stay Lengths for given (I^2 + J^2) *to the IOR*—continued

(Units are feet and decimals of a foot)—*continued*

	0 **5**	**1** **6**	**2** **7**	**3** **8**	**4** **9**
+2500	+47·500	+47·509	+47·519	+47·528	+47·538
+2505	+47·547	+47·557	+47·566	+47·576	+47·585
+2510	+47·595	+47·604	+47·614	+47·623	+47·633
+2515	+47·642	+47·652	+47·661	+47·671	+47·680
+2520	+47·690	+47·699	+47·709	+47·718	+47·727
+2525	+47·737	+47·746	+47·756	+47·765	+47·775
+2530	+47·784	+47·794	+47·803	+47·812	+47·822
+2535	+47·831	+47·841	+47·850	+47·860	+47·869
+2540	+47·878	+47·888	+47·897	+47·907	+47·916
+2545	+47·926	+47·935	+47·944	+47·954	+47·963
+2550	+47·973	+47·982	+47·991	+48·001	+48·010
+2555	+48·020	+48·029	+48·038	+48·048	+48·057
+2560	+48·067	+48·076	+48·085	+48·095	+48·104
+2565	+48·114	+48·123	+48·132	+48·142	+48·151
+2570	+48·160	+48·170	+48·179	+48·189	+48·198
+2575	+48·207	+48·217	+48·226	+48·235	+48·245
+2580	+48·254	+48·263	+48·273	+48·282	+48·291
+2585	+48·301	+48·310	+48·319	+48·329	+48·338
+2590	+48·347	+48·357	+48·366	+48·375	+48·385
+2595	+48·394	+48·403	+48·413	+48·422	+48·431
+2600	+48·441	+48·450	+48·459	+48·469	+48·478
+2605	+48·487	+48·497	+48·506	+48·515	+48·524
+2610	+48·534	+48·543	+48·552	+48·562	+48·571
+2615	+48·580	+48·590	+48·599	+48·608	+48·617
+2620	+48·627	+48·636	+48·645	+48·654	+48·664
+2625	+48·673	+48·682	+48·692	+48·701	+48·710
+2630	+48·719	+48·729	+48·738	+48·747	+48·756
+2635	+48·766	+48·775	+48·784	+48·793	+48·803
+2640	+48·812	+48·821	+48·830	+48·840	+48·849
+2645	+48·858	+48·867	+48·877	+48·886	+48·895
+2650	+[illegible]·904	+48·913	+48·923	+48·932	+48·941
+2655	+48·950	+48·960	+48·969	+48·978	+48·987
+2660	+48·996	+49·006	+49·015	+49·024	+49·033
+2665	+49·042	+49·052	+49·061	+49·070	+49·079
+2670	+49·088	+49·098	+49·107	+49·116	+49·125

Appendix D

Spinnaker Stay Lengths for given ($I^2 + J^2$) to the IOR—continued

(Units are feet and decimals of a foot)—*continued*

	0	1	2	3	4
	5	6	7	8	9
+2675	+49·134	+49·144	+49·153	+49·162	+49·171
+2680	+49·180	+49·189	+49·199	+49·208	+49·217
+2685	+49·226	+49·235	+49·244	+49·254	+49·263
+2690	+49·272	+49·281	+49·290	+49·299	+49·309
+2695	+49·318	+49·327	+49·336	+49·345	+49·354
+2700	+49·363	+49·373	+49·382	+49·391	+49·400
+2705	+49·409	+49·418	+49·427	+49·437	+49·446
+2710	+49·455	+49·464	+49·473	+49·482	+49·491
+2715	+49·500	+49·509	+49·519	+49·528	+49·537
+2720	+49·546	+49·555	+49·564	+49·573	+49·582
+2725	+49·591	+49·601	+49·610	+49·619	+49·628
+2730	+49·637	+49·646	+49·655	+49·664	+49·673
+2735	+49·682	+49·691	+49·701	+49·710	+49·719
+2740	+49·728	+49·737	+49·746	+49·755	+49·764
+2745	+49·773	+49·782	+49·791	+49·800	+49·809
+2750	+49·818	+49·827	+49·837	+49·846	+49·855
+2755	+49·864	+49·873	+49·882	+49·891	+49·900
+2760	+49·909	+49·918	+49·927	+49·936	+49·945
+2765	+49·954	+49·963	+49·972	+49·981	+49·990
+2770	+49·999	+50·008	+50·017	+50·026	+50·035
+2775	+50·044	+50·053	+50·062	+50·071	+50·080
+2780	+50·089	+50·098	+50·107	+50·116	+50·125
+2785	+50·134	+50·143	+50·152	+50·161	+50·170
+2790	+50·179	+50·188	+50·197	+50·206	+50·215
+2795	+50·224	+50·233	+50·242	+50·251	+50·260
+2800	+50·269	+50·278	+50·287	+50·296	+50·305
+2805	+50·314	+50·323	+50·332	+50·341	+50·350
+2810	+50·359	+50·368	+50·377	+50·386	+50·395
+2815	+50·404	+50·413	+50·422	+50·431	+50·440
+2820	+50·448	+50·457	+50·466	+50·475	+50·484
+2825	+50·493	+50·502	+50·511	+50·520	+50·529
+2830	+50·538	+50·547	+50·556	+50·565	+50·574
+2835	+50·582	+50·591	+50·600	+50·609	+50·618
+2840	+50·627	+50·636	+50·645	+50·654	+50·663
+2845	+50·672	+50·681	+50·689	+50·698	+50·707

Spinnaker Stay Lengths for given (I^2 + J^2) to the IOR—continued

(Units are feet and decimals of a foot)—*continued*

	0 5	1 6	2 7	3 8	4 9
+2850	+50·716	+50·725	+50·734	+50·743	+50·752
+2855	+50·761	+50·769	+50·778	+50·787	+50·796
+2860	+50·805	+50·814	+50·823	+50·832	+50·841
+2865	+50·849	+50·858	+50·867	+50·876	+50·885
+2870	+50·894	+50·903	+50·911	+50·920	+50·929
+2875	+50·938	+50·947	+50·956	+50·965	+50·973
+2880	+50·982	+50·991	+51·000	+51·009	+51·018
+2885	+51·027	+51·035	+51·044	+51·053	+51·062
+2890	+51·071	+51·080	+51·088	+51·097	+51·106
+2895	+51·115	+51·124	+51·133	+51·141	+51·150
+2900	+51·159	+51·168	+51·177	+51·186	+51·194
+2905	+51·203	+51·212	+51·221	+51·230	+51·238
+2910	+51·247	+51·256	+51·265	+51·274	+51·282
+2915	+51·291	+51·300	+51·309	+51·318	+51·326
+2920	+51·335	+51·344	+51·353	+51·363	+51·370
+2925	+51·379	+51·388	+51·397	+51·405	+51·414
+2930	+51·423	+51·432	+51·441	+51·449	+51·458
+2935	+51·467	+51·476	+51·484	+51·493	+51·502
+2940	+51·511	+51·519	+51·528	+51·537	+51·546
+2945	+51·554	+51·563	+51·572	+51·581	+51·589
+2950	+51·598	+51·607	+51·616	+51·624	+51·633
+2955	+51·642	+51·651	+51·659	+51·668	+51·677
+2960	+51·686	+51·694	+51·703	+51·712	+51·720
+2965	+51·729	+51·738	+51·747	+51·755	+51·764
+2970	+51·773	+51·782	+51·790	+51·799	+51·808
+2975	+51·816	+51·825	+51·834	+51·843	+51·851
+2980	+51·860	+51·869	+51·877	+51·886	+51·895
+2985	+51·903	+51·912	+51·921	+51·929	+51·938
+2990	+51·947	+51·956	+51·964	+51·973	+51·982
+2995	+51·990	+51·999	+52·008	+52·016	+52·025
+3000	+52·034	+52·042	+52·051	+52·060	+52·068
+3005	+52·077	+52·086	+52·094	+52·103	+52·112
+3010	+52·120	+52·129	+52·138	+52·146	+52·155
+3015	+52·164	+52·172	+52·181	+52·190	+52·198
+3020	+52·207	+52·215	+52·224	+52·233	+52·241

Appendix D

Spinnaker Stay Lengths for given ($I^2 + J^2$) to the IOR—continued

(Units are feet and decimals of a foot)—*continued*

	0 5	1 6	2 7	3 8	4 9
+3025	+52·250	+52·259	+52·267	+52·276	+52·285
+3030	+52·293	+52·302	+52·310	+52·319	+52·328
+3035	+52·336	+52·345	+52·354	+52·362	+52·371
+3040	+52·379	+52·388	+52·397	+52·405	+52·414
+3045	+52·422	+52·431	+52·440	+52·448	+52·457
+3050	+52·465	+52·474	+52·483	+52·491	+52·500
+3055	+52·508	+52·517	+52·526	+52·534	+52·543
+3060	+52·551	+52·560	+52·569	+52·577	+52·586
+3065	+52·594	+52·603	+52·611	+52·620	+52·629
+3070	+52·637	+52·646	+52·654	+52·663	+52·671
+3075	+52·680	+52·689	+52·697	+52·706	+52·714
+3080	+52·723	+52·731	+52·740	+52·749	+52·757
+3085	+52·766	+52·774	+52·783	+52·791	+52·800
+3090	+52·808	+52·817	+52·825	+52·834	+52·843
+3095	+52·851	+52·860	+52·868	+52·877	+52·885
+3100	+52·894	+52·902	+52·911	+52·919	+52·928
+3105	+52·936	+52·945	+52·953	+52·962	+52·970
+3110	+52·979	+52·988	+52·996	+53·005	+53·013
+3115	+53·022	+53·030	+53·039	+53·047	+53·056
+3120	+53·064	+53·073	+53·081	+53·090	+53·098
+3125	+53·107	+53·115	+53·124	+53·132	+53·141
+3130	+53·149	+53·158	+53·166	+53·175	+53·183
+3135	+53·192	+53·200	+53·208	+53·217	+53·225
+3140	+53·234	+53·242	+53·251	+53·259	+53·268
+3145	+53·276	+53·285	+53·293	+53·302	+53·310
+3150	+53·319	+53·327	+53·336	+53·344	+53·352
+3155	+53·361	+53·369	+53·378	+53·386	+53·395
+3160	+53·403	+53·412	+53·420	+53·429	+53·437
+3165	+53·445	+53·454	+53·462	+53·471	+53·479
+3170	+53·488	+53·496	+53·504	+53·513	+53·521
+3175	+53·530	+53·538	+53·547	+53·555	+53·563
+3180	+53·572	+53·580	+53·589	+53·597	+53·606
+3185	+53·614	+53·622	+53·631	+53·639	+53·648
+3190	+53·656	+53·664	+53·673	+53·681	+53·690
+3195	+53·698	+53·707	+53·715	+53·720	+53·732

Spinnaker Stay Lengths for given (I^2 + J^2) to the IOR—continued

(Units are feet and decimals of a foot)—*continued*

	0 5	1 6	2 7	3 8	4 9
+3200	+53·740	+53·749	+53·757	+53·765	+53·774
+3205	+53·782	+53·790	+53·799	+53·807	+53·816
+3210	+53·824	+53·832	+53·841	+53·849	+53·858
+3215	+53·866	+53·874	+53·883	+53·891	+53·899
+3220	+53·908	+53·916	+53·925	+53·933	+53·941
+3225	+53·950	+53·958	+53·966	+53·975	+53·983
+3230	+53·991	+54·000	+54·008	+54·017	+54·025
+3235	+54·033	+54·042	+54·050	+54·058	+54·067
+3240	+54·075	+54·083	+54·092	+54·100	+54·108
+3245	+54·117	+54·125	+54·133	+54·142	+54·150
+3250	+54·158	+54·167	+54·175	+54·183	+54·192
+3255	+54·200	+54·208	+54·217	+54·225	+54·233
+3260	+54·242	+54·250	+54·258	+54·267	+54·275
+3265	+54·283	+54·291	+54·300	+54·308	+54·316
+3270	+54·325	+54·333	+54·341	+54·350	+54·358
+3275	+54·366	+54·375	+54·383	+54·391	+54·399
+3280	+54·408	+54·416	+54·424	+54·433	+54·441
+3285	+54·449	+54·457	+54·466	+54·474	+54·482
+3290	+54·491	+54·499	+54·507	+54·515	+54·524
+3295	+54·532	+54·540	+54·549	+54·557	+54·565
+3300	+54·573	+54·582	+54·590	+54·598	+54·606
+3305	+54·615	+54·623	+54·631	+54·639	+54·648
+3310	+54·656	+54·664	+54·672	+54·681	+54·689
+3315	+54·697	+54·705	+54·714	+54·722	+54·730
+3320	+54·738	+54·747	+54·755	+54·763	+54·771
+3325	+54·780	+54·788	+54·796	+54·804	+54·813
+3330	+54·821	+54·829	+54·837	+54·846	+54·854
+3335	+54·862	+54·870	+54·878	+54·887	+54·895
+3340	+54·903	+54·911	+54·920	+54·928	+54·936
+3345	+54·944	+54·952	+54·961	+54·969	+54·977
+3350	+54·985	+54·993	+55·002	+55·010	+55·018
+3355	+55·026	+55·034	+55·043	+55·051	+55·059
+3360	+55·067	+55·075	+55·084	+55·092	+55·100
+3365	+55·108	+55·116	+55·125	+55·133	+55·141
+3370	+55·149	+55·157	+55·165	+55·174	+55·182

Appendix D

Spinnaker Stay Lengths for given ($I^2 + J^2$) *to the IOR*—continued

(Units are feet and decimals of a foot)—*continued*

	0 5	1 6	2 7	3 8	4 9
+3375	+55·190	+55·198	+55·206	+55·215	+55·223
+3380	+55·231	+55·239	+55·247	+55·255	+55·264
+3385	+55·272	+55·280	+55·288	+55·296	+55·304
+3390	+55·313	+55·321	+55·329	+55·337	+55·345
+3395	+55·353	+55·361	+55·370	+55·378	+55·386
+3400	+55·394	+55·402	+55·410	+55·418	+55·427
+3405	+55·435	+55·443	+55·451	+55·459	+55·467
+3410	+55·475	+55·484	+55·492	+55·500	+55·508
+3415	+55·516	+55·524	+55·532	+55·540	+55·549
+3420	+55·557	+55·565	+55·573	+55·581	+55·589
+3425	+55·597	+55·605	+55·614	+55·622	+55·630
+3430	+55·638	+55·646	+55·654	+55·662	+55·670
+3435	+55·678	+55·687	+55·695	+55·703	+55·711
+3440	+55·719	+55·727	+55·735	+55·743	+55·751
+3445	+55·759	+55·768	+55·776	+55·784	+55·792
+3450	+55·800	+55·808	+55·816	+55·824	+55·832
+3455	+55·840	+55·848	+55·856	+55·865	+55·873
+3460	+55·881	+55·889	+55·897	+55·905	+55·913
+3465	+55·921	+55·929	+55·937	+55·945	+55·953
+3470	+55·961	+55·969	+55·977	+55·986	+55·994
+3475	+56·002	+56·010	+56·018	+56·026	+56·034
+3480	+56·042	+56·050	+56·058	+56·066	+56·074
+3485	+56·082	+56·090	+56·098	+56·106	+56·114
+3490	+56·122	+56·130	+56·138	+56·147	+56·155
+3495	+56·163	+56·171	+56·179	+56·187	+56·195
+3500	+56·203	+56·211	+56·219	+56·227	+56·235
+3505	+56·243	+56·251	+56·259	+56·267	+56·275
+3510	+56·283	+56·291	+56·299	+56·307	+56·315
+3515	+56·323	+56·331	+56·339	+56·347	+56·355
+3520	+56·363	+56·371	+56·379	+56·387	+56·395
+3525	+56·403	+56·411	+56·419	+56·427	+56·435
+3530	+56·443	+56·451	+56·459	+56·467	+56·475
+3535	+56·483	+56·491	+56·499	+56·507	+56·515
+3540	+56·523	+56·531	+56·539	+56·547	+56·555
+3545	+56·563	+56·571	+56·579	+56·587	+56·595

Spinnaker Stay Lengths for given ($I^2 + J^2$) *to the IOR*—continued

(Units are feet and decimals of a foot)—*continued*

	0	**1**	**2**	**3**	**4**
	5	**6**	**7**	**8**	**9**
+3550	+56·603	+56·611	+56·619	+56·627	+56·635
+3555	+56·643	+56·651	+56·659	+56·667	+56·674
+3560	+56·682	+56·690	+56·698	+56·706	+56·714
+3565	+56·722	+56·730	+56·738	+56·746	+56·754
+3570	+56·762	+56·770	+56·778	+56·786	+56·794
+3575	+56·802	+56·810	+56·818	+56·826	+56·834
+3580	+56·841	+56·849	+56·857	+56·865	+56·873
+3585	+56·881	+56·889	+56·897	+56·905	+56·913
+3590	+56·921	+56·929	+56·937	+56·945	+56·952
+3595	+56·960	+56·968	+56·976	+56·984	+56·992
+3600	+57·000	+57·008	+57·016	+57·024	+57·032
+3605	+57·040	+57·047	+57·055	+57·063	+57·071
+3610	+57·079	+57·087	+57·095	+57·103	+57·111
+3615	+57·119	+57·127	+57·134	+57·142	+57·150
+3620	+57·158	+57·166	+57·174	+57·182	+57·190
+3625	+57·198	+57·205	+57·213	+57·221	+57·229
+3630	+57·237	+57·245	+57·253	+57·261	+57·269
+3635	+57·276	+57·284	+57·292	+57·300	+57·308
+3640	+57·316	+57·324	+57·332	+57·339	+57·347
+3645	+57·355	+57·363	+57·371	+57·379	+57·387
+3650	+57·394	+57·402	+57·410	+57·418	+57·426
+3655	+57·434	+57·442	+57·449	+57·457	+57·465
+3660	+57·473	+57·481	+57·489	+57·497	+57·504
+3665	+57·512	+57·520	+57·528	+57·536	+57·544
+3670	+57·551	+57·559	+57·567	+57·575	+57·583
+3675	+57·591	+57·599	+57·606	+57·614	+57·622
+3680	+57·630	+57·638	+57·646	+57·653	+57·661
+3685	+57·669	+57·677	+57·685	+57·692	+57·700
+3690	+57·708	+57·716	+57·724	+57·732	+57·739
+3695	+57·747	+57·755	+57·763	+57·771	+57·778
+3700	+57·786	+57·794	+57·802	+57·810	+57·817
+3705	+57·825	+57·833	+57·841	+57·849	+57·856
+3710	+57·864	+57·872	+57·880	+57·888	+57·895
+3715	+57·903	+57·911	+57·919	+57·927	+57·934
+3720	+57·942	+57·950	+57·958	+57·966	+57·973

Spinnaker Stay Lengths for given ($I^2 + J^2$) to the IOR—continued

(Units are feet and decimals of a foot)—*continued*

	0 5	1 6	2 7	3 8	4 9
+3725	+57·981	+57·989	+57·997	+58·004	+58·012
+3730	+58·020	+58·028	+58·036	+58·043	+58·051
+3735	+58·059	+58·067	+58·074	+58·082	+58·090
+3740	+58·098	+58·106	+58·113	+58·121	+58·129
+3745	+58·137	+58·144	+58·152	+58·160	+58·168
+3750	+58·175	+58·183	+58·191	+58·199	+58·206
+3755	+58·214	+58·222	+58·230	+58·237	+58·245
+3760	+58·253	+58·261	+58·268	+58·276	+58·284
+3765	+58·292	+58·299	+58·307	+58·315	+58·323
+3770	+58·330	+58·338	+58·346	+58·354	+58·361
+3775	+58·369	+58·377	+58·384	+58·392	+58·400
+3780	+58·408	+58·415	+58·423	+58·431	+58·439
+3785	+58·446	+58·454	+58·462	+58·469	+58·477
+3790	+58·485	+58·493	+58·500	+58·508	+58·516
+3795	+58·523	+58·531	+58·539	+58·547	+58·554
+3800	+58·562	+58·570	+58·577	+58·585	+58·593
+3805	+58·600	+58·608	+58·616	+58·624	+58·631
+3810	+58·639	+58·647	+58·654	+58·662	+58·670
+3815	+58·677	+58·685	+58·693	+58·700	+58·708
+3820	+58·716	+58·724	+58·731	+58·739	+58·747
+3825	+58·754	+58·762	+58·770	+58·777	+58·785
+3830	+58·793	+58·800	+58·808	+58·816	+58·823
+3835	+58·831	+58·839	+58·846	+58·854	+58·862
+3840	+58·869	+58·877	+58·885	+58·892	+58·900
+3845	+58·908	+58·915	+58·923	+58·931	+58·938
+3850	+58·946	+58·954	+58·961	+58·969	+58·977
+3855	+58·984	+58·992	+59·000	+59·007	+59·015
+3860	+59·022	+59·030	+59·038	+59·045	+59·053
+3865	+59·061	+59·068	+59·076	+59·084	+59·091
+3870	+59·099	+59·106	+59·114	+59·122	+59·129
+3875	+59·137	+59·145	+59·152	+59·160	+59·168
+3880	+59·175	+59·183	+59·190	+59·198	+59·206
+3885	+59·213	+59·221	+59·229	+59·236	+59·244
+3890	+59·251	+59·259	+59·267	+59·274	+59·282
+3895	+59·289	+59·297	+59·305	+59·312	+59·320

Spinnaker Stay Lengths for given (I^2 + J^2) *to the IOR*—continued

(Units are feet and decimals of a foot)—*continued*

	0 5	1 6	2 7	3 8	4 9
+3900	+59·327	+59·335	+59·343	+59·350	+59·358
+3905	+59·365	+59·373	+59·381	+59·388	+59·396
+3910	+59·403	+59·411	+59·419	+59·426	+59·434
+3915	+59·441	+59·449	+59·457	+59·464	+59·472
+3920	+59·479	+59·487	+59·495	+59·502	+59·510
+3925	+59·517	+59·525	+59·532	+59·540	+59·548
+3930	+59·555	+59·563	+59·570	+59·578	+59·586
+3935	+59·593	+59·601	+59·608	+59·616	+59·623
+3940	+59·631	+59·639	+59·646	+59·654	+59·661
+3945	+59·669	+59·676	+59·684	+59·691	+59·699
+3950	+59·707	+59·714	+59·722	+59·729	+59·737
+3955	+59·744	+59·752	+59·759	+59·767	+59·775
+3960	+59·782	+59·790	+59·797	+59·805	+59·812
+3965	+59·820	+59·827	+59·835	+59·842	+59·850
+3970	+59·858	+59·865	+59·873	+59·880	+59·888
+3975	+59·895	+59·903	+59·910	+59·918	+59·925
+3980	+59·933	+59·940	+59·948	+59·955	+59·963
+3985	+59·971	+59·978	+59·986	+59·993	+60·001
+3990	+60·008	+60·016	+60·023	+60·031	+60·038
+3995	+60·046	+60·053	+60·061	+60·068	+60·076
+4000	+60·083	+60·091	+60·098	+60·106	+60·113
+4005	+60·121	+60·128	+60·136	+60·143	+60·151
+4010	+60·158	+60·166	+60·173	+60·181	+60·188
+4015	+60·196	+60·203	+60·211	+60·218	+60·226
+4020	+60·233	+60·241	+60·248	+60·256	+60·263
+4025	+60·271	+60·278	+60·286	+60·293	+60·301
+4030	+60·308	+60·316	+60·323	+60·331	+60·338
+4035	+60·346	+60·353	+60·361	+60·368	+60·375
+4040	+60·383	+60·390	+60·398	+60·405	+60·413
+4045	+60·420	+60·428	+60·435	+60·443	+60·450
+4050	+60·458	+60·465	+60·473	+60·480	+60·487
+4055	+60·495	+60·502	+60·510	+60·517	+60·525
+4060	+60·532	+60·540	+60·547	+60·555	+60·562
+4065	+60·569	+60·577	+60·584	+60·592	+60·599
+4070	+60·607	+60·614	+60·622	+60·629	+60·636

Appendix D

Spinnaker Stay Lengths for given ($I^2 + J^2$) *to the IOR*—continued

(Units are feet and decimals of a foot)—*continued*

	0 5	1 6	2 7	3 8	4 9
+4075	+60·644	+60·651	+60·659	+60·666	+60·674
+4080	+60·681	+60·689	+60·696	+60·703	+60·711
+4085	+60·718	+60·726	+60·733	+60·741	+60·748
+4090	+60·755	+60·763	+60·770	+60·778	+60·785
+4095	+60·793	+60·800	+60·807	+60·815	+60·822
+4100	+60·830	+60·837	+60·845	+60·852	+60·859
+4105	+60·867	+60·874	+60·882	+60·889	+60·896
+4110	+60·904	+60·911	+60·919	+60·926	+60·933
+4115	+60·941	+60·948	+60·956	+60·963	+60·970
+4120	+60·978	+60·985	+60·993	+61·000	+61·007
+4125	+61·015	+61·022	+61·030	+61·037	+61·044
+4130	+61·052	+61·059	+61·067	+61·074	+61·081
+4135	+61·089	+61·096	+61·104	+61·111	+61·118
+4140	+61·126	+61·133	+61·140	+61·148	+61·155
+4145	+61·163	+61·170	+61·177	+61·185	+61·192
+4150	+61·199	+61·207	+61·214	+61·222	+61·229
+4155	+61·236	+61·244	+61·251	+61·258	+61·266
+4160	+61·273	+61·281	+61·288	+61·295	+61·303
+4165	+61·310	+61·317	+61·325	+61·332	+61·339
+4170	+61·347	+61·354	+61·361	+61·369	+61·376
+4175	+61·384	+61·391	+61·398	+61·406	+61·413
+4180	+61·420	+61·428	+61·435	+61·442	+61·450
+4185	+61·457	+61·464	+61·472	+61·479	+61·486
+4190	+61·494	+61·501	+61·508	+61·516	+61·523
+4195	+61·530	+61·538	+61·545	+61·552	+61·560
+4200	+61·567	+61·574	+61·582	+61·589	+61·596
+4205	+61·604	+61·611	+61·618	+61·626	+61·633
+4210	+61·640	+61·648	+61·655	+61·662	+61·670
+4215	+61·677	+61·684	+61·692	+61·699	+61·706
+4220	+61·713	+61·721	+61·728	+61·735	+61·743
+4225	+61·750	+61·757	+61·765	+61·772	+61·779
+4230	+61·787	+61·794	+61·801	+61·808	+61·816
+4235	+61·823	+61·830	+61·838	+61·845	+61·852
+4240	+61·860	+61·867	+61·874	+61·881	+61·889
+4245	+61·896	+61·903	+61·911	+61·918	+61·925

Spinnaker Stay Lengths for given ($I^2 + J^2$) *to the IOR*—continued

(Units are feet and decimals of a foot)—*continued*

	0 5	1 6	2 7	3 8	4 9
+4250	+61·932	+61·940	+61·947	+61·954	+61·962
+4255	+61·969	+61·976	+61·983	+61·991	+61·998
+4260	+62·005	+62·013	+62·020	+62·027	+62·034
+4265	+62·042	+62·049	+62·056	+62·063	+62·071
+4270	+62·078	+62·085	+62·093	+62·100	+62·107
+4275	+62·114	+62·122	+62·129	+62·136	+62·143
+4280	+62·151	+62·158	+62·165	+62·172	+62·180
+4285	+62·187	+62·194	+62·201	+62·209	+62·216
+4290	+62·223	+62·230	+62·238	+62·245	+62·252
+4295	+62·259	+62·267	+62·274	+62·281	+62·288
+4300	+62·296	+62·303	+62·310	+62·317	+62·325
+4305	+62·332	+62·339	+62·346	+62·354	+62·361
+4310	+62·368	+62·375	+62·383	+62·390	+62·397
+4315	+62·404	+62·411	+62·419	+62·426	+62·433
+4320	+62·440	+62·448	+62·455	+62·462	+62·469
+4325	+62·476	+62·484	+62·491	+62·498	+62·505
+4330	+62·513	+62·520	+62·527	+62·534	+62·541
+4335	+62·549	+62·556	+62·563	+62·570	+62·578
+4340	+62·585	+62·592	+62·599	+62·606	+62·614
+4345	+62·621	+62·628	+62·635	+62·642	+62·650
+4350	+62·657	+62·664	+62·671	+62·678	+62·686
+4355	+62·693	+62·700	+62·707	+62·714	+62·722
+4360	+62·729	+62·736	+62·743	+62·750	+62·758
+4365	+62·765	+62·772	+62·779	+62·786	+62·793
+4370	+62·801	+62·808	+62·815	+62·822	+62·829
+4375	+62·837	+62·844	+62·851	+62·858	+62·865
+4380	+62·872	+62·880	+62·887	+62·894	+62·901
+4385	+62·908	+62·916	+62·923	+62·930	+62·937
+4390	+62·944	+62·951	+62·959	+62·966	+62·973
+4395	+62·980	+62·987	+62·994	+63·002	+63·009
+4400	+63·016	+63·023	+63·030	+63·037	+63·045
+4405	+63·052	+63·059	+63·066	+63·073	+63·080
+4410	+63·087	+63·095	+63·102	+63·109	+63·116
+4415	+63·123	+63·130	+63·137	+63·145	+63·152
+4420	+63·159	+63·166	+63·173	+63·180	+63·187

Spinnaker Stay Lengths for given ($I^2 + J^2$) *to the IOR*—continued

(Units are feet and decimals of a foot)—*continued*

	0 **5**	**1** **6**	**2** **7**	**3** **8**	**4** **9**
+4425	+63·195	+63·202	+63·209	+63·216	+63·223
+4430	+63·230	+63·237	+63·245	+63·252	+63·259
+4435	+63·266	+63·273	+63·280	+63·287	+63·295
+4440	+63·302	+63·309	+63·316	+63·323	+63·330
+4445	+63·337	+63·344	+63·352	+63·359	+63·366
+4450	+63·373	+63·380	+63·387	+63·394	+63·401
+4455	+63·408	+63·416	+63·423	+63·430	+63·437
+4460	+63·444	+63·451	+63·458	+63·465	+63·473
+4465	+63·480	+63·487	+63·494	+63·501	+63·508
+4470	+63·515	+63·522	+63·529	+63·536	+63·544
+4475	+63·551	+63·558	+63·565	+63·572	+63·579
+4480	+63·586	+63·593	+63·600	+63·607	+63·615
+4485	+63·622	+63·629	+63·636	+63·643	+63·650
+4490	+63·657	+63·664	+63·671	+63·678	+63·685
+4495	+63·693	+63·700	+63·707	+63·714	+63·721
+4500	+63·728	+63·735	+63·742	+63·749	+63·756
+4505	+63·763	+63·770	+63·777	+63·785	+63·792
+4510	+63·799	+63·806	+63·813	+63·820	+63·827
+4515	+63·834	+63·841	+63·848	+63·855	+63·862
+4520	+63·869	+63·876	+63·884	+63·891	+63·898
+4525	+63·905	+63·912	+63·919	+63·926	+63·933
+4530	+63·940	+63·947	+63·954	+63·961	+63·968
+4535	+63·975	+63·982	+63·989	+63·996	+64·003
+4540	+64·011	+64·018	+64·025	+64·032	+64·039
+4545	+64·046	+64·053	+64·060	+64·067	+64·074
+4550	+64·081	+64·088	+64·095	+64·102	+64·109
+4555	+64·116	+64·123	+64·130	+64·137	+64·144
+4560	+64·151	+64·158	+64·165	+64·172	+64·180
+4565	+64·187	+64·194	+64·201	+64·208	+64·215
+4570	+64·222	+64·229	+64·236	+64·243	+64·250
+4575	+64·257	+64·264	+64·271	+64·278	+64·285
+4580	+64·292	+64·299	+64·306	+64·313	+64·320
+4585	+64·327	+64·334	+64·341	+64·348	+64·355
+4590	+64·362	+64·369	+64·376	+64·383	+64·390
+4595	+64·397	+64·404	+64·411	+64·418	+64·425

Spinnaker Stay Lengths for given $(I^2 + J^2)$ *to the IOR*—continued

(Units are feet and decimals of a foot)—*continued*

	0 5	1 6	2 7	3 8	4 9
+4600	+64·432	+64·439	+64·446	+64·453	+64·460
+4605	+64·467	+64·474	+64·481	+64·488	+64·495
+4610	+64·502	+64·509	+64·516	+64·523	+64·530
+4615	+64·537	+64·544	+64·551	+64·558	+64·565
+4620	+64·572	+64·579	+64·586	+64·593	+64·600
+4625	+64·607	+64·614	+64·621	+64·628	+64·635
+4630	+64·642	+64·649	+64·656	+64·663	+64·670
+4635	+64·677	+64·684	+64·691	+64·698	+64·705
+4640	+64·712	+64·719	+64·726	+64·733	+64·740
+4645	+64·747	+64·753	+64·760	+64·767	+64·774
+4650	+64·781	+64·788	+64·795	+64·802	+64·809
+4655	+64·816	+64·823	+64·830	+64·837	+64·844
+4660	+64·851	+64·858	+64·865	+64·872	+64·879
+4665	+64·886	+64·893	+64·900	+64·907	+64·914
+4670	+64·921	+64·927	+64·934	+64·941	+64·948
+4675	+64·955	+64·962	+64·969	+64·976	+64·983
+4680	+64·990	+64·997	+65·004	+65·011	+65·018
+4685	+65·025	+65·032	+65·039	+65·046	+65·052
+4690	+65·059	+65·066	+65·073	+65·080	+65·087
+4695	+65·094	+65·101	+65·108	+65·115	+65·122
+4700	+65·129	+65·196	+65·143	+65·150	+65·156
+4705	+65·163	+65·170	+65·177	+65·184	+65·191
+4710	+65·198	+65·205	+65·212	+65·219	+65·226
+4715	+65·233	+65·239	+65·246	+65·253	+65·260
+4720	+65·267	+65·274	+65·281	+65·288	+65·295
+4725	+65·302	+65·309	+65·316	+65·322	+65·329
+4730	+65·336	+65·343	+65·350	+65·357	+65·364
+4735	+65·371	+65·378	+65·385	+65·391	+65·398
+4740	+65·405	+65·412	+65·419	+65·426	+65·433
+4745	+65·440	+65·447	+65·454	+65·460	+65·467
+4750	+65·474	+65·481	+65·488	+65·495	+65·502
+4755	+65·509	+65·516	+65·522	+65·529	+65·536
+4760	+65·543	+65·550	+65·557	+65·564	+65·571
+4765	+65·578	+65·584	+65·591	+65·598	+65·605
+4770	+65·612	+65·619	+65·626	+65·633	+65·639

Appendix D

Spinnaker Stay Lengths for given $(I^2 + J^2)$ *to the IOR*—continued

(Units are feet and decimals of a foot)—*continued*

	0 5	1 6	2 7	3 8	4 9
+4775	+65·646	+65·653	+65·660	+65·667	+65·674
+4780	+65·681	+65·688	+65·694	+65·701	+65·708
+4785	+65·715	+65·722	+65·729	+65·736	+65·742
+4790	+65·749	+65·756	+65·763	+65·770	+65·777
+4795	+65·784	+65·791	+65·797	+65·804	+65·811
+4800	+65·818	+65·825	+65·832	+65·838	+65·845
+4805	+65·852	+65·859	+65·866	+65·873	+65·880
+4810	+65·886	+65·893	+65·900	+65·907	+65·914
+4815	+65·921	+65·928	+65·934	+65·941	+65·948
+4820	+65·955	+65·962	+65·969	+65·975	+65·982
+4825	+65·989	+65·996	+66·003	+66·010	+66·016
+4830	+66·023	+66·030	+66·037	+66·044	+66·051
+4835	+66·057	+66·064	+66·071	+66·078	+66·085
+4840	+66·092	+66·098	+66·105	+66·112	+66·119
+4845	+66·126	+66·133	+66·139	+66·146	+66·153
+4850	+66·160	+66·167	+66·173	+66·180	+66·187
+4855	+66·194	+66·201	+66·208	+66·214	+66·221
+4860	+66·228	+66·235	+66·242	+66·248	+66·255
+4865	+66·262	+66·269	+66·276	+66·283	+66·289
+4870	+66·296	+66·303	+66·310	+66·317	+66·323
+4875	+66·330	+66·337	+66·344	+66·351	+66·357
+4880	+66·364	+66·371	+66·378	+66·385	+66·391
+4885	+66·398	+66·405	+66·412	+66·419	+66·425
+4890	+66·432	+66·439	+66·446	+66·452	+66·459
+4895	+66·466	+66·473	+66·480	+66·486	+66·493
+4900	+66·500	+66·507	+66·514	+66·520	+66·527
+4905	+66·534	+66·541	+66·547	+66·554	+66·561
+4910	+66·568	+66·575	+66·581	+66·588	+66·595
+4915	+66·602	+66·608	+66·615	+66·622	+66·629
+4920	+66·636	+66·642	+66·649	+66·656	+66·663
+4925	+66·669	+66·676	+66·683	+66·690	+66·696
+4930	+66·703	+66·710	+66·717	+66·724	+66·730
+4935	+66·737	+66·744	+66·751	+66·757	+66·764
+4940	+66·771	+66·778	+66·784	+66·791	+66·798
+4945	+66·805	+66·811	+66·818	+66·825	+66·832

Spinnaker Stay Lengths for given $(I^2 + J^2)$ *to the IOR*—continued

(Units are feet and decimals of a foot)—*continued*

	0	1	2	3	4
	5	**6**	**7**	**8**	**9**
+4950	+66·838	+66·845	+66·852	+66·859	+66·865
+4955	+66·872	+66·879	+66·886	+66·892	+66·899
+4960	+66·906	+66·913	+66·919	+66·926	+66·933
+4965	+66·940	+66·946	+66·953	+66·960	+66·967
+4970	+66·973	+66·980	+66·987	+66·994	+67·000
+4975	+67·007	+67·014	+67·020	+67·027	+67·034
+4980	+67·041	+67·047	+67·054	+67·061	+67·068
+4985	+67·074	+67·081	+67·088	+67·094	+67·101
+4990	+67·108	+67·115	+67·121	+67·128	+67·135
+4995	+67·142	+67·148	+67·155	+67·162	+67·168
+5000	+67·175				

APPENDIX E

Laundering and dry cleaning of Terylene sails

STORAGE

All sails should be folded or rolled in a manner which avoids sharp creases as far as possible. Sails made from Terylene polyester fibre should be stored under well-ventilated, clean conditions, and dampness which may encourage the growth of mildew should be avoided as far as possible. Whilst mildew growths do not affect the strength of Terylene fabrics, they can cause stains which are unsightly and not readily removed.

WASHING

Small sails can be washed in the bath, and large ones on a clean concrete washdown, using a scrubbing brush and hose where necessary. Terylene sails should be washed in water as hot as the hand can bear and containing soap and washing soda, or any proprietary brand of liquid detergent. At localized areas where soiling is particularly heavy neat liquid detergent can be applied and the treated sail left overnight before washing.

If general soiling is persistent and difficult to remove, the sails may be steeped overnight in cold water containing 1 lb of sodium metasilicate/gallon (100 g/litre). Stainless steel, porcelain or enamel vessels should be used and *not* vessels made of aluminium or galvanized iron. Do not allow the solution to come in contact with galvanized luff wires, hanks or alloy slides. After this treatment the sail should be drained but not rinsed, and then given a warm handwash as described above, with light scrubbing.

REMOVAL OF STAINS

The suggestions below refer to white undyed sailcloth material. Coloured sails which have become abnormally stained should be dealt with by an experienced finisher or dry cleaner, especially when solvents or bleaching agents are involved in the stain-removal technique. Stains should be removed as soon as possible after they appear.

Blood

Soak the stained portion in cold water containing half a cupful of ammonia to half a gallon of water. If residual stains are still present after this treatment, damp the stain with a 1 per cent solution of pepsin in water acidified with a few drops of dilute hydrochloric acid, allow to stand without drying out for 30 minutes, and then rinse thoroughly.

Mildew

Scrub lightly with a dry stiff brush to remove as much of the mould growth as possible and then steep the stained portion for 2 hours in a cold solution of bleach (sodium hypochlorite) at a strength of approximately 1 per cent available chlorine. A proprietary brand of bleach such as Domestos may be used, 1 part of Domestos being added to 10 parts of water. Wash thoroughly in water and repeat the treatment if necessary. If after the final washing there is any residual smell of chlorine this may be removed by immersing for a few minutes in a 1 per cent solution of sodium thiosulphate (photographers' hypo). Rinse finally with water.

Oil, Grease, and Waxes

Small stains of this nature can be removed by dabbing with trichloroethylene or by the use of proprietary stain removers. Heavy staining is best removed by brushing on a mixture of detergent and solvent. This can be prepared by dissolving 1 part of Lissapol NX in 2 parts of benzene or toluene. Alternatively a proprietary brand such as Polyclens may be used. These 'solvent/detergent' mixtures should be brushed well into the fabric, left for about 15 minutes and then washed off with warm water. A well-ventilated place should be selected for carrying out this treatment, and precautions should be exercised if the solvents are inflammable. These treatments will remove oils, greases, petroleum jelly and most lubricating mixtures, but they will not remove stains caused by the fine metallic particles often associated with lubricants. Such stains can be removed by methods described below, after the oil or grease has been eliminated.

Metallic Stains

Stains caused by metals, in the form of rust, verdigris or finely divided particles, can be removed by either of the following methods (do not allow the solution to come into the contact with galvanized iron or copper):

(*a*) Immerse the stained portion in a 5 per cent solution of oxalic acid dissolved in hot water (1 oz. of oxalic acid dissolved in each pint of hot water). The hands and the fabrics should be washed very thoroughly after using oxalic acid solutions, as this chemical is poisonous.

(*b*) Immerse the stained portion in a warm solution containing 2 parts of concentrated hydrochloric acid per 100 parts of water. Wash off thoroughly with water.

Appendix E

Pitch and Tar

Organic solvents such as perchloroethylene, trichloroethylene, trichloroethane (Genklene), solvent naphtha or white spirit may be dabbed on to the stain to effect removal. Again care should be taken to work in a well-ventilated position, and due precautions should be observed when using inflammable solvents.

Varnish

Dab the stain first with trichloroethylene and then with a mixture of equal parts of acetone and amyl acetate. Shellac varnish is easily removed with alcohol or methylated spirit. Paint strippers based on alkalis should not be used on Terylene.

Adhesive Numbers

To remove adhesive numbers, soak in benzene until the glue is softened. After peeling off the numbers, remove the glue from the sail with a rag dipped in benzene.

All information in this section is given in good faith, but without warranty. Freedom from patent rights must not be assumed.

'Terylene' is the registered trade mark of the Imperial Chemical Industries Limited for their polyester fibre.

'Lissapol' and 'Genklene' are registered trade marks, the property of Imperial Chemical Industries Limited.

'Domestos' is a registered trade mark, the property of Domestos Ltd.

'Polyclens' is a registered trade mark, the property of Polycell Products Ltd.

Reprinted by kind permission of I.C.I. Fibres Limited, Harrogate, Yorkshire.

APPENDIX F

Thread and needle sizes to use for hand sewing two thicknesses of cloth

Cloth weight	*Thread weight*	*Needle size*
1–3 oz	Use machine thread	Domestic or no. 19
3–4 ,,	ditto	19 or 18
4–6 ,,	2 lb (light)	18 or 17
6–8 ,,	4 lb (medium)	18 or 17
8–11,,	6 lb (,,)	17
11–15,,	6 lb (,,)	16
15–21,,	8 lb (heavy)	15

When sewing three or four thicknesses of cloth, use a size larger needle and thread than the table.

If repairing head, tack or clew (six or more thicknesses), use two sizes larger needle and one size heavier thread than the table.

If working an eye, use a heavier thread and space out stitches.

If roping, use a size heavier thread, and blunt the point of a size larger needle than the table.

Modern sailcloth is so closely woven that the threads are packed one on the other in a tight weave, so that each pass of the needle carries a high risk of cutting individual yarns, particularly in the lighter cloths where the weave is usually closest. Therefore the fewer stitches in any repair job, the less the chance of weakening the cloth. It is thus a general principle that any hand sewing should be restricted to the fewest stitches possible – which is another way of saying that modern practice is to keep stitches large and widespread, using doubled twine if necessary.

APPENDIX G

Measurement of sails

Introduction

The aim of sail measurement rules is to provide a framework within which sails can be made under certain predetermined restrictions. At one extreme the class may wish to encourage development and experiment, while at the other it may try to produce strictly one-design sails, so that racing depends on other factors. In any case some form of control is usually necessary and there are many inherent problems in administering rules.

Not only does the concept of the ideal sail shape vary from helmsman to helmsman, but two sails made to exactly the same pattern by the same Sail Maker may vary in flow – and sometimes even in outline. Indeed, the same sail will alter its shape when set on two different boats, due to variations in rig and tune.

The method of roping a sail will alter its characteristics. A taped sail will pull fairly easily to its full size on the floor, while one which has been cut to the same size and had a rope machined on will be harder to pull out; hand roping will make it harder still. In addition, the amount and thickness of the tabling will change a sail's characteristics, and so will the way in which the cloths have been laid. If the edge to be measured has a good deal of bias to its cloth, with a light tabling, the Sail Maker will allow more for stretch than if there were no bias and a stout tabling. Finally, the human element also plays its part in producing different sails to the same pattern.

It is easy to see, therefore, how two similar sails will fail to measure the same under the hands of different Measurers, working in different circumstances – perhaps on a lawn in one case and on a flat concrete or wooden surface in the other.

Cloth

Synthetic sailcloth varies from bolt to bolt, even within the same batch from a particular maker. This means that different results may stem from the cloth. Nylon is subject to moisture and temperature changes: a cold damp sail will elongate, and a hot dry one will shrink. So whether your spinnaker measures to the rule sometimes depends on the weather. On moist days, some owners place their sails in laundry driers to remove any dampness just before measuring, or they lay them in the sun on top of the heated body of a car. The difference in length can be as much as 2½ per cent, which is 6 in. in 20 ft.

Measurers

Before he starts, therefore, the unfortunate Measurer has a difficult task. If to this is added the fact that he seldom has good conditions in which to work, such as a wooden surface with prickers so that he can peg out the sail, it is easy to see why anomalies sometimes occur. Rules should therefore be worded so as to be capable of easy interpretation.

Secondly, the Measurer must follow precisely any instructions about tension to apply along the edge being checked. This usually says something about 'tension adequate to remove [all] wrinkles adjacent to the measurement being taken'. I have put the word 'all' in brackets because it is not always included. The IYRU Sail Measurement Instructions include it (and also state that sails should be completely dry), and this means that some hand-roped sails must be anchored firmly at one end and pulled out with a block and tackle.

Failure to observe this requirement strictly can also lead to trouble with the minimum luff length of headsails which have their luff wire loose inside the tabling, or which are made to slide loose over the luff wire. Even more liable to error are headsails which have a roped luff. I recall a Measurer coming into the loft one day to recheck a Dragon genoa with a rope luff which he had failed to pass as being under size on the luff. The sail had not been altered, and we set it up together, anchored at the tack and with a purchase at the head. When the luff was pulled to the minimum length according to the rules there were minute wrinkles still discernible along the luff tabling, which did not disappear completely until another two inches had been pulled. To show how the sail would go further, we pulled it another four inches, and it was obvious that it would have gone more had it not been for a checkwire. Yet the Measurer had not been able to pull the sail even as far as the minimum distance with a straight pull by hand along the luff. Incidentally, I sailed with that genoa the next day, and it did not set at all well until pulled nearly to the maximum; the minimum position produced a very poor shape.

Datum Points

Having established how the measurements should be taken, we must decide where the measurement datum points shall be. As fast as rules appear stating that certain points shall be used, such as centre of eye or point of intersection of the two edges concerned, owners find new ways round them. Nor must I absolve the Sail Makers in this respect; they are often guilty of finding a loophole, so that they can squeeze more area out of a particular rule. The Snipe is a fine example of how the rule has been abused. As a result of measuring between eyes, extra area has gradually been achieved by insetting the eyes into the sail. The point has now been reached where there are distances limiting the amount by which a measurement eye may be inset, and the eye has, in some cases, lost its identity as a halyard or tack attachment, being merely worked into the sail as a measurement datum point, while another eye near to it does the utilitarian work.

The IYRU Sail Measurement Instructions lay down a guide to Measurers in respect of these datum points, in case a particular rule is vague on the subject. They should be carefully studied by any class drawing up new rules or revising old ones. These instructions are printed at the end of this appendix, and I would principally commend to your attention the wording 'Due, however, to the various methods of making the corners of headsails, a Measurer shall if he considers that a sail is measured either favourably or unfavourably by this method, use a different method as follows'. It then goes on to detail the method. The point I am making is that this eminently sensible paragraph gives the Measurer latitude to use his own initiative in doubtful cases. In other words, differences caused by the human element can be allowed for by intelligent use of the human element.

One-design Sails

We have already seen that there are plenty of obstacles to achieving one-design sails. The best way to solve the problem is to appoint a sole Sail Maker to the class, and to freeze the design of the sails, such as has been done in Great Britain by the Firefly Association, and in France and elsewhere by the 420 class. This is as near as you will ever get, but do not expect perfection.

Measurement by Area

There are many rules which claim to measure area, but there are few which really include everything. Most classes in this category allow mainsail rounds to be added free to the nominal area, thus encouraging a large roach in an attempt to get as big a sail as possible. Where a class seriously intends to measure everything, it must rely largely on the Sail Maker. Once the rope has been put on to a sail, it is hard to measure the luff and foot rounds accurately, so the sizes should be checked in the loft before roping (and the rules should stipulate this).

When we come to a more numerous class like the Shearwater III catamaran, however, which is spread across the country and has periodic meetings where boats come from far and wide, we are up against a different problem. Whereas a single fleet in a particular port can and does accept the vagaries of its own Measurer, on the grounds that his particular likes and dislikes are the same for everybody, when several fleets are gathered together some sails may be oversize according to strict interpretation of the rules – particularly where there is unrestricted choice of Sail Makers (for they also have their human failings). It therefore becomes necessary to try and measure the whole area of a roped sail laid on the yacht club floor. This requirement is highlighted by the International Catamaran rules, where sails are required to be within a certain total area depending on the size of the boat – and area of spars has to be measured as well. No less a person than Austin Farrar spent a great deal of time drafting the latter rules, and he would be the first person to admit that they are not perfect. How, for instance, does a Measurer verity the extra area incorporated in a mainsail with a baggy foot, once the sail has been roped? A shelf can be fairly determined, but a roped mainsail with a great deal of foot round or a lot of broad seam in the tack area becomes virtually impossible to measure.

Those classes considering adopting a full area measuring system would do well to study the International Catamaran rules, and incorporate the appropriate passages, for they make the best of an extremely difficult requirement.

Restricted Classes

Most classes are content to mark black bands on the spars in order to limit the luff and foot of the mainsail, and then to allow luff, foot and leech rounds as 'free' area. Maximum permissible leech round is controlled by means of cross measurements, usually at half height and sometimes three-quarter and even quarter heights as well. Within this framework, a class can be as liberal or tight as it likes. The following are some of the variations, all of which measure fore-and-aft sails in a similar way:

1. Sails can all be to the same nominal plan, with reasonable tolerances, as with the Dragon.

2. They can be allowed to vary as between mainsail and headsail, provided a certain area is not exceeded; this total may vary according to:

   (i) the size and shape of the boat (e.g. 5·5 metre);
   (ii) the overall height of the sailplan (e.g. Merlin Rocket);

(iii) or it may be a certain fixed total figure regardless of any latitude in size and shape of boat or rig (e.g. 12 ft National).

3. Total measured area depends on hull form. Mainsail bands and foretriangle are measured, but any headsail may be set in the foretriangle (e.g. 12 metre).

4. Total measured area is fixed, regardless of hull form. Mainsail bands and foretriangle are measured, but any headsail may be set in the foretriangle (e.g. 14 ft International).

5. The area may be varied with a wide tolerance, but the chosen figure reflects in the yacht's handicap (e.g. I O R).

All these different rules rely on a similar form of measurement, and the following are some of the points to consider. Not all of them apply to all of the above classifications.

Sizes

Mainsail. We have seen that the best system of measuring a mainsail is that of painting limiting marks on the spars, beyond which the extremities of the sail are not allowed to extend. This has the advantage of being constant, accurate and easily checked. The leech can be measured or not, as the rules require. If it is to be included, it should be from the forward top corner of the headboard (i.e. the point which lies nearest to the upper black band) to the clew. Some classes take the top datum as the rear upper corner of the headboard, and some extend the triangle and measure to the apex.

Headsail. A headsail with a fixed wire luff presents little problem, as it will usually lie on the floor in its fully extended shape provided the luff is set taut. Sails with the wire loose inside the tabling, those with a luff which can slide or adjust over the wire, and those with roped luffs need careful attention.

Cross Measurements. Limiting cross measurements are not usually needed on headsails, as they are not normally allowed battens to extend the leech outside the line of the natural triangle. It is not wise to demand that a mainsail cross measurement shall be taken at a certain distance down from the head or up from the tack, because this brings in the question of how much tension should be applied to the luff while determining the position. The surest way is to fold the head to the tack to establish the half height, but do not then take the cross measurement at rightangles to the luff, because the luff is seldom a straight line from which a rightangle can be taken. It is better to make a second fold head to clew and mark the leech similarly to the luff, and then measure between these two points. If you already have a rule which demands a measurement taken at rightangles to the luff, and you do not want to change for fear of altering the effect of the rule, then the simplest way of taking the measurement is to fold head to tack as before. The two parts of the luff rope should then lie one on top of the other for not less than three feet either side of the fold, and the measurement taken along the resulting fold. Threequarter and quarter heights can be similarly taken.

If you are establishing precise maxima for a particular class, remember to make allowance for luff rounds: the more luff round in a sail, the less roach can be put on for a given cross measurement. It is therefore wise to see that several sails are checked before finalizing a figure, and to ensure that a number of them are ones which have been made for stiff masts. Stiff masts will require less luff round and thus confer more roach, so that a limit established solely through bendy mast sails may well result in too much roach when a sail for a stiffer spar is used.

Where a tack does not present an easily definable point, such as in many Finns which are rounded in this area and may have two or three eyes instead of the usual one, special arrangements are necessary. The IYRU recommends that the sail be pulled under a tension of 10 lbs and the cross measurement distance measured down from the head. This is a poor compromise, but the best which can be achieved under the circumstances.

Battens. Battens are usually limited in length. Some few classes also limit their width, and this is a sensible precaution to close a possible loophole. They should also be required to divide the leech into approximately equal parts, with a specific tolerance mentioned. It would be wise to say whether these divisions should be taken along the straight line head to clew, or along the edge of the sail itself; it is not important which is chosen, but along the edge of the sail gives a little more necessary latitude. Battens should be required to be approximately at rightangles to the leech, save the bottom one which is often preferred parallel to the boom so that it can be rolled in if necessary. Be careful to allow a sail with less than the maximum number of battens, for this can be no advantage but may be necessary when reefing.

Headboard. The headboard should be limited, either to a maximum dimension in any direction, or to one taken at rightangles to the mast, preferably the latter.

Strengthening Patches

Despite rules to the effect that no stiffening material may be incorporated in a sail, mainsail clew patches and spinnaker head patches get stiffer and stiffer. There should be a limit on their size and a reminder that only patches 'consistent with normal good sailmaking practice' should be used.

Racing Numbers

Racing number rules should conform with IYRU requirements, which is to say that they should be a certain minimum height and width, and that those on the starboard side should be higher up the sail than those on the port. Another requirement is that they shall be placed at approximately two-thirds of the sail above the boom. The cult of setting the number low in the sail may be smart and *avant-garde*, but it is of no help to the harassed race officer trying to identify your boat in a forest of sails, especially if half the racing number is obscured through reefing. The number should serve a utilitarian and not a decorative purpose.

THE MEASUREMENT INSTRUCTIONS OF THE INTERNATIONAL YACHT RACING UNION

SECTION III – SAIL MEASUREMENT

1. GENERAL

(1) Sails shall be measured in a dry state laid on a flat surface with just sufficient tension to remove wrinkles across the line of the measurement being taken.

(2) Sails shall be flexible, soft and capable of being easily stowed. The body of the sail shall be so constructed that it may be folded flat in any direction, other than in way of windows and corner stiffening as defined below, without cracking or otherwise permanently damaging the sail or its reinforcement. Reinforcement of any fabric having the effect of stiffening the sail is permitted only within a distance from each corner of 150 mm plus 3 per cent of the length of the luff of the sail. Other reinforcement, as a continuation of corner stiffening or elsewhere, comprising not more than two additional layers of material having the same weight as the body of the sail, is permitted provided that it can be folded as described above and is not stiffened by the addition of bonding agents, close stitching, or otherwise. Glued seams shall not be considered as stiffening provided that they can be folded as described above. Normal tabling at the edges of the sail is permitted provided that it is not stiffened.

Spinnakers may have reinforcement patches in the lower two-thirds of the sail for use with a recovery line.

(3) The term 'sail' shall be taken to include the headboard, tabling,

SAIL REINFORCEMENT AND ADVERTISING MARKS FOR INTERNATIONAL ONE-DESIGN CLASSES

This table is included as a guide and reference should be made to the Class Rules. All measurements are millimetres unless otherwise shown.

Class	*Maximum permitted distance of 'stiffening' from corner of sail (150 mm plus 3 per cent of luff length) (See paragraph III.1 (2))*			*Maximum permitted distance of sail maker's mark from tack (Racing Rule 26 refers)*	
	Mainsail	*Headsail*	*Spinnaker*	*Mainsail*	*Headsail*
Cadet	260	225	240	300	300
Contender	325	—	—	405	—
Dragon	425	350 (genoa)	360	520	530
Enterprise	320	265	280	400	300
Finn	Head 200* Tack 320* Clew 300*	—	—	490	—
5-0-5	345	290	Head 230 Clew 300	430	345
Fireball	320	280	280	425	300
Flying Dutchman	450*	450*	450*	425	520
Flying Junior	295	265	260	365	295
470	325	275	280	400	300
420	300	255	270	360	300
Lightning	370	315	330	455	350
OK Dinghy	315	—	—	405	—
Optimist	205	—	—	300	—
Snipe	1 ft. 0 in.	10$\frac{3}{8}$ in.	—	1 ft. 3 in.	11$\frac{3}{4}$ in.
Soling	405	365	370	480	400
Star	1 ft. 5 in.	1 ft. 1$\frac{1}{2}$ in.	—	2 ft. 0 in.	1 ft. 1$\frac{1}{4}$ in.
Tempest	380*	340*	330*	510	375
Tornado	595*	440*	—	355	300
Vaurien	305	260	260	330	240

* See Class Rules.

bolt and foot ropes (or tapes). It shall not include cringles which are wholly outside the sail.

(4) In sails where, under class rules, windows are permitted, or not specifically prohibited, the total area of the transparent material of such windows shall not exceed one per cent of the nominal area of the sail or 0·3 m², whichever is the greater. The nominal area of the sail shall be taken as ½ (length of luff × length of foot). Windows shall not be placed closer to the luff, leech or foot than 150 mm.

(5) Openings in the sail, in addition to the normal cringles and reefing eyelets, are permitted provided that the sail is flat in the vicinity of the openings.

(6) When batten pockets are measured the maximum inside dimensions shall be taken, ignoring the effect of any elastic or other retaining devices. The length shall be taken from the aft edge of the sail.

(7) Sails passing round a stay or spar and attached back on themselves by stitching, zipper or similar device shall be considered to be double luffed sails.

(8) If the luff of the sail is not attached to a spar or luff wire, a check wire, minimum diameter 1·25 mm, shall be securely fastened to the head and tack cringles. The length of the luff shall be measured with sufficient tension to straighten this check wire.

Section III.1(8) shall only apply to spinnakers which are required to have check wires. Headsails are not normally required to have check wires although the measurer has to be satisfied that the luff cannot be stretched to exceed the maximum dimension permitted by the class rules.

(9) Where sails are set on spars, measurement bands shall be marked on the spars, so that they are clearly discernible whilst racing. The inside edges of these bands shall define the limits to which the sail may be set.

(10) The area of the fore-triangle of formula and development classes shall be measured in accordance with the instructions contained in Section III.4.

2. MAINSAILS

(1) Definitions

(i) Head – The head shall be taken as the highest point of the sail projected perpendicular to the luff or its extension.

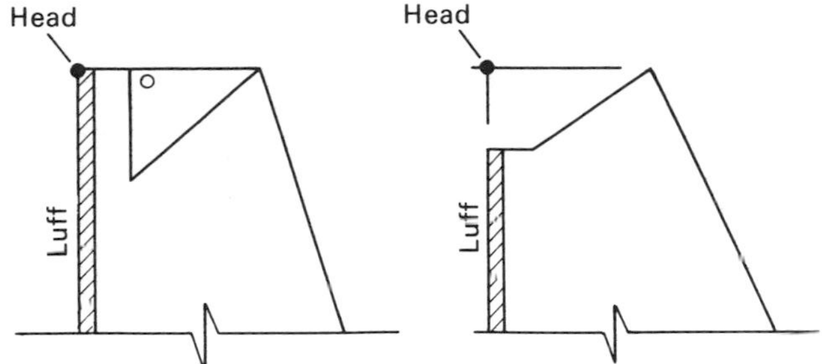

(ii) Clew – The clew shall be taken as the aftermost part of the sail projected to the foot or its extension.

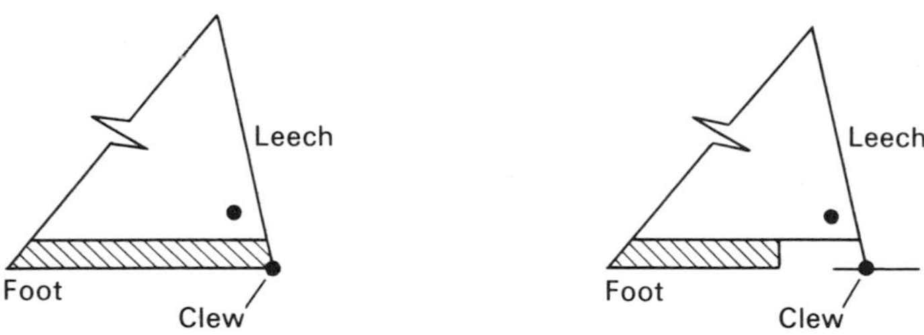

(2) Measurements

(i) Leech

The length of the leech shall be taken as the straight distance between the head and the clew.

(ii) Luff

The length of the luff shall be taken as the distance on the mast between the upper edge of the lower measurement band and the lower edge of the upper measurement band.

For double luff sails which envelop the mast the length of the luff shall be taken as the distance on the mast between the upper edge of the lower band and the highest point of the mast.

(iii) Foot

(*a*) For sails set on a boom, the length of the foot shall be taken as the distance between the inner edge of the boom measurement band and the aft side of the mast and track, excluding any local curvature, measured with the boom fore and aft and at right angles to the mast.

For sails which envelop the boom completely the length of the foot shall be taken as the distance between the aft side of the mast, as defined above, and the aft end of the boom.

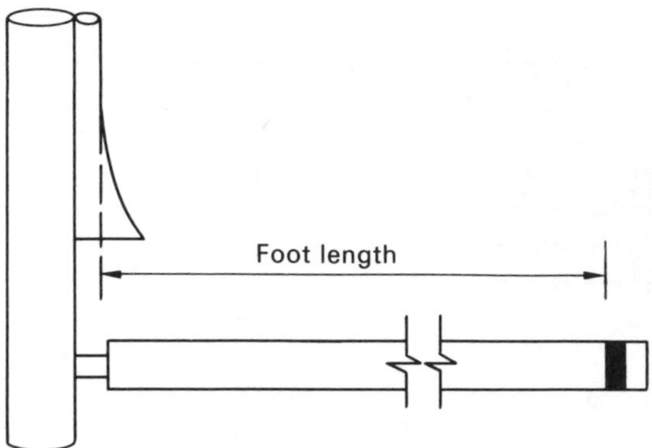

(*b*) For a loose-footed sail the length of the foot shall be taken as the distance from the aft upper edge of the lower measurement band on the mast to the clew. The measurer shall indelibly record the foot length on the sail and on the boom, as near to the clew as possible, to define the limit of the foot.

Where a loose-footed sail projects beyond the end of the boom the measurer shall record the foot length indelibly on the sail and this dimension shall be recorded on the yacht's certificate.

(iv) Cross Widths

The cross measurements shall be the distance from the leech measurement points, as defined below, to the nearest point on the fore edge of the sail including the bolt rope. The points on the leech from which the cross measurements are taken shall be determined bridging any hollows in the leech with straight lines.

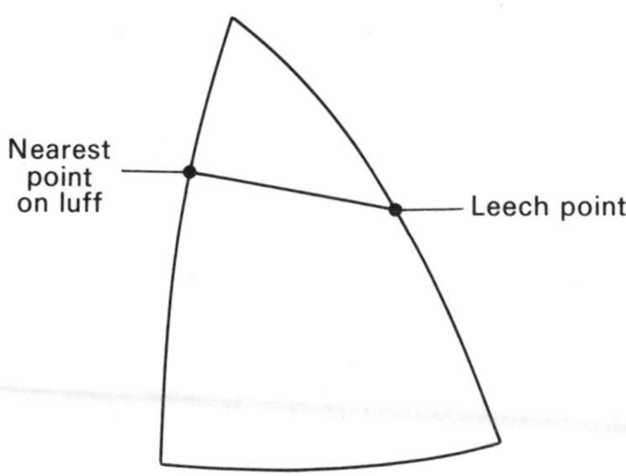

The mid-point of the leech shall be determined by folding the head to the clew and the quarter and three-quarter leech points by folding the clew and the head to the mid-point of the leech.

3. HEADSAILS

(1) The length of the luff shall normally be the distance between the lowest part of the sail on the luff rope at the tack and the highest point of the sail on the luff rope at the head.

Owing, however, to the varying methods of making the corners of headsails, a measurer shall, if he considers that a sail is measured either favourably or unfavourably by this method, use a different method as follows:

The point of measurement at the tack shall be the point where the extension of the luff meets the extension of the foot, ignoring any round or hollow to the foot, and the point of measurement at the head shall be the point where the extension of the luff meets the extension of the leech, ignoring any round or hollow of the leech.

If the cloth is not permanently attached to a luff wire, the measurer shall be satisfied that the luff cannot be stretched to exceed the maximum dimension permitted by the rules.

(2) The length of the leech shall normally be the distance between the lowest part of the sail directly below the centre of the clew cringle and the highest part of the sail at the head.

(3) The length of the foot shall normally be the distance between the lowest point of the sail on the luff rope and the outer edge of the sail directly aft of the centre of the clew cringle.

(4) The measurement from clew to luff shall normally be between the outside edge of the clew and the nearest point on the luff.

(5) Centre Measurement

The mid-point of the foot shall be determined by placing the centre of the clew cringle over the centre of the tack cringle and tensioning both halves of the foot equally. The length of the centre measurement shall be taken as the distance between the highest point of the sail on the luff and the lowest edge of the sail at the mid-point of the foot. For the purpose of taking the centre measurement there shall be no tension along the luff, leech or foot.

N.B. – In 3(2), (3) and (4) the measurer shall measure in a similar way as in the alternative method laid down in 3(1) if he considers it proper to do so.

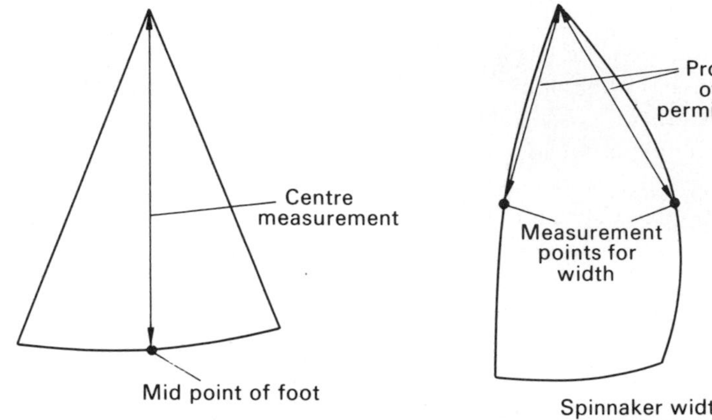

4. AREA OF FORE-TRIANGLE

For classes which require the area of the fore-triangle to be calculated, the base 'J' and the height 'I' shall be measured.

'I' shall be measured from the deck (or such other point as the class rules require) along the fore side of the mast to the intersection of the aft edge of the forestay and the forward face of the mast.

'J' shall be measured horizontally from the fore side of the mast to the intersection of the aft edge of the forestay (extended if necessary) and the deck.

Where there is more than one forestay the measurements shall be taken to the foremost stay on which a headsail is set.

Where there is no forestay and the headsail is set flying the measurements shall be taken to the line of the forward edge of the luff of the foremost headsail (extended if necessary).

5. SPINNAKERS

(1) The spinnaker shall be measured folded along its centreline with the leeches together.

(2) The length of the leeches shall be taken as the distance between the highest point of the sail at the head and the lowest point of the sail on the leech, measured round the edge of the sail.

(3) The half-width of the foot shall be taken as the distance between the lowest points on the centre fold and leech, measured round the foot of the sail.

(4) The length of the centre fold shall be taken as the distance between the head and the mid-point of the foot, measured round the fold of the sail.

(5) The half-height half-width shall be taken as the distance between the points on the leech and the centre fold which are, measured in a straight line, half the maximum permitted leech length from the head.

(6) The three-quarter height half-width shall be taken as the distance between points on the leech and the centre fold which are, measured in a straight line, one quarter of the maximum permitted leech length from the head.

SECTION IV – SAIL AREA MEASUREMENT

1. GENERAL

(1) The intention is to establish a reliable and simple method of measuring the area of the sail plan, including spars. This method produces consistent results not dependent on variations in roping tensions or sophisticated measuring equipment.

(2) The principle of the measurement of the area of a mainsail, and of a headsail roped for a luff spar, is to use measurement bands, or measurement bands and the foot length recorded on the sail, to obtain the area of the main triangle and to add (or subtract) the area of the rounds on the luff, leech and foot.

(3) In the case of a sail set into a groove on a spar that area obscured within the groove shall not be included when calculating the area.

(4) The area of any holes in the sail shall not be deducted from the measured area.

(5) The term 'sail' shall be taken to include the headboard and tabling. It shall not include bolt or foot ropes or cringles which are wholly outside the sail.

2. SPARS

(1) The area of that part of any spar, including the luff spar of a headsail, which projects above the sheerline, shall be measured. Fairings added to a spar shall be measured as part of the spar. The area of the spar shall be taken as the overall length multiplied by the mean half girth. The girth shall be the distance from the centreline round the spar and back to the centreline. Sufficient girth measurements shall be taken for a reasonable mean dimensions considering the profile of the spar. If the profile of the spar is not uniform it shall be divided into its constituent lengths and the area of each length determined and added together.

(2) A spar which supports the rig, but on which no sail is set directly, e.g. a bipod straddling the hulls or a structure aft to support a

main staysail shall not be measured for area if the length of the major axis is less than one-and-a-half times the length of the minor axis.

3. AREA OF A SAIL SET ON A SPAR

(1) Area of Main Triangle

The area of the main triangle shall be calculated from the following formula or by a scale drawing.

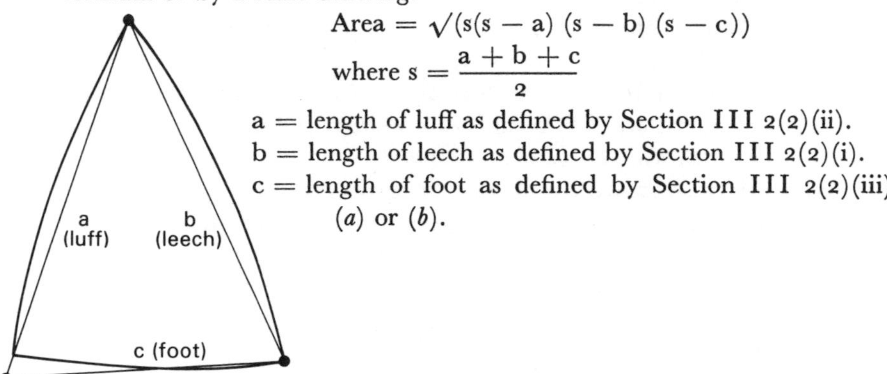

$$\text{Area} = \sqrt{(s(s - a)\,(s - b)\,(s - c))}$$

$$\text{where } s = \frac{a + b + c}{2}$$

a = length of luff as defined by Section III 2(2)(ii).
b = length of leech as defined by Section III 2(2)(i).
c = length of foot as defined by Section III 2(2)(iii) (*a*) or (*b*).

(2) Area of Luff, Leech and Foot Rounds

(i) The area of the rounds on the luff, leech and foot shall be calculated from measurements taken with the sail pegged out on a flat surface with just sufficient tension to remove waves or wrinkles from the edge rounds and to spread the sail substantially flat. Battens shall be set in their pockets. Once the sail has been pegged out in this way all the required measurements shall be taken and no alterations to the tension shall be made.

Needles shall then be fixed at the head and clew so that the distance between them is the same as the length of the leech. A third needle shall be fixed at a point the lengths of the luff and the foot as used in calculating the area of the main triangle, from the head and clew respectively. A thin thread shall be stretched round these needles to define the main triangle. The rounds on the luff, foot and leech shall then be measured and the areas calculated as defined below.

(ii) The area of the luff and foot rounds shall be taken as two-thirds of the product of the chord of the round and the perpendicular offset. The luff and the foot round chords shall be taken as the distance between the points at which the edge of the sail and the thread defining the luff and foot of the main triangle intersect. The perpendicular offsets shall be the distance between the points on this thread mid-way between the luff and foot measurement points and the nearest edge of the sail.

(iii) The area of the leech round shall be taken as $\frac{L}{4}(1{\cdot}16X + Y + 1{\cdot}16Z)$ where L is the chord length of the leech. The leech round chord shall be taken as the distance between the points at which the edge of the sail and the thread defining the leech of the main triangle intersect. X, Y and Z shall be the perpendicular offsets between the points of this thread at $\frac{1}{4}$, $\frac{1}{2}$ and $\frac{3}{4}$ of the distance between the leech measurement points and the edge of the sail.

(iv) If any round is not a fair curve the area shall be determined by dividing the sail up into right-angled triangles or quadrilaterals as appropriate.

4. AREA OF A SAIL NOT SET ON A SPAR

The sail shall be pegged out on a flat surface with just sufficient tension to remove waves or wrinkles from the edge rounds and to spread the sail substantially flat. Battens (if any) shall be set in their pockets.

A thread shall be stretched between needles, inserted to define the head, clew and tack. The length of the luff, leech and foot shall be taken as the straight distance between these points and the area calculated using the formula in section IV.3.

The areas of the rounds shall be calculated in the manner described in section IV.3(2).

5. AREA OF A SPINNAKER

(1) The area of the spinnaker shall be taken as:

$F \times L + 2/3\,(G - F)L$

where F = half-width of the foot as defined by Section III.5(3).

L = leech length as defined by Section III.5(2).

G = half-height width.

(2) The half-height width (G) shall be taken as twice the distance between the mid-point of the leeches and the nearest point on the centrefold. The mid-point of the leech shall be determined by measuring half the length of the leech from the head round the edge of the sail.

APPENDIX H

Altering sail sizes

It is easier to cut down the size of a sail than to increase it. Nevertheless, our examination of the effect of bias stretch shows us that great care has to be taken not to leave the leech, in particular, with the cloths at too great an angle. A secondary factor to consider is the shaping which has been built in through broad seam and round; the cutting should remove as little of this as possible.

The following drawings show most of the more usual ways in which sails can be made smaller, and some of the more practicable ones in which they can be increased. I have assumed horizontally cut mainsails and spinnakers, and mitre cut headsails in every case.

1

Mainsails

Shorten Luff and Leech. There is a danger of upsetting the upper leech due to excessive bias at the head. Suggested safe maximum reduction is 5 per cent of the luff. Flow at luff and foot is undisturbed. Batten pockets and perhaps racing number may be disturbed. *Cost:* low. Headboard and pockets to move, leech to fair.

2

Shorten Luff and Leech. No disturbance to leech or flow. Amount of reduction dictated by resulting rise of boom as tack angle changes. Batten pockets may have to be repositioned to keep spacing even; also racing number possibly. *Cost:* medium. Headboard and pockets to move, luff to re-rub and re-rope.

Shorten Luff Only. Disturbs broad seam at tack and foot. Clew will droop. *Cost:* low. Foot to re-rope and new tack eye to work. Clew should not be disturbed.

3

Shorten Luff and Leech. Disturbs tack seam and foot seam. Foot is also very slightly shortened. Batten pockets may have to be repositioned to keep spacing even. *Cost:* low. As above, but new clew eye to work.

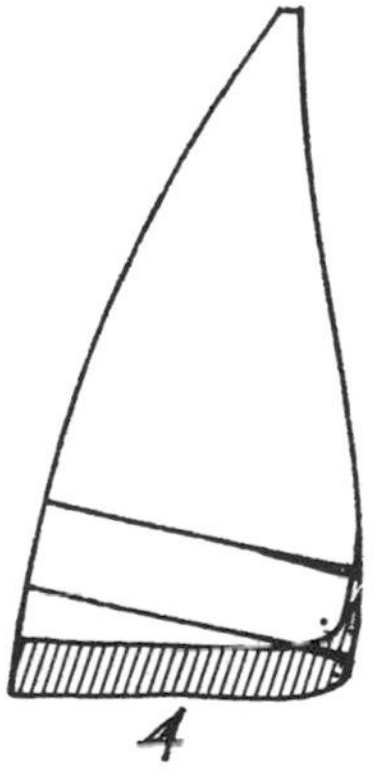

4

Shorten Luff, Leech and Foot. If strip to be taken off is nearly parallel, bias should be undisturbed, but there is always a danger when cutting a leech that its set will be spoiled. Shorter foot will alter batten length if IOR. All pockets must be moved anyway, so they can easily be shortened at the same time. Racing number may have to be moved. *Cost:* medium. Cut and re-rub whole leech, move batten pockets, drop headboard, new clew eye.

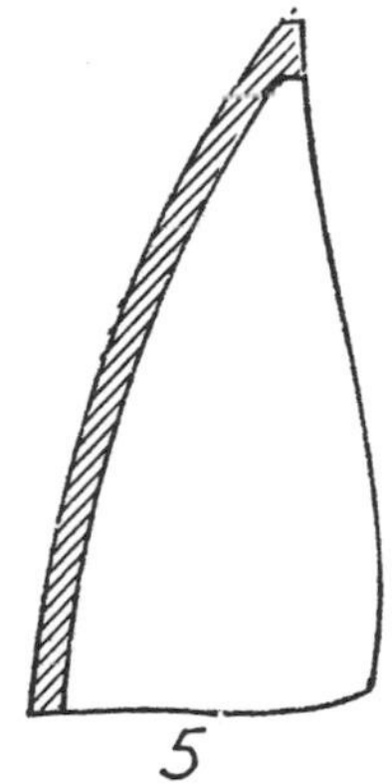

5

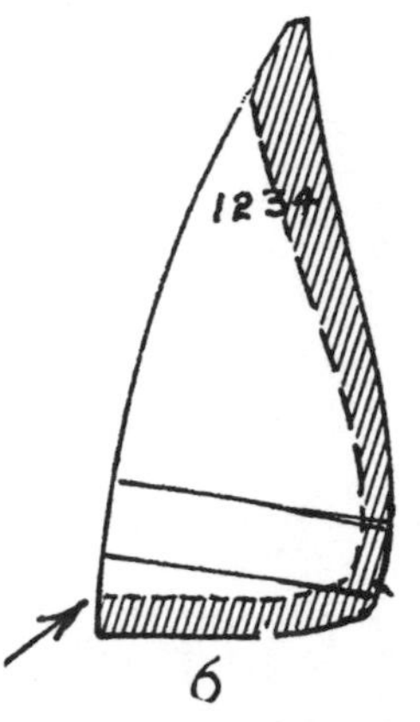

6

Leech can be shortened further without shortening luff, by cutting up at clew.

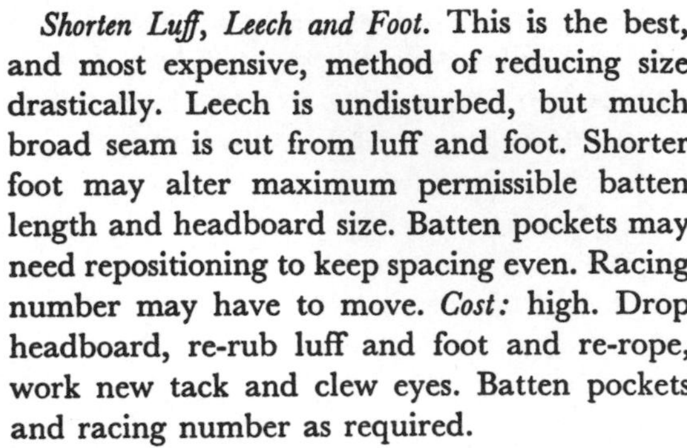

Shorten Luff, Leech and Foot. This is the best, and most expensive, method of reducing size drastically. Leech is undisturbed, but much broad seam is cut from luff and foot. Shorter foot may alter maximum permissible batten length and headboard size. Batten pockets may need repositioning to keep spacing even. Racing number may have to move. *Cost:* high. Drop headboard, re-rub luff and foot and re-rope, work new tack and clew eyes. Batten pockets and racing number as required.

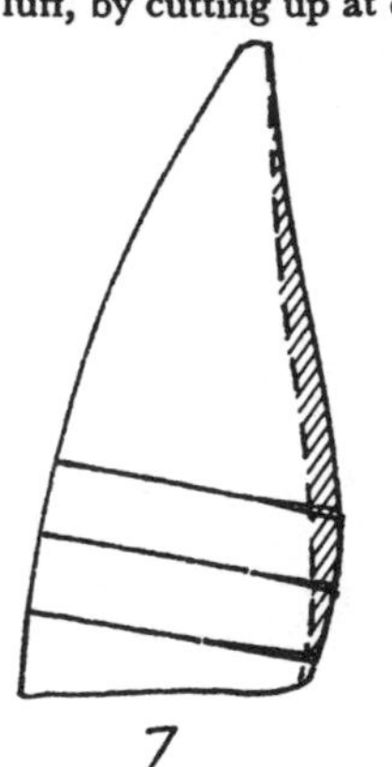

7

Shorten Foot. Cuts out much broad seam at luff. Boom will droop. Shorter foot may alter maximum batten length and headboard size. Should be able to leave headboard undisturbed if it is not now too big. *Cost:* low to medium. Take off rope, cut and re-rub luff, new tack eye to work, re-rope luff.

8

Shorten Luff, Leech and Foot. Cuts out much luff seam. Reduction may not result in same tack angle, so boom may rise or droop. Shorter foot may alter maximum permissible batten length and headboard size. Batten pockets may need repositioning to keep spacing even, and racing number may have to move. *Cost:* medium. Luff rope to come off, drop headboard, re-rub luff, new tack eye, batten pockets to move, re-rope.

Shorten Foot and Leech. Danger of upsetting lower leech due to excessive bias. Suggested safe maximum reduction is 5–10 per cent of foot length. Shorter foot may alter maximum permissible batten length and headboard size. Should be able to leave headboard undisturbed if it is not now too big. Lower batten pockets will move in, according to how high up the leech has to be faired. *Cost:* low. Cut and re-rub leech, shift pockets, new clew eye.

9

Shorten Leech Only. No danger to leech or shape. Batten pockets may need repositioning to keep spacing even. *Cost:* low. Take rope off foot, cut and re-rub foot, re-rope. New clew eye, batten pockets as required.

10

Lengthen Luff. This is major surgery, and much depends on exact lay of cloths and degree of lengthening. Sometimes three or four inches can be gained on the foot as well, by allowing the tack to go forward by this amount into the new cloth. Batten pockets will need repositioning, and reef points may be spoiled. *Cost:* high. Take off luff rope, rip tack seam, put in new cloth, cut and rub new luff, re-rope luff, new tack eye, drop headboard (this can often be moved complete with head patch and top cloth), rub new leech.

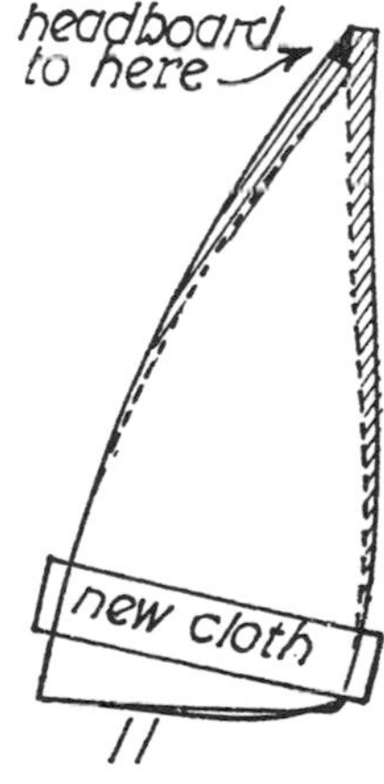

11

Headsails

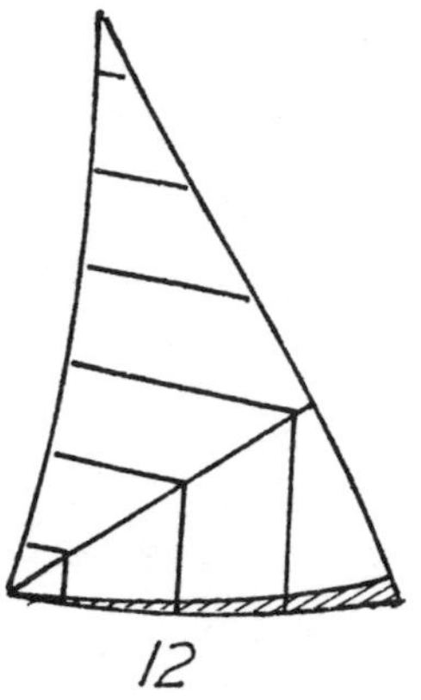

Shorten Luff Only. Slight danger of upsetting the foot due to excessive bias. Clew will drop, as leech is not shortened, so sheet lead goes forward. *Cost:* low. Cut and rub new foot, shorten luff wire, work new tack eye.

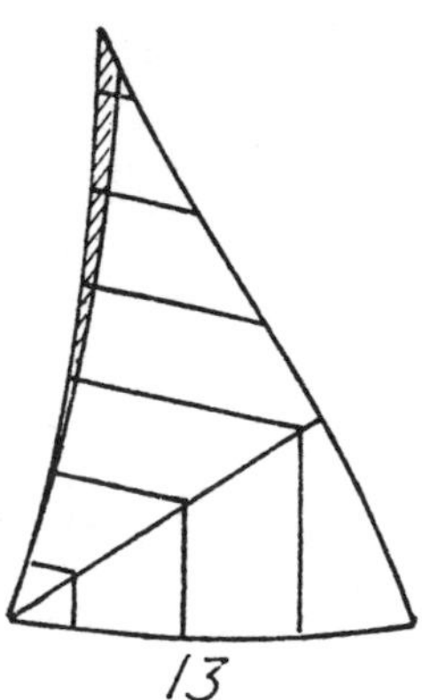

Shorten Luff and Leech. Danger of upsetting leech if too much is cut, due to excessive bias at head. Suggested safe maximum is 5 per cent of luff length. No side effects from this cut, as the sheet lead stays the same. *Cost:* low. Cut and rub new leech, shorten luff wire, work new head eye.

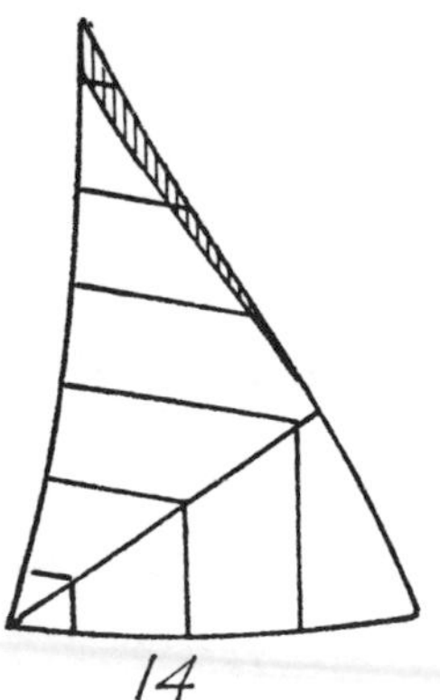

Shorten Luff and Leech. No danger to leech or foot. Clew will rise, and sheet lead goes aft. *Cost:* medium. Cut and re-rub luff, take out, shorten and replace luff wire, work new head eye.

Shorten Luff, Leech and Foot. No danger to leech or foot. Clew and sheet lead will move according to whether strip cut off is a parallel piece or not. *Cost:* medium. Cut and re-rub luff, take out, shorten and replace luff wire. Work new head and tack eyes.

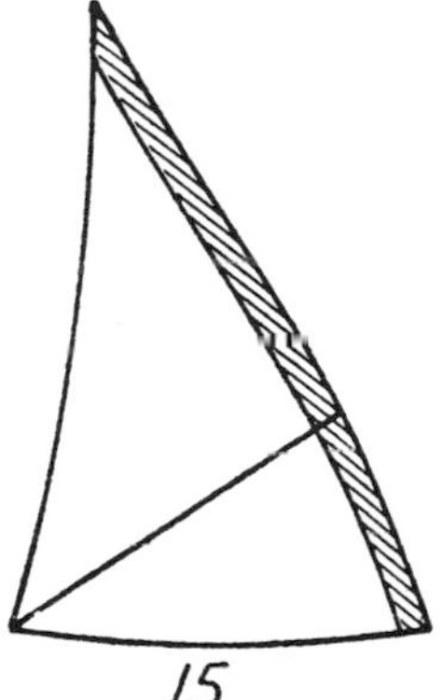

15

Shorten Foot Only. No danger to flow. Clew will drop so sheet lead will move forward. Depending on angle of the foot, so the luff may shorten slightly as well. *Cost:* low. Cut and re-rub luff. Take out and shorten luff wire slightly (or let it run out at the tack), work new tack eye.

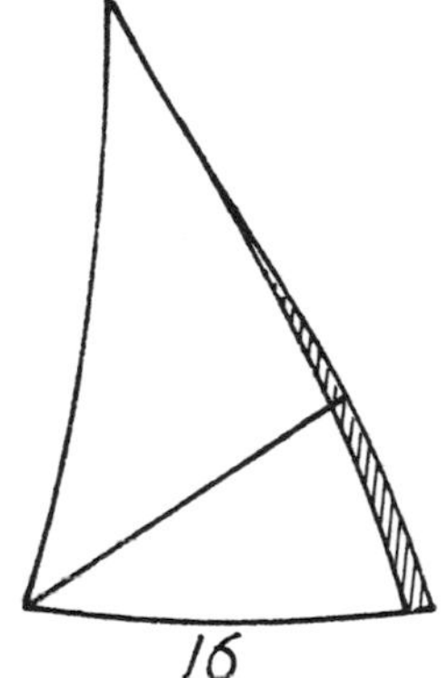

16

Shorten Foot Only. Danger of upsetting leech if too much is cut, due to excessive bias. Suggested safe maximum is 5 per cent of leech length. Clew comes off mitre: this is not a good method but can be done if clew not more than 5 per cent of foot from mitre, and it is then adequately reinforced. Sheet lead goes forward. *Cost:* low. Cut and re-rub leech. Work new clew eye.

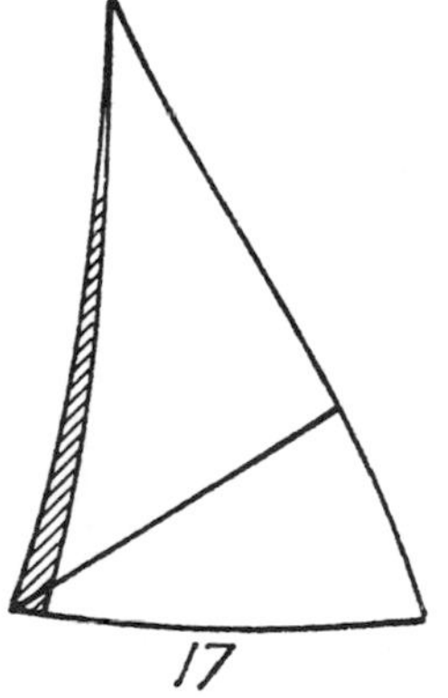

17

18

Shorten Leech Only. Slight danger of disturbing foot due to bias. Clew comes off mitre, see remarks immediately above. Sheet lead goes aft. *Cost:* low. Cut and re-rub foot, work new clew eye.

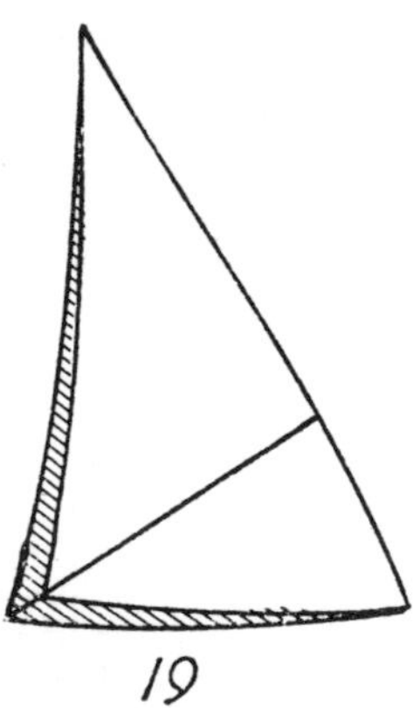

19

Shorten Leech and Foot. Danger to leech and foot due to bias. Suggested maximum safe cut is 5 per cent of foot length up the mitre. Sheet lead stays the same. *Cost:* medium. Cut and re-rub leech and foot, work new clew eye.

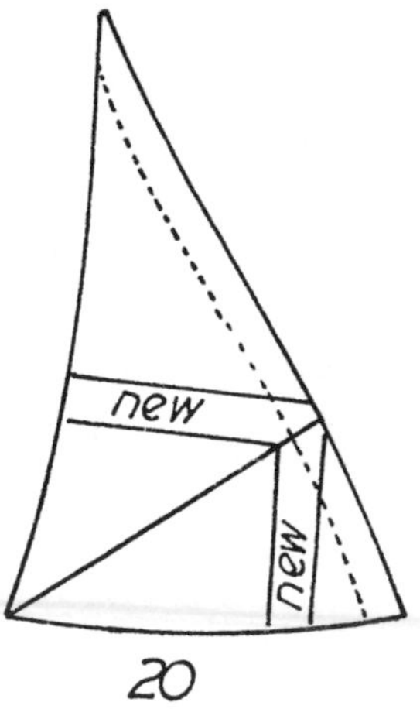

20

Enlarge Headsail. This again is major surgery. Usually all three dimensions, luff, leech and foot, will have to be made bigger together, and then the sail cut again to the required new sizes. This usually means a new luff wire, and the clew will move (and the sheet lead with it) according to the final size of the sail. *Cost:* high. Remove luff wire, rip two seams, insert two new cloths (or part cloths), re-rub sail to new sizes, put in new luff wire, work head and tack eyes.

Headsail Clew Angle

The important point about cutting down a headsail into a smaller sail, besides bias angle, is the angle made by the clew. If this is the same as the original sail, the sail will cut by the luff to desired shape within its overall size.

It is sometimes desired to alter the angle at the clew of a particular headsail. This involves ripping the mitre seam, and then overlapping the two halves at one end or the other. The result is a shortening of at least two of the sides of the sail, which then has to have its luff re-rubbed. The two illustrations at 22 and 23 are of the headsail at 21 above, with narrower and wider clew angles respectively. *Cost:* This sort of alteration is, in itself, a major job, but it is often combined with an enlargement of the sail along the lines of 20; this makes it a very expensive modification indeed. It is usually confined to headsails of at least 40 ft on the luff, because below this size it would be almost as cheap to have a new sail made from scratch.

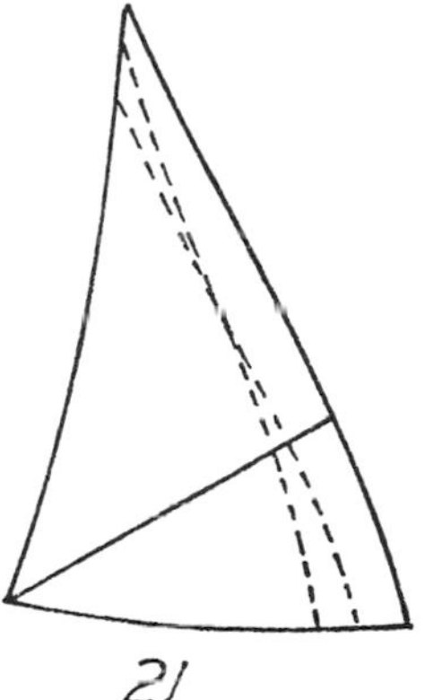

21

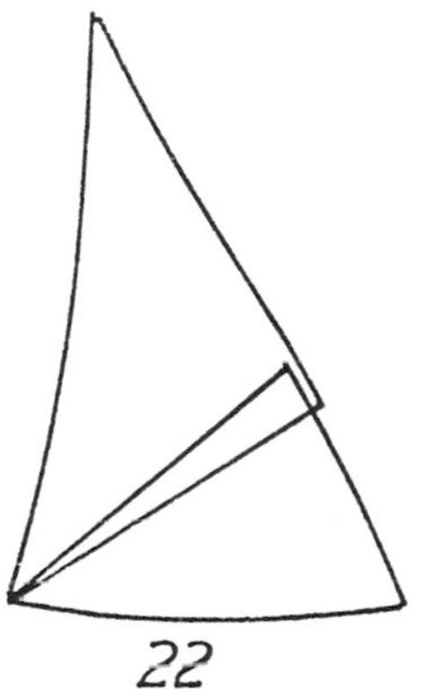

22

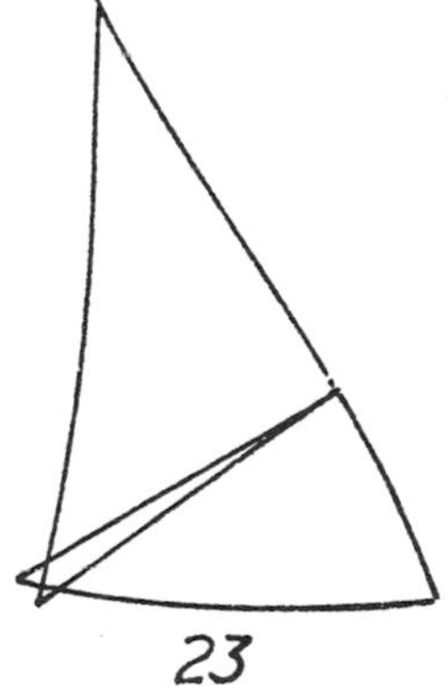

23

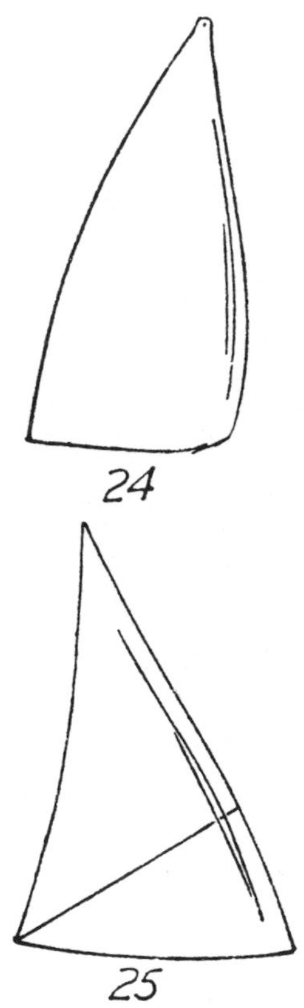

Flattening Mainsails and Headsails

Flattening sails is a common requirement and, as explained on page 273, an easy one. The sail is first set up for examination, and a decision taken as to how much luff round to remove. This is then done by pleating out the required amount, tapering away to nothing at either end. It has the advantage that it can be removed again by simply cutting the stitches to leave a double row of stitch holes which cause no harm. It is not easy to pleat less than ½ in., because this becomes ¼ in. on each side of the pleat, which must also taper to zero at either end. There is a minor risk of small creases radiating from the start and finish, where the pleat fades away to nothing. *Cost:* low. The examination of the sail takes the time here, and the decision on how much to pleat takes the skill. A Sail Maker will not normally charge for these items for one of his own sails. If the sail is by another maker, however, be prepared for a higher charge, which might be termed the consultation fee.

Making Mainsails and Headsails Fuller

It is not easy to make a sail fuller; the cloth is not there to provide the extra flow. It is not practicable to add a long strip up the luff, as this would set up counter stresses due to conflicting warp and weft. The best way to do the job is in combination with an alteration along the lines of pages 380/383 above, where the sail is taken apart and a new cloth inserted; this often gives the chance of increasing luff round in the process, but it is an expensive business if no alteration in size is required. See also pages 288 to 293.

Spinnakers

Make Narrower. A vertical section is cut from the centre of the sail; if necessary a seam has to be made (such as when cutting an orbital spinnaker in this way). *Cost:* low. The racing number is lifted, cut the centre seam and remake it, replace the racing number.

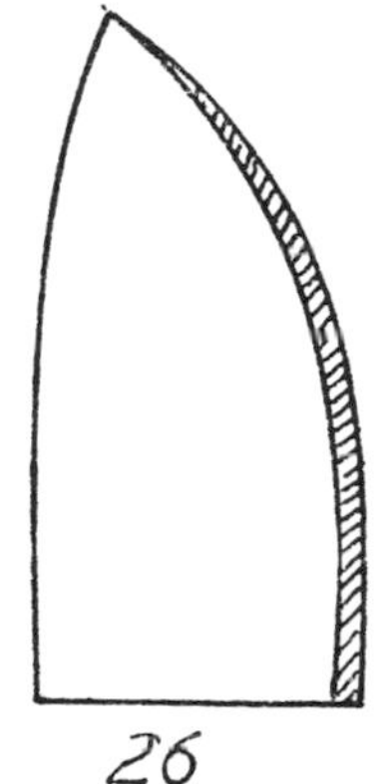

26

Make shorter. A parallel piece is cut across the sail in the lower half, where there is normally no broad seam. Leave the foot and clews intact, so that the whole section can be sewn back to the shortened sail. *Cost:* low. Cut out the required section, shorten the wires or tapes, and rejoin sail.

Parallel piece cut out across this point, and sail rejoined.

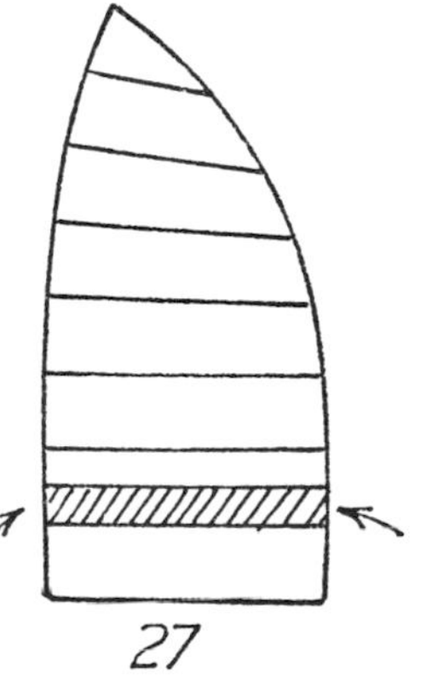

27

Make Wider. It is possible, of course, to add a short length to each cloth at the centre seam. This is however, a costly business and no less likely to spoil the set of the altered sail because of the great amount of sewing involved. One vertical panel can be inserted in the middle of the sail with surprisingly good results. The shaping in the upper half of the sail will be disturbed, but the elastic nature of nylon seems to allow it to absorb the clash of bias angles which is inevitable. *Cost:* medium. Remove the racing number, rip the centre seam, insert a carefully tapered new cloth down the middle, re-sew the racing number.

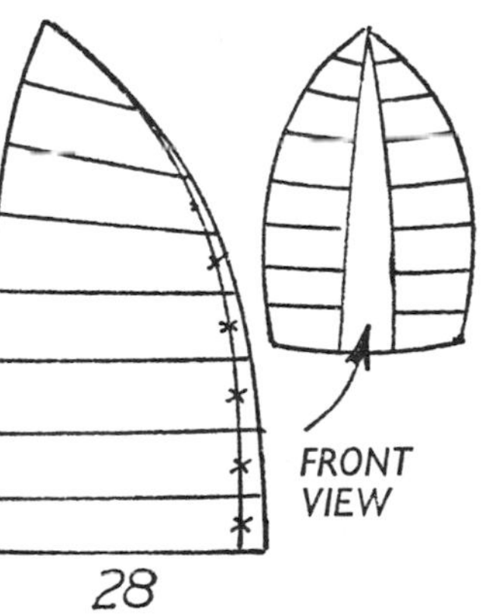

28

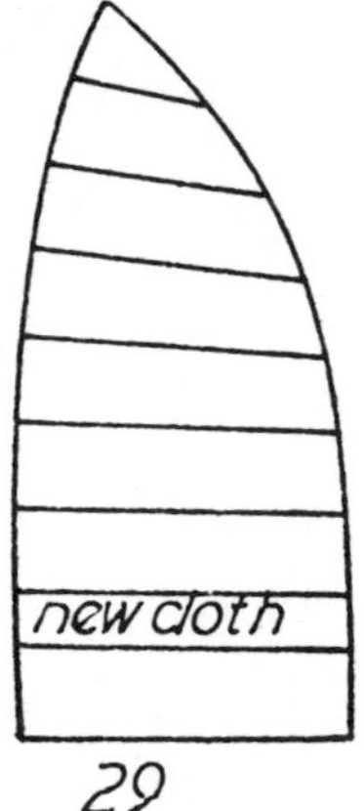

Make Longer. This is a comparatively simple operation with no attendant dangers. It is virtually the reverse of the case where the sail is made shorter. *Cost:* medium. Rip a lower seam, insert a new panel of the correct width, splice or Talurit/Nicopress (with a double ferrule) an extra length of wire in the stays, or increase the length of the tapes if there is no wire.

APPENDIX I

'Mystere', sailplan and measured sail area plotted against IOR rating

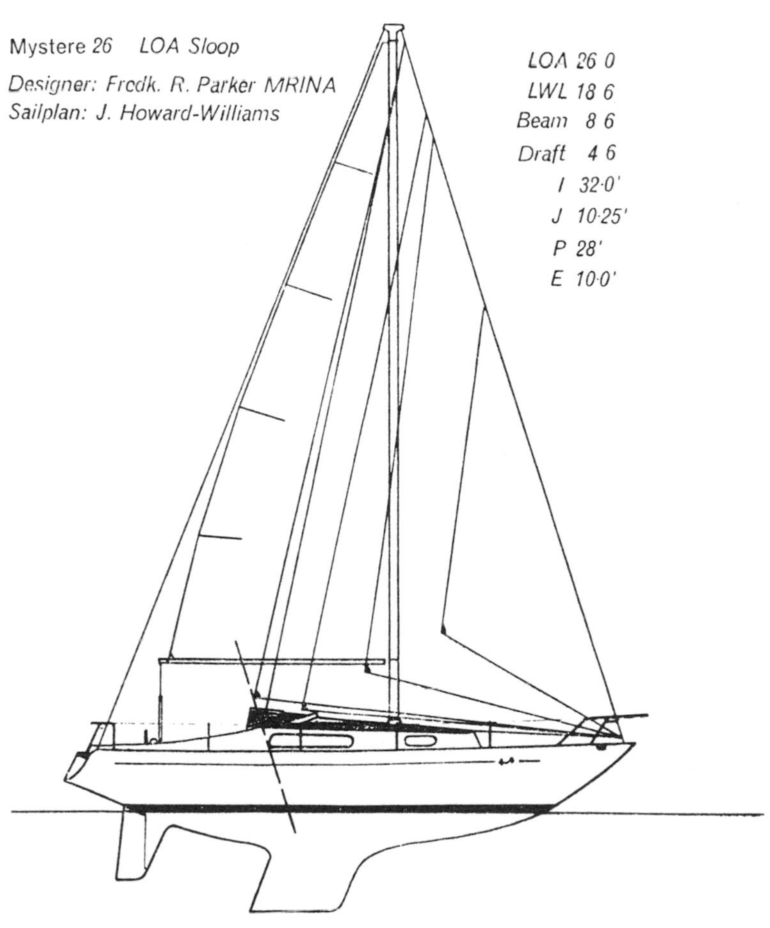

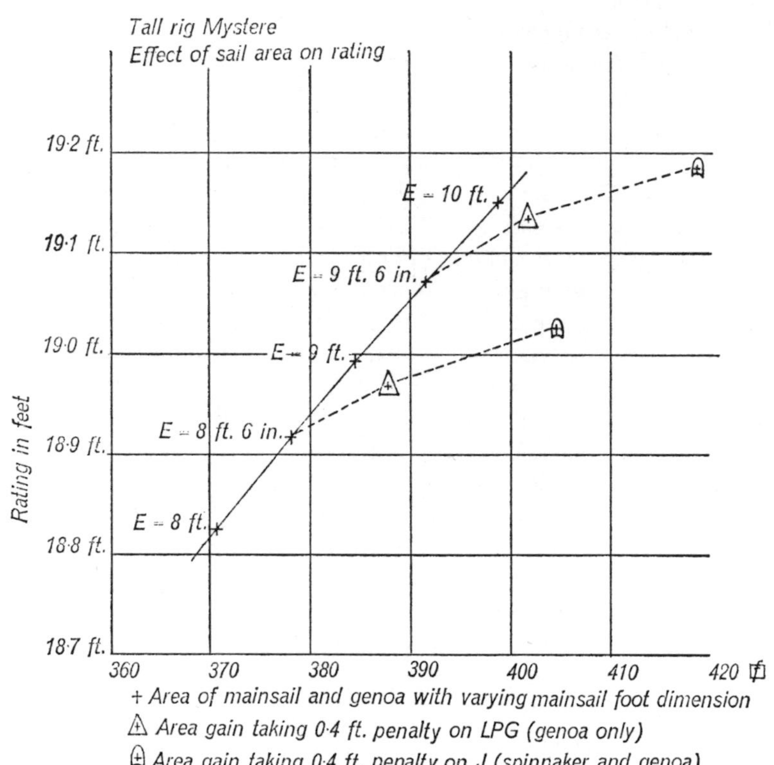

+ Area of mainsail and genoa with varying mainsail foot dimension

Area gain taking 0·4 ft. penalty on LPG (genoa only)

Area gain taking 0·4 ft. penalty on J (spinnaker and genoa)

APPENDIX J

Measuring a yacht for new sails

When a yacht needs new sails and a sailplan does not exist, it will be necessary to measure her if the sails are to fit. It is best if the measurements to be taken are written down beforehand, when there is time to consider what is going to be needed. Working to a list should help to avoid omissions, and the appropriate items should be extracted from the full table at the end of this Appendix. The following comments may be helpful.

General. Always write down the full distance you find, and either make any allowances for sheave clearance afterwards when you come to draw up the sailplan, or else make it clear that no allowance has been made. Measurements from the masthead can be taken shackling the wire or tape to the appropriate halyard and hauling it aloft. Care should be taken, not only to avoid the wrong rope (topping lift for main halyard), but also to ensure that the halyard is hoisted hard up and made fast securely, so that it does not creep down between two different measurements supposedly from the same point. Be accurate, and watch out for sag caused by the wind, as this can make quite a difference over 40 or 50 ft. It is best to fit a rope downhaul alongside a measuring wire or tape, otherwise you may find it difficult to pull down the halyard afterwards. Take too many rather than too few measurements. A steel tape measure is better than a linen one, for the latter may stretch even if it is reinforced; a measuring wire is best of all for it will sag less in a wind, but I realize this sort of equipment is not in common supply.

Jib. The spinnaker halyard may be used if it is more convenient, and if it leads from nearly the same point aloft. You are really measuring the foretriangle here, to establish mast rake and maximum luff distance. Measure to bowsprit end, stem head, forestay on deck and tack fitting, as these will be at least several inches different; don't forget the vertical measurement to the deck, which is the 'I' measurement (you may have to make an estimate of the coachroof here). Many large yachts have a forestay fitting which precludes hanks or snap hooks near the tack, and this is useful to know.

Staysail. The same measurements from aloft are needed as for the jib, with the addition of the one to the clew in the sailing position if a boom staysail is used. In the latter case make sure that tack and clew fittings are noted (the jaw width can also be important in some yachts), together with the travel of the clew outhaul slide if one is used. You will see in the table that the maximum and minimum distances from tack eye to clew eye duplicate this measurement, but it is vital to know it, and there is no harm in being doubly sure. There may, of course, be no travel at the clew, in which case there will be only one measurement from eye to eye. If the staysail is fitted to a boom with slides, a sample will ensure a correct fit. You would be surprised at the number of people who tell their Sail Maker that they need 'one inch slides'; this does not tell him whether the slides are internal or external, or whether the track or the slides are one inch (a $\frac{7}{8}$ in. internal slide fits a 1 in. external track, and a 1 in. external slide fits a $\frac{7}{8}$ in. internal track). In addition, an external track may not be deep enough to take a particular internal slide which would jam. Thus, if a sample slide is not available, measure the depth of the track as well as the width (a piece of paper pressed over the end of a track section will press the correct imprint into the paper), and also note the amount of room between the underside of the track and the mast if external slides are involved; some heavy slides have thick flanges which will not pass between the track and the mast if there is little room.

Mainsail and Mizzen. Make sure that the luff measurement is taken with the gooseneck in the lowest position, and make a note of the amount of vertical travel. While the wire or tape is aloft, it is quite easy and quick to take the distances vertically to the deck, to the mizzenmast at the deck, and to the counter; none of these is essential, but they will all help to draw up the plan of the boat. The distance from the head to the clew in the sailing position should be taken to the same point you use when measuring the boom from tack eye to clew eye, with the clew in the outermost position if there is an adjustment. Check before taking the leech distance that the boom is the right height to clear the deckhouse or heads in the cockpit. The tack knock back is the distance from the tack of the main or mizzen to the aft face of the mast in question; this is usually $1\frac{1}{4}$ to $1\frac{3}{4}$ in. where there is no roller boom, but varies from 4 in. to 8 or 9 in. for a roller boom, depending on the type of gear fitted. The Sail Maker must know this distance so that he can cut away the tack by the correct amount, in order that the sail shall set properly at the tack and shall not exceed the black band at the clew. If the main halyard is not available for any reason, you can always use the flag halyard, but try and gauge the resulting difference in the distance aloft. Once again it is preferable to supply a sample slide to ensure correct fit; check that luff and foot are not different in this respect. Some boats are fitted with mast ramps, where the track is led away from the mast just above the tack, so that it fairs nicely towards the tack fitting if this is set back for a roller gear. Draw a quick picture of this ramp, showing how high above the tack it starts and finishes, and its vertical distance to the mast at its lowest point. If there is no ramp, the track sometimes finishes well above the tack, so the Sail Maker will need to know not to fit a slide below a certain point. For a grooved mast, substitute the height of the groove entry above the tack for this measurement.

Gaff Sails. If an old sail is available, it should be bent to the spars and hoisted for measuring, as it will correctly give the gaff height and angle even if the sail is a little short on the foot and head. If there is not one, you must hoist the gaff and boom to the best estimate of their sailing positions. In either case two tapes or wires should be used, one attached to the throat and one to the peak. It is important that the distance from peak to tack and clew, and from throat to tack and clew should be taken simultaneously with the gaff and boom at a constant height and angle. Have a good look at the throat eye when the gaff is hoisted, to see whether it is out of line with the rest of the luff and/or head. Don't forget to count the mast hoops. Measure also the top and bottom of the protecting band on the mast in way of the gaff jaws when hoisted, to ensure that the checkwire which will be fitted to the luff will leave the throat correctly positioned at the mast.

Hull. The overall and waterline lengths are usually known without measurement, and a sufficiently accurate guess can be made at the overhangs with the aid of the tape measure on the deck. These details will be necessary for the outline of the hull, as will the freeboard at several convenient points. Freeboard can be established by tying a suitable weight on to the wire or tape, and lowering over the side until the end just touches the water. This establishes the sheer line, which is important for a low cut genoa. Deckhouse details are needed so that the right amount of clearance can be kept between the top of it and the boom. Having settled the outline of the hull itself, don't forget the locations of the various stays and masts where they meet the deck, and the jib fairleads. Note that the measurements from mast to stem, and 'J' are not necessarily the same for a sloop, but establish the position of the forestay on deck in relation to the stem head. Spreaders are not essential, but useful when determining the genoa leech and whether also a particular sail, perhaps an intermediate genoa, will sheet inside the upper shrouds and under the lower spreaders. The mast and boom circumferences have been included in case it may be necessary to make a sail cover for the main or mizzen.

Interpretation. When drawing the plan, start at the waterline and work upwards until the hull is complete. Next settle the position of the masts at deck level, and then establish their rake. There will be a discrepancy at the masthead due to the use of two different halyards (jib and main), and you must allow for the shackle and splice together with the thickness of the mast. Draw all measurements with a soft pencil and the right position should soon be manifest. If one distance is wrong it will be shown up by the fact that all the others are mutually corroborating without it. It is for this purpose that too many measurements are better than too few.

When deciding how big to make the stretched sizes of a mainsail or mizzen to a plan established on these lines, due allowance should be made for clearance at the masthead for the halyard splice and shackle; it is possible that two large wooden blocks with their attendant shackles and eyes may have to be accommodated between the sheave and the headboard. A suitable minimum allowance is 2 per cent of the total distance from sheave to tack, which is 6 in. on a 25 ft luff and 1 ft on a 50-ft luff.

Measuring Old Sails. Sometimes old sails are taken as a pattern for size. This is all right for headsails, which spread on the floor to their full size, but a mainsail will not do so without being stretched on the luff and foot. This can only be properly achieved on the spars, and the sail makes a poor pattern on its own, even if it is made of Terylene or Dacron. It is thus preferable to measure the spars along the lines I have just given, because too great a variation will occur if the sail itself has to be measured.

An exception to this rule is the use of an old headsail to establish the size of a new one. The old sail is hoisted on the boat, and the place where the clew of the new headsail is desired can be given by reference to the old one. The instructions to the Sail Maker will then give the sizes of the old sail (luff, leech and foot) and the fact that the clew of the new sail should come, say, 6 in. further aft and 3 in. lower than the old one. If the luff needs to be longer, this can also be compared with the old sail.

APPENDIX J

Boat measurement table

	Inner jib	*Outer jib*
JIB		
Halyard in sheave to deck (vertical) ('I').		
Halyard in sheave to bowsprit end.		
Halyard in sheave to stem head.		
Halyard in sheave to forestay on deck.		
Halyard in sheave to tack fitting.		
First hank up from tack (to clear turnbuckle, etc.).		
STAYSAIL		
Halyard in sheave to deck (vertical).		
Halyard in sheave to stem head.		
Halyard in sheave to forestay on deck.		
Halyard in sheave to tack fitting.		
Halyard in sheave to clew in sailing position.		
Boom: tack eye to clew eye.	*Max.*	
	Min.	
Boom: clew lashes or outhaul slide. Slide travel.		
Boom: reef cleats from clew in max. position.		
Foot: loose, lacing or slides. No. and type of slides.		
First hank up from tack (to clear turnbuckle, etc.).		

	Mizzen	*Main*
MIZZEN/MAINSAIL		
Halyard in sheave to tack in lowest position.		
Halyard in sheave to deck (vertical).		
Halyard in sheave to clew in sailing position.		
Halyard in sheave to mizzen mast at deck (main only).		
Halyard in sheave to counter.		
Tack knock back (distance tack to aft face of mast).		
Luff groove, lacing or slides. No. and type of slides.		
Foot groove, lacing or slides. No. and type of slides.		
Mast ramp details, or distance up groove starts.		
Gooseneck travel.		
Boom: roller or fixed.		
Boom: reef cleats from clew in max. position.		
Boom: tack eye to clew eye. *Max.*		
Min.		
Boom: clew lashes or outhaul slide. Slide travel.		

GAFF SAILS (*Extra to above*)

Gaff throat eye to peak eye.
Peak to tack in sailing position.
Peak to clew in sailing position.
Throat to tack in sailing position.
Throat to clew in sailing position.
Distance throat in sailing position is offset from true.
Number of mast hoops.
Gaff laces, groove or slides. No. and type of slides.
Mast band to tack. { *Top* / *Bottom* }

HULL

Pulpit and guard rail height. Continuous YES/NO.
Length overall (with/without bowsprit).
Length water-line.
Bow overhang.
Stern overhang.
Freeboard at bow.
Freeboard at mainmast.
Freeboard at mizzen mast (or other convenient point).
Freeboard at stern.
Mast to stemhead.
Bowsprit length.
J measurement (mast to outer stay at deck/bowsprit).
Mast to middle stay at deck.
Mast to inner stay at deck.
Distance between masts.
Mizzen mast to counter.
Deckhouse height above deck.
Jib fairleads aft of mast (max. and min. if on track).

	Mizzen	*Main*
Mast circumference at tack.		
Boom circumference at tack.		
Boom circumference at clew.		
Upper spreaders above the deck, and width.		
Lower spreaders above deck, and width.		

APPENDIX K

Beaufort Wind Scale

Beaufort number	*Wind speed*				*Seaman's term*	*Estimating wind speed*	
	knots	*mph*	*metres per second*	*km per hour*		*Effects observed at sea*	*Effects observed on land*
0	under 1	under 1	0·0–0·2	under 1	Calm	Sea like mirror	Calm; smoke rises vertically
1	1–3	1–3	0·3–1·5	1–5	Light air	Ripples with appearance of scales; no foam crests	Smoke drift indicates wind direction; vanes do not move
2	4–6	4–7	1·6–3·3	6–11	Light breeze	Small wavelets; crests of glassy appearance, not breaking	Wind felt on face; leaves rustle; vanes begin to move
3	7–10	8–12	3·4–5·4	12–19	Gentle breeze	Large wavelets; crests begin to break; scattered whitecaps	Leaves, small twigs in constant motion; light flags extended
4	11–16	13–18	5·5–7·9	20–29	Moderate breeze	Small waves, becoming longer; numerous whitecaps	Dust, leaves, and loose paper raised up; small branches move
5	17–21	19–24	8·0–10·7	30–38	Fresh breeze	Moderate waves, taking longer form; many white horses; some spray	Small trees in leaf begin to sway
6	22–27	25–31	10·8–13·8	39–50	Strong breeze	Larger waves forming; white horses everywhere; more spray	Larger branches of trees in motion; whistling heard in wires
7	28–33	32–38	13·9–17·1	51–61	Near gale	Sea heaps up; white foam from breaking waves begins to be blown in streaks	Whole trees in motion; resistance felt in walking against wind
8	34–40	39–46	17·2–20·7	62–74	Gale	Moderately high waves of greater length; edges of crests begin to break into spindrift; foam is blown in well-marked streaks	Twigs and small branches broken off trees; progress generally impeded
9	41–47	47–54	20·8–24·4	75–87	Strong gale	High waves; sea begins to roll; dense streaks of foam; spray may reduce visibility	Slight structural damage occurs; slates blown from roofs
10	48–55	55–63	24·5–28·4	88–101	Storm	Very high waves with overhanging crests; sea takes white appearance as foam is blown in very dense streaks; rolling is heavy and visibility reduced	Seldom experienced on land; trees broken or uprooted; considerable structural damage occurs
11	56–63	64–72	28·5–32·6	102–116	Violent storm	Exceptionally high waves; sea covered with white foam patches; visibility still more reduced	
12	64–71	73–82	32·7–36·9	117–132	Hurricane	Air filled with foam; sea completely white with driving spray, visibility very seriously affected	Very rarely experienced on land; usually accompanied by widespread damage
13	72–80	83–92	37·0–41·4	133–148			
14	81–89	93–103	41·5–46·1	149–166			
15	90–99	104–114	46·2–50·9	167–183			
16	100–108	115–124	51·0–56·0	184–200			
17	109–118	125–136	56·1–61·2	201–219			

Bibliography

Cornelius Shields on Sailing *Cornelius Shields* 1965

Expert Dinghy Racing *Paul Elvström* 1963

Manual of Yachting and Boat Sailing and Naval Architecture 11th Ed. *Dixon Kemp* 1913

Further Offshore *John Illingworth* 1970

Race Your Boat Right *Arthur Knapp Jnr* 1963

Racing Dinghy Handling *Ian Proctor* 1948

Sailing Boats *Uffa Fox* 1959

Sailing Ships and their Story *E. Keble Chatterton* 1909 New Edition 1923

Sailing Ships, their History and Development *Science Museum* 1932 Reprinted 1962

Sailing Theory and Practice *C. A. Marchaj* 1964

Sailing to Win *Robert Bavier* 1948

Sailor's Word Book *Admiral W. H. Smyth* 1867

Sail Power *Wallace Ross* 1975

Ship, The *Björn Landström* 1961

Story of Sail *G. S. Laird Clowes* 1936

Technical Report of the Aeronautical Research Committee 1931–32 Vol I *H.M.S.O.* 1933

Tom Diaper's Diary *Tom Diaper* 1950

Voiles et Gréements *Pierre Gutelle* 1968

Wind Tunnel Technique *R. C. Pankhurst and D. W. Holder* 1952

Working in Canvas *P. M. Blandford* 1965

Yacht Racing. The Aerodynamics of Sails and Racing Tactics *Manfred Currey* 1928

Yacht Sails – their Care and Handling *Ernest Ratsey and Ham de Fontaine* 1957

Amateur Yacht Research Society Papers 1955–1964

Davidson Laboratory, Stevens Institute of Technology, Technical Memoranda 1935–1955

Bibliography

Sailing Yacht Performance *John C. Sainsbury* 1962
Southampton University Yacht Research Papers 1960–1964

Numerous articles and letters in
Yachting *U.S. Magazine* 1959–1966
Yachting World *British Magazine* 1959–1966
Yachts and Yachting *British Magazine* 1959–1966
Yachtsman *British Magazine* 1959–1966

Index

Numbers in **bold** type refer to diagrams; Plates are photographs

Index

NOTES

NOTES

NOTES

NOTES

NOTES

NOTES